Mao, Stalin and the K

This book examines relations between China and the Soviet Union during the 1950s, and provides an insight into Chinese thinking about the Korean War.

This volume is based on a translation of Shen Zihua's best-selling Chinese-language book, which broke the Mainland Chinese taboo on publishing non-heroic accounts of the Korean War. The author combined information detailed in Soviet-era diplomatic documents (released after the collapse of the Soviet Union) with Chinese memoirs, official document collections and scholarly monographs, in order to present a non-ideological, realpolitik account of the relations, motivations and actions among three Communist actors: Stalin, Mao Zedong and Kim Il-sung.

This new translation represents a revisionist perspective on trilateral Communist alliance relations during the Korean War, which sheds new light on the origins of the Sino-Soviet split and relations between China and North Korea. It features a critical introduction to Shen's work and the text is based on original archival research not found in any other book in English.

This book will be of much interest to students of Communist China, Stalinist Russia, the Korean War, Cold War Studies and International History in general.

Shen Zhihua is professor of history at East China Normal University and Director of the Cold War History Studies Center on the Shanghai campus. He is also an adjunct professor of history at Peking University. He is author of several books on the Cold War in Chinese.

Neil Silver is a retired U.S. diplomat who worked in, on and around China. He served in embassies in Beijing, Tokyo and Moscow, including as Minister-Counselor for Political Affairs in Beijing and Tokyo, and in the State Department, worked on Chinese, Japanese, Korean, and Southeast Asian affairs.

Cold War History Series
Series Editors: Odd Arne Westad and Michael Cox

In the new history of the Cold War that has been forming since 1989, many of the established truths about the international conflict that shaped the latter half of the twentieth century have come up for revision. The present series is an attempt to make available interpretations and materials that will help further the development of this new history, and it will concentrate in particular on publishing expositions of key historical issues and critical surveys of newly available sources.

Reviewing the Cold War
Approaches, Interpretations, Theory
Edited by Odd Arne Westad

Rethinking Theory and History in the Cold War
The State, Military Power and Social Revolution
Richard Saull

British and American Anticommunism before the Cold War
Marrku Ruotsila

Europe, Cold War and Coexistence, 1953–1965
Edited by Wilfried Loth

The Last Decade of the Cold War
From Conflict Escalation to Conflict Transformation
Edited by Olav Njølstad

Reinterpreting the End of the Cold War
Issues, interpretations, periodizations
Edited by Silvio Pons and Federico Romero

Across the Blocs
Cold War Cultural and Social History
Edited by Rana Mitter and Patrick Major

US Internal Security Assistance to South Vietnam
Insurgency, subversion and public order
William Rosenau

The European Community and the Crises of the 1960s
Negotiating the Gaullist challenge
N. Piers Ludlow

Soviet–Vietnam Relations and the Role of China, 1949–64
Changing alliances
Mari Olsen

The Third Indochina War
Conflict between China, Vietnam and Cambodia, 1972–79
Edited by Odd Arne Westad and Sophie Quinn-Judge

Greece and the Cold War
Frontline state, 1952–1967
Evanthis Hatzivassiliou

Economic Statecraft during the Cold War
European responses to the US trade embargo
Frank Cain

Macmillan, Khrushchev and the Berlin Crisis, 1958–1960
Kitty Newman

The Emergence of Détente in Europe
Brandt, Kennedy and the formation of Ostpolitik
Arne Hofmann

European Integration and the Cold War
Ostpolitik–Westpolitik, 1965–1973
Edited by N. Piers Ludlow

Britain, Germany and the Cold War
The search for a European Détente 1949–1967
R. Gerald Hughes

The Military Balance in the Cold War
US perceptions and policy, 1976–85
David M. Walsh

The Cold War in the Middle East
Regional conflict and the superpowers 1967–73
Edited by Nigel J. Ashton

The Making of Détente
Eastern and Western Europe in the Cold War, 1965–75
Edited by Wilfried Loth and Georges-Henri Soutou

Europe and the End of the Cold War
A reappraisal
Edited by Frédéric Bozo, Marie-Pierre Rey, N. Piers Ludlow and Leopoldo Nuti

The Baltic Question during the Cold War
Edited by John Hiden, Vahur Made and David J. Smith

The Crisis of Détente in Europe
From Helsinki to Gorbachev, 1975–85
Edited by Leopoldo Nuti

Cold War in Southern Africa
White power, black liberation
Edited by Sue Onslow

The Globalisation of the Cold War
Diplomacy and local confrontation, 1975–85
Edited by Max Guderzo and Bruna Bagnato

Yugoslavia and the Soviet Union in the Early Cold War
Reconciliation, comradeship, confrontation, 1953–1957
Svetozar Rajak

The End of the Cold War in the Third World
New perspectives on regional conflict
Edited by Artemy Kalinovsky and Sergey Radchenko

Mao, Stalin and the Korean War
Trilateral communist relations in the 1950s
Shen Zhihua; translated by Neil Silver

Mao, Stalin and the Korean War

Trilateral communist relations in the 1950s

Shen Zhihua
Translated by Neil Silver

Routledge
Taylor & Francis Group

LONDON AND NEW YORK

First published in Chinese in 2003 as "Mao Zedong, Stalin yu
Chaoxian zhanzheng" by Guangdong renmin chubanshe
[Guangdong People's Publishers]
Revised edition published in 2007

First published in English in 2012
by Routledge
2 Park Square, Milton Park, Abingdon, Oxon OX14 4RN

Simultaneously published in the USA and Canada
by Routledge
711 Third Avenue, New York, NY 10017

Routledge is an imprint of the Taylor & Francis Group, an informa business

British Library Cataloguing in Publication Data
A catalogue record for this book is available from the British Library

Library of Congress Cataloging-in-Publication Data
Shen, Zhihua, 1950–
[Mao Zedong, Sidalin yu Chaoxian zhan zheng. English]
Mao, Stalin and the Korean War : trilateral communist relations in
the 1950s / [Zihuha Shen] ; translated by Neil Silver.
  p. cm. – (Cold war history series)
  Translation of: Mao Zedong, Sidalin yu Chaoxian zhan zheng.
  Includes bibliographical references and index.
  1. Korean War, 1950-1953. 2. China–Foreign relations–Soviet
  Union. 3. Soviet Union–Foreign relations–China. I. Title.
  DS918.8.S5413 2012
  951.904'22–dc23   2012000374
ISBN: 978-0-415-74812-4 (pbk)
ISBN: 978-0-415-51645-7 (hbk)
ISBN: 978-0-203-11220-5 (ebk)
Typeset in Baskerville
by Wearset Ltd, Boldon, Tyne and Wear

First issued in paperback in 2013

Contents

7   North Korea crosses the 38th parallel   133

8   China decides: "whatever the sacrifice necessary"   149

9   A new stage in Sino-Soviet cooperation   178

Translator's acknowledgments and thoughts

I found Shen Zhihua's *Mao, Stalin and the Korean War* at a local Chinese book fair. I was impressed with its non-ideological, realpolitik analysis of the relations among the leaders of China, the Soviet Union and North Korea before and during the Korean War. An example of post-Mao, post-revolutionary Chinese history and international relations writing, Shen's book sold about 100,000 Chinese copies in authorized and pirated editions, crossing the line between scholarly monograph and popular history. I felt it should be available for foreign readers, both for its intrinsic value as a key to understanding hitherto obscure "Red" diplomatic and political maneuvering at the time of the Korean War, and as a window into how some Chinese now write about what were once sensitive and even taboo topics.

This translation would not have been finished without the encouragement and support of a number of individuals and institutions. First of all, I have to thank Shen Zhihua for his consistent encouragement and help in resolving a number of practical issues, from the English translation of Russian and Korean names rendered into Chinese to the provision of documents not otherwise available to me. Likewise, I am deeply indebted to Yang Kuisong for permission to adapt and use as an introduction his review of Shen's book.

Throughout my translation project, two persons, Xia Yafeng and Lauren Marcott, have served faithfully and diligently as readers and editorial advisers. Sarah Cheeseman skillfully edited the final text. I cannot thank them enough for the help they offered, especially in my moments of indecision about how to proceed in the face of editorial hurdles. Despite their good advice, any errors are due to my own lack of diligence.

Allen Whiting read my translation at a very early stage. His balanced but encouraging comments about the virtues and defects of Shen's book led me to refashion Shen's five chapters into nine thematically focused chapters, cut tangential information and add other devices (see Endnotes). I hope these changes will make this translation more accessible to readers. James Hershberg's curiosity about how Shen's peers in China reviewed his book led me to Yang Kuisong's review and my decision to use it as an introduction. I have done this to raise cautionary flags over some of Shen's analysis.

Fortunately, two major sources of Chinese books and journals are in my backyard, the Chinese collection in the Gelman Library of The George Washington University and the Asian Reading Room at the Library of Congress. Among the always helpful librarians at these collections, the Asian Reading Room's J. J. Zhang stands out as the most generous with his time and advice.

Though a long-distance relationship, some of my warmest regards are for the researchers at the Slavic Reference Center at the University of Illinois at Urbana-Champaign. After I stumbled over the Center's notice in a professional journal, I sent in a number of puzzling requests for the original Russian source of material used by Shen in vaguely sourced Chinese translations, and held my breath. Amazingly, the Center's researchers tracked down the sources of this material, including an interview with Stalin first published in LOOK! Thank you Kit Condill, Joe Lenkart and Helen Sullivan.

I wish to acknowledge and thank Christian Ostermann and the Cold War International History Project (CWIHP) at the Woodrow Wilson Center for International Scholars for permission to use in whole or in part their translations of Russian documents that have been posted on the CWIHP digital archive website. I also wish to thank the Cold War International History Project and the National Security Archive for giving me access to copies of untranslated Russian documents.

Many others have helped me with advice, encouragement and introductions along the way, notably Steven Levine, John Merrill, J. Stapleton Roy, Kathryn Weathersby and Arne Westad.

As I translated Shen's book, I came to some conclusions. My suspicion that some of Shen's analysis of Stalin's motives for supporting the war rests on shaky ground has been well addressed in Yang's introduction. Yang also usefully pointed out that Mao Zedong and Zhou Enlai, in particular, were drawn to the idea of joining the Korean War when the U.S. and its allies were pinned inside the Pusan perimeter prior to the Inchon landing. Shen subsequently explored this issue in great depth (in a 2009 Taiwan journal article), reaching conclusions parallel to those outlined earlier by Yang (see Selected Bibliography and Suggested Further Reading). It turns out that while Mao and Zhou were intrigued with the idea of boosting China's international prestige by adding a "China factor" to the war at this point, neither Stalin nor Kim Il-sung was eager for or even open to Chinese military intervention before the Inchon landing sent North Korean forces reeling northward. Though unfulfilled, Mao's eagerness to join the fight before Inchon undercuts to some degree the view generally espoused by Shen, namely that China's entry into the Korean War (albeit after Inchon) reflected a realpolitik, national interest calculus versus an ideologically motivated decision.

Finally, after plowing all available ground, Shen finds no strong evidence that Stalin briefed Mao on his reaction to Kim Il-sung's entreaty to war before Mao left Moscow in February 1950. Whatever the perhaps forever unknowable facts, Mao seemed far from surprised when Kim came to brief him about Stalin's support for the war plan in May 1950. Though it is only a feeling and not an established fact, it seems that Mao, and to some extent Zhou Enlai, knew or suspected more than they were willing to share with their Chinese leadership peers at key points prior to the outbreak of the Korean War. It also seems that Mao did not think deeply, if he thought at all, about possible conflict between Kim's war plan and China's own goal of "recovering" Taiwan at an early date.

As Richard Haass commented about a more recent war: "All wars are fought three times. There is the political struggle over whether to go to war. There is the physical war itself. And then there is the struggle over differing interpretations of what was accomplished and the lessons of it all."

Neil Silver
McLean, Virginia

Introduction

Yang Kuisong[1]

After many twists and turns, Shen Zhihua's *Mao Zedong, Stalin and the Korean War* has at long last been published in China.[2] This is good news in the Chinese academic world. The Korean War occurred more than half a century ago, and the leaders who were personally involved in the war are now all dead. With the end of the Cold War and the collapse of the Soviet Union, the archives of the main participants in the war, the Soviet Union and the United States, have now both been opened. Foreign scholars have enthusiastically published the fruits of their research in the newly opened Russian archives. For some time, Chinese scholars have not been shy in voicing their opinions, but it has, in fact, been very hard for them to publish the results of their research openly in China. Shen was one of the first Chinese scholars to work on the Korean War. His book demonstrates his skill in collecting and using Russian archival material. Academic colleagues interested in the Korean War can now acquaint themselves with the facts and conclusions culled by Chinese scholars from the trove of recently declassified Russian documents.

Shen focuses on the Soviet factor behind the outbreak of the war and China's decision to dispatch troops "to resist America and assist Korea." The book tries especially hard to explain the relationship of the Sino-Soviet alliance concluded in February 1950 to the outbreak of the war four months later, and the challenges posed to the new Sino-Soviet alliance by reverses in the war. Frankly speaking, although this book does examine the role and effect of the war on the then new Sino-Soviet alliance, it mainly examines the Korean War, what Chinese call the "War to Resist America and Assist Korea," that is to say, why Kim Il-sung launched the war, and why Mao felt he was compelled to deploy Chinese troops. What role did Stalin play in all this? Why did he support the Korean War? How did the Korean War break out? Why did China finally send troops?

For many decades these questions have puzzled scholars and officials worldwide. Even in China and the Soviet Union, two of the main protagonists, most leaders had no clear idea what had happened. The Korean War broke out in June 1950. Only ten years later, in June 1960, even some who had been personally involved in discussions and decisions about the war were not clear on the cause for the outbreak of the war and the background to China's troop deployment. On June 22, 1960, Soviet Communist Party Chairman Nikita Khrushchev met in Bucharest, Romania with a Chinese Communist Party delegation led by Politburo member Peng Zhen. The two traded charges, with Khrushchev accusing Mao of sharing responsibility for starting the war, and Peng categorically rejecting this accusation.

Let's take a look at how they argued:

KHRUSHCHEV: We can talk in this small group. The Korean War was started by North Korea, with the approval of the Soviet Union and China.

PENG: That's wrong. We didn't agree. I was involved in the Politburo discussions. I know the issue.

KHRUSHCHEV: We've also seen the documents. Mao Zedong agreed.

PENG: I have to make two things clear: first, we didn't know about the outbreak of the Korean War beforehand, and, second, after the war started you sent your ambassador to our Central Committee, saying it was not possible for the Soviet Union to send its forces, and that Stalin was thinking of asking us to send troops.

KHRUSHCHEV: If at the time we had been in charge and not Stalin, this war would not have been fought, but if Mao Zedong had not agreed, Stalin would not have done what he did. The Korean War was launched only after Stalin and Mao Zedong both approved.

PENG: What you said is wrong. Comrade Mao Zedong was against the war. As Comrade Mao Zedong told Stalin in Moscow, if a war is fought, the issue won't be South Korea, but rather the American imperialists. The issue won't be whether or not South Korea can be captured, but rather whether North Korea can be held. Comrade Mao Zedong also shared this view with Comrade Kim Il-sung. After the Korean War started, Stalin said that if the Soviet Union sent in troops this would mean a world war, and he therefore asked China to send troops. And this is the reason we agreed to send troops. I was in the Politburo discussions at the time.

KHRUSHCHEV: You're talking about events that happened after the war broke out. The issue is that Stalin and Mao Zedong both signed off on launching the war.

PENG: What you said does not fit the facts. You're just spinning a story. I was in the discussions. From start to finish, we believe it was Comrade Stalin who agreed. Comrade Kim Il-sung has the most authority to speak to this question.

KHRUSHCHEV: You're probably younger than I am. How old are you?

PENG: Fifty-eight.

KHRUSHCHEV: You are younger than I am, but your memory is not as good as mine.

PENG: My memory is very good. I remember very clearly, since I participated in the Politburo discussions. We conveyed our views to Stalin.

KHRUSHCHEV: You're a master of hindsight. Chinese are good at this.

PENG: You're wrong. We actually said this to Stalin.

KHRUSHCHEV: He didn't listen to what others said. He had already turned himself into an icon.

PENG: We were not satisfied with Stalin. We had our grievances....

KHRUSHCHEV: (repeating himself) Stalin and Mao Zedong jointly approved the Korean War.

PENG: That's absolutely wrong. Comrade Mao Zedong offered his views. You can ask other comrades who participated in the discussions at the time. Then you'll understand.

KHRUSHCHEV: Let's not talk about the dead. I say the fault lies with Stalin and Mao Zedong.

PENG: Totally wrong. You have people who participated in the event and should be able to testify. I'll say it again. What you say is completely wrong.[3]

Clearly, in 1960, in a restricted setting, Chinese and Soviet leaders acknowledged privately that North Korea started the Korean War by attacking across the 38th parallel. They were arguing about whom to blame for the decision to start the war. Khrushchev held that Stalin and Mao jointly gave the green light to Kim Il-sung to launch the war. However, Peng firmly believed that Mao did not agree and even opposed starting the war, and that China was kept in the dark about details regarding the actual launch of the war.

Shen's book provides a relatively clear answer. It points out that all the war planning and the implementation of the war plan was accomplished secretly between Stalin and Kim Il-sung, that is, between Moscow and Pyongyang. China neither participated in nor was informed in any detail about the war plan and its implementation. Therefore, Khrushchev's contention that Stalin and Mao jointly signed off and jointly decided on launching the war is untenable. Second, however, Mao knew that Kim Il-sung had a war plan; Stalin informed Mao of the plan. At Stalin's request, Kim visited Beijing on May 13, 1950 to seek Mao's views on launching the war. When Mao then had Premier and Foreign Minister Zhou Enlai check Stalin's intentions through Soviet Ambassador Roshchin, Stalin told Mao that though he had approved the North Korean military unification plan, "[T]he question should be decided finally by the Chinese and Korean comrades together, and in case of disagreement by the Chinese comrades the decision ... should be postponed pending further discussion."[4] Clearly, after Stalin agreed to the North Korean plan, Mao and his Chinese comrades did not object. Therefore, when Khrushchev said that, "if Mao Zedong had not agreed, Stalin would not have done what he did," he was speaking factually.

Sometimes history is complicated.

-2-

Why did Stalin on the one hand plan a war to unify Korea with Kim Il-sung behind the backs of the Chinese while on the other hand insist that Kim get Chinese approval? Stalin clearly could not ignore the Treaty of Friendship, Alliance and Mutual Benefit that China and the Soviet Union had concluded on February 14, 1950. As stipulated in the treaty, if either party entered a state of war, the other party was bound to render effective assistance. Though the Korean War might not directly involve the Soviet Union in a state of war, as the main war planner, supporter and weapons supplier, it could not avoid some risk. Furthermore, if anything went wrong in the Korean War, it would bring a great deal of trouble to China just across the Yalu River. Stalin could not act selfishly and completely ignore his new ally, China.

But people usually ignore another question. Why did Stalin approve a Korean action that even Mao, who believed in "taking power through arms, and resolving issues through war," thought was somewhat risky? If we want to be clear about this, we need to look at Shen's analysis and narration of how Soviet attitudes toward Korea evolved in the years after the end of World War II. If we pay close attention to this evolution, we discover that in the early postwar years Stalin had no intention of challenging the United States in Korea. But the unexpected success of the Chinese revolution and his new alliance with Communist China led Stalin to change his cautious approach to Soviet policy in the Far East.

Why was Stalin's performance so different in Europe and Asia? Simply put, for the Soviet Union, the postwar strategic center of gravity was in Europe. Toward the distant Far East, Stalin's policy was to stay on the defensive. In accord with its demands at the 1945 Yalta Conference, the Soviet Union would be satisfied acquiring special rights in Northeast China and pocketing South Sakhalin and the Kuril Islands from Japan. As the war drew to a close, Stalin made no special demand at Yalta regarding Korea, and was ready to allow an independent Korean government, albeit one "friendly" to the Soviet Union, to take over after the end of a postwar U.S.–Soviet–British–Chinese four-power trusteeship in Korea.

By 1948, the United States and the Soviet Union were locked in a sharp confrontation in Europe, even as Soviet policy in the Far East remained extremely cautious. In Asia, the Soviets did not see themselves as a match for the United States. According to Shen,

> Stalin never considered setting up an Eastern European-style satellite state in Korea or North Korea. The Soviet Union first urged that Soviet and American forces withdraw simultaneously from the Korean peninsula. Later, it announced that Soviet occupation troops would unilaterally withdraw from North Korea, and promised to grant full, autonomous political power to the (North) Korean people to a much greater degree than it had granted in some Eastern European countries.

In order to avoid provoking the United States, Stalin even opposed diplomatic relations of an alliance nature with the Democratic People's Republic of Korea, not to speak of accepting responsibility for its unification goal.[5]

-3-

That Stalin did not want to provoke the United States in the Far East in the immediate postwar period is not news. As remembered by many Chinese (Communists) of an older generation, at the end of the Anti-Japanese War (World War II), in 1945, Stalin opposed Mao's revolution. Those familiar with postwar Chinese Communist history know the story of how the Soviet Red Army chased the Eighth Route Army out of the cities in Northeast China when Chinese Communist forces entered the Northeast before the Nationalist Army. In the opinion of many Chinese Communist leaders, until the spring of 1949, (when the Chinese Communists were on the cusp of victory in the civil war), Stalin still feared U.S. intervention in China and, therefore, promoted the idea that the Communists and the Nationalists could divide and rule China north and south of the Yangtze River, respectively.

If Stalin feared American intervention in Asia, then why did he suddenly change his attitude in early 1950, and why was he then willing to run the great risk of war with the United States by supporting Kim's Korean unification plan? Most scholars believe that President Harry Truman's January 5 and Secretary of State Dean Acheson's January 12, 1950 statements excluding the Korean peninsula and Taiwan from the U.S. Pacific defense perimeter flashed a misleading signal to Stalin. Shen stakes out a very different and very controversial view.

Going against mainstream scholarship, Shen portrays the shift in Stalin's attitude toward Korea not as rooted in these U.S. leadership statements, but rather in the Soviet leader's analysis of the consequences of the new Sino-Soviet alliance for Soviet interests.

> The role of the Chinese revolution and the Sino-Soviet alliance in spurring changes in Stalin's Korean and Far Eastern policies, however, is not necessarily as thought by some scholars, namely, that since the Soviet Union felt its position in the Far East was now stronger, it follows that Moscow was more confident it could confront and defeat U.S. power on the Korean peninsula.
>
> Actually, the opposite was true. The change in the political regime in China and the signing of the new Sino-Soviet treaty made Stalin wonder if Soviet interests in the Far East were threatened or, possibly, even lost.... As far as Moscow was concerned, the establishment of New China was like a dual-edged sword.... The new alliance surely strengthened Soviet political power in Asia. But, in establishing the alliance, Stalin was forced to give up most of the political and economic rights

and interests that he had wrested from Chiang Kai-shek in 1945. It is therefore possible to conclude that Stalin's motive for changing his Korean policy in early 1950 was based on a desire to maintain and protect Soviet political and economic interests in Asia, especially in Northeast Asia. This was the crux of the issue for Stalin.[6]

What important rights might be lost? Based on articles in the 1950 treaty, "In the short space of three years, the Soviet Union would lose" access to the Pacific Ocean through control of the Chinese Changchun Railway and the ice-free port of Lushun, rights that it had acquired at Yalta and in the 1945 Sino-Soviet treaty. As Shen argues:

> It would be obvious to Stalin that if war broke out on the Korean peninsula, whatever the result, the Soviet strategic goal in the Far East – acquisition of an ocean outlet and an ice-free port – would be guaranteed. If the war ended in victory, the Soviet Union would control the whole Korean peninsula, and the ports of Inchon and Pusan would replace Lushun and Dalian.... Even if the war went poorly, the Soviet Union would achieve what it wished, since a tense situation in Northeast Asia would force China to ask Soviet forces to stay in Lushun and Dalian. Moreover, based on the new Sino-Soviet agreement, in the event of war, the Soviet Army had the right to use the Changchun Railway, and, if this happened, the Changchun Railway would, of course, remain under Soviet control.[7]

In analyzing Stalin's thinking, Shen argues that the Soviet leader was following the Czarist Russian tradition of seeking an ice-free port on the Pacific. This analysis is logical. Whether at Yalta, or in sending troops to Northeast China, Stalin didn't mince words. The Soviet Union's war aim vis-à-vis Japan was to restore the rights and interests that Czarist Russia had lost in the 1904–05 Russo-Japanese War. The most important of these rights was access to and use of an ice-free ocean outlet on the Pacific – the port of Lushun in Northeast China.

However, when considered together with the voluminous material that Shen has appended to his book,[8] it is clear that what is stated above is merely one aspect of the story of early Sino-Soviet relations. After deeper research, it seems that Shen has concluded that things were much more complex than he originally thought. Most obviously, if Stalin feared that China would quickly become strong and powerful, at a time when the Soviet Union still had not recovered from the devastation of World War II, why did he send so many experts and so much aid to assist poor, backward China to establish its own industrial base? Stalin was not so generous to the fraternal (Soviet satellite) nations of Eastern Europe.

More importantly, if Stalin had not been willing to cede rights to the Chinese Changchun Railway and Lushun port, he could have held out, sticking to the argument he had used when he first met Mao. If he had held to the argument that scrapping the old Sino-Soviet treaty would cause political and diplomatic problems for the Soviet Union, Mao likely would have tactfully accepted this explanation. This would have been much easier than launching a dangerous war. However, Stalin, not Mao, was the first to propose that Soviet forces withdraw from Lushun. According to the record of Mikoyan's January 1949 discussions with Mao, and the exchange of cables between Mao and Stalin, it is clear that the Chinese Communist leadership believed that the Soviet military should not withdraw precipitously from Lushun. Mao even repeated this request when he met Stalin in Moscow. It was Stalin, with his strong memory of the February 1946 China-wide anti-Soviet demonstrations (after details of a secret Yalta agreement on Soviet rights in China were leaked), who realized that if the Soviet Union continued to occupy Lushun with the Chinese Communists now in power, this would undermine the image of the Soviet Union and the Chinese Communist Party in Chinese public opinion. He therefore expressed his intent to withdraw.

The Soviet Union's geographical position and its newly acquired global great power status determined that it would do everything in its power to gain unimpeded access to the Pacific Ocean by means of an ice-free Pacific naval base. Even after the Korean War, the Soviet Union set up a long-wave radio station in China, and proposed that the Soviet Union, China and Vietnam establish a joint submarine force. And, as late as the 1970s, it acquired a naval base on Camranh Bay in Vietnam. All of this was aimed at affording its freedom of naval access to the Pacific. We therefore cannot ignore this motive in Stalin's support for the Korean War.

But this was not the only reason, and I'm afraid not the main reason, for the war. The risk and the price of resorting to war to gain or to hold onto a warm-water ocean port were just too great. Moreover, Stalin was always careful and calculating. He would surely understand that if the Korean War was lost, and all of the Korean peninsula fell into American hands, the Lushun naval base would be worthless. Moreover, should the Americans stand at the Tumen River (on the northern border of North Korea), the Soviets would fear that even the use of Vladivostok would become problematical. What, then, would be the significance in keeping Lushun? And, if the war was won, was there any guarantee a unified Korea would lease its own ice-free ports? Even if it did, who could guarantee that, like the Chinese, the Koreans would not one day want to control their own ports?

-4-

What, then, were the main reasons that impelled Stalin in 1950 to dare to support the Korean War? We can delve into the circumstances confronting Stalin based on Shen's analysis in this book. After Stalin was forced to back down from the Berlin crisis, he obviously felt that Soviet power was unable to openly confront the United States in Europe. Since U.S. pressure in Europe and the Middle East was just too great, he turned in another direction to divert U.S. power. In Asia, Stalin had formerly maintained a moderate policy, and had not created trouble. There had been no place to turn for help in Asia, and he had feared the danger of a two-front war. Now, however, he dared to plot an offensive and challenge the Americans. He calculated that with the success of the Chinese revolution, New China (the People's Republic of China) could pin down American power in Asia and lighten its pressure in Europe and the Middle East. Stalin handed the Chinese Communists the responsibility for guiding and assisting Communist parties in Asia,[9] and, with this goal in mind, assertively sought to help China restore its economy and build its industries.

Mao, Stalin and the Korean War acknowledges this change in Stalin's attitude toward the Chinese revolution. Shen explains how prior to late 1948, Stalin had suggested a compromise between the Nationalists and the Communists in order to stabilize the situation in China and protect Soviet rights and interests in Northeast China. However, as described by Shen, with the unexpected Chinese Communist gains in the civil war, Stalin lost little time in using every means he could, short of outright, open support, to help his "Chinese comrades."

Why did Stalin attach so much importance to the victory of the Chinese revolution? First, China was very big. As the largest country in Asia, the victory of the Chinese revolution undoubtedly was a great blow and not insignificant threat to American power in the Pacific. Second, China's example would inspire others. If the United States, which had provided significant wartime assistance to Nationalist China, a strategically valuable ally, did not dare to intervene in the end on behalf of the Nationalists, would it dare intervene in other Asian national revolutions? If most Asian countries emulated China and rose in revolution, would the United States have the strength to match the Soviet Union?

It seems clear that the victory of the Chinese revolution and the birth of New China in October 1949, and then the Sino-Soviet alliance signed in February 1950, shifted the Asian power balance between the Soviet Union and the United States. It also changed Stalin's hitherto consistently cautious attitude on issues in the Far East. This is not to say that Stalin changed from the defensive to the offensive overnight. Stalin would still not allow the Soviet Union to take on great risks. However, he seemed to believe that through China, and with China out in front, he could cause trouble for the United States. And, therefore, he not only did not fear China's development, but on the contrary, he wanted to help China achieve more rapid development, so it could spread its influence, promote revolution in Asia and check the United States.

Is there a basis to support this conclusion? Yes, there is. The most pertinent proof is that when Liu Shaoqi visited Moscow in July 1949, Stalin explicitly proposed a division of labor between the two communist parties, with the Chinese Communist Party guiding and assisting other Asian communist parties toward revolution through the example and experience of the Chinese revolution. In fact, Stalin appeared more enthusiastic and engaged on the issue of Asian revolution than his Chinese Communist guests. For example, in January 1950, Stalin suddenly started to ignore real conditions in Japan and India, and give gratuitous advice to the communist parties in these countries.

On January 6, the journal of the Cominform[10] (Communist Information Bureau) criticized the Japanese Communist Party not only for failing to oppose the American occupation of Japan, but also for its policy line that as long as the U.S. occupation forces remained in Japan, Japan might possibly peacefully adopt socialism.[11] In reaction to this criticism, Japanese Communist Party leaders defended their policy, arguing in print that the Cominform had not considered Japanese conditions. At this point, Stalin mobilized Mao Zedong to direct *Renmin ribao* (People's Daily) to publish an editorial supporting the Cominform's position. The Chinese Communist Party flagship publication criticized the Japanese Communist Party's peaceful transition policy, telling the Japanese party that it "must instruct the [Japanese] people in revolutionary spirit … launch a resolute struggle against U.S. imperialism and … end the U.S. occupation and reactionary rule."[12]

In the face of joint Soviet–Chinese pressure, the Japanese Communist Party accepted Cominform advice and changed its policy. Its leaders went underground, and the party turned from "peaceful revolution" to urban and rural guerilla warfare. In the same period, buoyed by the success of his new Chinese allies, Stalin launched a similar attack on the leadership of the Indian Communist Party.

-5-

Stalin was not radicalized overnight on the Korean issue just because he signed a new treaty with China under which Lushun would revert to China in a few years. As we have seen, from 1948 on, he began to reevaluate his attitude and to gradually provide greater support for the Chinese Communists. But only in January 1950 did Stalin fundamentally change his policy to promote revolution throughout Asia. Stalin's shift from his previous opposition to war in Korea to support for the North Korean invasion of South Korea was part of this overall policy reversal.

Why did this happen in January 1950 and not before or after? Shen is certainly correct in stressing that this happened at this time because Stalin had decided to conclude a new treaty with China. Before this, though Stalin had a favorable view of the Chinese revolution, and, moreover, had started to provide massive support to it from 1948 onward, he was still extremely careful, fearing he might aggravate the British and Americans. Therefore, he did all he could to hide his growing and now finally total support for the Chinese Communists. Why was Stalin so fearful of the

United States and Britain on Far Eastern issues? One key reason was the Yalta Agreement, specifically with respect to the Soviet acquisition of former Japanese territory. On December 16, 1949, the day Mao arrived in Moscow, Stalin made this point clearly.

Stalin told Mao that the 1945 bilateral treaty with the Nationalists was concluded on the basis of the Yalta Agreement. And, the Soviet postwar acquisition of South Sakhalin and the Kuril Islands was also based on the Yalta Agreement. If the 1945 Sino-Soviet treaty was abrogated, and a new bilateral treaty was concluded, said Stalin, this would undermine the Soviet Union's legal position, "since a change in even one point could give America and England the legal grounds to raise questions about modifying ... provisions concerning the Kuril Islands, South Sakhalin, etc."[13]

Two weeks later, Stalin, caught in an historical vortex, finally thought the issue through. On January 2, 1950 he sent then First Deputy Premier Vyasheslav Molotov along with Politburo member Anastas Mikoyan to see Mao to convey that he (Stalin) and the Soviet Communist Party Politburo had decided to conclude a new treaty with China, the Yalta Agreement be damned. Obviously, if Stalin wanted to depend on Chinese support, he needed to establish an alliance relationship with Mao. If he rigidly adhered to the Yalta Agreement, it would be impossible to transform China into a truly significant ally. Compared with any lingering attachment in Asia to the Yalta Agreement – which had already been shot through with holes by the Chinese revolution – it was obviously now more in the Soviet interest to sign a treaty with Mao. It was clear from the struggle in Europe with the United States that it was only a matter of time before the Cold War spread to the Far East. Without China's support the Soviet Union would be in a passive position in Asia. If Stalin wanted to draw on China's strength to check the United States in the Far East, he could not remain bound by the Yalta Agreement. How could shrewd Stalin let Mao go away disgruntled and not find a way to turn Mao into his ally?

The lure of the benefits from relations with China and the great hope he invested in China's revolutionary experience prodded Stalin to make up his mind, bury his concern over any possible American and British reaction, and sign a new treaty with China. And, only when he allied with China and leaned on it to promote Asian revolution was Stalin in a position to urge the Japanese, Indian and other Asian Communist parties to follow China on the road to armed revolution. In this situation, when he learned that Kim Il-sung had once again proposed to unify Korea by military means, Stalin was inclined to change his formerly negative attitude and agree without hesitation to Kim's request.

At a January 17, 1950 lunch, an agitated and excited Kim Il-sung first told two Soviet Embassy counselors and then the Soviet ambassador that following China's successful liberation, the next issue was how to liberate the people in southern Korea. He could hardly sleep at night when he thought of unifying Korea. But the last time he had visited Moscow and raised the issue, Stalin had merely told him that he could counterattack South Korea if Syngman Rhee's forces attacked North Korea. The problem was that Rhee had not launched an offensive attack and thus the issue of Korean national unification had dragged on without resolution. He needed to see Stalin again to seek guidance on the liberation of the South by the People's Army.

In line with his existing instructions, Soviet Ambassador Shtykov replied cautiously to Kim. But to Shtykov's surprise, after receiving his report, Stalin responded on January 30, 1950 that he now wanted to help Kim.

> I understand the dissatisfaction of Comrade Kim Il-sung, but he must understand that such a large matter in regard to South Korea such as he wants to undertake needs large preparation. The matter must be organized so that there would not be too great a risk. If he wants to discuss this matter with me, then I will always be ready to receive him and discuss it with him. Transmit this to Kim Il-sung and tell him that I am ready to help him in this matter.[14]

It's not hard to see that the situation in Asia changed dramatically in January 1950. The unexpected change flowed from Stalin's decision to abandon the Yalta Agreement and ally with China. All the subsequent moves, his promotion of armed revolution in Japan and India, and his willingness to help Kim Il-sung unify Korea through the force of arms, followed from Stalin's new sense of freedom of action in Asia.

-6-

Since Stalin had decided to go on the attack, why did he not tell Mao, who was then still in Moscow, that he was ready to help Kim?

Shen offers some explanations.

First: Since Mao had asked Stalin to assist in the liberation of Taiwan and Stalin had turned him down, it would be very hard for Stalin to convince Mao to agree to support military measures in Korea. And, pending in-depth discussions with Kim, Stalin was not in a position to seek Mao's opinion on launching a war in Korea.

Second: Stalin was worried that Mao would oppose his decision and, should the situation become difficult, Mao would refuse to be drawn in and would not accept Moscow's direction.

Third: Stalin would be keeping Mao in the dark only for a time. In the end, Stalin would still seek Mao's agreement, since he had to take precautions against any possible U.S. intervention. As a countermeasure, Stalin hoped that China would take responsibility and its military forces would contend with any American threat.

I fundamentally agree with Shen's first point, but believe something more needs to be said about his second and third points.

In July 1949 Stalin and Liu Shaoqi had agreed to a division of labor between the Soviet and Chinese Communist parties, with the Chinese taking responsibility for other Asian communist parties, and the Soviets taking responsibility for communist parties on other continents. But there was an important exception. Moscow had nurtured the North Korean party, the Korean Worker's Party, since the Soviet occupation of Korea, and this remained a Soviet responsibility. In the division of labor in Asia, Stalin was not required to consult China in any detail on the Korean issue.

We cannot say with any surety that in the period before Stalin met Kim and agreed on military action, Stalin did not tell Mao what was on his mind because he lacked confidence in Mao. While Mao was in Moscow, Stalin's discussions with Kim were in the future, with a decision on an offensive pending. Therefore, Stalin understandably would not at this juncture tell Mao in any detail what he was thinking with regard to Kim's plan. At the same time, as far we presently know, there is no definitive proof that Stalin and Mao did not discuss the Korean question in detail in Moscow. In *Mao, Stalin and the Korean War,* Shen refers to the fact that Stalin and Mao "possibly" discussed the Korean question or, again, "discussed the Korean question" in Moscow, but states that "details are unknown." Therefore, we have no basis to conclude that the two leaders were in disagreement over Kim's plan to unify Korea by force.

Actually, on the basic principle of using military force in Korea, even if we do not know what Stalin and Mao talked about, we can infer with some certainty that there would be no basic disagreement between the two. To say that Mao might oppose the offensive would mean at the most that he would oppose the timing of an offensive. By 1950, like Stalin, Mao clearly believed that the unification of Korea could only be accomplished through a war of liberation. Mao spoke to the Koreans on this point a year earlier, cautioning Kim Il-sung's secret envoy, Kim Il, in April 1949 that no offensive against the South should be launched in 1949, that a North Korean offensive against the South could only be considered after the end of the Chinese civil war, and only then after consultations with Moscow. And, in spring 1950 Mao was mentally prepared to discuss the issue with Kim Il-sung. In fact, when North Korean Ambassador Li Juyeon met with Mao (likely in April 1950) to discuss Kim's intended visit to see Mao, Mao told Li that, "[If] you intend to begin military action against the South in the near future, then [Kim and I] should not meet officially. In such a case the trip should be unofficial."[15]

There is the question of when Stalin should report the situation to Mao and whether he should consider the issue of secrecy. As Shen points out, the Korean War was the first major international issue to confront the Sino-Soviet alliance, and a major test of this alliance relationship. Furthermore, Korea adjoined China's main industrial base in the Northeast. There was every reason for Stalin to report to Mao that he and Kim were ready to implement such an important military plan. But we need to understand that Stalin was a very cautious and calculating person. Before even settling on the kernel of a plan through discussion with Kim, Stalin would not lightly reveal his personal thoughts to others. And even when the kernel of a plan was developed, Stalin would still carefully think through the situation before deciding when to tell Mao. Thus, only after Kim visited Moscow and Stalin and Kim agreed on an offensive did Stalin instruct Kim to go to Beijing to talk with Mao and gain his acquiescence. For Stalin, this was taking a big risk.

Why do I say this? According to Anastas Mikoyan, Stalin trusted Mao (by early 1949), but had no similar confidence that the Chinese Communist leadership as a whole was capable of protecting secrets. Mikoyan recounts that in January 1949, when Stalin was consulting secretly with Mao by cable on how to respond to Chiang Kai-shek's request to the Soviet Union, the United States and Britain to mediate between the Nationalists and the Communists, U.S. Ambassador Leighton Stuart unexpectedly acted first, telling the Nationalists that the U.S. did not want to mediate. This produced a strong reaction in the Kremlin, where it was widely believed there must have been a leak regarding the Stalin–Mao exchanges on the mediation issue from within the Chinese Communist leadership. Stalin specifically asked Mikoyan to convey the high importance he (Stalin) placed in the protection of secrets by the Chinese Communist Party. Although Mao told Mikoyan there was no possibility of a leak of his exchanges with Stalin, Mikoyan was not convinced.[16] In the same period, Stalin received a report from his personal representative in China, I. V. Kovalev, that the Chinese Communist leadership was internally complicated, with some pro-U.S. tendencies.[17] In view of this situation, we may have reason to believe that Stalin did not strive to pull the wool over Mao's eyes. On the contrary, to prevent Mao from feeling he was not being taken seriously, Stalin took the considerable risk, at least as he likely saw it, of giving Mao a heads-up on the Korean War, a secret military move of major significance.

To come up with logical explanations for the actions of calculating leaders, scholars often too easily ascribe the qualities of circumspection, far-sightedness and command brilliance, in other words, the ability to plan for every eventuality and weigh the merits of every possibility beforehand. But, sometimes this does not accord with reality. Many historical events actually occur based on accidental factors. Many historical figures were far less crafty and sagacious than we believe today. To think that Stalin, before the outbreak of the Korean War, had planned that if the United States intervened, he would let China take the responsibility of sending troops to confront the United States is, perhaps, to deify Stalin. This leads some people easily to the misinterpretation that Shen agrees with the idea that Stalin supported the Korean War in order to drag China into the war and drive a wedge between China and the United States. And, this, in fact, is not Shen's viewpoint. In his book, Shen makes it very clear that before the outbreak of the war, and during the planning for the war, Stalin actually gave very little careful thought to the possibility of a direct U.S. intervention.

U.S. forces were stationed in South Korea from September 1945 until June 1949. When the Korean War broke out, there was still a U.S. military advisory group in South Korea helping to train South Korean forces. Normal logic would dictate that if North Korea launched an offensive, and South Korea faced a crisis, given the American government's confrontational attitude toward the Soviet Union in Europe and the Middle East, there was a good possibility that it would intervene with its troops in Korea. Most people today would view it as extremely logical to think that Stalin would have planned from the outset to send the Chinese to confront the Americans if there was a setback in the war.

However, sometimes history is strange and puzzling. Looking through all the documents and historical material, we can find no evidence that Stalin ever considered the possibility that the U.S. would intervene militarily with its own forces. Kim Il-sung had even said that Stalin believed that the Americans would not intervene. We can find no indication in the blitzkrieg offensive plan devised by the Soviet generals who helped North Korea plan for its offensive or in the reams of now available intelligence and operational reports exchanged before the war between the Soviet Union and North Korea that these two countries prepared in any way for a possible U.S. intervention. This would be inconceivable had Stalin given any thought at all to the possibility of a U.S. intervention. And this explains perfectly why, before seeing Mao at Stalin's request, Kim was so confident that he did not need to ask China for any assistance. It also explains why, after the war broke out and American forces intervened, as Shen notes, Moscow and Pyongyang were so surprised, even to the extent that Stalin did not know whether the North Koreans planned to continue or temporarily halt their advance, and whether they would be frightened by U.S. bombing. As a result, the advance of the Korean People's Army was clearly stymied, and, after occupying Seoul, it temporarily halted its advance. To continue its offensive, a little over a week after starting the war, the Korean People's Army was forced on the fly to quickly and completely reorganize its command structure. This situation raises big questions about the theory that Stalin strived to use the Korean War to drive a wedge between the United States and China.

-7-

If Stalin wasn't so brilliant and far-sighted on the Korean issue, what about Mao? On the basis of currently available documentation, at the very least Mao gave somewhat more thought to the possibility of foreign intervention than Stalin. However, he fixated largely on Japan and not on the United States. Shen quotes Mao's comments on the issue in some detail. In late April 1949, in meeting with the Director of the Political Department of Korean People's Army, Kim Il, Mao said that, when the Americans leave, if war breaks out on the Korean peninsula and drags on, Japan might intervene. And, should the Americans leave Korea and the Japanese not step in behind them, if the North launches an attack on the South, the Japanese might still become involved, since "MacArthur can quickly send Japanese troops and arms to Korea."[18] When Mao met with North Korean Ambassador Li some weeks before Kim Il-sung's May 1950 visit, he went so far as to say that, "As regards the Americans, there is no need to be afraid of them. The Americans will not enter a third world war over such a small territory."[19]

As far as can be documented, Mao raised the possibility of a U.S. military intervention on only one occasion, on May 15, 1950, while discussing the North Korean plan with Kim Il-sung. Mao once again first asked about the possibility the Japanese would intervene. Kim replied that there was no possibility that Japan (i.e., the Japanese government) would get involved, but he could not exclude the possibility that the U.S., still occupying Japan, might dispatch 20,000–30,000 Japanese troops. However, said Kim, the introduction of Japanese troops would have no decisive effect on the progress of the war. If Japanese forces joined in the war, the Korean People's Army would fight even more fiercely. Mao said that under existing circumstances there was no possibility that Japan would get involved, but should 20,000–30,000 Japanese troops join the fight, the war could become protracted.

Mao then changed the subject and suggested that if U.S. forces intervened, China would send troops to help North Korea. Since the Soviet Union had an agreement with the United States regarding the 38th parallel, said Mao, it was not possible for Moscow to intervene, but China was under no such obligation, and could help Korea. Kim tactfully declined Mao's suggestion, since he believed there was no possibility the Americans would intervene. But Mao persisted, indicating that if North Korea launched its war on the South after China occupied Taiwan, China would be able to provide abundant assistance. But, since North Korea had already decided to go to war, the two countries shared the task with respect to the fight, so China agreed and would provide whatever assistance was necessary.

"Should American forces intervene, China will deploy its troops to help Korea."[19] Mao said this and was prepared to do it. But his promise stirred up considerable unease inside the Chinese Communist Party leadership. As recounted in *Mao, Stalin and the Korean War*, Zhou Enlai's July 2 discussion with the Soviet ambassador conveyed a sense of the angst and dissatisfaction in the Chinese leadership that the North Koreans had launched their offensive without regard to the possibility of an American intervention. But take a look at early August. When the North Korean offensive had advanced toward Pusan and the Tsushima Strait, and was bearing down on the U.S. Army, with only about 100 sq km to go, within the Chinese Communist Politburo, there was a growing itch to join in the final fight. Mao stated that China should prepare to assist North Korea with its People's Volunteers. Even more ambitiously, Zhou Enlai said that, "To gain victory, we need to add the China factor. After the China factor is added, there may be a change in the international situation." However, in early October, when the whole war situation was reversed by the American landing at Inchon, the main force of the Korean People's Army was on the point of collapse, and the U.S. and South Korean forces seemed on the verge of quickly sweeping past the 38th parallel, most members of the Chinese Communist Party leadership initially treated Mao's proposal to deploy Chinese forces with reserve.

The step-by-step explanation of the process by which the Chinese decided to join the war and the evolution of Chinese attitudes as described in *Mao, Stalin and the Korean War* is convincing, logical, dramatic and on target. Shen, by consulting and comparing a large number of Russian and Chinese documents, along with memoirs of leaders during the Korean War, has meticulously, boldly and engagingly sketched the whole process. Though Shen is known as a specialist in Soviet studies, his grasp of the background to Chinese decision-making and investigation into Chinese psychology is his strongest point, surpassing his passages regarding the motivations of Stalin and Kim. Perhaps, after all, it is easier for Chinese to capture and describe the motivations of other Chinese than to fathom and sketch the motivations of foreigners. This reminds us that despite the fairly large release of Russian documentation on the Korean War, it is still very hard to peer into Stalin's internal world and to fully comprehend the reasons for his miscalculations.

1 Stalin

From Yalta to the Far East

Stalin played a pivotal role in two major events in East Asia in the mid-twentieth century: the formation of the Sino-Soviet alliance, which lasted in any practical sense for only a decade, and the Korean War, whose effects have long outlasted the Cold War. Stalin's influential role derived from his leadership of the international Communist movement and the Soviet Union's enhanced global status as a result of World War II.

In the immediate postwar years, Soviet policies toward both China and Korea aimed to foster regional stability within the Yalta system, vital, in Moscow's view, to promoting Soviet economic interests and security goals in the Far East. In this light, Stalin's alliance with newly communist China in February 1950 and his April 1950 green light for Kim Il-sung's attack on South Korea (in June) constituted sharp breaks with the strategies and policies he had adopted in 1945.

Until 1950, Soviet policies toward China and Korea were not closely linked. But after Stalin decided in early 1950 that "there has been a shift in the international situation," his policies created – in actuality if not in intent – an inherent link between his China and Korea policies. To grasp the significance of this change, we need to delve into the origin and motivation of Stalin's early postwar policies in the Far East.

Soviet postwar foreign policy goals

With the end of World War II, twentieth-century international relations entered a new phase. The early postwar years were a time of transition, of realignments in the international political order and strategic redefinitions by all the major powers, setting the parameters for future events by channeling the course the major powers would take. Consequently, an appraisal of Stalin's early postwar foreign policy and strategy can clarify the evolution of Soviet policy toward China and Korea, including the objective conditions and subjective motivations that led the Soviet Union and Communist China to form their alliance.

Scholars around the world have long probed Stalin's postwar foreign policy from two different viewpoints. One view is that Stalin had an aggressively ambitious program, seeking to control and expand his spheres of influence. The other view is that Stalin resorted to moderate, cautious and defensive political countermeasures.[1] Before the dissolution of the Soviet Union, however, scholars representing these points of view, whether traditionalists or revisionists, had virtually no access to Soviet archives; their conclusions were based mainly on analysis of public statements and actions of Soviet leaders.

Now, with Russia's opening of its Soviet-era archives to foreign view, scholars have begun to reexamine Stalin's postwar foreign policy. Some now believe that Stalin's postwar behavior was eccentric and capricious, that Soviet foreign policy was aimless and freighted with inertia, and that its policies toward both Europe and the Far East were "blind" and "lacked any internal linkages." Others believe that the political aim of Stalin's foreign policy was simply to protect Soviet vested interests and spheres of influence, that he had no intention of fanning world revolution, that he did not want to directly confront the West and that, for a time, he thought Soviet security goals could be harmonized with the West in line with Yalta and Potsdam principles. In this view, faced with an increasingly tense situation in relations with the West, Stalin was at a loss over what to do. The Chinese Communist victory in 1949 then had a major impact on Stalin, and the new Sino-Soviet alliance in turn really stoked Soviet conflict with the United States.[2]

These views, however, do not fully and accurately reflect the strategic objectives of immediate postwar Soviet foreign policy. Without sketching the meandering evolution of Stalin's foreign policy in this period, it is hard to understand the essence of Soviet foreign policy and the reasons behind shifting Soviet policies toward China and Korea.

A juggling act: peaceful coexistence, world revolution and realpolitik

Peering through the dense, roiling fog of history, we can discern three strategic aspects or levels that shaped postwar Soviet foreign policy – peaceful coexistence, world revolution and national security interests.

First was peaceful coexistence. As Stalin said after World War II:

> In the most strenuous times during the war the differences in government did not prevent our two governments [the U.S. and the USSR] from joining together and vanquishing our foes. Even more so it is possible to continue this relationship in time of peace.[3]

This view was based on wartime cooperation, especially on the "Yalta system" forged by the leaders of the United States, Great Britain and the Soviet Union at the summit meeting held at Yalta on the Crimean peninsula in February 1945.

The Yalta Conference shaped the postwar world order. After Germany's surrender, the Potsdam Conference in July 1945 confirmed and amplified the results of the Yalta Conference. Based on the reach of their political and military power, the three major allied countries divided up what became the spheres of influence of the Soviet Union in the East and the United States and Great Britain in the West. Many scholars hold that Stalin was satisfied with the Yalta system, both in form and content. The structures built into this system all fit well with Russia's traditional national security strategy of using space to buy time, i.e., creating broad buffer zones around its national perimeter to guarantee sufficient time for maneuver and preparation against possible threats.

Later Georgian Communist Party First Secretary Akaki Mgeladze and then Foreign Minister Vyacheslav Molotov told the following anecdote: After the war, a map showing the new borders of the Soviet Union was brought to Stalin's dacha. Stalin pinned it to the wall and said to those around him:

> Let's take a look. What do we have here? In the north, everything is as it should be. Finland offended us, so we have pushed our border away from Leningrad. Poland's coast has long been Russian territory! Now it's ours again. Our Byelorussians now all live together, as do our Ukrainians and Moldovans. The situation in the West is normal.

As Stalin spoke, he turned and pointed to the Soviet Union's eastern border. "What's the situation here? The Kurils are back with us, and Sakhalin is all ours. Just look at how good things are! Lushun is ours, as is Dalian." Stalin next drew a circle around China with his pipe. "The Changchun Railway is also ours; there's no problem with China or Mongolia." Then he pointed south of the Caucasus. "But I don't like our border here."[4]

Stalin's tour d'horizon puts the Soviet Union's postwar situation in good perspective.

Except for Stalin's disappointment with the border "south of the Caucasus," through the war and the Yalta system the Soviet Union had gained new political rights and interests. From Finland through the three Baltic states to Eastern Europe, and from the Near East to Mongolia, onto Northeastern China, and the northern part of the Korean peninsula, and to the islands north of Japan, Stalin had achieved Russia's long-standing strategic goal of building broad national security buffer zones all around it. Therefore, Stalin, above all, needed to maintain peaceful coexistence with the Western capitalist world. Only then could he guarantee the vested interests of the Soviet Union at the lowest possible cost.

Yet, from the perspective of world revolution, the Soviet Union's highest strategic goal, peaceful coexistence was still only a temporary goal. Stalin held that the socialist Soviet Union would inevitably eliminate the capitalist world, and, further, that this historical mission of the Soviet Union and the world proletariat could only be achieved through revolution. As Stalin put it prior to World War II,

What do all these facts show? That the stabilization of capitalism is coming to an end, that the upsurge of the mass revolutionary movement will increase with fresh vigor ... the bourgeoisie will seek a way out through a new imperialist war ... the proletariat, in fighting capitalist exploitation and the war danger, will seek a way out through revolution.[5]

After the war, Stalin again proposed the theory of the general crisis of capitalism, asserting that,

Marxists have declared more than once that the capitalist system of world economy harbors elements of general crises and armed conflicts and that, hence, the development of capitalism in our time proceeds not in the form of smooth and even progress but through crises and military catastrophes.[6]

Capitalist crisis leads to war, war brings on revolution and revolution upends the capitalist world; this is the logic of Stalin's general crisis theory. In line with this world view, Soviet foreign policy should be encompassed within an overall system of world revolution, whether the world situation is characterized by peace or war. If Stalin's theory is followed to its logical end, peaceful coexistence should be subordinated to world revolution; it is only a partial, temporary goal within the overall strategic goal of world revolution.

But Stalin's consistent guiding principle was to put Soviet national security interests at the heart of his foreign policy and strategy. The theoretical basis for this guiding principle was Stalin's "theory of socialism in one country." Therefore, with respect to basic Soviet foreign policy goals – i.e., the promotion of Soviet national security interests – world revolution was merely a means or perhaps a partial and temporary goal within its external strategy. Under Lenin, the Russian Bolshevik party defined its task as international revolution, liberating all of mankind through a worldwide revolutionary upsurge, and even eliminating national borders. In actuality, however, by the time Stalin emerged supreme, Great Russian chauvinism was already deeply rooted in the Soviet Communist Party.

Before the war, when the Soviet Union was surrounded by capitalist states, Stalin held that the defense of Soviet national interests was not only the starting point for Soviet foreign policy, but also the goal of struggling proletariats and proletarian parties around the world. This belief enabled Stalin to sign the Soviet–German Non-aggression Pact, ruthlessly divide Poland, establish an "Eastern Front," sign a Neutrality Pact with Japan, launch a war on Finland under false pretenses and ultimately dissolve the Communist International (Comintern).

Stalin believed that Soviet national interests equated with the interests of socialism and the fundamental interests of mankind. Therefore, his logic went, the interests of world revolution should be subordinated to Soviet national interests. Whether and when the people of a country should rise in revolution, and whether or not the Soviet Union should support a given national liberation movement, depended on whether or not a revolutionary movement was helpful in promoting Soviet national interests. This was Stalin's unwavering logic.

To summarize, in Stalin's three-dimensional structure of foreign policy aims, Soviet national security always occupied the highest place. In dealing with postwar international relations, depending on time and place, Stalin sometimes used the need for peaceful coexistence as a reason to adjust policy, and sometimes fanned world revolution for his political objectives. These moves were always temporary and changeable; his goal was to guarantee Soviet national security interests. Everything was ultimately subordinated to Soviet foreign policy aims.

From opportunistic cooperation to outright confrontation

From this starting point, Stalin's postwar foreign policy evolved gradually from maintaining great power cooperation and limited expansionism toward stark bloc-on-bloc confrontation.

Immediately after the war, Stalin wanted to maintain the cooperative partnership that he had forged with the Western allies during the war in order to strengthen political benefits the Soviet Union had gained in the Yalta and Potsdam agreements. The passive Soviet reactions to the Greek revolution, the Chinese revolution, the communist movement in Western Europe and other issues in 1945 make this clear. Stalin maintained this foreign policy direction based on the following considerations:

First, as a result of World War II, the Soviet Union had become a political and military world power, but still faced an enormous task of recovery and development. Soviet postwar economic strength then was simply no match for the Western countries led by the United States. The reconstruction task required cooperation with the United States and other Western countries to assure the peaceful external environment needed by the Soviet Union to rebuild and expand its devastated domestic economy.

Second, Stalin's policy of diplomatic cooperation was based on his belief that for a period after the war, there was no possibility another world war would erupt. Stalin formulated a two-tiered definition of a new world war, either one between capitalist countries or one between capitalist countries and the Soviet Union. He argued that,

> [W]ar with the U.S.S.R. ... is more dangerous to capitalism than war between capitalist countries; for whereas war between capitalist countries puts in question only the supremacy of certain capitalist countries over others, war with the U.S.S.R. must certainly put in question the existence of capitalism itself.

But the Soviet Union would not attack the capitalist countries.[7] Under these conditions, it was crucial for the Soviet Union to continue to cooperate diplomatically with the West.

Third, the Yalta system guaranteed the Soviet Union's postwar international position and national security interests. As Stalin saw it, the Soviet Union's postwar spheres of influence were established through an international cooperative process with its (then) Western allies. In order to uphold the Yalta system, Soviet foreign policy must be based on cooperation with the West.

In sum, the Yalta system guaranteed the Soviet Union's vested interests, but they could be assured only by a cooperative policy. Yet divisions were inherent in this cooperation. Latent conflict over national interests aside, there were other reasons:

First of all, owing to their differing ideologies, value systems and social systems, the Soviet Union and the Western powers stood in diametrical opposition. Their wartime alliance had been built on specific historical conditions dictated by their joint opposition to common threats. With the end of the war, their enemies were vanquished, and, therefore, the historical mission of their alliance and the reason for its existence was over.

Next, though President Roosevelt and Stalin both advocated a policy of cooperative great power global dominion, Roosevelt, having seen the drawbacks of the post-World War I Versailles agreements, sought to ensure peace and stability through organizations such as the United Nations. Roosevelt aimed to use such organizations to coordinate international affairs among the big powers. Roosevelt believed that American interests could be assured by relying on American economic power and the Open Door policy. But other Western leaders, notably Prime Minister Churchill, shared neither Roosevelt's political power nor his innovative thinking. On issues where Roosevelt might tolerate or ignore Stalin, his successor, President Truman, and other Western leaders were drawn to oppose Stalin. Roosevelt's death arguably darkened prospects for great power cooperation.

Finally, by contrast with the intent that underlay Roosevelt's cooperative policy, the great power cooperation advocated by Stalin – at its core – continued the traditional international practice of distributing the spoils of war among the victors, in this case dividing up global spheres of power. In substituting the Yalta system for the prewar Versailles agreements, Stalin's intent was to build a new world order based on shared Soviet–American world dominion.

Having been encircled for decades by the capitalist world, and seeing itself constrained and discriminated against, the Soviet Union had long nursed its lonely grievances. The rise of Russian revanchism as a result of Czarist Russia's defeat in the Russo-Japanese War (1904–05), of course, fed into these feelings. As a result, Stalin's World War II victories filled him with a new feeling of superiority. As a victor, the Soviet Union could now join in world domination. Because of this, and despite the fact that it pursued a policy of big power cooperation, the Soviet Union often showed an itch to expand, especially in places not covered by the Yalta and Potsdam agreements.

Theoretically, if the Soviet Union and the West had scrupulously abided by the principle of peaceful coexistence, even if the two sides could not share the same kind of wartime alliance relationship, they still could have at least maintained a normal cooperative relationship. However, owing to the reasons noted above, in the new postwar world order, the standpoints and viewpoints of the Soviet Union and the West were poles apart. Both sides viewed the other as rivals, and did all they could to check and harm the other side. Both sides jockeyed to strengthen their own international position and to change the world to accord with their values and modes of thought. As a result, it was hard to avoid rising discord and conflict.

Conflict between the Soviet Union and the Western powers first arose over Eastern Europe. Eastern Europe bordered the Soviet Union's European heartland, and, historically, Eastern Europe had often been the corridor through which foreign enemies had invaded Russia. Consequently, Eastern Europe was the key prize sought by Stalin in constructing Soviet postwar security buffers and spheres of influence. The core of this policy was to use the Soviet Red Army's advance into Eastern Europe to support Eastern European communist parties in setting up pro-Soviet governments and Soviet-style structures. This gained at one stroke two great strategic goals of Soviet foreign policy, guaranteeing its national security and promoting world revolution. Therefore, on the question of Eastern Europe, the Soviet Union would not yield an inch to the United States and the Western countries.

As early as the Yalta Conference Stalin had made it clear that he would not tolerate any challenge to his power in Eastern Europe. He flatly rejected the American proposal to replace the Soviet-sponsored Lublin Provisional Government with an alternative Polish provisional government. In September 1945 the Soviet Union similarly rebuffed an American request to reconstitute the Romanian and Bulgarian governments. And, on the German question, the Soviet aim was to turn the Soviet zone of occupation into a forward buffer to guarantee the security of the western part of the Soviet Union. The Soviet Union sought to strengthen its zone, to maximize its influence in Germany and to prevent the formation of a Western-leaning independent government in the Western-occupied zones.

The hard-line attitude of the Western powers toward Stalin's actions in Eastern Europe reflected their unhappiness and misgivings. But there was little they could do under the Yalta system. Eastern Europe was now effectively in the Soviet sphere of influence, and, even should the West react, it would look weak.

The issues that sparked conflict and led to policy changes on both sides occurred in those areas that had not been defined or adjusted under the

Yalta agreements, most prominently, Turkey and Iran. It was in these areas that Stalin expressed his own dissatisfaction, along with expansionist intentions.

Czarist Russia and the European great powers had historically contested for control of the Near East. From the nineteenth century on, Czarist Russia had single-mindedly sought to control the Dardanelles, the strait linking the Black and Aegean Seas, and to gain an ice-free ocean port in the Persian Gulf to the south in Iran. After World War II, Turkey and Iran also occupied a fairly important place in Stalin's foreign policy. If the Soviet Union could gain political and economic rights and interests in these countries, this would not only guarantee the security of its southern border, but would also gain bases from which to make further moves toward the Mediterranean Sea and Indian Ocean. However, under the Yalta agreements, neither Turkey nor Iran was in the Soviet sphere of influence. So Stalin's designs evoked strong Western responses.

Soviet pressure to gain footholds in Turkey and Iran had a major impact on postwar relations between the Soviet Union and the West. Two studies of these events[8] led to the following conclusions:

First, though Stalin's actions in the Near East were motivated by the Soviet Union's desire to expand its sphere of influence in the region, he did not want to change his fundamental policy of cooperation with the West. He clearly did not foresee Western reactions to his actions when they went beyond the Yalta agreements. Therefore, when faced with a stiff attitude from the United States and Britain, the Soviet Union retreated and compromised. The Soviet Union's military withdrawal from Iran, like its military withdrawals from Northeast China and, later, from North Korea, showed that there were limits to Stalin's expansionism. In these situations, he wanted to avoid direct confrontation and conflict, especially with the United States.[9]

Second, the Soviet Union's diplomatic moves strengthened coordination and consensus in the West. The rise in the postwar position of the United States and the decline in British and French power led to some contradictions among the Western countries. This was evident in the fairly large differences between the United States and Great Britain over the Turkish and Iranian questions. But Soviet actions in this period caused all the Western countries to feel under threat. This promoted Western unity. To some significant extent, against the backdrop of the West's long-standing, inherent anti-Communist ideology, the Soviet Union's postwar diplomatic actions on its periphery strengthened Western collective consciousness and quickened the formation of the Western anti-Soviet alliance.

Third, the Soviet Union's diplomatic actions hastened the revision of Western policy toward the Soviet Union. The two Near East incidents finally brought about the rupture of what was already a shaky cooperative relationship between the Soviet Union and the West, deepening mutual suspicion, hostility and confrontation. Churchill's "Iron Curtain" speech, even with its strong ideological color, evoked no strong response in the United States and in other Western countries. But American diplomat George Kennan's "Theory of Containment" and President Truman's policies show that the Soviet Union's actions in the Near East caused the big Western countries to feel their own interests had been violated. This brought about a revision in their policy toward the Soviet Union. The confrontations over Turkey and Iran thus paved the way toward formation of antagonistic blocs between the Soviet Union and the West.

Soviet setbacks in Turkey and Iran led Stalin to conclude that the Soviet Union could no longer go it alone in international affairs, and that, to contend with the United States and its Western allies, he needed to coordinate and unite the power of the Soviet Union with the Eastern European countries now under his control. Not long after the Soviet Union withdrew from Iran, around the end of May and the beginning of June 1946, in talks with Yugoslav and Bulgarian leaders, Stalin broached the idea of establishing a Communist Information Bureau to coordinate policy. He later took up the idea again in the spring of 1947 with Polish United Workers' Party leader Wladyslaw Gomulka.[10] This shows that Stalin was thinking, albeit in embryonic form, of an over-arching framework for collective diplomatic confrontation with the West.

In this period, the hardening U.S. and Western diplomatic attitude caught Soviet attention. Soviet ambassador to Washington Nikolai Novikov's lengthy September 1946 analysis of U.S. foreign policy demonstrates Soviet concern over changing American policy, and to a certain extent laid the basis for Stalin's adjustment of his policy toward the United States.[11] As set out by Ambassador Novikov, "The foreign policy of the United States, which reflects the tendencies of American monopolistic capital, is characterized in the postwar period by a striving for world supremacy." In line with its " 'hard-line' policy with regard to the Soviet Union,"

> [I]n the postwar period the United States no longer follows a policy of strengthening cooperation between the Big Three (or Four) but rather has striven to undermine the unity of these countries. The objective [is] to impose the will of other countries on the Soviet Union.

If George F. Kennan's famous 8,000-word telegram laid the theoretical basis for America's Soviet containment policy, then Novikov's analysis, which was circulated at almost the same time, played a similarly important role as a guide to a Soviet hard-line, counterattack policy toward the United States.

In Stalin's eyes: Marshall Plan equals containment

What really brought about a fundamental change in Soviet postwar foreign policy, however, was the Marshall Plan unveiled in June 1947. Though

President Truman had announced his Truman Doctrine only shortly before, Stalin had seen the Truman's speech as mere rhetorical posturing about how the United States would carry out its "containment" policy toward the Soviet Union.[12] But Stalin concluded that the Marshall Plan was a substantial U.S. move to establish an anti-Soviet bloc, by – what Stalin could not tolerate – trying to bring Eastern Europe under Western influence, and by assisting and rearming the Soviet Union's old enemy, Germany (i.e., Western Germany).[13]

The Soviet Union's response to the Marshall Plan brought a major change in its foreign policy. To guarantee that Eastern Europe would support the Soviet Union in creating a strong interest group opposed to the West, Stalin decided that he needed to unify and harmonize the actions of the governments and communist parties in Eastern Europe in reaction to the Marshall Plan. As soon as the Soviet Union decided to oppose the Marshall Plan, and it did at first hesitate and send mixed signals, it fired off urgent cables to Eastern European Communist Party leaders on July 8 and 9 suggesting they reject invitations and boycott the Paris Conference to discuss the Marshall Plan. When the Czechoslovaks nonetheless indicated they were eager to join the Marshall Plan, Stalin summoned Czechoslovak leaders to Moscow, browbeating them into accepting the Soviet position, as he did as well with the Poles.[14] In late July 1947, when the Yugoslav and Bulgarian leaders announced that they were consulting on a bilateral Treaty of Friendship, Cooperation and Mutual Assistance, Stalin sternly criticized this "hasty" and "erroneous" action, emphasizing that it "had not been coordinated with the Soviet government."[15]

To resist the Marshall Plan and to strengthen Soviet influence and control over Eastern Europe, between July 10 and August 28 the Soviet government signed bilateral trade agreements with Bulgaria and five other Eastern European countries, the so-called Molotov Plan. The Molotov Plan solidified economic relations between the Soviet Union and the Eastern Europe countries, brought them into the Soviet Union's orbit and established a Soviet–Eastern European economic group in opposition to Western capitalism.

Stalin's answer: Cominform conformity in Europe

The Soviet foreign policy change was signaled organizationally through a new international communist coordinating mechanism, the Information Bureau of the Communist and Workers' Parties, the Cominform. But, in marked contrast with the prewar Communist International, or Comintern, the postwar Cominform was limited to Europe, and was clearly formed in response to the threat posed to Soviet interests by the Marshall Plan. The Cominform was not intended as a harbinger of world Communist revolution. Rather, Stalin sought a coordinating mechanism to strengthen control over Eastern Europe and the non-ruling communist parties of Western Europe.[16]

There were two policy consequences of the Cominform. Soviet-style political regimes replaced democratic multi-party coalition governments in Eastern Europe. And, criticism was leveled at the French and Italian Communist parties for clinging to their strategy of legal, parliamentary struggle. Moscow and its proxies urged instead that the Western European communist parties employ strikes and other revolutionary actions against their countries' capitalist governments. With the Cominform, and in the wake of the Marshall Plan, Soviet foreign policy abandoned great power cooperation, and was now oriented toward bloc-on-bloc struggle with the West.[17]

Rooted in the confrontation between the United States and the Soviet Union, the Cold War was manifested in geopolitical and ideological struggle. As a result of World War II, the United States and the Soviet Union were political and economic superpowers. Bursting forth from the Western hemisphere, the United States abandoned its traditional isolationism. East of the American homeland, in postwar Europe, depleted powers, notably Great Britain, France and Italy, were forced to depend on American economic and military power. To America's west, a defeated Japan together with a weak China and a weak Philippines provided a golden opportunity and space for the United States to insert itself into Asia. The Soviet Union, for its part, had moved beyond its prewar "isolated island" position. On one side, having sent its armies into Europe and liberated the Eastern European countries, the Soviet Union now occupied a vast security belt. On the other side, as it expanded eastward, it promoted (recognition of) Mongolian independence (in its diplomacy with the U.S. and China), and dominated Northeast China and North Korea. It still coveted the Near East. Thus, the United States and the Soviet Union, geopolitical rivals, confronted each other on the Eurasian land mass.

Ideologically, the United States and the Soviet Union were locked in confrontation. The United States, flying the flag of "freedom" and "democracy," and paving the way with its dollars and occupying armies, became the leader of the capitalist world alliance, seeking to bring the whole world into a U.S.-style "Free World." For its part, the Soviet Union, waving the banner of "proletarian internationalism," strove to bring the recently liberated "democratic" (Eastern European) countries and newly independent post-colonial countries into its orbit, and lead all of humanity toward Stalinist-style communism.

Relative Soviet moderation in the Far East

But, the Cold War did not emerge in lockstep fashion around the world. It developed eastward from Europe toward Asia.

Whether Stalin shifted his diplomatic measures globally from peaceful coexistence to world revolution, or whether he used different measures simultaneously in different countries and regions, his basic aim was to maintain and expand Soviet spheres of influence, and to ensure Soviet national security interests. As the Soviet Union's domestic economy revived and developed, and the international situation changed, the direction of Soviet foreign policy gradually changed from moderation toward a hard line, and, in the main, from great power cooperation toward bloc-on-bloc confrontation.

This does not mean every element of Soviet policy changed. Europe was still the center of gravity of Soviet foreign policy. Soviet policy toward Asia more often than not complemented its European policy. Consequently, Stalin's Asia policy evolved neither simultaneously with nor completely in accord with his European policy. The opposite happened. To concentrate power in Europe to confront the United States and the West, in Asia, the Soviet Union maintained a relatively moderate and conservative policy, albeit one based principally on expediency.

Until 1950, in contrast to the direct bloc-on-bloc confrontation that characterized the international situation in Europe, in the Far East, the United States and the Soviet Union maintained an attitude of restraint, especially in their policies toward Korea and China. In the end, however, Soviet policy in Asia also shifted toward toughness and confrontation. In 1950, under the premise of "the change in the international situation," the Far East became the cockpit of an explosive crisis involving the United States and the Soviet Union.

2 Korea

The evolution of Soviet postwar policy

When the allied victory in Europe was assured, the United States, proceeding from its conflicting aims of limiting its casualties in its final Pacific assault and reining in Soviet postwar expansion in the Far East, urgently sought a Soviet commitment that it would join in the war against Japan – along with a clarification of Moscow's political conditions. Stalin did not commit himself quickly. Only at Yalta did the Soviet Union clarify its main political condition for joining in the war against Japan: restoration of the Russian sphere of influence as it was under the Czars, before Russia's defeat in the 1904–05 Russo-Japanese War. Later, with the rapid change in the war situation, especially after the success of the U.S. atomic bomb test, the United States was no longer as keen for the Soviet Union to move into Asian affairs. But, after the United States dropped its atomic bombs on Japan, when the Pacific situation was then already settled, Moscow, without reaching agreement in its negotiations with the Chinese Nationalist government, and without receiving clear guarantees with respect to its political condition for joining in the war in the Far East, hastily sent its troops into Northeast China, launching a full-scale attack on the Japanese Army and thereby gaining a favorable diplomatic position based on its military presence.[1]

As stipulated in the Yalta agreements, the Soviet Union aimed to recover the Kuril Islands, South Sakhalin and nearby islets, all of which had been occupied by Japan since the Russo-Japanese War. The Soviets also wanted to join in the occupation of Japan. The achievement of this latter aim would depend on the unfolding of American and Soviet military power in the Far East. As a result of the contest of wills between the U.S. and the Soviet Union in Asia, the Soviets were not able to share in the occupation of Japan. However, events in Korea played out differently.

The 38th parallel: a hastily drawn line

Even as the American military was still fighting in the archipelago off the southern main islands of Japan, the Soviet Army entered the Korean peninsula in force. Japan's unconditional surrender after the U.S.

dropped its two atom bombs and the Soviet Union attacked the Japanese Army in Northeast China created a power vacuum on the Korean penin-sula. The United States had no alternative but to propose that it and the Soviet Union jointly occupy Korea, with the two allied powers accepting the surrender of Japanese forces in Korea north and south of the 38th par-allel, respectively.[2]

On August 15, 1945 President Truman notified Stalin that he had approved "General Order Number One" for the surrender of Japanese forces that was to be promulgated by the Supreme Commander for the Allied Powers, General Douglas MacArthur. One of the items in the order established the 38th parallel on the Korean peninsula as the line of demar-cation between the American and Soviet zones for the purpose of accept-ing the Japanese surrender.

On August 16 Stalin replied that he "had nothing against the substance of the order," but then reminded President Truman of the Soviet Union's demand to acquire all the Kuril Islands, as agreed to at Yalta, and further, made a strong, insistent case for the Soviet occupation of northern Hokkaido. In an August 18 reply to Stalin, Truman agreed to modify Order Number One to include the Kuril Islands in the area to be surren-dered to the Commander-in-Chief of the Soviet Forces in the Far East. However, he rebuffed Stalin with respect to northern Hokkaido, assuring him only that "General MacArthur will employ Allied token forces, which of course, includes Soviet forces, in so much of a temporary occupation of Japan proper as he considers it necessary ... to accomplish our Allied sur-render terms."[3]

On September 2, after the Japanese surrender ceremony on the battle-ship Missouri in Tokyo Bay, General MacArthur issued "General Order Number One," including the change requested by Stalin with respect to the Kurils and the language Stalin had agreed to with respect to the divi-sion of Korea. By the time the order to accept the surrender reached the Soviet combat zone in Korea, some units of the Soviet forces had already crossed the 38th parallel, and were moving on the road toward Seoul. But, as soon as they received the order regarding the demarcation line, these Soviet units swiftly withdrew north of the 38th parallel. On September 6, U.S. forces entered and garrisoned Seoul.[4]

While the United States hastily proposed the 38th parallel to limit the expansion of the Soviet sphere of influence on the Korean peninsula, the Soviet Union, considering deeper political issues, was very happy with the 38th parallel plan. But Washington was thinking about the Korean ques-tion, while, as we have noted, Stalin's eyes were fixed on northern Hokkaido. Then State Department adviser Colonel Dean Rusk, who came up with the 38th parallel proposal, estimated that had the Soviet Union, based on its military posture, refused to accept the 38th parallel and pro-posed a more southern line of demarcation, from a practical standpoint, the U.S. would have been forced to accept such a revised plan. But, Stalin did not do this, rather he agreed without hesitation to the 38th parallel plan. Stalin's action both surprised Rusk at the time[5] and later puzzled some scholars.[6]

Stalin loses his bid to gain a foothold in Japan

Indeed, in the last stages of World War II, the Soviet Army was in an unprecedentedly strong position, leading Stalin to assert smugly that, "This war is not as in the past; whoever occupies a territory also imposes on it his own social system. Everyone imposes his own system as far as his army can reach."[7] Then, why did Stalin accept the 38th parallel? As a politician, Stalin had a deeper consideration. He accepted the 38th parallel proposal as a bargaining ploy.

In Stalin's August 16 reply to Truman accepting the American surrender plan, he had proposed two important revisions: (1) that all of the Kuril Islands should be turned over to Soviet military occupation, and (2) that northern Hokkaido, one of the four Japanese main islands, should be turned over to Soviet military occupation. Stalin especially stressed the importance of the second point, noting that: "As is known, in 1919–21 the Japanese occupied the whole of the Soviet Far East. Russian public opinion would be gravely offended if the Russian troops had no occupation areas in any part of the territory of Japan proper." Finally, in a tone that allowed for no debate, Stalin told Truman that, "I am most anxious that the modest suggestions set forth above should not meet with any objections."[8] Clearly, Stalin was hoping to exchange U.S. occupation of Korea south of the 38th parallel for Soviet occupation of a portion of Japan well to the north of the 38th parallel.

Based on the American experience with the division of Germany, however, the United States could only limit the further expansion of Soviet power in East Asia by unilaterally occupying Japan. The United States might abandon Korea, but it was determined not to let the Soviet Union have a hand in Japan. Truman, in his August 18 reply to Stalin, agreed to Stalin's first revision, designating the Kuril Islands as an area within which the Soviet Union would accept the Japanese surrender. This had already been clearly stipulated at Yalta. But, as we have seen, Truman parried Stalin's second requested revision, that Soviet forces be allowed onto the Japanese main islands, saying merely that Soviet forces might play a "token" role in the occupation of Japan.[9]

On the one hand, Stalin in his August 22 reply expressed regret that the United States had rejected the Soviet request, while, on the other hand, even before sending his reply, on August 20 Stalin ordered Soviet Army and naval forces to land on and garrison Hokkaido, giving as a reason that Hokkaido was north of the 38th parallel. The Soviet representative to MacArthur's headquarters, Lt. General Derevyanko, called on General MacArthur and asserted that, whether or not the U.S. agreed,

Soviet forces would land on and garrison Hokkaido. MacArthur rejected this on the spot: "I told him that if a single Soviet soldier entered Japan without my authority, I would at once throw the entire Russian (*sic*) Mission, including himself, into jail."[10] The strong American reaction stymied the Soviet plan to take over Hokkaido, and, since Stalin had already agreed to the division of the Korean peninsula, what was done could not be undone. He was forced to accept a *fait accompli*, ceding the southern part of Korea to the United States and putting off the Korea question off until the future. As will be seen, this opportunity only came in 1950.

Wartime Korean trusteeship planning

The Yalta plan for Korea called, however, not for a divided occupation by the United States and the Soviet Union, but rather for a four-power trusteeship comprised of the United States, the Soviet Union, China and Great Britain. At a meeting between the American and Soviet leaders at Yalta, President Roosevelt had raised the issue of territorial trusteeships, proposing that, until the Korean people were ready for self-government, Korea should be administered under a trusteeship composed of a Soviet, an American and a Chinese representative. When Roosevelt said a trusteeship might last twenty to thirty years, Stalin countered "the shorter the period the better." Probably owing to British Foreign Secretary Anthony Eden's March 1944 rejection of an American proposal to put Korea and Indochina under postwar trusteeships, Roosevelt told Stalin that he felt it was not necessary for Great Britain to join in a trusteeship for Korea.

Stalin agreed to the trusteeship plan, but proposed that the British should be invited to join in the Korea trusteeship. Thus, the plan for a postwar Korean provisional trusteeship by China, the United States, the Soviet Union and Great Britain was fixed at Yalta. In referring to the territories that would be under trusteeships, conference documents do not go into specifics about the Korean trusteeship, merely noting that the issue of trusteeships would be a "matter of subsequent agreement."[11] When Truman sent his adviser, Harry Hopkins, to Moscow in May 1945, shortly after he took office as president, Stalin reaffirmed his agreement to a four-power trusteeship for Korea.[12]

Nevertheless, while Soviet authorities were not oblivious to the Korean issue, it was not high on their agenda, and, at the time, they had no firm policy for postwar Korea. A June 1945 paper drafted in the Soviet Foreign Ministry Second Far Eastern Division laid out Soviet thinking on Korea in the months after the Yalta Conference.[13] Prepared as background for Soviet negotiators at the Potsdam Conference, the paper stressed that, except for normal trade relations, "Japan must forever be excluded from Korea;" that "the independence of Korea must be effective enough to prevent Korea from being turned into a staging ground for future aggression against the

USSR;" that Soviet security in the Far East would be guaranteed by "friendly and close relations between the USSR and Korea;" that this "must be reflected in the formation of a [future] Korean government;" and that, if a trusteeship were established, the Soviet Union "must ... participate prominently in it."[14] This paper shows that the Soviet government was highly focused on great power rivalry in the Far East. Moscow still considered Japan to be a threat, so it wanted to prevent Japan from again turning Korea into a springboard for expansion on the Asian continent. However, the Soviet Union did not seek unilateral occupation or control of Korea, though, over the longer term, it desired the formation of a Korean government that would have "close, friendly relations" with the Soviet Union.

Early Soviet occupation policy

Through the end of 1949, Soviet policy toward Korea can be divided into three stages: first, cooperating with the United States through the trusteeship to establish a unified Korean government friendly to the Soviet Union; second, when this failed, strengthening the political and economic power of the North Korean administration, and, on this basis, promoting unification through an election aimed at forming a unitary Korean government that would maintain friendly policies toward the Soviet Union; and, third, following the election held in South Korea and the establishment of the Republic of Korea, working to establish an independent North Korean government that met Soviet needs, and, on this basis, to confront the United States.

As foreshadowed above, Soviet Foreign Ministry documents indicate that as late as September 1945 the Soviet government had no fixed political plan for resolving the Korean issue. The Soviet Union at this point supported the trusteeship system as a means to counter American gains in the Pacific and to promote Soviet interests. As outlined in a Foreign Ministry position paper:

> The occupation of Korea by Soviet troops in the zone north of the 38th parallel must be kept for the same period of time as the American occupation of the remaining part of Korea.... Upon the conclusion of the occupation regime, presumably after two years, Korea must become a trust territory of the four powers, with the apportionment of three strategic regions, Pusan, Chejudo, and Inchon, which must be controlled by the Soviet military command. Insisting on the apportionment for the USSR of the strategic regions in Korea, we can exert pressure on ... the Americans, using their wish to receive for themselves strategic regions in the Pacific Ocean. In case the proposal about granting the Soviet Union these strategic regions in Korea meets with opposition, it is possible to propose joint Soviet-Chinese control over these strategic regions.[15]

These documents indicate that in September 1945 Moscow's objective was to safeguard Soviet strategic interests in Northeast Asia through joint management over Korea. Stalin's aim was not to gain control over the whole Korean peninsula as he had done, for instance, with Poland in Europe. At the outset, Stalin did not intend to divide the Korean peninsula or to unilaterally occupy North Korea. To the contrary, he was implementing a much more complex strategy. Under the premise of controlling some militarily important positions, his strategy called for balancing Soviet and American interests and influence on the Korean peninsula.[16]

At least through the end of 1945, Soviet policy aimed to use both the Soviet position of strength and a policy of cooperation with the United States to establish a unified Korean government that was friendly to or at least not antagonistic toward the Soviet Union. A Foreign Ministry background paper by (former) Soviet ambassador to Japan Jacob Malik, "On the Question of a Unified Korean Government," indicates that in December 1945 the Soviet Union was prepared to adopt election procedures to establish a Korean provisional government. The paper argued that "It would not be politically wise for the Soviet Union to oppose the establishment of a unified Korean government," and further recommended: (1) Support and announce the restoration of Korean independence and sovereignty. (2) Pledge support for the establishment of a Korean provisional government with the participation of all Korean social and political organizations. (3) All of these organizations should elect a provisional committee to prepare for the convocation of a constitutional conference. (4) Before a constitutional conference is convened, in all regions, democratic meetings among workers, peasants, intellectuals, teachers, employees, hired workers and other groups should be held to discuss and propose representatives to the constitutional convention and candidates to be officials of a unified Korean government. (5) Set up a special unified liaison committee of representatives of the Soviet Union and the United States (if possible also to include representatives from China and Great Britain) to take the responsibility for this organizational work. (6) Set up a Soviet–U.S. mixed commission composed of Soviet Army Headquarters and U.S. Army Headquarters representatives to resolve urgent issues arising from the Soviet and American garrisoning of forces in Korea.[17]

To further cooperate with the United States, the Soviet Union did not at first put a Communist in charge of the provisional government in northern Korea. Sixty-six officers of the 88th Route Army Korean battalion led by Kim Il-sung (who had been trained in the Soviet Far East) were on the Soviet cargo ship *Pugachev* that docked in Wonsan on October 10, 1945. But when the Administrative Bureau of the five provinces of northern Korea was set up on November 19, nationalist leader and Pyong'an Namdo Provincial People's Committee leader Cho Man-sik, not Kim Il-sung, was elected chairman. In this period, Soviet occupation authorities did not support Korean Communist Party propaganda, agitation and other activities in the U.S. occupation zone in South Korea. Soviet Communist Party Central Committee International Bureau documents indicate that in the fall of 1945, though the Soviet authorities actively reorganized and guided the activities of the Korean Communist Party in the North, they did not extend this activity south of the 38th parallel.

The Korean Communist Party headquarters in this period was located in Seoul. Korean Communist Party Chairman Pak Hon-yong only later went to North Korea where he was appointed vice premier and foreign minister. Despite sabotage and pressure from anti-Communist organizations in South Korea, Soviet occupation authorities in the North repeatedly turned down Korean Communist Party requests for help, even demurring from approaching U.S. occupation authorities to allow the Korean Communist Party to engage in legal activities. Instead, the Soviets asked the Korean Communists in the South to cooperate with U.S. occupation authorities, lecturing them that

> the correct strategic line can take place only through a correct understanding of the international position of Korea.... The ideals of the United States, the leader of capitalism, and the Soviet Union, the fatherland of the proletariat, are to be expressed in Korea without contradiction.

U.S. occupation policy in the South was running into strong opposition in this period and Korean Communist Party activities might have strengthened the party's position there, but reports from Korea in 1945 contain no mention of Soviet support for propaganda or agitation work in the southern part of Korea.[18]

Soviet economic policies in Korea in 1945 also indicate that Stalin then had no plans for a long-term occupation of the Korean peninsula or North Korea. In a briefing paper for the December 1945 Moscow Foreign Ministers' Conference entitled "A Report on Japanese Military and Heavy Industry in Korea," Soviet Foreign Ministry adviser S. P. Suzdalev provided a detailed list of Japanese assets left in Korea and offered three recommendations:

> (1) Japanese military and heavy industries in Korea were set up and maintained to serve Japan's aggressive policy. Soviet occupation authorities must take these industries out of Japanese hands. (2) All Japanese military industry and heavy industries in northern Korea should be considered spoils of war belonging to the Red Army, since all of these enterprises, to a certain degree, served the Japanese Imperial Army in fighting the Red Army. The Red Army made very heavy sacrifices to take these enterprises out of Japanese hands. (3) Finally, Japanese military and heavy industries in northern Korea must be turned over as a part of the reparations to the Soviet Union to

compensate for the destruction inflicted by Japan on the Soviet Union, including the harm inflicted by Japan's intervention in the Soviet Far East between 1918 and 1923.[19]

Soviet occupation authorities assured the people of North Korea that they would "guarantee protection of the properties of all Korean enterprises and will assist you in every manner possible to maintain the regular activities of your enterprises." On September 20 Stalin issued an order to the Soviet Far East Army Commander, General A. M. Vasilevsky, the Military Council of the Maritime Military Region and the Military Council of the 25th Army to protect

> the private property of North Korean citizens … safeguard normal functioning of industrial, trade, municipal, and other enterprises … [and o]rder the troops in North Korea to obey discipline strictly, not insult the population and behave correctly.[20]

However, from October through mid-December 1945 "the Soviets seemed to lose control of their troops," who, in this period, engaged in wanton depredations against Japanese and Koreans. As they had done with many Japanese colonial-era factories in Manchuria, "the Soviets carted off many North Korean factories." American intelligence concluded that the Soviet actions indicated that "the Russians would not intend to remain in North Korea," probably believing "that Korea could be unified under the four-powers' trusteeship."[21]

However, the Soviet Union also calculated that it would be very hard to work with the United States to establish a unified Korean government friendly to the Soviet Union. As Soviet Foreign Ministry Second Far Eastern Division Deputy Director Zabrodin wrote:

> [T]he question is extremely complex, because of the multiplicity of political parties and groups, the lack of unity among them, and the solicitations of the United States…. Meanwhile, the character of the future government of Korea [will determine] the question of whether Korea will in the future be turned into a breeding ground of anxiety for us in the Far East or into one of the strong points of our security in the Far East.

Zabrodin concluded that a Korean government could be established in one of two ways:

> (1) The creation of a Korean government on the basis of agreement between the governments of the USSR, USA and China. In the formation of [this] government, the introduction … of Communists and genuinely democratic elements will meet with strong opposition from

the Korean reactionary elements, since the government will undoubtedly be inclined in favor of closer relations with the Soviet Union. It also goes without saying that these reactionary elements will find support among the governments of the USA and China. (2) The convening of a Representative People's Assembly, to which must be elected representatives of the entire Korean people (excluding traitors), by means of universal, secret and equal voting. The People's Assembly must proclaim a Korean Republic and create a Korean People's Government.[22]

Soviet–American face-off in Korea

Indeed, the United States and the Soviet Union locked in sharp conflict over how and what kind of unitary, provisional Korean government to establish. After the United States moved toward a hard-line policy in South Korea, and especially after the U.S.–Soviet Joint Commission fell into deadlock in early 1946, the Soviet Union began to change its initial policy of cooperation with the U.S. aimed at forming a unified Korean government. Instead, it began to assist in the political and economic development of North Korea, aiming to bolster the North with the goal of eventually establishing a unified Korean government friendly to the Soviet Union through national, peninsula-wide elections. In the short term, the Soviets therefore adopted Zabrodin's second option.

Soviet occupation authorities in North Korea quickly strengthened their political and administrative control. After the Soviet Red Army fought its way into Korea, it set up military management organizations called garrison headquarters in all provinces and administrative organizations under its control, 113 in all. In this early period, the only task of the garrison headquarters was to oversee property and arms seized from the Japanese. However, after the August 15th liberation of Korea, various autonomous management organizations were quickly set up throughout Korea, including so-called People's Committees, which gradually took on responsibility for local management. These indigenous Korean local organizations filled the power vacuum left by the collapse of Japanese control, acting to protect public installations, transportation facilities and enterprises, and stabilizing society.

After the U.S. Army entered South Korea, it also set up a military government, but unlike the Soviets in the North, it banned the People's Committees. Soviet military occupation authorities shortly thereafter reorganized the People's Committees in North Korea, renaming them People's Political Committees. By the end of August 1945, the reorganization of the People's Political Committees in the northern zone of occupation was basically complete. Every member of the People's Political Committees was either a nationalist or Communist, and Soviet occupation authorities either directly or indirectly controlled these committees through their local garrison headquarters. Later, the duties of the local garrison headquarters were sharply expanded to include all aspects of the work of the local People's Political Committees, thereby implementing a regime similar to military control.[23]

In October 1945 Marshal K. A. Meretskov, Commander of the Maritime Military District of the Soviet Far Eastern High Command, authorized Col. General I. M. Chistiakov, Commander of 25th Army, the Soviet Army of occupation in North Korea, to set up a Civil Administration. Chistiakov in turn appointed Major General A. A. Romanenko as commanding officer of the new Soviet Civil Administration. Compared with the U.S. military government in South Korea, the Soviet 25th Army Civil Administration was fairly small. But, with the help of Communist Party members in the People's Political Committees, the Soviet Army firmly controlled the economic and political life of North Korea.[24]

At the beginning of 1946, during talks in the U.S.–Soviet Joint Commission, the situation became very complex, leading to sharp political conflict. On the one hand, the U.S. military government attempted to shift the balance of power among various political forces in southern Korea. It outlawed the Communist Party, strengthened state security organs and encouraged moderate leftists to join in an American-controlled coalition of leftists and rightists, all aimed at creating a political base wide enough to hold a general election under southern control. Soviet occupation authorities meanwhile were supporting their own political regime in North Korea, preparing to establish a central provisional government in the North.

Communist North Korea: born and nurtured

A Korean Provisional People's Committee to govern northern Korean was announced on February 8, 1946. In the new northern regime, Kim Il-sung replaced Cho Man-sik. Cho, a respected anti-Japanese nationalist leader, had made no secret that he viewed the Soviets as occupiers on a par with the Japanese. Col. General Terentii Shtykov (who, in time, became the de facto "supervisor of Soviet-sponsored state-building in North Korea" and later the first Soviet ambassador to North Korea) had reported that Cho was "nationalistic" and "anti-Soviet," and recommended that he be replaced by Kim. Stalin agreed, reportedly noting that, "Korea is a young country. It needs a young leader."[25]

The Provisional People's Committee in the North was thus a creature of the Soviet occupation authorities. The archives of the former Soviet Communist Party Central Committee in Moscow hold a large volume of material related to Soviet drafts of a constitution and legal statutes for the North Korean regime as well as many reports concerning Soviet assistance in training political leaders and technical personnel, and in establishing Soviet-style propaganda and social organizations in North Korea.[26]

As their influence spread, Soviet occupation authorities gradually relaxed their direct control and management in the North. After the Soviets authorized establishment of the Korean Provisional People's Committee in February 1946, the Soviet Civil Administration staff was sharply reduced. According to an American intelligence report, in September 1946 there were about 200 Soviet officers in the Civil Administration headquarters, with the number dropping to 60 by December 1946. A British source estimated that the number of Soviet advisers to the North Korean central government fell to about 30 by April 1947.[27]

In the same period, the number of Soviet occupation forces was likewise sharply cut. Local security police took over when the Soviet Army began to withdraw in December 1946. As the North Koreans increased their own military and police forces, Soviet occupation troops were reduced from 40,000 in 1946 to 10,000 in 1947. On April 3, 1947 Soviet 25th Army Commander Col. General Chistiakov was replaced by a lower ranking officer, Lt. General G. P. Korotkov.[28]

Russian archives bear out that, compared with the very difficult political problems encountered by the United States in South Korea, Soviet control over North Korea was much more effective, and Soviet policies and principles were conscientiously carried out. In a February 20, 1947 letter to Stalin, the newly established Korean People's Committee stated that, "[T]he Korean people impatiently await the unification of South and North Korea and the rapid creation of a unified democratic provisional government of Korea." Similarly, the Presidium of the Korean People's Committee responding to a letter from Molotov on March 1, 1947 stated that, "[C]onsidering that Korea has until now not been unified, the people of North Korea are applying all their efforts to realize national unification of the country and creation of a democratic government based on Moscow's decision." On August 15, 1947, the anniversary of the liberation of Korea, responding to greetings from Soviet Foreign Minister Molotov, Kim Il-sung stated that,

> [Y]our greeting … increases our belief that at the soonest possible time a united democratic Korean government will be created and Korea will be a fully independent state. I am convinced that as a result of the efforts of the Soviet Union and you personally, the question of the creation of a Provisional Democratic government for Korea will be resolved in the spirit of the Moscow agreement of the three Foreign Ministers, which responds to the interests of the entire Korean people."[29]

To strengthen North Korea's economic position, the Soviet Union changed its predatory economic policy and began providing economic assistance. Meretskov and Col. General Shtykov in a May 12, 1947 joint telegram to Stalin stated that,

Without the help of Soviet or other foreign specialists, North Korean industry and rail transport cannot operate. We must without delay send Soviet engineers and technicians to North Korea, not only to help the People's Committee to turn around the management of industry and transportation, but also to strengthen our government's future position and influence in Korea.

If Soviet experts do not arrive in North Korea before the unification of North and South Korea and the establishment of a Korean provisional government, the Korean provisional government, which will depend on foreign technical assistance, will inevitably invite American technicians to work in Korea. This will strengthen American influence in Korea and harm our national interest. Therefore, we beseech you to issue an instruction to send Soviet experts to North Korea at the earliest opportunity.[30]

This document by the Soviet military occupation authorities clearly shows the new point of departure for Soviet policy toward Korea. In reaction, Molotov added this comment: "Comrade Stalin, I believe we must support this proposal." Though Stalin's comment is hard to make out on a copy of this document, it is clear that he approved the proposal.

In sum, during 1946 and 1947, though the United States and the Soviet Union both now realized that there was no way for them to continue to cooperate under the trusteeship arrangement, this recognition had not yet led to the logical conclusion that independent governments should be established in the South and the North. In this period the Americans and the Soviets continued to work through Koreans under their control to hold a general election and thereby establish a unified Korean provisional government favorable to their respective interests. Scholars differ on whether it was the Americans or the Soviets who first decided to establish an independent government on the territory under their control.[31] We can conclude, however, that once events reached this point, at a time of sharpening U.S.–Soviet confrontation in Europe, the division of the Korean peninsula and the Korean people was predestined.

Division cemented: the ROK and the DPRK are established

Shortly after the Republic of Korea (ROK) was established in South Korea (August 15, 1948), the Democratic People's Republic of Korea (DPRK) was established in the North (September 10, 1948), receiving Soviet recognition and assistance. Stalin informed Kim Il-sung on October 12, 1948 that:

The Soviet government unswervingly upholds the right of the Korean people to form their own unified, independent state, welcomes the formation of the Korean government, and wishes it victory in its effort to revive the Korean nation and develop democracy. The Soviet government is prepared to establish diplomatic relations with the Democratic People's Republic of Korea, to exchange ambassadors, and, simultaneously, to establish appropriate economic relations.[32]

The Soviet Union clearly hoped North Korea would develop and strengthen, check American influence on the peninsula, and create a protective security screen for the Soviet Union in the Far East.

Stalin's fundamental Korea policy, however, had not changed. Even though there was no longer any way to cooperate with the United States in Korea, the Soviet Union had no desire for open conflict with the United States in Korea. Rather, Moscow's aim was to establish a Korean government friendly toward the Soviet Union. But, whereas it had formerly envisaged a friendly, neighboring state covering the whole Korean peninsula, this was now only to be in northern Korea. The reason was simple: In 1948, when the Americans and the Soviets were in sharp conflict in Europe, Stalin could not afford to put Korea at the top of his agenda. The Soviet Union's Europe-first foreign policy and its need, above all, to recover from the tremendous human and material harm inflicted on it by World War II, dictated that it place Northeast Asia in a subordinate position.

Stalin never considered setting up an Eastern European-style satellite state in Korea or North Korea. The Soviet Union first urged that Soviet and American forces withdraw simultaneously from the Korean peninsula. Later, it announced that Soviet occupation troops would unilaterally withdraw from North Korea, and promised to grant full, autonomous political power to the (North) Korean people to a much greater degree than it had granted in some Eastern European countries. In order to avoid provoking the United States, Stalin even opposed diplomatic relations of an alliance nature with the Democratic People's Republic of Korea, not to speak of accepting responsibility for its unification goal.

Stalin sidesteps an alliance with the DPRK

Once Kim Il-sung's government was established, his next order of business was to form an alliance relationship with the Soviet Union that he could rely on to strengthen the North's position and influence in his effort to unify Korea. Kim floated this request while preparing for an official visit to the Soviet Union, but Stalin expressed no interest. A January 19, 1949 report to Moscow from Soviet ambassador to Pyongyang Terentii Shtykov concerning the Korean delegation's Moscow visit makes the Soviet position clear:

> Regarding Kim Il-sung's desire to conclude a Treaty of Friendship and Mutual Assistance with the Soviet Union during his visit, I explained

to Kim Il-sung and [Foreign Minister] Pak Hon-yong that at this time, with the country divided in two, it is not advisable to conclude such a treaty. It might be used by the South Korean reactionaries to oppose the Government of the Democratic People's Republic of Korea.

My explanation made Kim Il-sung and Pak Hon-yong a little uneasy. Kim Il-sung hemmed and hawed in explaining his reasons for concluding a treaty. To bolster his argument, he said that the Chairman of the Presidium of the Supreme People's Assembly, Kim Doobong, had repeatedly raised the question of concluding a Treaty of Friendship and Mutual Assistance with the Soviet Union, and that if, for whatever reason, a treaty cannot be concluded, then a secret agreement on Soviet assistance to Korea should be signed. After my additional explanation, Kim Il-sung and Pak Hong-yong agreed that now is not the time to raise the question of concluding a Treaty of Friendship and Mutual Assistance.[33]

As a result, when Kim visited Moscow in March 1949, he merely signed an economic and cultural agreement with the Soviet Union.

Some Russian scholars believe that Kim took the opportunity of his visit to lobby Stalin in favor of using military force to unify Korea, though this claim is disputed by a participant in the March 1949 Stalin–Kim meeting. Those who claim Kim raised the issue of using military force say that he suggested that the situation then opened up the possibility and even required the use of force to unify Korea. But, according to this account, Stalin did not agree, citing the North's inferior military position, the Soviet–American 38th parallel agreement, and possible U.S. intervention. Stalin reportedly suggested, however, that if the South attacked the North, the North could launch a counterattack and try to unify Korea.[34] In interviews in 1993 and 1994, Mikhail (M. S.) Kapitsa, Stalin's interpreter in the March 1949 meeting, asserted there was absolutely no discussion then about resorting to military action.[35]

A report in *U.S. News and World Report* (1993, no. 8) claimed that Stalin compelled Kim to prepare a plan for an attack on the South, that Soviet Armed Forces Minister Bulganin led a group of high-level advisers in another meeting with Kim, and that a war plan was then drawn up, but the report's author provided no evidence to support his assertions and the report lacks all credibility.[36] What can be believed is that, in early 1949, Stalin had no serious discussion with Kim concerning the use of military force on the Korean peninsula, and that, at a minimum, he did not agree to North Korea taking such an action.

In sum, the Soviet Union first agreed to a trusteeship system, then supported the establishment of a unified Korean government, albeit one friendly to the Soviet Union, and finally assisted North Korea in establishing an independent government. However, while the tactics of Soviet policy toward Korea changed, the basic goal remained the same: to maximize

Soviet control and influence on the Korean peninsula while avoiding any direct conflict that would lead the United States to adopt in reaction an overly hard-line policy. This policy was remarkably similar in approach and result to American postwar policy in Korea.[37] At a time when Soviet foreign policy was generally evolving from great power cooperation to bloc-on-bloc confrontation, its policy in the Far East remained anchored in the Yalta system. In the early postwar years, Soviet policy sought to limit confrontation and conflict in Asia to the lowest possible level. This point is also borne out in Soviet early postwar policy toward China.

3 China

Twists and turns of Soviet postwar policy

Stalin's postwar Far East strategy had two goals toward China. First, he sought to erase Mongolia from China's (political–historical) map and to secure its uncontested independence, thereby creating a broad security zone south of the Soviet Union. Second, he wanted to restore the Czarist-era sphere of influence in Northeast China, gaining access to an ice-free outlet on the Pacific. Stalin informed the United States of his first goal in a December 14, 1944 meeting with Ambassador to Moscow W. Averell Harriman. Stalin nailed down America's agreement to these Soviet goals in a February 8, 1945 meeting with President Roosevelt at Yalta as well as in the Yalta agreements. At the same time, Stalin reciprocated the U.S. assurances. Soviet postwar China policy would support Chiang Kai-shek's Nationalist government and discourage Chinese Communist revolutionary activity.[1]

Hemming in Chiang Kai-shek, the United States and the Soviet Union used sticks and carrots to prod the Nationalist government to accept Soviet conditions. After the Soviet Red Army moved into Northeast China in force, Chiang Kai-shek had little choice but to conclude the August 1945 Sino-Soviet Treaty of Friendship and Alliance.[2] On the basis of this treaty, which was to be in force for 30 years, the two sides also signed "An Agreement on the Chinese Changchun Railway," "An Agreement on Dalian," "An Agreement on Lushun Port," and other associated documents.

Moscow's gains in Northeast China paramount

By these agreements, the Soviet Union regained all the rights that Czarist Russia had lost in Northeast China as a consequence of the Russo-Japanese War of 1904–05. The Changchun Railroad would now be jointly owned and operated by China and the Soviet Union, with the Changchun Railway Bureau Director seconded from the Soviet Union. Dalian was declared a free port, with the port manager also seconded from the Soviet Union. All imported and exported goods destined for the Soviet Union that went through Dalian or over the Changchun Railway were to be free of customs duties, unlike similar goods destined for other parts of China. Lushun was designated as a Chinese–Soviet joint use naval base, the chairman of the naval base commission was to be seconded from the Soviet Union, and the most important civilian administrative personnel in Lushun were subject to appointment and removal by Soviet military authorities.[3]

Right down until a new Sino-Soviet treaty was signed (with the People's Republic of China in 1950), the main goal of Soviet policy toward China was to ensure the rights enumerated above. To accomplish this goal, Stalin made some concessions and assurances to Chiang Kai-shek. He recognized Chiang as China's leader, and (in the immediate postwar period) advised the Chinese Communist Party to submit to the Nationalist government's unified leadership.

Communists and Nationalists position for Civil War

As China's anti-Japanese struggle (i.e., World War II) came to a close, the Chinese Communist Party and its military, though still relatively weak vis-à-vis the Nationalist Army, had achieved unprecedented strength, and now constituted a serious threat to Nationalist Party rule over China. According to prominent Chinese scholar Zhang Baijia, when Mao Zedong turned his attention to what to do in the postwar period, he was of two minds.

Mao faced two theoretically antithetical options: long-term Nationalist–Communist cooperation aimed at the peaceful reconstruction of China or a possible break in Nationalist–Communist relations and renewed civil war. On the eve of the end of the war, a central tenet of Chinese Communist strategy implied that it would work toward a cooperative, peaceful relationship. In late April 1945, at the opening of the Chinese Communist Party Seventh Congress, Mao defined the world's main decisive and controlling factor as the unity of the three great powers: Great Britain, the United States and the Soviet Union. Because of this favorable international situation, he proposed, the Nationalist Party might make concessions and compromise with the Chinese Communist Party. Postwar China, therefore, might move toward democracy, abolish one-party rule, implement democratic reforms, and establish a unified, multi-party government, all leading, step-by-step, to the (Communist) political goal of implementing "New Democracy" nationwide.

However, if the Communist Party was prepared to work hard for peace, the Nationalists, by contrast, were looking to rely above all on military force. This was based on a pure power calculation: the Nationalists were relatively strong, and the Communists were still relatively weak. But, based on trends, the Nationalists' decline was obvious, while the Communists had growing momentum on their side. The Nationalists, to maintain their monopoly on national political power, intended to use their existing military superiority to check the strengthening Communist position. The Nationalists wanted at the very least to quickly reduce Communist power to the point where it could no longer pose a threat. The Communists, on the other hand, wanted to postpone a showdown as long as possible, to avoid a setback, to develop further, and to assure final victory.[4]

In this situation, one of Chiang Kai-shek's main policy goals was to limit Soviet support for the Chinese Communists. In early July 1945, after the start of Chinese–Soviet negotiations, Stalin proposed that China recognize Mongolian independence. Chiang Kai-shek demanded as "a condition of exchange" for the Nationalist government's recognition of independent Mongolia that "the Soviet Union, in the future, not support the Chinese Communists or the Xinjiang rebellion," and provide assurances concerning "the sovereignty and administrative integrity of [China's] three Northeast provinces." Chiang Kai-shek also had China's delegation head, Song Ziwen, further clarify to the Soviet Union the Nationalist government's conditions that,

> The Chinese Communist Party must strictly follow central government military and political orders, that is, all parties must strictly follow national laws; however the government will treat all equally without discrimination, and once a national assembly is convened, and a government is reorganized, it will accept them into the Executive Branch, though certainly not in a unity government.[5]

Since Stalin had already made this commitment to the United States, he readily accepted Chiang Kai-shek's conditions.

Stalin enunciated three principles concerning Nationalist–Communist relations: First, "China can only have one government, led by the Nationalist Party," though it should allow the Communist Party and others to participate in the government. Second, "the Chinese Government is highly justified in requiring unified, national military and government regulations," and its unwillingness to establish a coalition government is a "legitimate demand." Third, all Soviet arms and other materiel "will be provided only to the Central Government, and it will not provide arms to the Communist Party." Stalin also added significantly that, "In China, there is the Nationalist Party. The other force is the Communist Party. But can the Communist Party overturn the government? ... If China and the Soviet Union are allies, then nobody can overturn the Chinese government."[6] Stalin's adoption of these measures to carry out his China policy cast a cloud over already unstable and unharmonious relations between the Chinese Communists and the Soviet Union.

Starting with the signing of the Sino-Soviet Treaty of Friendship and Alliance with the Nationalist government in August 1945 through signing of the Sino-Soviet Treaty of Friendship, Alliance and Mutual Benefit with Communist China in February 1950, Soviet policy toward China and its relations with the Chinese Communist Party went through numerous twists and turns.

Roots of Moscow's distrust of the Chinese Communists

From 1934, when Mao Zedong led the Red Army on the Long March to Yan'an and restored contacts with the Soviet Union and the Communist International (Comintern), relations between the Chinese Communist Party and the Soviet Union were fraught with mutual distrust and discord. First, there was conflict over the strategy of subordination to the international united front and the Comintern advocated by Moscow-returnee Wang Ming and Mao's policy of party autonomy during China's anti-Japanese united front period.

Later, once the Soviet Union and the Comintern came to terms with Mao's leadership of the Chinese Communist Party, conflict arose over wartime strategy and tactics. As Hu Qiaomu, Mao's secretary, recalled,

> When a Soviet representative arrived in Yan'an, he immediately asked why the Chinese Communist Party did not mass its military force against the Japanese. The Soviet goal was for the Chinese Communist Party to field a large military force to remove Soviet concern over its rear area [i.e., over Japanese forces in northern China]. But the Chinese Communist Party then insisted on waging guerilla warfare, since it was incapable of large-scale warfare. The Soviet Union was very unhappy with this state of affairs, believing that the Chinese Communist Party did not want to support the Soviet Union.[7]

To a large degree, Mao's dogged insistence on an independent, autonomous political stance for the Chinese Communist Party was aimed as much at managing relations with Stalin and the Soviet-led Comintern as it was at managing domestic relations with the Nationalists. The Chinese Communist Party's evasion of Moscow's directives aroused Stalin's deep dissatisfaction and suspicion.[8] In Moscow's view, Mao's Yan'an party rectification (purge) campaign (launched in February 1942) and the elevation of Mao Zedong Thought at the Chinese Communist Party Seventh Congress (convened in April 1945) were aimed at rooting out Soviet influence within the Chinese Communist Party.[9] Against this background, it is therefore not surprising that Stalin told U.S. Ambassador W. Averell Harriman on June 22, 1944 that the "Chinese Communists are not real Communists, they are 'margarine' Communists," implying that once conditions improved they would abandon Communism.[10] Relations between the Chinese and Soviet Communist leaders became even more complex and strained after the Soviet Red Army invaded Northeast China in August 1945.

Chinese Communists try to anticipate Soviet postwar policy

Nevertheless, when the Chinese Communists were forming their strategy and policies for the final stage of the anti-Japanese struggle, they did not know that Stalin had already decided to throw his support to the Chinese Nationalist government. Mao thought the Soviet Union would help the Chinese Communist Party once the war was over. In his final remarks to the Seventh Party Congress in May 1945, he expressed the "great hope [that] the international proletariat and the great Soviet Union will help us," and his belief that "help will surely come from the international proletariat, otherwise Marxism doesn't work."[11] Expecting that a Soviet troop deployment into Northeast China would help their party, the Chinese Communists adopted an activist policy, expanded areas under their control, preparing for armed conflict with the Nationalist Party.

On August 11, 1945 the Chinese Communist Party Central Committee sent the following message to its regional party committees:

> Following the Soviet entry into the war, Japan has announced its surrender. The Nationalist Party is actively preparing to 'regain lost ground' in our liberated areas, and gain fruit from the victory over Japan. The battle for control will be intense.... [O]ur party's task is two-fold: (a) In the present stage, we have to concentrate our main strength to force the [Japanese] enemy and [its] puppet regimes to surrender to us. In light of actual conditions, we must attack those forces which will not surrender, gradually annihilate them, forcibly expand our liberated areas, occupy all the large and small cities and main transportation routes which we can or should occupy, seize weapons and supplies, and give a free hand to grass-roots armed mass organizations, all without the least hesitation.... (b) In the coming stage, the Nationalist Party may launch a large-scale offensive against us. Our party must prepare to mobilize our military forces and deal with a civil war ... on a scale that will be dictated by circumstances.[12]

CCP leaders now focused their attention on the post-Japanese surrender situation in Northeast China, moving People's Liberation Army units toward and into the Northeast. From Yan'an, Zhu De ordered units under Lü Zhengcao from Shanxi and Suiyuan into Chahar and Jehol, units under Zhang Xueshi from Hebei and Chahar into Jehol and Liaoning, units under Wan Yi from Shandong and Hebei into Liaoning, and units under Li Yunchang from the Hebei–Jehol–Liaoning border area into Liaoning and Jilin.[13]

At the same time the Chinese Communists adopted an offensive strategy in northern and central China. On August 20 Mao cabled the CCP's Central China Bureau that,

> Your planned uprising in Shanghai is absolutely correct. We look forward to the thorough implementation of your plan, and will send strong armed forces into the city to help. If conditions are right for uprisings in other cities, act accordingly.

The same day Mao cabled CCP party bureaus in Shanxi, Chahar and Hebei provinces directing that,

> You should swiftly organize armed uprisings … in Peiping, Tianjin, Tangshan, Baoding, and Shijiazhuang, seizing the chance to launch coordinated uprisings … to take these cities, the most important of which are Peiping [now Beijing] and Tianjin.[14]

Stalin warns Chinese Communists against civil war

Chinese Communist preparations to launch a broad offensive against the Nationalists quickly came into conflict with the Soviet Union's China policy. By this time, the Soviets had signed the Sino-Soviet Treaty on Friendship and Alliance with the Nationalists. The Soviet Red Army was not in Northeast China to promote the Chinese Communist revolution. At this point, U.S. Ambassador to China Patrick Hurley and Chiang Kai-shek proposed Nationalist–Communist peace talks, inviting Mao to Chongqing.[15]

In two telegrams sent to the Chinese Communist leadership in mid-August 1945 Stalin insisted that China had to avoid civil war, which, he asserted, would lead to national catastrophe, and urged Mao to attend the Chongqing talks promoted by Hurley and Chiang. Mao was angry over this arm-twisting, but joint Soviet and American diplomatic pressure forced a change in Chinese Communist strategy.[16]

Given limited Chinese Communist strength at the time, there was no way to successfully carry out an offensive strategy absent Soviet assistance. Mao decided therefore to attend Chongqing talks with Chiang, while also revising his strategy of attacking large cities. On August 21 Mao cabled the party's Central China Bureau canceling the planned uprising in Shanghai, explaining that an uprising of this type would turn into an attack against Chiang. On August 22 the CCP Central Committee and Central Military Commission likewise rescinded instructions to occupy large cities.[17]

On August 23 Mao made a lengthy speech at an enlarged Politburo meeting: "The present situation is that the war with Japan is over and we have entered the stage of peaceful reconstruction." Mao continued that conditions allowed for two possibilities: one was that the Chinese Communist Party could take over some big cities, the other was that they wouldn't, and Mao admitted that it then looked like they wouldn't. They had tried to take over some large cities, but had failed. There were two reasons: one was that the Soviet Union, bound by the Chinese–Soviet Treaty of Friendship and Alliance, could not help the Chinese Communists; the other was that Chiang was using his internationally recognized status as head of the legal government of China to force the Japanese to surrender only to his Nationalist forces. The Chinese Communists were therefore entering the period of peaceful reconstruction without having taken any major cities.

As for the Chongqing talks, Mao proposed that, "Comrade Zhou Enlai immediately proceed to the negotiations, talk two days and then return. [Ambassador] Hurley and I will then go. We cannot put this off. We have to go, but I don't think there is any danger."[18] In an August 26 speech, Mao raised the possibility of Communist territorial concessions during the Chongqing talks that would involve Communist pullbacks from areas in southern China in exchange for Nationalist political concessions and/or territorial concessions to the Communists elsewhere.[19]

Chinese Communists deploy forces to Northeast China

Based on experience, Chinese Communist leaders already thought that Soviet help to the Chinese Communist Party would be limited. Even before the Soviet Union sent its troops into Northeast China, while Nationalist representatives were in Moscow talking with Stalin, Wang Ruofei, then a CCP representative charged with foreign affairs work, offered his analysis of these talks. Wang noted that the treaty that the Soviets would be signing with the Nationalists would naturally not be one "under which the Soviet Union can freely support the Communist Party against the Nationalist Party." However, Soviet concessions to the Nationalists would not go beyond two limits, he argued. The Soviets would not tolerate the emergence of a pro-American, fascist government in China, and the Soviets would not restrict the development of the Chinese Communists, even if they might not be willing to assist the Chinese Communists.[20] Wang's assessment proved to be quite accurate.

The Chinese Communists calculated, however, that despite strains with the Soviet leader and limits on Soviet China policy dictated by the international situation in the Far East, the two Communist parties nevertheless shared a common ideology. Moreover, the Chiang Kai-shek government's reliance on the United States provided some hope for the Chinese Communists that, as they became stronger, the Soviet Union would lighten and then abandon its restrictions on them. Therefore, Chinese Communist policy at this time was based on the calculation that it might gain Soviet support and assistance by reaching out and coordinating closely with Soviet positions and actions in China.

While carefully staying in step with the Soviet Red Army in the Northeast and managing the Chongqing talks, the CCP decided to deploy its forces rapidly into the Northeast, seeking to occupy a wide swath of the countryside, including small and medium-sized cities. As laid out in an August 29 Central Committee message to local party branches, bound by Soviet treaty obligations to the Nationalist government, "The [Soviet] Red Army will undoubtedly refrain from formally consulting with us or assisting us when our party and army enter the three northeastern provinces." However, continued the message, as long as Chinese Communist military actions in the Northeast "do not directly affect the Soviet Union's treaty obligations, the Soviet Union will turn a blind eye and give us great sympathy."[21] Another Central Committee message instructed that,

> [I]n the name of the Northeast Volunteer Army, you can unofficially, surreptitiously, and indirectly seize cities and rural areas unoccupied by the Soviet army, and you should send cadres into the cities you cannot reach to make unofficial contact with the Red Army.[22]

Conflicting Soviet signals

And yet, at the time, Chinese Communist leaders after all were still unclear about overall Soviet policy toward China. At this juncture, the Soviet Union was requesting that Nationalist troops enter the Northeast in accord with Soviet commitments made to the United States and Chiang Kai-shek, including in the August 1945 Sino-Soviet treaty. Stalin told Ambassador Harriman on August 27 that he hoped the Nationalist government "would send Chinese troops in the near future to take over from the Russians in keeping order and controlling Japanese saboteurs." Harriman reported to Secretary of State James Byrnes that he believed that the Soviet Union wanted to withdraw from Manchuria within three months, and he therefore recommended that the Chinese government give "immediate consideration" to deploying troops to the Northeast.[23]

Stalin sought comprehensive implementation of the guarantees contained in the Yalta Agreement, i.e., restoration of all the rights in China that Czarist Russia had lost as a result of the Russo-Japanese War. Ideological considerations were at best of small political importance in Stalin's handling of relations with the Nationalist government. Thus, whether the Soviet Red Army would "leave alone" or provide "sympathy to" Chinese Communist forces in Northeast China would be decided solely on the basis of Soviets' needs as related to the Nationalist government in China and the United States internationally. As a result, Chinese Communist policy toward the Northeast had to constantly adapt as Soviet attitudes changed.[24]

By early September 1945, Chinese Communist forces from North China were already closing in on or had entered the Northeast. On September 11, the Central Committee cabled its Shandong Bureau that,

> According to an investigative report by a person sent to Dalian by the East Shandong party committee, the situation in the Northeast is going quite well now for our party and army. To take advantage of the situation before the Nationalist Party and army arrive in the Northeast (it is estimated they will not arrive in the short term), and to enhance quickly our force level and strengthen our position in the Northeast, the Central Committee has decided to redeploy from Shandong four divisions (twelve regiments), totaling 25,000 to 30,000 soldiers, to

arrive in the Northeast in groups by sea, and to send [PLA Political Commissar] Xiao Hua to provide unified leadership at the front.[25]

Soviet Red Army forces occupying Northeast China were not all on the same page when it came to understanding and implementing Moscow's immediate postwar China policy. Some Soviet Red Army units, such as those at Shanhaiguan, Dalian and Shenyang, expressed support for the Chinese Communist forces,[26] while elsewhere, conflict and friction grew between Chinese Communist and Soviet Army units. There are many anecdotal Chinese accounts of such conflict, and documentary evidence of this friction has also been found recently in Russian archives.

In early September 1945 the Manchurian Committee of the Third Unit of the CCP Shandong Bureau sent a letter to the Soviet Communist Party complaining about poor Soviet Army discipline and conduct in Northeast China. It asked the Soviet Army not to disarm Chinese Communist forces entering Northeast China, and, further, to provide these forces with arms, printing equipment and paper. These requests did not elicit a favorable response. Soviet military authorities refused to provide printing equipment and paper to the Chinese Communists, prohibited Chinese Communist activities in Soviet-occupied areas, and reminded the Chinese Communists that these questions would be decided by Chiang Kai-shek's government.[27]

To clarify the Soviet stance and coordinate with the Chinese Communists, two high-ranking Soviet military officers representing Marshal Rodion Malinovsky, the Soviet Red Army commander in the Northeast, flew to Yan'an on September 14. These Soviet officers conveyed Malinovsky's oral message that neither the Nationalist Army nor the Chinese Communist Eighth Route Army should enter the Northeast before the Soviet Red Army withdrew, and asked People's Liberation Army Commander-in-Chief Zhu De to order the withdrawal of Eighth Route Army units that had reached Soviet-occupied areas near Shenyang, Dalian, Changchun and Pingquan. They also informed the CCP that the Red Army would soon withdraw. Then China could decide how Chinese forces should enter the Northeast, and the Soviet Union would not interfere in this Chinese internal matter.[28] Faced with this situation, the Chinese Communist Party Central Committee's strategic plan for gaining control of the Northeast projected "a long-term struggle with the Nationalist Party," noting that forces entering the Northeast "need to concentrate on key cities and rural areas contiguous with the Soviet Union, Korea, Mongolia and Jehol to establish bases for long-term competition, and then to struggle for control of the major cities along the South Manchuria railway."[29]

Shortly thereafter, the Five Power Foreign Ministers' meeting in London ended in failure. The Soviet Union and the United States were unable to coordinate their positions on the Far Eastern question, and the Soviet Union refused to join the Far Eastern Consultative Commission.

The United States was concerned that the Soviet Union would use the Sino-Soviet treaty to control Northeast China, and repeatedly sought a Soviet public guarantee that it would act in accord with the "Open Door" principle.

Soviets react to specter of U.S. influence in Northeast China

When U.S. naval ships began to carry large numbers of Nationalist troops to ports in North and Northeast China, the Soviets expressed deep concern and great displeasure. In October the Soviets were offended when a U.S. warship landed without prior notice in Dalian and its commanding officer went on land to investigate the situation. Infuriated, Marshal Malinovsky repeatedly raised this incident in stern terms with Nationalist government officials. Zhang Jia (Chang Kia-ngau), a Nationalist Chinese representative in talks with Malinovsky, observed in his diary that, "The Soviets are unwilling to have us rely on the United States to transport our troops. In other words, they are unwilling to have the United States acquire a foothold in the Northeast."[30]

Displeased by American moves in Northeast China, Stalin adjusted his Far Eastern strategy. To resist American pressure and put the brakes on the Nationalists, the Soviet Union not only prevented Nationalist forces from landing in Northeast China ports, but also indicated its support for a Chinese Communist takeover of the Northeast. In early October the Soviet Army proposed to the Chinese Communist Party Northeast Bureau and the CCP Central Committee that they deploy 200,000 to 300,000 troops to secure the Northeast, with the Soviet Army providing a large amount of military equipment. In late October a Soviet Army representative encouraged the Northeast Bureau: "[In the Northeast] you should take control and act ... [to] quickly send personnel to control large industrial cities and industries." Furthermore, he continued, the Chinese Communists "can gradually take the reins of the government," with the Soviet Army coordinating with Communist forces to fight the Nationalist army.[31] The Soviet Army representative even proposed that the Chinese Communist Central Committee might move to Northeast China.

Influenced by the new Soviet policy, on October 16 and 19 and November 1 the Chinese Communist Party Central Committee sent a series of instructions to its field military units directing them to "change the former dispersal plan," "resolutely and completely annihilate Chiang forces from whatever direction they enter the Northeast," concentrate Chinese Communist main forces along the line from Jinzhou, through Yingkou, to Shenyang, and, "above all, defend Liaoning and Andong [Dandong], and then seize control of the whole Northeast." The overall CCP strategy was to seize the Northeast and consolidate in North and Central China.[32]

To implement this task, the Chinese Communists sorely needed the Soviets to provide more help. Consequently, the Central Committee asked the Soviet Army to postpone its withdrawal from the Northeast and prevent Nationalist forces from landing in Northeast ports and taking political power. The Soviets said it would be difficult to postpone their withdrawal, but they agreed that before they withdrew, they would not allow Nationalist forces to be airlifted to Changchun. The Soviet Army was ready, moreover, to provide weaponry, communications and transportation equipment to the Chinese Communist forces, to allow the Chinese Communist forces free rein in areas where the Nationalist forces had landed, and, in Changchun, to allow the Chinese Communists to replace all the city department heads, albeit not the mayor.[33] Also, undoubtedly owing to Soviet cooperation with the Chinese Communists, Nationalist forces were unable to land at Dalian, Yingkou or Huludao.

Under Nationalist pressure, Soviets restrict Chinese Communists

In quick order, however, Soviet policy in the Northeast shifted again. The Soviets aimed on the one hand to prevent the insertion of American power into the Northeast, and on the other hand to apply pressure on the Nationalists. A Soviet representative was negotiating at this time with the Nationalist government concerning the turnover of the Northeast and bilateral economic cooperation. The Nationalists were demanding that the turnover of the Northeast be completed before signing a bilateral economic cooperation agreement, and the Soviets were demanding the exact opposite. Both sides held their ground.[34]

Chiang Kai-shek's countermove effectively employed an array of sticks and carrots. To put pressure on the Soviets, on the one hand, he ordered the withdrawal of the Nationalist field headquarters in the Northeast, while, at the same time, he offered some economic concessions, thereby seeking to elicit Soviet political reciprocity. Sure enough, Chiang's strategy worked.

On November 17 the Soviet ambassador to China informed the Nationalists that:

> Chinese government troops can land without hindrance in [Changchun] and Mukden [Shenyang]. The Soviet Army will give them the assistance needed.... The Soviet Army strictly adheres to the Sino-Soviet treaty. With respect to the Communist Party in Manchuria, in the past the Soviet Army has not given it any assistance, and this continues to be the case.... If the Chinese government desires ... the Soviet Army ... can postpone [its evacuation] for one or two months.

On November 20, the Soviet ambassador informed the Nationalist Foreign Ministry that, "The Soviet government has instructed its Air Force command to take measures necessary to guarantee the unhindered landing of Chinese troops in [Changchun] and Mukden [Shenyang]."[35]

After reaching agreement with Chiang Kai-shek, the Soviet Union again restricted Chinese Communist activities in the Northeast. On November 19 Soviet military authorities in the Northeast informed the Chinese Communist Northeast Bureau that, in accord with the Sino-Soviet Treaty of Friendship and Alliance, the Soviet Union would be turning over the Changchun Railway and cities along the railway to the Nationalists, and therefore requested that Chinese Communist forces withdraw 50 km behind the rail line, that they not enter the area under Soviet Army occupation, and that they not fight with the Nationalists before the Soviet Army withdrew from the Northeast. The Soviet representative threatened that, "armed force would not be spared, if needed" to uphold Soviet interests, including to expel Chinese Communist forces. Shortly afterwards, the Soviet Army demanded that the Chinese Communists desist from undertaking activities in major cities that would undermine the Sino-Soviet treaty.[36] In early December, Foreign Minister Molotov instructed the commanding officer of the Lushun naval base not to allow Chinese forces – Nationalist or Communist – to enter the Soviet base. He stressed that, "[Soviet military authorities] must resolutely oppose all Communist attempts to restructure political and economic life inside the naval base as they have done in their own base areas."[37]

At the same time this was occurring, in early and mid-November 1945, two Nationalist armies were transported on 31 U.S. ships from Kowloon in Hong Kong and Haiphong in Vietnam to Qinhuangdao. In succession, they attacked and occupied Shanhaiguan, Suizhong, Jinzhou and strategic points the Communist Eighth Route Army had seized from Japanese-allied puppet armies. In the face of this sudden change in circumstances, the Chinese Communists again adjusted their plans.

Chinese Communists reassess policy in the Northeast

On November 20 and 28, the Chinese Communist Party Central Committee sent two instructions to the Northeast Bureau. One directed that the Northeast Bureau "quickly set up consolidated bases in eastern, northern and western Manchuria, and strengthen work in Jehol and eastern Hebei." The other noted that, given the actions of the Soviet occupation authorities, the Chinese Communist leadership acknowledged that "an independent Northeast" was impossible, and that the Chinese Communist main forces should again disperse "to seize small and medium-sized cities, secondary rail lines and rural areas; work to create base areas; and carry out long-term planning."[38]

CCP Politburo member Chen Yun and his colleagues on the frontline in Northeast China, Gao Gang and Zhang Wentian acknowledged that the fundamental goal of Soviet China policy was to uphold the Soviet Union's own interests. In a November 30 report to the Central Committee, they pointed out that the goal of Soviet policy was "to preserve peace in the Far

East and world peace," that Soviet policy toward the Nationalists and the Communists in the Northeast would shift from time to time in support of this goal, and that the Chinese Communist Party should be prepared for a long struggle with the Nationalists in the Northeast. In sum, they argued, the Chinese Communist Party should "avoid placing all [its] hopes on Soviet assistance."[39] The term "preserve peace" was merely a Chinese Communist mantra to save Soviet face. The abandonment of any illusions about Soviet assistance by the Chinese Communist leadership indicates that these leaders essentially understood the motivation of Stalin's Far Eastern policy.

By December 1945, there had been a change for the better in relations between the Soviet Union and the Nationalist government. In the December 1945 Moscow Conference of Foreign Ministers, the Soviet Union and the United States were again on the same page with respect to China, with both countries pledging support for a unified, Nationalist-led government. Foreign Minister Molotov reiterated Soviet support for Chiang Kai-shek and promised that Soviet and American aims were the same "on the issue of support for China's central government."[40]

Stalin spelled out this position in a December 30 meeting with Chiang Kai-shek's son, Chiang Ching-kuo. Stalin told the younger Chiang that the Soviet Union had had three representatives in Yan'an, but withdrew them all since it disagreed with the Chinese Communist Party's move to scuttle the Chongqing talks. The Soviet Union stood by the spirit of the Moscow Conference of Foreign Ministers, said Stalin. The Chiang Kai-shek government was the only legal Chinese government. China could not have two governments and two armies. The Chinese Communists were not members of the Soviet Communist Party, and the Comintern no longer existed. Without a request from the Chinese Communist Party, the Soviet Union would not give it advice. And, since the end of the Chongqing talks, the Chinese Communists had not asked for Soviet advice. The Soviet Union was not happy with Chinese Communist actions. If they asked for Soviet advice, the Soviet Union would recommend that the Chinese Communists act in the spirit of what had been shared with Chiang Ching-kuo. The Chinese Communists wanted to enter Manchuria, but the Soviet Union had not allowed that.[41]

As this indicates, the Soviet Union had some reason to believe then that its interests in the Far East could be realized through accommodation with the United States and the Chiang Kai-shek government. Thus, when General George Marshall arrived in China (in late December 1945) to mediate Nationalist–Communist relations, the Soviet Union not only rejected the Chinese Communist suggestion that Moscow join in Marshall's mediation effort, but urged the Chinese Communists to stop the civil war and cooperate with the Nationalists to achieve democratic reforms. Moscow warned the Chinese Communists that under no circumstances should they fight in Northeast China, lest "all their forces be annihilated and this action provoke the great danger that the American military might enter Manchuria."[42]

Mao Zedong was so unhappy with the Soviet position that he decided to indicate that he was inclined to strengthen relations with the United States. Mao had Zhou Enlai convey to General Marshall on his behalf that, "When I [Mao] go abroad, I want to go first to the United States." Hu Qiaomu later explained that, while it was tactically expedient to make this political gesture toward the United States, on another plane, this statement reflected unhappiness with the Soviet Union and a desire to attract U.S. assistance.[43]

Faced with this situation, the CCP Central Committee re-emphasized its strategy toward Northeast China, i.e., that it would work to establish strong bases far from big cities and main transportation lines in the Northeast.[44] In other words, the Chinese Communists would depend on their own strength and prepare for a long struggle with the Nationalists for control of the Northeast.

Renewed Soviet–Nationalist tensions

In the spring of 1946, important developments forced the Soviet Union to withdraw its troops from the Northeast and scale back its expectations with respect to its economic position in Northeast China.

First, Sino-Soviet negotiations on economic cooperation in the Northeast fell into stalemate. The disagreements revealed a wide gap between Nationalist Chinese and Soviet ideas over the scope of bilateral economic cooperation. Though the Soviet Union scaled back its demands for joint management of enterprises, China made no concessions with respect to a large number of heavy industrial, aviation and river navigation enterprises. The two sides clung to opposing positions on whether the chairmen and managers of joint enterprises should be appointed by the Chinese or Soviet sides. The two sides also again disagreed over the timing of the signing of the economic cooperation agreement. The Soviets wanted to sign an agreement before its troops withdrew from China, and China wanted to sign after the Soviet Army withdrew. As the date of the Soviet withdrawal (February 1, 1946) drew near, there was no substantial progress on Sino-Soviet economic cooperation.

In pursuit of its economic interests in the Northeast, the Soviet Union repeatedly threatened Nationalist China that it would not withdraw its troops if the issue of economic cooperation was not resolved. The Nationalist government, bitter over its earlier concessions in the Northeast, vacillated between soft and hard-line tactics. Chiang Kai-shek finally decided that, "If the Soviets do not withdraw their troops, then we will not advance or discuss the issue of economic cooperation. We will shelve it and see what happens."[45] This "cool management" tactic left the Soviets to make their intentions clear while the Nationalists appealed for international support.

When Soviet forces continued to occupy the Northeast after February 1, 1946, Chinese (Nationalist) negotiators left Changchun, and Sino-Soviet economic negotiations broke off. The Soviets later asked that the negotiations resume. The Chinese government refused, but stated that it would consider the Soviet request if negotiations were moved to Chongqing. With no resolution in sight, the deadline both sides had set for the Soviet troop withdrawal passed, putting the Soviets on the diplomatic defensive.[46]

The issue of the Northeast then came to U.S. and wider international attention. After the U.S. learned about the background of the Sino-Soviet economic negotiations, on February 9, it sent notes to the Chinese and Soviet governments asserting that their discussion of joint management of industrial and mining operations in the Northeast infringed on the "Open Door" policy. Great Britain threw its support behind the U.S. position. General Marshall encouraged the Chinese government to resist Soviet pressure and to make no commitments with respect to "war spoils" or economic cooperation. Marshall told Foreign Minister Wang Shijie that, "Time was running against the Soviet [Union], since the longer her troops remain in Manchuria, the more clearly she becomes a deliberate treaty wrecker in the eyes of the world." On February 13, Secretary of State Byrnes cabled Wang suggesting that if the Soviet Union's economic demands in Northeast China touched on the question of reparations, they should be referred to the Far Eastern Commission for decision.[47] The internationalization of the question of Sino-Soviet economic cooperation forced the Soviet Union to confront the issue with the United States and Great Britain, further pressuring the Soviets to make a difficult choice.

At the same time, the rise of anti-Soviet sentiment in China also increased pressure on the Soviets to withdraw from the Northeast. On February 11, 1946, to force the Soviet Union into an early withdrawal, the United States and Great Britain published previously secret details regarding the treatment of the Far East at the Yalta Conference. Shortly thereafter, Nationalist Chinese newspapers published information about Soviet economic demands and the suspension of the Soviet troop withdrawal, stirring enormous Chinese popular anger.

Massive anti-Soviet demonstrations broke out in Chongqing, Changchun, Nanjing and other large cities, demanding the Soviets withdraw immediately from the Northeast. Taking advantage of the situation, Chiang Kai-shek made a strong statement reiterating that the Chinese government enjoyed complete sovereignty over Manchuria. Nationalist newspapers then seized on a January 16, 1946 incident in which Zhang Xinfu, a member of the technical staff involved in the turnover of the Northeast to the Nationalists, was (mortally) wounded (by a Soviet soldier), thus further stoking strong anti-Soviet sentiment.[48]

Forced to withdraw, Soviets tilt to the Chinese Communists

Given these circumstances, it was imperative that Soviet forces withdraw from the Northeast. Stalin, however, was not happy to abandon the economic benefits he had been on the verge of gaining, and he was especially keen on seeing that the United States did not use the Soviet troop withdrawal to gain a foothold in the Northeast. Though Stalin publicly paid lip service to America's "Open Door" policy, he felt, of course, that the U.S. policy was designed for its own selfish reasons, warning the Nationalists that, "[T]he Open door policy … is an instrument of imperialist aggression. Therefore, while opening its doors, China also should be prepared to close its doors."[49]

In early 1946, after U.S. Special Envoy General Albert Wedemeyer announced that the United States would transport Nationalist General Du Yuming's troops to Northeast China, Marshal Malinovsy candidly told Nationalist representative Zhang Jia that the Soviet Union had consistently opposed the insertion of U.S. power into the region. Zhang wrote in his diary that, "Now that the United States has gone a step further in indicating its intention to support Chinese [Nationalist] military power in the Northeast, Soviet concern and jealousy are bound to increase."[50]

The Soviet Union was now clearly concerned with, in its view, the American military's intrusion into Northeast China. As Stalin had made clear to Chiang Ching-kuo in their December 30, 1945 meeting, the Soviet Union was not willing to countenance an American or any other foreign military presence in Manchuria, the "Soviet zone."[51] And now, the Soviet Union itself could neither continue to militarily occupy Manchuria nor rely on Nationalist cooperation to check the insinuation of U.S. power into Northeast China. Therefore, it once again revised its policy, seeking now to gain its objectives by assisting the Chinese Communist Party in Northeast China.

Chinese Communists fill vacuum in the Northeast

Accordingly, the Soviet Red Army now withdrew precipitously from Shenyang, Siping and other large cities, affording Chinese Communist forces the opportunity to enter and fill the vacuum. On March 8, 1946, a Soviet Army representative officially informed the CCP Northeast Bureau that the Soviet Red Army would be withdrawing from Fushun, Jilin and Shenyang, that the Red Army would not turn these areas over to the Nationalists, and that the Chinese Communists were free to act.[52] And, in fact, on March 9, without warning, Soviet occupation authorities in Shenyang received orders to withdraw from Shenyang within two days, leaving Shenyang Garrison Commander I. Kovtun-Stankovich surprised.[53]

Soviet occupation authorities turned over control of some areas to Chinese Communist forces, notably areas outside the Chinese Changchun

Railroad and South Manchurian Railroad rights of way.[54] On the verge of their withdrawal, Soviet Army authorities suggested that once they withdrew, the Chinese Communists were free to fight it out for control along the Changchun railway, and indicated that they supported CCP seizure of Changchun, Harbin and Qiqihar.[55] Responding to a request by Xiao Jingguang, Commander of the South Manchuria Military District of the (CCP-controlled) Northeast Democratic Alliance Army and Han Guang, CCP Secretary in Dalian, Soviet military authorities turned over to Communist forces about 50 railroad box cars of captured Japanese arms along with 20 trucks that had been shipped to the Northeast from Chongjin in North Korea.[56]

In response the Soviet policy shift, the Chinese Communists once again significantly readjusted their plans for Northeast China. By early 1946 Chinese Communist leaders had gained a good grasp of the complex international background to the Northeast China issue.

At this point, in conjunction with a Nationalist–Communist agreement on a ceasefire throughout China with the (significant) exception of the Northeast, Chiang Kai-shek asked the Soviet Army to defer its withdrawal, while simultaneously asking the United States to transport 250,000 Nationalist troops quickly to the Northeast to occupy Shenyang, Anshan, Yingkou and other large cities. Seeking to take advantage of the opportunity presented by the ceasefire in the rest of China, Chiang wanted to launch a large-scale advance in the Northeast to wipe out Chinese Communist forces or to push them into far-off mountainous areas. Chiang hoped thereby to put the Chinese Communists in an unfavorable position as a prelude to resolving the Northeast issue by negotiations.

The CCP Central Committee laid out the new situation in a March 5, 1946 instruction to the CCP Northeast Bureau. Drafted by Liu Shaoqi, the instruction noted that the Soviets were seeking "economic cooperation" in the Northeast, but had so far been rebuffed by Chiang and the Americans. Meanwhile, the Nationalists were fanning a nationwide anti-Soviet movement. In response, the Soviet Red Army had postponed its withdrawal. As long as Chiang and the Americans were contending with the Soviet Union over the Northeast, accommodation between the Chinese Communists and the Nationalists was impossible. But, in view of the Nationalist-led anti-Soviet movement, the Soviet Red Army might be more willing to help the Chinese Communists. The Northeast Bureau should, therefore, hold discussions with Soviet authorities and report the result of these discussions to the Central Committee. Citing past experience, however, the Central Committee warned that the Northeast Bureau had to be very clear in these discussions, since, "in the future, when the Soviet Union resolves the issue of economic cooperation [in the Northeast], it might once again favor Chiang."[57]

The chance to occupy key positions in the Northeast following the Soviet troop withdrawal was a golden opportunity for the Chinese

Communists. Mao was prepared to exploit this opportunity with or without Soviet support. On March 15, he cabled Zhou Enlai, then in Chongqing negotiating with the Nationalists, that, "You cannot allow the Nationalists to garrison Harbin, and must do all you can to see that neither side garrisons Fushun or Yingkou." Mao stressed that Zhou should not listen uncritically to Soviet advice, terming the Soviets overly soft. In a March 16 instruction, Mao told Zhou that the CCP should make no territorial concessions unless it received corresponding Nationalist political, military and territorial concessions.[58]

While stressing that there should be no unreciprocated concessions in the Chongqing negotiations, the CCP Central Committee ordered its forces in the Northeast to quickly undertake strong military measures. On March 24, Mao instructed the Northeast Bureau that,

> Our party's policy is to do all we can to seize Changchun and Harbin, along with the entire Chinese Eastern [Chinese Changchun] rail line, and to spare no sacrifice to prevent the occupation of Changchun, Harbin, and the China Eastern rail line by Chiang's army.

Quickly contact the Soviet occupation authorities, ordered Mao,

> to permit our side to send forces to occupy Changchun and Harbin and the entire Chinese Eastern rail line ... [m]obilize all you have to firmly control the Sipingjie region. If reactionary forces advance north, thoroughly annihilate them, preventing their advance on Changchun.... Our main forces in South Manchuria must resolutely wipe out any enemy advance on Liaoyang, Fushun, and related areas.

On March 25, Mao reiterated to the Northeast Bureau that until there was a ceasefire in the Northeast, "You must make every effort and spare no sacrifice to protect strategic positions, especially in North Manchuria." As for Changchun, Harbin, Qiqihar and related areas, "Within a day or two of the Soviet Army's withdrawal, you must control them ... to prevent the [tripartite U.S.–Nationalist–Communist] ceasefire small teams, on their arrival, from handing them over to Nationalist occupation."[59]

Chinese Communist forces at this point were now able to take advantage of the opportunity presented by the fact that while the Soviet Army had already withdrawn from the Chinese Changchun railway, the Nationalist army was still held up in western Manchuria. Chinese Communist forces thus quickly took over a number of southern Manchuria cities with substantial industrial bases, including Andong, Benxi, Liaoyang, Haicheng, Fushun and Tonghua. In mid-March, Communist forces occupied Siping, and, in mid- and late April, they occupied the key cities of Changchun, Harbin and Qiqihar, wiping out more than 30,000 Manchurian "puppet" troops and armed bandits who were being used by the Nationalists. At this point, the whole section north of Kaiyuan on the Changchun rail line was under Chinese Communist control. Now, with North Manchuria securely at their back and controlling internal lines of communication, Mao was resolved to engage the Nationalists in strategic battles. In an April 19 instruction to the Chongqing CCP delegation, Mao summed up his guidance in a slogan, "Fight over every inch; never retreat." In an April 20 telegram to the Northeast Bureau and Lin Biao, Mao proposed a policy of preparing "to turn Changchun into Madrid."[60]

Chinese Communist Party's policies in the Northeast at this time were not entirely dependent on Stalin's policies, but they were clearly closely linked to Soviet support. This policy convergence caused Mao to overestimate Chinese Communist military power, and to make the error of engaging the Nationalists in decisive combat in strategic areas. In mid-1946, as a result of engaging in decisive, main force battles with the Nationalists near Siping, Lin Biao's forces suffered heavy losses and were forced to withdraw in defeat.[61] Chinese Communist leaders thereby realized that,

> Though we have taken the two large cities of Changchun and Harbin, our first priority is in the rural areas and in the small and medium-sized cities.... We must delay the outbreak of national civil war as long as possible. [Our army's] main force must not be afraid of losing areas, retreating, and leaving the enemy far behind, in order to gain time to rest and reequip, and to restore morale.... Our party must prepare for a prolonged fight.[62]

Enhanced Chinese Communist stature in Soviet eyes

After the Soviet Army withdrew from China, there was a major shift in the interactions between the Soviet Union and the Chinese Communists. Before it withdrew its army, the Soviet Union, with 1,000,000 men occupying Northeast China, was able to pursue its Far Eastern strategic interests based on its strategic superiority in the Northeast. The Chinese Communists and their military forces were then only a bargaining chip in Stalin's negotiations with the Nationalist government, and not a very important bargaining chip at that. But, after the Soviet Red Army withdrew, the Chinese Communists were the only factor the Soviets could use in their China policy to check the Nationalist government's policy toward the Soviet Union and American power in China. As Chinese Communist military strength grew, this factor grew more attractive in Stalin's eyes.

At the end of 1946, Soviet trade organizations openly established economic relations with the CCP-controlled Northeast People's Democratic Administrative Commission, and the Soviet Union provided economic aid to the Northeast liberated area. These moves reflected the beginning of a "turn" in Soviet policy toward China. This does not mean, however, that the Soviet Union now moved to total support for the Chinese Communist Party.

Stalin wanted to maintain relations with the Chinese Communists and assist them in order to strengthen their power to check the United States and Chiang. But, on the other hand, the Soviets still hoped to maintain the Yalta system in Asia and to guarantee the Soviet Union's political and economic interests in China as recognized in the 1945 Sino-Soviet Treaty of Friendship and Alliance. This balance required normal relations with the Nationalist government and the maintenance of a certain distance from the Chinese Communists. Once the Soviet Union rejected the Marshall Plan and stirred up the Berlin crisis, Stalin was forced to focus on the confrontation with the United States in the West. But in the East, he still maintained a situation of relative détente. This meant that Stalin was not in a position to throw his full support to the Chinese Communists in their armed struggle to seize power even if he had wanted to do so.

The Chinese Communist Party policy toward the Soviet Union was now also nuanced and independent. Mao held that the Chinese Communist revolution must stand on its own feet. The Soviet troop withdrawal from Northeast China only strengthened the Chinese Communists in their belief that they had to rely on their own resources to win revolutionary victory.

Mao's policies now were not simply reactions to Stalin's wishes. However, Mao realized that only the Soviet Union would support the Chinese revolutionary cause, and he therefore needed to show respect for the Soviet Union as the leader of world communism. As a consequence, after the Soviet Red Army withdrew from the Northeast, the Chinese Communist Party stepped up the frequency of its requests for instructions and its reports to Stalin. While the Chinese Communists were forced to adjust their strategy in response to changing Soviet policy in the early postwar period (late 1945 through early 1946), from the second half of 1946 until the end of 1948, however, Soviet–Chinese Communist relations featured greater subtlety and complexity.

From the outset of the Chinese civil war in 1945, the Soviet Union's China policy generally paralleled that of the United States. However, the Soviet Union sometimes played up its minor role in mediation between the Nationalists and the Communists, seeking thereby to strengthen its influence on "the China question" vis-à-vis the United States. Likewise, Moscow pursued a pattern of subtle political duality: criticizing American interference in Chinese domestic politics, while still signaling its intention to coordinate with the U.S. on China policy.

In December 1946, Stalin told Elliott Roosevelt, former President Roosevelt's son, that the Soviet Union was "ready to pursue a common policy with the United States in Far Eastern questions."[63] Foreign Minister Molotov, in an April 1947 letter to Secretary of State George C. Marshall (who had ended his mediation of the Nationalist–Communist civil war and returned to Washington in his new role), reaffirmed that Stalin's "common policy" referred to decisions adopted at the December 1945 Big Three foreign ministers' meeting regarding China: "In its relations with China, the Soviet Government has upheld and upholds a policy of non-interference in China's internal affairs."[64] On the one hand, the Soviet government supported and assisted the Chinese Communist administration in northern Manchuria and secretly supported Chinese Communists in Soviet-occupied Dalian and Lushun.[65] On the other hand, Soviet military occupation authorities repeatedly invited the Nationalists to send a negotiating team to Lushun. In April 1947, Soviet military authorities met with Nationalist representatives on the question of the northern "border" of the Lushun base, and, in June 1947, entertained a high-level Nationalist delegation sent from Nanjing.[66]

Moscow offers to mediate between Nationalists and Communists

In the summer of 1947, however, the Chinese people's war of liberation (i.e., the Chinese Communist offensive against the Nationalists) advanced in ways that were problematical with respect to the Soviet goal of stability in the Far East. Soviet policy toward China then shifted to promoting peace talks between the Nationalists and the Communists. In October 1947, Soviet ambassador to Iran Ivan Sadchikov proposed to his Chinese counterpart in Tehran, Ambassador Zheng Yitong, that the Soviet Union mediate an end to the Chinese civil war. The Soviet ambassador tried to convince Ambassador Zheng that the downturn in Soviet–American relations need not lead to a similar worsening in Chinese–Soviet relations. Sadchikov told Zheng that Japanese and American imperialism were common enemies of the Soviet Union and China, and that American policy in pursuit of a peace treaty with Japan conflicted with Soviet and Chinese interests. China and the Soviet Union could hold talks regarding Xinjiang, Manchuria, and the conflict between the Nationalists and the Communists, added Sadchikov.[67]

According to telegrams from American Ambassador Leighton Stuart to the State Department, (then) Soviet Military Attache General N. V. Roshchin, prior to his return to Moscow in January 1948, had raised the issue of possible Soviet mediation between the Nationalists and the Communists. Nationalist intelligence had reportedly intercepted a telegram from Moscow ordering its embassy in Nanjing to "bring about some arrangement between [the] Kuomintang and [the] Communists." Consequently, in his farewell call on General Zhang Zhizhong, Roshchin signaled that the Soviet Union wanted to arrange peace talks between the Nationalists and the Communists.

After Roshchin returned to China in February in his new role as Soviet ambassador, Stuart reported that, "the return of Roshchin as Ambassador may mean a Soviet desire to mediate at this time." On the other hand, "Chinese concurrence in [the] appointment of Roshchin does not necessarily mean [the] Chinese Government has [the] immediate intention of seeking Soviet mediation." Stuart argued that "[mediation] is consistent with general Soviet ... aims...." From the Chinese government's standpoint, said Stuart,

> Soviet mediation might before long become necessary and even desirable. From [the] American standpoint any Soviet injection into [the] Chinese situation has objections ... though we can see a possible situation where such a Soviet move might be turned to our advantage.[68]

From Roshchin's return to China on February 22, 1948 through early 1949, he worked hard to curry contacts with high Nationalist officials. In June 1948, Roshchin proposed to a Chinese Nationalist Defense Ministry official that talks be held to prevent the appearance of a "Cold War" between China and the Soviet Union. He recommended that both sides work to find a common position on a Chinese–Japanese treaty, and promised non-interference in China's internal affairs, increased commercial loans to the Nationalists and mutually beneficial economic development projects along the Chinese–Soviet border.

According to Roshchin, the Soviet Union sought to resist the influence of British and American imperialism, and believed widespread investment in China would create conditions for China to industrialize as Japan had done during the Meiji Restoration. Roshchin said that if (Nationalist) China accepted his suggestion, they could easily resolve all of the difficult issues in Sino-Soviet relations. If China did not adopt his suggestion, however, the Soviet Union might be forced to establish a "buffer zone" along its border with China to protect Soviet national security interests.[69]

When Roshchin met with Chinese Foreign Minister Wang Shijie in August 1948, he reiterated that the Soviet Union wanted to mediate the Nationalist–Communist conflict and was willing to provide material assistance to the Nationalists. The diplomatic record confirms that Chiang Kai-shek accepted Stalin's invitation to visit Moscow that September. Ambassador Roshchin set up this (ultimately aborted) trip through Chiang Ching-kuo.[70]

In meeting with Nationalist officials, Roshchin suggested that one reason the Soviets were interested in mediating the Chinese civil war was their fear that Mao "might take a course of action similar to that of Tito." Ambassador Roshchin sought support for his efforts from the American Embassy. There is evidence that his mediation efforts were looked upon favorably by Nationalist officials.[71] To the extent that Stalin's goals in this period tended to be similar to U.S. China policy, Soviet diplomatic activity clearly ran counter to Chinese Communist Party wishes.

Mao wary of Soviet intent

By early 1946, Mao Zedong had concluded that Soviet and Chinese Communist aims were not necessarily in alignment. The Soviets sought accommodation in Asia, while the Chinese Communists sought to survive and to develop through domestic struggle. Therefore, in April 1946, Mao came up with a new formulation, that while the Soviet Union and the United States sought mutual accommodation, this did not mean that the people of other countries (including China) had to pull back and compromise in their internal struggles. On the contrary, they should engage in all-out revolutionary struggle against domestic reactionary opponents. In Mao's final twist, Soviet–U.S. accommodation, in fact, was only possible under the conditions created by the global revolutionary struggle.[72]

Mao thus justified an independent road for the Chinese Communist revolution. Confronting an international situation characterized by apparent compromise between the Soviet Union and the United States, the Chinese Communists needed to struggle for their own goals. With the justification of this theoretical formula, Mao underscored the need for Chinese Communist self-reliance in preparation for a long struggle with the Nationalists over Northeast China. As Mao explained (in July 1946) to Luo Ronghuan, deputy political commissar of the Northeast Democratic Unity Army (who was about to leave for medical treatment in the Soviet Union), "We have to rely mainly on ourselves in the struggle for the Northeast [so don't place] too many demands [on the Soviets]."[73]

By summer 1948, the People's Liberation Army had achieved many important victories, decisively changing the Chinese situation on the ground. Even earlier, in December 1947, Mao had reported to Stalin that the Chinese revolution had reached a turning point. The People's Liberation Army had by then pushed back the Nationalist Army and was on the offensive.[74]

Chinese Communists advance, Stalin recalibrates

Even while Ambassador Roshchin was working to curry favor with Nationalist officials, changes on the ground in China and the fortune of the Chinese revolution forced Stalin to reevaluate his China policy. In April 1948, the Soviet Foreign Ministry instructed its Nanjing Embassy to: (1) adopt a policy of restraint in dealing with the Chinese government and its officials, stressing Soviet non-interference in Chinese domestic affairs; (2) carefully investigate and report on the measures and changes undertaken by the Chinese government in foreign and defense policy and domestic affairs; (3) pay close attention to factional struggle within the Chinese government and the Nationalist Party, and its political aims; (4) carefully study American policy toward China, especially to expose its support for Chiang Kai-shek's anti-Soviet measures; (5) strengthen contacts with

"democratic and progressive" figures, while maintaining a cautious attitude; (6) assure Soviet interests in China; and (7) use various channels
and means to strengthen propaganda friendly to the Soviet Union.[75]

In May 1948, Stalin showed Mao's telegram asking for assistance to his
confidant and personal adviser on China, I. V. Kovalev, stating that,

> Of course we will give New China all the help in our power. If social-
> ism is victorious in China, and our countries take the same path, then
> the global victory of socialism will be assured. We will then never con-
> front the threat of unforeseen difficulties. Therefore, we must do all
> we can to help the Chinese Communists.[76]

Stalin reiterated this assessment a few days later, just before Kovalev left
for China.

During 1948, Soviet trade greatly increased with the Communist-
controlled area in Northeast China. Trade between Soviet foreign trade
organizations and the Chinese Communist-controlled Northeast Area
People's Democratic Authority grew from 93 million rubles in 1947 to 151
million rubles in 1948.[77] Local Chinese Communist officials in the Northeast also petitioned Moscow for economic assistance. In September 1948,
Lin Biao, commander of Chinese Red Army forces in the Northeast and a
CCP Northeast China Bureau secretary, asked Stalin to send 100 Soviet
technical advisers and engineers. In October, Gao Gang, also a CCP
Northeast China Bureau secretary, appealed to Stalin for railway equipment and 20,000 tons of cotton. And in December, Gao Gang again
appealed to Soviet officials in Northeast China to supply railway and elec-
trical generating equipment.[78]

In June 1948, at the invitation of the Northeast Liberated Area People's
Democratic Authority, the Soviet government sent a Soviet railway specialist group including 50 engineers, 52 technicians, and 220 technical personnel and skilled workers. This group brought technical equipment,
including an emergency repair train, a caisson, a crane, and other
machinery and material needed for railway reconstruction: metal com-
ponents, steel rails, bridges and steel beams. Soviet aid helped greatly in
restoring railways in the Northeast Liberated Area. By December 15, 1948,
15,000 km along the Manchurian railway mainlines had been restored as
well as 120 large and medium-sized bridges totaling more than 9,000
meters in length. These included the 987-meter Songhua River Number 2
Bridge, the 320-meter Yinma River Bridge on the Harbin–Changchun line,
the 440-meter Songhua River Bridge on the Jilin–Changchun line, and 12
more large and medium-sized bridges.[79]

With the CCP's steady advance toward victory in the civil war, Mao paid
increasing attention to relations with the Soviet Union, especially as he
considered his party's future foreign policy needs as a governing party. A
sign of Mao's growing attention to Soviet policy direction was the CCP's

pro-Soviet shift in its stance toward Yugoslavia. After Soviet relations with Yugoslavia plummeted, on June 28, 1948, the Soviet-directed Cominform issued a resolution condemning the Yugoslav Communist Party.[80] In quick order, on July 1, 1948, the CCP, while not a Cominform member, issued a resolution supporting the Soviet position against Tito's Yugoslavia Communist Party.[81]

CCP First Vice Chairman Liu Shaoqi's November 1, 1948 anti-Tito article, "On Internationalism and Nationalism," which reaffirmed Chinese Communist support for the Soviet position, was widely published in China. Liu asserted that the world was divided into two camps, and that "neutrality" was impossible. The question of whether or not to ally with the USSR, Liu said, was a "dividing line between revolution and counter-revolution."[82]

Mao asks to visit Moscow, Stalin cautiously delays

From spring 1948, Mao repeatedly asked to visit Moscow. China's civil war had now reached a decisive stage. The Chinese Communists were now strong enough to hold their own in talks. Anticipating his future government's foreign policy needs, Mao wanted to strengthen ties with Moscow and seek its assistance.

Mao's visit to Moscow was set for mid-July 1948, but in a telegram dated April 26, 1948 Mao wrote Stalin that he had decided to visit Moscow "before the agreed date" to seek advice from the CPSU Central Committee on political, military, economic and other issues. If possible, he also wanted to visit the countries of Eastern Europe. Stalin, as he had on at least one earlier occasion, first agreed to Mao's visit and then demurred.[83]

On May 10, Stalin suggested that Mao delay his departure:

> In connection with … events in the regions where you will be staying and … the advance by troops under [Nationalist General] Fu Zuoyi … we are worried [about] your absence … and also about the safety of your journey. Would it not be better … to postpone your visit to us for awhile.…

Mao agreed, thanking Stalin for his advice and concern.[84] However, on July 4, Mao again proposed to visit the Soviet Union. On July 14, Stalin again begged off, asking his representative, Andrei Orlov, to tell Mao that,

> In view of the start of the grain harvest, top party officials are leaving for the provinces in August, and will remain there until November. Therefore, the Central Committee requests Comrade Mao Zedong to delay his visit to Moscow until the end of November in order to have the opportunity to meet with all top party comrades.

Orlov told Moscow that based on his long acquaintance with Mao, his smile and comment ("fine, fine") on hearing this message "in no way indicated that he was pleased with the telegram." In fact, his bags were packed, he was prepared to travel and he had not expected to be rebuffed.[85]

Yet with an eye toward the looming need to manage external relations, the closer the Chinese Communists came to power, the more Mao felt the need to strengthen and clarify relations with the Soviet Union. Mao again raised the issue of visiting Moscow. On August 28, 1948, Orlov reported to Moscow following a conversation with Mao that, "whereas in 1947 he had not been in any hurry to visit Moscow, now the situation had changed, and he wished to leave for Moscow as soon as possible."

On September 28, Mao again cabled Moscow that,

> On a number of questions it is essential that I report personally to the [CPSU] Central Committee and to the boss.... I request that you convey this to the Central Committee and to comrade the boss. I sincerely hope they will give us instructions.[86]

Thus, in sincere, respectful language, Mao communicated the CCP's desire to receive Moscow's guidance on important issues and its wish to maintain unity with the Soviet Union. In day-to-day operations, Mao did not follow Moscow in all things; but he recognized that after victory in the Chinese civil war, he would need strong relations with the Soviet Union to manage domestic economic reconstruction and to play on the international stage.

Stalin's view of the Chinese Communists at this point now shifted in a major way. His repeated refusals to meet personally with Mao reflected his cautious approach. This did not mean, however, that the Soviet leader would continue to refuse high-level contact with the Chinese Communists. Therefore, when Mao asked to visit Moscow at the end of December, the CPSU Politburo countered by deputing Politburo member and Stalin confidant Anastas Mikoyan to travel secretly to China early in the New Year to see Mao and other CCP leaders. Mikoyan's goals were to understand Chinese Communist intentions and to convey Soviet views on issues Mao had raised or would raise in these talks.[87]

At the end of 1948, both Stalin and Mao knew they had to reach out and draw closer, though differences and contradictions remained between the two.

4   Paving Mao's road to Moscow

The Chinese Communist Party and the Soviet Union brought profoundly different interests, views and goals to the table as they forged their alliance, starting with their secret talks in January–February 1949 and ending, after the Chinese Communist Party took power in October 1949, with signing of the Sino-Soviet Treaty Friendship, Alliance and Mutual Assistance in February 1950.

Countering the United States, their common enemy, was the motivating factor and shared goal that led to their alliance. In the face of possible U.S. interference, Mao sought Soviet assistance to complete the huge job of unifying China, including Taiwan, and to rebuild China's devastated economy. Stalin wanted to draw on China's strength to check U.S. power and influence in Asia, while avoiding any direct involvement in a possible Chinese–U.S. military conflict.

Yet, the birth of New China under the Communists and the renewed claims that flowed from Communist China's sovereignty claims also threatened the rights and privileges that the Soviet Union had only recently gained in the Far East at Yalta and as a result of 1945 Sino-Soviet Treaty of Friendship and Alliance with the Nationalist government.

These differing approaches – toward the United States and their conflicting national interests – underlay the goals and conditions present at the birth of the Sino-Soviet alliance. They were also unacknowledged, looming factors that led over time to increasing tension and discord in the alliance. In two sets of meetings between high-level Chinese and Soviet party leaders during 1949, and then during Mao's Moscow visit later that year and into early 1950, consensus as well contradictions were evident. Nevertheless, there was a shift in the way the two countries' common and divergent purposes played out. The trend was clear: Mao had chosen to "lean to one side," the Soviet side.

Mikoyan's secret visit to Mao's headquarters

By the winter of 1948–49, the situation in the Far East had changed dramatically. The Chinese Communist Party now controlled half of China and, for the first time, was a factor in the overall Asian power balance. Stalin sat up and took notice. On his behalf, in early 1949, then Foreign Minister Vyachaslev Molotov and Deputy Foreign Minister Andrei Vyshinsky cabled a new instruction to Stalin's confidant in China, I. V. Kovalev: "From now on, in all matters concerning China, communicate only with comrade Filippov [Stalin]."[1] Yet, despite Stalin's increasing attention to the rapid shift in power in China, it was still far from clear what he would do as the Chinese Communists approached victory in the Chinese civil war.

Despite the Soviet Union's thickening involvement with and support for the Chinese Communists, as long as the Soviet Union retained diplomatic ties with the Nationalist government, which it did to the very end, the Soviet role in China remained ambiguous. During January 1949, for instance, just before Stalin's secret envoy, Anastas Mikoyan, set off for the Communist base in Xibaibo, there was a flurry of diplomatic activity after Chiang Kai-shek's January 8, 1949 attempt to interest the great powers in mediating Nationalist–Communist peace talks. Against this background, telegrams flew back and forth between Stalin and Mao, with Stalin initially counseling Mao to adopt a less than categorically negative approach toward Chiang's proposal. Mao vigorously deflected Stalin's advice, finally telling the Soviet leader that the Chinese people should resolve their own problems without foreign intervention.

By the time Mikoyan arrived in Xibaibo on January 31, 1949, Stalin and Mao had reached agreement on the issue of handling the Nationalist government peace talks proposal, with Stalin bowing to Mao's desire for the Soviet Union to stay out of this affair and let the Chinese Communist revolution run its course. Mikoyan spoke with Mao and an array of other high-level Chinese Communist leaders, leaving on February 7 after a week of intensive discussions.

Mao was Mikoyan's main interlocutor, lecturing him almost non-stop for three full days, February 1–3, on Chinese conditions and the CCP's positions and policies. According to Mao's Russian interpreter, Shi Zhe, Mikoyan did not appear to enjoy Mao's rambling, didactic discourses. However, through his talks, Mikoyan gained an understanding of the situation in China and in the Chinese Communist Party.[2]

Conditions in China aside, the main issues between the Soviet Union and the Chinese Communists were over Northeast China, principally how to handle the Lushun naval base leasehold and jurisdiction over the Chinese Changchun Railway; whether "Outer Mongolia" should remain independent; and the degree of Soviet influence in Xinjiang, all issues foreshadowed in the 1945 Sino-Soviet Treaty of Friendship and Alliance signed with the Nationalist government. Compared with Mongolia and Xinjiang, the most difficult and ultimately most contentious issue was to involve the balance of Soviet and Chinese interests in Northeast China.

Mongolia: Soviet Nyet on return to China

Mao early on tactfully raised the issue of Mongolia, indicating that China would like to reclaim Outer Mongolia (the Mongolian People's Republic). The Soviet reaction was firm. Stalin forestalled Mao's approach by raising the opposite question – of Outer Mongolia annexing China's Inner Mongolia region. As recounted by Mikoyan in a 1960s-era report to the CPSU Central Committee, Stalin's message to Mao was that,

> The leaders of Outer Mongolia support the unification of all the Mongolian regions of China with Outer Mongolia to form an independent and united Mongolian state. The Soviet government does not agree with this plan, since it means taking a number of regions from China, although this plan does not threaten the interests of the Soviet Union. We do not think that Outer Mongolia would agree to surrender its independence in favor of autonomy within the Chinese state, even if all the Mongolian regions are united in one autonomous entity.

Faced with this stiff message, Mao dropped the issue, noting merely that he would "take note [and] not raise the question of the unification of Mongolia."[3] Plainly, Stalin dug in his heels and stared down the Chinese Communists on Mongolia, just as he had with the Nationalists during negotiations on the 1945 Sino-Soviet treaty.

Xinjiang: Soviets pledge non-interference

When Chinese Communist leaders raised the issue of Soviet influence in Xinjiang, Mikoyan stated categorically that the Soviet Union had no territorial ambitions there. Mikoyan reported to Moscow that, "Mao entertained suspicions regarding our plans in Xinjiang. He spoke of an independence movement in the Ili district of Xinjiang," and noted that local insurgents reportedly had acquired Soviet-made artillery, tanks and planes, and that there was a local autonomous Communist Party. According to Mikoyan,

> I told him quite clearly that we do not support the independence movement of the Xinjiang peoples, and even less do we wish to make any claims as regards Xinjiang territory, believing that Xinjiang was and should remain part of China.[4]

The Soviet Union had long-standing interests in Xinjiang. While the 1945 Sino-Soviet treaty had not touched on Xinjiang, during treaty negotiations, Stalin had foresworn support for Xinjiang independence as a trade-off for Chiang Kai-shek's agreement to recognize (Outer) Mongolian independence.[5] Nevertheless, the Nationalists later had been forced to turn back a Soviet attempt to guarantee its interests in Xinjiang through a treaty with a regional government there.[6]

It was impossible to overlook the fact that Moscow exercised considerable influence in the Xinjiang region through a significant Soviet minority presence.[7] Soviet influence and control was exercised through the Association of Soviet Citizens Abroad, "a country within a country," not through occupation of territory or by treaty. Stalin was thus in a good position to concede on Xinjiang, and thereby deprive the Chinese Communists of any justification to put Xinjiang on the agenda.

Northeast China: feeling each other out

On the sensitive issue of Soviet rights in the Northeast, Mao and Mikoyan took a cautious, exploratory approach. Mao explained that some non-Communist Chinese questioned why the Soviet Union should retain the Lushun naval base after the CCP came to power. Noting that there were Communists in both China and the Soviet Union, Mao said this made possible the Soviet retention of the Lushun naval base, and, in fact, the CCP favored Soviet retention of the base until China could stand up to Japanese aggression. Then the Soviet Union itself would no longer need the base. Mao thus tactfully indicated China should eventually reclaim the Lushun naval facility, but in the near future had no plan to do so.

Mikoyan told Mao that the Soviet Union had decided to withdraw its forces from Lushun as soon as Japan signed a peace treaty and the U.S. withdrew its forces from Japan. However, should the CCP believe it appropriate for Soviet forces to withdraw immediately from the Lushun area, the Soviet Union was prepared to do so. This offer was disingenuous, however, since it was clear that the Chinese Communists had no desire to see the immediate withdrawal of Soviet naval forces at Lushun.

As expected, as soon as Mao and other CCP leaders heard the Soviet position, they responded that it was not possible for Soviet forces to withdraw immediately from the Lushun naval base, since this would only benefit the U.S. Mao proposed to maintain secrecy, wait until Communist power was firmly established and then reconsider the issue once China, with Soviet assistance, was again on its feet. Mao said that the Chinese people appreciated the 1945 Sino-Soviet treaty, but once China was in a better situation, the two countries could sign a mutual assistance treaty similar to the Soviet–Polish treaty. To Mikoyan "[I]t was clear that [Mao] had some tactical considerations ... he did not want to reveal."[8] Later events bore out Mikoyan's insight.

Stalin worried most about the Changchun Railway. According to I. V. Kovalev, who accompanied Mikoyan in Xibaipo, "On more than one occasion, [Stalin] sent me radio telegrams asking what the true feelings of the Chinese comrades were toward the Changchun Railway Treaty and whether or not they felt it was really equitable."[9] Mikoyan told Chinese

Communist leaders that the Soviet Union did not regard the Changchun Railway Treaty as unequal,

> since this railway was built with mainly Russian resources.... It is possible that in this treaty the principle of equity is not adhered to perfectly, but we are prepared to discuss this question with our Chinese comrades and resolve it in a fraternal manner.

Referring vaguely to "minor discrepancies in determining property rights" that needed resolution, Mao noted that some former railway enterprises had been confiscated by the Nationalists and then returned to the railway by the Chinese Red Army (People's Liberation Army) when it took control, leading to public criticism that the Nationalists had confiscated these enterprises in accord with the 1945 Sino-Soviet treaty while the Chinese Communists had violated the treaty. Mao proposed that CCP Manchuria party chief Gao Gang and Kovalev jointly study the issue and report to their respective party central committees.[10]

Though Stalin was quite worried about the fate of the 1945 Sino-Soviet treaty, Chinese Communist leaders in the Xibaibo meetings expressed no clear opinion about the treaty, likely since they had not yet had a chance to study the issue carefully. They focused instead on gaining greater Soviet economic and military assistance.

Chinese Communists seek enhanced military and economic aid

In a February 1 meeting, Zhou Enlai and Chinese Red Army (People's Liberation Army) Commander-in-Chief Zhu De raised the urgent need for Soviet military equipment and advice, including anti-tank guns, tanks and equipment for explosives and weapons production, as well as advisers on military training, organization and weapons production. Zhou also sought Soviet steel rails, gasoline, motor vehicles and other machinery and materiel.

During a February 2 meeting, Zhu De and Central Committee member Ren Bishi stressed how the Soviet Union might help China economically. Ren sketched CCP plans to turn the Northeast into a national military industrial base for motor vehicles, airplanes, tanks and other military equipment production, and floated three ways the Soviets could help: through loans, joint economic ventures and Soviet-run concessionary enterprises. He also solicited Soviet help in exploiting rare mineral resources in Northeast China, including uranium, magnesium, molybdenum and aluminum, noting that Japan had extracted a ton of uranium from the Northeast. If the Soviet Union was interested, China could also consider joint development ventures or invite the Soviet Union to run concessionary enterprises to exploit these mineral resources. Stressing that industrial development in the Northeast required skilled experts, and noting that China was still employing Japanese specialists at the Anshan Steel works, Ren asked the Soviet Union to send at least 500 economic specialists to China.

In a February 3 meeting, CCP First Vice Chairman Liu Shaoqi proposed that the Soviet Union assist China's industrial development by sharing socialist economic development experience and providing economic literature, experts, technicians and capital. He pressed Mikoyan to indicate how much economic aid the Soviet Union could provide so China could factor this into its economic plans. Mikoyan agreed in principle to provide Soviet experts and other help in arms production, suggesting the Chinese Communists draw up a list of what they sought, since he had to refer specific questions to Moscow.[11]

While Chinese Communist leaders clearly urgently sought Soviet assistance, Mao asserted that he would not take offense if Moscow could not provide loans or other assistance. However, Mao still pressed the Soviet Union to provide military materiel as soon as possible, and proposed to send a delegation to Moscow to sign a loan agreement and discuss other issues.[12]

Mikoyan's reaction to Chinese Communist policies

Based on Mikoyan's reports, the following were the policies adopted or being considered by the CCP in early 1949 along with Mikoyan's reaction and advice:

First, the Chinese Communists thought at that point (i.e., in early 1949) that it was not urgent to take Nanjing, Shanghai and other big Chinese cities, since they lacked sufficient expertise and wherewithal to supply China's big cities. Mikoyan, relaying CPSU Central Committee advice, urged the CCP to rapidly occupy China's larger cities "to strengthen the party's proletarian base."

Second, Mao boasted that, "Chinese peasants have more social consciousness than all American workers and many British workers." Mikoyan felt the Mao and the CCP were over-reliant on the party's rural base.

Third, Mao was reluctant to quickly establish a government after taking Nanjing, the Nationalist capital, since any such government would, he thought, necessarily be a coalition government, which Mao feared would lead to confusion. Mikoyan urged Mao to establish a coalition-based revolutionary government right after occupying Nanjing or Shanghai, arguing that this would strengthen the Communist Party's hand, domestically and internationally.

Fourth, Mao was inclined not to pursue early foreign (i.e., non-Soviet bloc) diplomatic recognition of a new revolutionary government, not refusing outright recognition if offered by other governments, but not agreeing to immediate diplomatic ties. This would give the new regime a freer hand in resolving issues involving foreign rights and interests in China. Mikoyan questioned this view.

Fifth, Mao repeatedly stressed that he wanted to accept the leadership and direction of the Soviet Communist Party, that he was Stalin's pupil, that he supported a pro-Soviet policy and, furthermore, that he appreciated Stalin's concern for the Chinese revolution.

Sixth, Liu Shaoqi said China's transition to socialism would be gradual, starting with greater planning, and with "the full offensive against capitalist elements" ten to 15 years off. Only then would China begin the transfer of industrial and commercial enterprises to state control. However, Liu asked for Soviet advice on this strategy.[13]

While Mikoyan's talks with the Chinese Communist leadership did not settle any practical issues, his long discussions with Mao, his wide contacts with other Chinese Communist leaders and – especially during this period – Stalin's frequent message exchanges with Mao provided both sides with a better understanding of each other's positions, intentions and demands, as well as differences of view. This greater understanding provided the basis for subsequent high-level exchanges, and was an important step toward the Sino-Soviet alliance that was consummated in February 1950.

Chinese Communist shifts after Mikoyan's visit

In the wake of Mikoyan's visit, Mao was more strongly convinced than ever that New China's economic development required an alliance with the Soviet Union. In his March 13, 1949 Final Report of the Second Plenum of the Chinese Communist Party Seventh Congress, Mao declared that,

> We cannot imagine being without the Soviet Union.... We must stand with the Soviet Union on the same front; we are allies. When we have a chance, we will make this clear in a statement; for now, we need to explain this to non-party persons, and make propaganda to this effect.

On April 3, the Chinese Communist Party with other ("democratic") Chinese parties issued a joint statement of opposition to the North Atlantic Treaty. This statement, drafted by Mao, was the first public recognition that the Soviet Union would be an ally of New China.[14] In a related move, while CCP leaders did not want to shut the door to the United States and other Western countries, to gain Stalin's trust, they frequently reported on developments in these relations and sought Moscow's guidance.

At this time, while the Chinese Communists were urgently seeking Soviet loans and assistance to revive China's economy, Soviet loans were not forthcoming.[15] Some CCP leaders allegedly considered accepting loans from capitalist countries, but Mao, arguing that the issue was very sensitive, sought Stalin's advice.

In mid-April, Stalin's confidant I. V. Kovalev reported to Stalin on his three-hour April 9 meeting with Mao, Zhu De, Zhou Enlai and Liu Shaoqi. Mao told Kovalev that the United States, using Citibank as a proxy, had offered to loan $100–300 million to the Chinese Communist Party. Mao said the CCP regarded this "as an attempt to lure us into this deal not for [China's benefit], but for the sake of getting American capitalism out of its crisis ... and enslaving the Chinese nation as they did under the Chiang Kai-shek regime." Mao informed Kovalev, however, that, in view of the capitalist countries' special economic interests in Shanghai, the CCP would communicate directly with them "in special cases while abstaining from any official legalization of these diplomatic relations."[16]

Reacting to this report, Stalin cabled Kovalev:

> When you meet Mao Zedong, tell him the following: First, we believe the Chinese People's Government should not refuse to establish formal relations with capitalist countries, including the United States, if these countries officially foreswear military, economic, and political support for Chiang Kai-shek and the Nationalist Government.... Second, we believe that, under the right conditions, China should not refuse to accept foreign loans from or trade with capitalist countries. The conditions for loans and trade should not impose a burden on China's economy and its financial development which could later be used to infringe on China's national sovereignty or its national industry.[17]

On the sensitive issue of Sino-American relations, Mao Zedong paid special attention to Moscow's opinion. Kovalev recalled that both before and after crossing the Yangtze, Mao Zedong and Zhou Enlai on a number of occasions provided him with information on relations with the United States and other Western countries, seeking Soviet advice.[18]

On May 23, Kovalev reported that Mao had briefed him on an early May meeting between CCP representative Huang Hua and U.S. Ambassador Leighton Stuart. Stuart reportedly said the U.S. no longer supported that Nationalists, offering this as proof that the U.S. Embassy had remained in Nanjing (after the Nationalist government withdrew to Guangzhou). He also reportedly stated that U.S. forces stationed in China (ground and naval) would be withdrawn as soon as the People's Liberation Army entered major cities (i.e., Qingdao and Shanghai), expressed hope for a widely representative coalition government, and pledged the United States would recognize and establish relations with a coalition government that was supported by the whole Chinese nation.

However, said Mao, Stuart's statements were at odds with General MacArthur's actions. Just recently, MacArthur had deployed two U.S. army regiments to Qingdao, and had strengthened U.S. naval forces at Shanghai. "Either Stuart was lying or the military (MacArthur) are ignoring the

State Department." Mao believed that Ambassador Stuart had "also lied about the Americans' alleged non-support for the Nationalist regime," which, said Mao, "is actively going on now." As for Stuart's statement that the U.S. and other Western embassies were staying in Nanjing, Mao said, "this is not in our interest either. We would be happy if all the capitalist embassies got out of China for good." In a May 26 message, Stalin asked Kovalev to convey his agreement with "Comrade Mao's assessment of American Ambassador Leighton Stuart," and that, "the [CPSU] Central Committee highly appreciates Comrade Mao Zedong's information."[19]

At the time, however, Soviet calculations were more complicated and nuanced than Mao thought. On the one hand, the Soviet leader did not welcome close contacts between the Chinese Communists and the United States. On the other hand, he was concerned that the United States would intervene militarily to thwart the Chinese Communist liberation effort. Stalin's main concern then was not that the Chinese Communists and the United States would establish relations, but rather that the Chinese Communists would engage in an extreme military action that would give the U.S. a pretext for intervening militarily in the Chinese civil war. Should the United States intervene militarily, the Soviet Union would face a hard choice: If it joined in this conflict, it would become embroiled in an Asian war with the United States; if it adopted an evasive stance, and the Chinese Communists were defeated by the United States, Soviet interests in northern China would be harmed.

Despite the debate among historians as to whether Stalin tried to stop the Chinese Communists from crossing the Yangtze, there is no available archival material directly touching on the issue. It is evident from Ambassador Roshchin's activities and Stalin's telegrams to Mao regarding the Soviet offer to mediate, however, that the Soviet Union would have been content had the Nationalists and the Communists ruled on opposite sides of the Yangtze. Therefore, there were grounds for Mao's repeated expressions in later years of resentment toward Stalin on this score. Hu Qiaomu's version, that while Stalin did not formally propose that Chinese Communist forces desist from attacking across the Yangtze, this is what the Soviet leader intended, is believable.[20] Soviet Ambassador Roshchin revealed a similar concern. As reported by a U.S. Embassy Minister-Counselor on April 1, 1949, before the Chinese Communist army crossed the Yangtze, Roshchin opined that, "when the Chinese Communists seized all of China, they would be 'riding the back of a tiger' and confronted with situations impossible of solution."[21]

Actually, perhaps the one "riding the back of a tiger" was Stalin. When in April 1949 the People's Liberation Army shelled the British frigate *Amethyst* and the cruiser *London*[22] during its campaign to cross the Yangtze, the British Conservative Party in an emergency cabinet meeting called for a declaration of war on Red China. I. V. Kovalev, then in Peiping, later said that Moscow's reaction made him feel "that we were facing a crisis.... With the Soviet military on the Liaodong peninsula, including the Soviet fleet at Lushun and other Pacific bases, on a war footing, we luckily avoided a conflict despite heightened tensions."[23]

Liu Shaoqi delegation to Moscow disguised as trade mission

Out of fear of provoking the United States, Stalin was still reluctant to have an overt, close relationship with the Chinese Communists. In his May 26, 1949 cable to Kovalev, Stalin had also cautioned that: "We believe now is not the right time to publicize the friendship between the Soviet Union and Democratic China."[24] Based on this cautious view, Stalin asked that the upcoming Chinese Communist delegation to Moscow to be led by Liu Shaoqi be portrayed to the foreign press as a Northeast China trade delegation led by Gao Gang.[25]

The delegation arrived in Moscow on June 26, 1949.[26] This visit was the most significant diplomatic move by the Chinese Communists before the establishment of the People's Republic of China. The delegation aimed to convey directly to Stalin Chinese Communist positions on key foreign and domestic issues, to strengthen relations with the Soviet Union, to pave the way for a meeting between Mao and Stalin, and to create the basis for a Sino-Soviet alliance. More concretely, the delegation sought access to Soviet economic development and management experience, and greater economic and military assistance. Over a month and a half, in numerous meetings with Stalin and other Soviet leaders, Liu for the most part achieved the purpose of this visit. Some issues, however, were left for Mao to resolve when he visited Moscow in the winter of 1949–50.

In Liu's meetings and in his extensive July 4 written report addressed to Stalin and the CPSU Central Committee, Liu briefed his Soviet hosts on China's domestic situation and the Chinese Communist strategy for establishing a new regime, and sought Soviet advice. Judging by Stalin's selective underlining, comments and questions on a Russian version of the July 4 report, the Soviet leader read it with great care and interest.[27] Among the topics covered in Liu's report were the potential applicability of the Chinese revolutionary experience to other "colonial and semi-colonial countries;" the CCP's plan to include non-Communist parties in a new coalition government; how the planned inclusion of China's "national bourgeoisie" in a CCP-controlled "people's dictatorship" would differ from Soviet-style "proletarian dictatorship;" the intended pro-Soviet tilt of New China's foreign policy; the increasing restrictions that would be placed over foreign economic, journalistic, charitable and educational organizations operating in China; and the CCP's cautious approach to establishing diplomatic relations with "imperialist" countries.

Fealty to Stalin proclaimed

On June 30, only a few days after Liu's delegation arrived in Moscow, Mao announced in his article "On the People's Democratic Dictatorship" that New China would implement a pro-Soviet foreign policy of "leaning to one side." In his July 4 report, Liu stressed the significance of Mao's statement:

> In our policy in international relations we shall certainly be at one with the USSR, and we have already made some explanations to this effect to the democratic parties and groups. (Yes!) [Note: Stalin's comments are in parentheses]. Some non-partisan people criticized our policy for its pro-USSR slant, but Comrade Mao Zedong told them that our policy would be leaning toward the USSR, for it would be an error should we not stand ... with the USSR ... but take a middle road. Upon such explanations all democratic parties and groups, jointly with the CCP, signed and published a statement against the North Atlantic Pact.

As an indication of Soviet gratitude, *Pravda* published Mao's "leaning to one side" article in a special edition on July 6.

Further conveying a strong sense of CCP fealty to the CPSU, Liu's July 4 report stated that,

> The Soviet Communist Party is the chief headquarters of the international communist movement.... [T]herefore, the CCP submits to decisions of the Soviet Communist Party.... (No!) If on some questions differences should arise between the CCP and the Soviet Communist Party, the CCP, having outlined its point of view, will submit and resolutely carry out decisions of the Soviet Communist Party. (No!) We believe it is necessary to establish closest mutual ties between the two parties [and] exchange appropriate authorized political representatives so as to ... achieve better mutual understanding between our parties. (Yes!)[28]

Though Stalin waved aside the CCP pledge that it would follow CPSU leadership, he seemed clearly moved by the Chinese Communist attitude. In relations between the CPSU and the CCP, said Stalin, his most important mistake had been to ask the Chinese Communist Party to compromise with the Nationalist Party in 1945. "Since we did not understand the situation, we gave the Chinese revolution bad advice, causing problems in your work, and interfering with you."

"There was no interference," said Liu. However, Stalin repeatedly apologized, saying that the Chinese Communist Party was a mature party; that it had achieved rapid political, theoretical and economic achievements;

and that he expected the Chinese Communist Party to stand in the front rank of the international Communist movement. "We are still your students," said Liu. Stalin responded that students can overtake their teachers, and when the center of revolution moved from Europe to the East, the Chinese Communist Party's historical responsibility would increase. The Soviet Union would fall behind, and China would advance rapidly and would overtake its teacher. The interpreter, Shi Zhe, believed that Stalin conveyed a sense of remorse and guilt.[29]

Stalin proposed an international division of "revolutionary" labor between China and the Soviet Union, with the CCP taking responsibility for mentoring national democratic revolutionary movements in Eastern colonial and semi-colonial countries where China's revolutionary experience was relevant. While China worked on revolution in the East, the CPSU would continue to work in the West.[30]

Stalin asserted that after the death of Marx and Engels, the Western European social democratic movement stagnated. As a result, the center of revolution had shifted to the eastward (i.e., to Russia), and, said Stalin, had now shifted again to China and East Asia:

> You should fulfill your [revolutionary] responsibility [in] East Asia. Maybe we Soviets are a bit stronger ... when it comes to ... Marxist theory. But when it comes to putting Marxist theory into practice, you have a lot of experience worthy of our study. We have already learned a lot from you.[31]

This was the first sign of Soviet respect for the Chinese Communist Party in the history of Sino-Soviet inter-party relations.

Chinese Communists reiterate need for Soviet aid

Grand strategizing aside, Liu's most important trip objective was to secure greater Soviet assistance to China's still unfinished revolution and, in the future, to its post-revolutionary economic redevelopment.

Stalin understood China's urgent need was for economic assistance. Deep into the evening of June 26 and the morning of June 27, only hours after the Chinese delegation arrived in Moscow, Stalin discussed Soviet assistance to China, reporting that the CPSU Central Committee had decided to provide a U.S. $300 million loan to the Chinese Communist Party at one percent interest, to be disbursed over five years in the form of equipment, machinery and commodities. China would then have ten years to repay the loan once it was fully allocated. Stalin proposed that the loan agreement could first be signed between the representatives of the CPSU Central Committee and CCP or, alternatively, between the Soviet government and the Northeast China government. After a coalition government was established in China, a state-to-state agreement could then be signed.

Stalin committed the Soviet Union to providing naval assistance, including experts and minesweepers to help clear mines around Shanghai, as well as to salvage sunken naval and commercial vessels. Stalin also promised that, "In response to your request for help in strengthening coastal defense at Qingdao, we can dispatch a naval force to Qingdao. But, it should be sent in the form of a visit after an all-China government is established."

Responding to the CCP delegation's request to establish an air link between Moscow and Peiping (now Beijing), Stalin said, "We have already made preparations, so we can start setting up this air route." He also agreed to help China establish an airplane assembly and repair facility.[32]

The Soviets further agreed to help establish a naval school at Lushun, set up coastal defenses, and build a rail line between Ulaanbaator in Mongolia and Zhangjiakou in China.[33]

Liu asked Stalin to help establish a Chinese People's Air Force, requesting 100–200 Yak fighters, 40–80 bombers, spare parts, and Japanese and German heavy bombs, and training of Chinese aviators at a Soviet air school. The Soviets agreed, but suggested an air school for Chinese aviators should be set up in China, rather than in the Soviet Union.[34] Responding to a CCP request for help in countering Nationalist air attacks, Stalin agreed to send Soviet air assets to provide defense around Lushun and Dalian. The two sides also discussed cooperation on intelligence and counter-espionage. When Gao and Liu complained that most of the Soviet intelligence network in China was unreliable and was, in fact, working for the United States and Chiang Kai-shek, and that a stop should be put to such uncontrolled activity, Stalin agreed, stating that: "The situation requires us to unify our intelligence efforts, and we are prepared to start immediately."[35]

Shortly after the delegation returned to China, the Soviet Union sped up assistance to the Chinese Communists. In September, the Soviet Council of Ministers decided to provide (Communist) China with 334 planes and artillery pieces, including 360 antiaircraft guns, all valued at U.S.$26,500,000. The Soviet Union later provided another U.S.$31,500,000 worth of arms and technical equipment, and steel rails and fixed equipment worth U.S.$6,300,000.[36]

Uncle Joe's advice on Xinjiang

Liu's visit also gained Soviet cooperation with regard to Xinjiang, an important factor in strengthening understanding between the CCP and the Soviet Union. While Stalin was sensitive about Soviet interests in Northeast China, he was avuncular and magnanimous when it came to Xinjiang, urging that,

> [The CCP] should not put off occupying Xinjiang, since delay could invite [British] intervention in Xinjiang. They could stir up the

Moslems, including the Indian Moslems, to continue the civil war against the Communist Party. This should not be allowed since Xinjiang has large petroleum reserves and cotton.... The proportion of [Han] Chinese is now less than five percent. After occupying Xinjiang you should bring this up to 30 percent.

To help China liberate (occupy) Xinjiang, Stalin offered to provide 40 fighter planes to "scatter and destroy" regional military leader Ma Bufang's cavalry.[37]

The Chinese leadership reacted quickly to Stalin's suggestion. Mao had planned to solve the Xinjiang issue in 1950 or 1951, but, after receiving Liu's report, Mao decided to move forward the date for the attack on Xinjiang. With Mao's instructions in hand, Liu told Stalin that Mao had agreed with his recommendation to speed up the occupation of Xinjiang and had "suggested that we clarify the issue of assistance on the part of Soviet aviation and troop airlift."[38]

On July 25, Mao informed Liu that following the occupation of the areas around Lanzhou in Gansu and Xining in Qinghai, the CCP could prepare to move on Xinjiang in the fall of 1949. At the same time, he instructed both Deng Liqun, who was then attached as a political secretary to the delegation, to hurry to Ili in Xinjiang to set up radio communications, and Peng Dehuai, then PLA military commander in Northwest China, to explore the possibility of occupying Xinjiang before the end of 1949.[39] With Soviet help, Deng Liqun set up radio communications from Ili to Mao and the Soviet Embassy, and met with reliable local leaders. A short time later in 1949, the Chinese Communist Party achieved a (mostly) political resolution of the Xinjiang question.[40]

Stalin's recommendation to move early into Xinjiang was not made out of concern over Chinese interests, but rather from concern that Western powers might infiltrate China's Northwest, which bordered on the Soviet Central Asian republics. Nevertheless, Stalin's advice was instrumental in promoting the CCP's largely bloodless occupation of Xinjiang.

The 1945 Soviet–Nationalist treaty and Northeast China

Liu and Stalin came to no decision as to whether or not to conclude a new Sino-Soviet treaty. As part of (what turned out to be) early stage negotiations with Chinese Communist leaders over terms of a new Sino-Soviet treaty, it was clear to Stalin that there would be a clash of interests over Soviet rights and interests in Northeast China. This was the same knotty issue that had been at the heart of the 1945 Sino-Soviet treaty negotiations with the Nationalist government.[41] And, it was precisely on issues related to Northeast China that negotiations between Stalin and Liu reached an impasse.

Mao, as the founder of New China, was determined to protect national sovereignty, and naturally wanted to rid China of all unequal treaties, including the 1945 Sino-Soviet treaty. And, Stalin, to protect Soviet interests in the Far East, wanted to uphold the existing 1945 bilateral treaty. This issue, then, was at the heart of the clashing interests between China and the Soviet Union. If the CCP leadership was not yet prepared to think through the issue when Mikoyan raised it in his visit to Xibaibo, later in 1949, as the CCP prepared to take power in China, Mao was forced to consider this extremely sensitive issue.

After Mikoyan left China, CCP leaders began to consider what to do about legacy Chinese treaties. Zhou told a group of non-Communist opinion leaders on April 17, 1949 that, "Some foreign treaties must be abrogated, while others need revision, and still others can be retained."[42] In discussing treaties that "need revision" or "can be retained," he was clearly thinking about the 1945 Sino-Soviet treaty.

Before the Chinese Communist delegation led by Liu set off for Moscow, Mao held a long discussion with Liu and CCP Soviet-expert Wang Jiaxiang (later the first ambassador to Moscow from the People's Republic of China). Wang raised two questions: what to do about the 1945 Sino-Soviet treaty once the Communists formed a new government, and how to handle Soviet requests to protect its former underground intelligence agents in China. According to Wang's recollection, Mao merely said, "We can talk about these two questions and see [what develops]".[43] The intention of the two sides, China and the Soviet Union, to feel each other out on the question of the 1945 bilateral treaty is reflected in Liu's July 4 report to Stalin and in Stalin's annotation on the report.

> In establishing their diplomatic relations, the USSR and New China will have to give closer attention to [the 1945 Chinese–Soviet Treaty]. [They could adopt] one of the following three options:
>
> 1   The new government of China will state its complete acceptance of this treaty as valid, without any amendments whatsoever.
> 2   Proceeding from the original text of the treaty, representatives of both governments will conclude a new treaty of friendship and alliance between the USSR and China, which, in conformity with the new situation, would be amended in style and substance.
> 3   Representatives of the governments of both countries will exchange notes to the effect that the present treaty temporarily remains what it is but state that they are prepared to revise it at an opportune moment.
>
> Which of the above three variants is good? (Settle the issue upon Mao Zedong's arrival in Moscow.)[44]

Forewarned by I. V. Kovalev's reporting from China, Stalin avoided the contentious Changchun Railway question in his meeting with Liu.

Mikoyan had conveyed the Soviet position in Xibaibo that the railway treaty was an equal treaty, and should therefore be upheld. While the CCP had subsequently not enunciated a clear position on the railway treaty issue, Kovalev reported that Gao Gang and Chen Yun, his CCP interlocutors on the Changchun railway issue, always insisted that the treaty was equal and satisfactory, but, in his opinion, "[T]he Chinese secretly wanted total control of the railroad and in practice were doing their best to wrest management of the line from Soviet personnel."[45]

Stalin knew that the Chinese Communists were not proposing an immediate Soviet withdrawal from the Lushun naval base. Therefore, he restated Mikoyan's rhetorical argument that the Chinese Communists should decide between two proposals. One was that the Soviet Union should not withdraw for the time being, since they were effectively blocking U.S. and Nationalist Chinese freedom of movement, thereby protecting Soviet interests and Chinese Communist interests. The other was that the Soviet Union should withdraw its forces immediately, thereby giving the Chinese Communists greater political room for maneuver. Since Dalian was a free port, said Stalin, China and the Soviet Union could operate it jointly even in the absence of diplomatic relations between China and third countries. On the 1945 Sino-Soviet treaty and what to do about it, Stalin noted that in his exchange of telegrams with Mao, he had already declared that the 1945 treaty was unequal. Since it was a product of relations with the Nationalists, it could not be otherwise. But, as noted above, Stalin brushed aside the three options for dealing with the 1945 treaty that Liu had proposed, saying simply that the issue should be decided when Mao visited Moscow.[46]

Though Liu said the old treaty could be extended, by presenting three options for addressing the issue of treaty extension, the CCP leadership indicated that it hoped to replace the 1945 treaty, while leaving substantial room for discussion. Stalin certainly understood this, but it is clear from what he said that he hoped to maintain the 1945 treaty as it was.

Stalin rebuffs request for aid to liberate Taiwan

During the Moscow talks, Taiwan emerged as a key point of contention between the Chinese Communist leadership and the Soviet Union, with Stalin neither prepared nor willing to give CCP leaders the help they sought to resolve the Taiwan issue.

Stalin repeatedly said that while he was not afraid of war, he was opposed to war, and would do everything he could to prevent war, since the Soviet Union needed 15 to 20 years of peace to rebuild its economy.[47] But for the CCP, the liberation of Taiwan, the elimination of Chiang Kai-shek and the unification of China were bedrock policies, and Mao was banking on Soviet help to take Taiwan.

In addressing the Taiwan issue in his July 4 report to Stalin, Liu tendentiously claimed that "Since part of the Guomindang [Nationalist] forces on the island of Taiwan might take our side, the liberation of Taiwan could take place even earlier than [autumn of 1949]."[48] Internally, in mid-July, Mao and other CCP leaders discussed creating an air fighter group to provide air cover for a summer 1950 Taiwan Strait crossing aimed at capturing Taiwan. This plan envisioned sending 300–400 military personnel to the Soviet Union for aviation training and the purchase of about 100 airplanes from the Soviet Union.[49] On July 26, the CCP Military Commission formed an air force leadership group comprised of the Central Military Commission's Air Force Office and the 14th Army Corps Headquarters and units under its control, and decided to send PLA Air Force Commander Liu Yalou and others to Moscow for detailed talks on the purchase of aircraft, the hiring of experts and advisers, and Soviet help in starting up an air school.[50]

Earlier, on July 25, Mao sent an instruction to Liu Shaoqi, arguing the necessity and urgency of occupying Taiwan:

> Great difficulties have mounted day by day in Shanghai since the [Nationalist] blockade began. To break the blockade, we must occupy Taiwan, but, without an air force, this is impossible. We would like you [Liu] to exchange ideas with Comrade Stalin on whether the USSR can help us, that is, train in Moscow 1,000 aviators and 300 airfield technicians within six to twelve months. Also, whether the USSR can sell us 100–200 fighter aircraft and 40–80 bombers to be used in the Taiwan operation. We would also like to ask for Soviet help in establishing a naval fleet. We expect to have occupied the whole of the Chinese mainland, except for Tibet, by the second half of next year.

Mao proposed that the Soviet Air Force help liberate Taiwan, though, characteristically, he couched the idea in a roundabout way.

> [I]f we employ Soviet help (that is, besides our request for Soviet help in training our aviators and selling us aircraft, we may have no choice but to ask the Soviet Union to send Soviet air force and naval experts, and aviators to join in military operations) in capturing Taiwan, could this harm American–Soviet relations?
>
> Please report all this to Comrade Stalin so he can consider our plans.... If these plans are generally acceptable, then we plan to send students to the USSR at once. Detailed aviator training plans are now being drawn up. We shall let you know later. After settling these issues, you can return to China.[51]

Despite his efforts, Liu was not able to secure Soviet help in a cross-Strait operation against Taiwan.

According to documents in the possession of I. V. Kovalev, in a telegram to Moscow before the Chinese Communist delegation left for

Moscow, Mao asked Stalin for Soviet air and naval support in the liberation of Taiwan, but did not receive a positive response. When Liu raised the issue again in Moscow, Stalin immediately turned down the idea. He told the Chinese delegation that the Soviet Union had suffered enormous damage during World War II, with the country in ruins from its western border to the Volga River. Soviet military support for an attack on Taiwan would mean a clash with American air and naval forces that could lead to a new world war. The Soviet Union had no reason to incur this risk. "If we, the leaders, do this," Stalin told Liu, "the Russian people would not understand us. Moreover, they may throw us out if we undervalue their wartime and postwar efforts and hardships." Stalin proposed to refer the question to an enlarged CPSU Politburo meeting. On July 27, he invited the Chinese delegation to the CPSU Central Committee headquarters. There, Liu, Gao Gang and Wang Jiaxiang joined in a meeting that included Marshals Nikolai Bulganin and Aleksandr Vasilevsky. After Stalin reiterated his earlier arguments, Liu withdrew China's request for direct assistance for an attack on Taiwan, indicating that the issue was now off the table.[52]

Clearly, the respective abilities of the Chinese Communist Party and the Soviet Union to satisfy the demands of the other side were limited by their calculation of global issues and their respective long-term objectives. Importantly, at the time, since the leaders of Communist China and the Soviet Union shared a common ideology and common strategic views on the international situation, an alliance served their mutual long-term interests. As a result, Mao (working through Liu) and Stalin strove to forge understanding on the key issues where they agreed, and to achieve cooperation where they could on issues where they disagreed. This effort was the basis for the overall success achieved in the meetings between Liu and Stalin.

From this viewpoint, Professor Chen Jian's conclusion is apt: After Liu's visit to Moscow,

> The framework of Sino-Soviet strategic cooperation had been established. Mao and the CCP leadership, knowing Stalin's attitude, became more confident in dealing with the United States and other 'imperialist' countries. To further change the 'leaning-to-one-side' approach from rhetoric to reality, the CCP leadership now had every reason increasingly to base the CCP's foreign policy on a strategic alliance with the Soviet Union.[53]

However, Liu's visit to Moscow had not resolved some basic issues related to conflicting national interests. Resolution of these issues awaited Mao's face-to-face meeting with Stalin.

5   Mao's trip to Moscow

Within weeks after the People's Republic of China was proclaimed on October 1, 1949, preparations unfolded for Mao Zedong's winter 1949–50 Moscow visit, during which Mao and Stalin took each other's measure and, after weeks of discussion, interspersed with sulking on Mao's part and deliberate reconsideration on Stalin's part, finally concluded a new Sino-Soviet treaty and formed an alliance.

Communist China and the Soviet Union built their alliance principally to manage the perceived American threat. The Chinese Communist Party, even as it seized and solidified power, needed Soviet support to check any U.S. intention to intervene in the Chinese civil war and to subvert the new Communist government. The Soviet Union, in the context of its global confrontation with the United States, needed China to counter American power in Asia. As characterized by Professor Arne Westad, the Sino-Soviet alliance was above all an anti-American coalition aimed at countering the postwar rise of the United States in Asia and the American-led world capitalist system.[1] On this point, China and the Soviet Union shared the same goal. But there was also an important economic imperative behind the Chinese Communists' desire to conclude an alliance with the Soviet Union. To revive China's economy, the Chinese Communists needed massive Soviet assistance.

Chinese economy in ruins

After winning the Chinese civil war, the new Chinese Communist government faced an economy in ruins and a host of unfulfilled tasks. Its leadership was fairly burning with impatience to revive the economy. China's confrontation with the West meant that its only hope was to gain Soviet assistance. The Chinese leadership therefore put its difficult situation on the front burner in talks with the Soviets.

On October 28, 1949 Chinese Government Administrative Council Vice Premier and Economic Commission Chairman Chen Yun told Soviet Ambassador Roshchin that China's financial and economic situation was "complicated and difficult." Foreign trade was at a standstill due to the

Nationalist coastal blockade. Of China's ports, only Tianjin was then handling a small amount of export–import trade. China lacked technical personnel to revive its economy. Chen claimed the new government had inherited only 20,000 engineers and technicians from the Nationalists, but most were allegedly "reactionary and pro-American." In the giant Anshan steel complex in the Northeast, 62 of the 70 engineers were Japanese, most of whom were "antagonistic toward Chinese, especially toward Communist Party members."[2]

A Soviet Embassy Counselor painted a similarly grim picture of the devastated Chinese economy diplomatic in a report filed in early 1950. When important industrial centers like Tianjin, Shanghai, Chongqing and Guangzhou had been liberated, he reported, over 75 percent of their industrial enterprises were idle. The retreating Nationalist Army left a landscape of destruction: bombed dams; tens of thousands of hectares of ruined fields; missing or bombed railway locomotives and carriages; ruined electric generating plants and warehouses; ruined transportation, telegraph and radio-communication equipment; and sunken ships. When the Nationalists abandoned Shanghai, they destroyed the international wireless station, blew up the main workshops at the Jiangnan Shipyard and the petroleum tanks at the Jiangwan airport, and scuttled four oil tankers and ten ferries. When they fled Wuxi, the Nationalist forces set fire to more than 1,000 trucks carrying industrial equipment from Shanghai. Of the more than 100 railway bridges between Wuhan and Guangzhou, more than 90 were bombed out. At Hankou, the Nationalists destroyed more than 30 ships and bombed out all the rail bridges linking the three Wuhan cities.[3]

Given their preoccupation with the economy and development, Chinese leaders put all their faith in an alliance with the Soviet Union. As Liu Shaoqi, then Vice Chairman of the Central People's government, said on October 5, 1949, only days after the proclamation of the People's Republic of China, "to unite with the Soviet Union [is] the fundamental state principle."[4]

However, Mao clearly knew he could not conclude a treaty with the Soviet Union by simply begging for assistance. He needed to explain to Stalin how a Sino-Soviet alliance would fundamentally benefit the Soviet Union, not merely benefit China. Mao indeed sent this kind of message. His starting point was to impress Moscow with the idea that to make political cause against the United States, the Soviet Union needed China to become stronger economically.

Li Kenong, head of the CCP Intelligence Bureau and Mao Zedong's liaison with the Soviet Embassy, warned Ambassador Roshchin on November 17, 1949 that the United States had "hatched a plan for the Chinese Communist Party to go over to the side of the Tito clique," and was seeking to expand U.S. "influence in China ... to destroy Sino-Chinese friendship." Li told Roshchin that imperialist propaganda claimed that the

Soviet Union was "seizing China's grain and natural resources," and that the "unequal" 1945 Sino-Soviet treaty had resulted in China losing all of its industrial equipment in Northeast China to the Soviet Union.[5]

There is no information at present that the U.S., in fact, had "hatched a plan for the Chinese Communist Party to go over to the side of the Tito clique," or how the Chinese Communists could possibly have known this. But, in delivering this news, Li Kenong was reminding Moscow that in its conflict with the U.S., it could not ignore China. Stalin long worried that Mao might tilt toward Tito, but the Soviet leader was also worried about New China's relations with the United States. Mao certainly believed this, telling Luo Longji, a Chinese Democratic League leader, that China was "unable to accept U.S. assistance [since this] would arouse Soviet suspicion."[6] Of course, Mao had to make China's position clear. So Chinese leaders told Moscow that the United States was not only continuing to assist the Nationalist remnants on Taiwan, but was also trying to organize counter-revolutionary organizations on the mainland. In sum, Mao sought to clearly differentiate China's positions toward the United States and the Soviet Union, stressing the importance of close Sino-Soviet ties. But, at the same time, Li's message hinted at Chinese Communist dissatisfaction with the 1945 Sino-Soviet treaty.

Trip preparations

Preparation for Mao's visit to the Soviet Union began in earnest in October 1949. The Chinese envisioned a three-month trip, the first month in the Soviet Union to sign a new Sino-Soviet treaty, the second month to tour through some Eastern European countries, and the third month to rest and recuperate at Sochi on the Black Sea. Stalin's confidant and liaison to Mao, I. V. Kovalev, at first recommended that Mao's trip be kept secret.[7]

On November 5, Kovalev conveyed Stalin's views, welcoming Mao's plan to visit Moscow. Mao said that he wanted to see Stalin in December in Moscow and pay his respects on Stalin's 70th birthday. Since many countries would be sending delegations to Stalin's birthday celebration, said Mao, his trip to Moscow could be open in character.

On November 8, Mao sent a telegram to Moscow on his trip, and on November 10, he sent Prime Minister and Foreign Minister Zhou Enlai to reiterate to Ambassador Roshchin not only that he (Mao) wanted to visit the Soviet Union, but also that he wanted to discuss the 1945 Sino-Soviet treaty. Zhou added that should Mao and Stalin decide to conclude a new bilateral treaty, he was also prepared to travel to Moscow.[8]

In a parallel approach, a November 9 telegram from the CCP Central Committee instructed Chinese Ambassador Wang Jiaxiang in Moscow to probe whether the Soviets would welcome Zhou's arrival together with Mao. This approach was meant to gauge where the Soviet leader stood on revising the 1945 treaty. After noting that the Chinese leadership had already asked Stalin through his personal representative, I. V. Kovalev, to decide the date for Mao's travel to Moscow, the telegram continued that, "As for whether Comrade Zhou Enlai should accompany Mao Zedong to Moscow, or whether the question of his visit and its timing should be fixed after Mao arrives in Moscow, please ask Stalin to consider and decide."[9] Ambassador Wang immediately conveyed this message to the CPSU Central Committee.[10] In reaction, Deputy Foreign Minister Andrei Gromyko suggested to Stalin that since the Chinese had raised the issue of the possible impact on the work of organizing the new Chinese government should Mao and Zhou travel together to Moscow, the Soviets should tell the Chinese that the Soviet government was prepared to accept whatever decision the Chinese made.[11] This Soviet maneuver was a way of hinting that the Soviet Union only wanted Mao to visit. The situation described above indicates that both sides clearly exchanged views before Mao's visit to Moscow about what he wanted to discuss; there was really no misunderstanding about what was up for discussion.

To sum up, Mao's goal in traveling to Moscow was, first, to secure as much Soviet economic assistance as possible, and second, to conclude an alliance with the Soviet Union, an alliance clothed in a new treaty. Mao, however, had absolutely no confidence in the outcome of his visit, since Stalin would not give him a clear answer on whether or not to bring Zhou to Moscow. Mao could only set out alone (i.e., without Zhou), ostensibly to offer birthday greetings to Stalin, but, in reality, to find out what cards Moscow was holding.

To further focus Stalin's attention on his upcoming visit, Mao summoned I. V. Kovalev on December 3, reporting that the Chinese Communist Party was coming under sharp domestic political pressure over his upcoming visit to Moscow. Mao said that China's non-Communist democratic parties opposed the visit, since, according to tradition, "foreign barbarians" always came to pay tribute to the Chinese emperor, not the other way around. They also feared that Mao's trip to Moscow would complicate China's relations with Western countries, and China would lose economic assistance from these countries.[12]

Mao's pre-visit concern was well founded; from the start, his visit was quite rocky. Shi Zhe, Mao's Russian interpreter in Moscow, believes that Mao and Stalin ran into difficulties and communication barriers at the start of their first meeting, since "neither Stalin nor Mao Zedong could fathom the other's psychology or intentions." This, claims Shi, led to misunderstandings, starting with Stalin's inability to understand what Mao wanted when he said that he wanted to go home with something that was "both pretty to look at and tasty."[13]

In contrast, Stalin's interpreter and Russian scholar, N. T. Fedorenko, has argued that Stalin and Mao "understood each other" from the start, and "calmly reached agreement, with no difference of opinion" in their discussions on the new treaty.[14] But the reality was the opposite. Dialogue between Stalin and Mao hit an impasse from the start. Other Russian scholars such as A. M. Ledovsky and B. T. Kulik have argued that Mao traveled to Moscow principally for rest and recuperation, and his later complaint about being cold-shouldered by Stalin is thus baseless.[15] Archival material, however, makes it abundantly clear that Mao, long before he left China, had already made the goal of his visit to Moscow very clear. He wanted to sign a new Sino-Soviet treaty of alliance.

Mao in Moscow

Mao reached Moscow on December 16, 1949; formal talks with Stalin started six hours later. According to the Soviet record, the two leaders disagreed in their first meeting over two important issues: what to do about the 1945 bilateral treaty, and the liberation of Taiwan. Though both leaders indicated they could make concessions with respect to the treaty, in fact, there was no meeting of the minds. On Taiwan, Stalin refused to offer direct assistance to China.[16]

When Mao started to recount the CCP Central Committee's discussion of the 1945 Sino-Soviet Treaty of Friendship and Alliance in the wake of Liu Shaoqi's summer 1949 Moscow visit, Stalin responded that, "This question we can discuss and decide." He noted that the two sides could continue with the old treaty, announce impending changes or make changes on the spot, but explained that,

> As you know, this treaty was concluded between the USSR and China as a result of the Yalta Agreement, which provided for the main points of the treaty (the question of the Kuril Islands, South Sakhalin, Port Arthur [Lushun], etc.). That is, the given treaty was concluded, so to speak, with the consent of America and England. Keeping in mind this circumstance, we, within our inner circle, have decided not to modify any of the points of this treaty for now, since a change in even one point could give America and England the legal grounds to raise questions about modifying ... provisions concerning the Kuril Islands, South Sakhalin, etc. That is why we searched to find a way to modify the current treaty ... by formally maintaining the Soviet Union's right to station its troops in Port Arthur [Lushun] while, at the request of the Chinese government, actually withdrawing the Soviet armed forces currently stationed there. One could do the same with the Chinese Changchun Railroad, that is, to effectively modify the corresponding points of the agreement while formally maintaining its provisions, upon China's request. If, on other hand, the Chinese comrades are not satisfied with this strategy, they can present their own proposals.

After Stalin set out the Soviet reluctance to change any of the formal provisions of the 1945 Sino-Soviet treaty, Mao conceded that, "The present situation with regard to the Chinese Changchun Railroad and Lushun corresponds with Chinese interests." He also conceded that,

> In discussing the treaty in China we had not taken into account the American and English positions regarding the Yalta Agreement. We must act in a way that is best for the common cause. The question merits further consideration.

Then, Mao asked, "Should not Zhou Enlai visit Moscow in order to decide the treaty question?" A message Mao had earlier sent before his trip to Moscow had explicitly stated that Zhou's responsibility in coming to Moscow would be to sign a treaty. Therefore, in raising the issue again, Mao was again signaling his intent to sign a new Sino-Soviet treaty. An unhappy Stalin responded that, "No, this question you must decide for yourselves. Zhou may be needed in regard to other matters." The record of the meeting indicates that on the Sino-Soviet treaty, though both sides stated that they could compromise, the Soviet Union wanted to maintain the old treaty, while China intended to sign a new bilateral treaty. This difference is obvious, though neither side stated its position baldly, since both sides wanted to preserve room for diplomatic maneuver.

When the discussion then turned to aid, trade and transport issues, Mao directed his comments to Taiwan, noting that, "We would also like to receive your assistance in creating a naval force." He explained:

> Nationalist supporters have built a naval and air base on the island of Taiwan. Our lack of naval forces and aviation makes the occupation of the island by the People's Liberation Army more difficult. With regard to this [issue], some of our generals have been voicing the opinion that we should request assistance from the Soviet Union, which could send volunteer pilots or secret military detachments to speed up the conquest of Taiwan.

Mao raised Taiwan after serious consideration, since, in meeting with Liu Shaoqi, Stalin had made it abundantly clear that the Soviet Union did not want to assist China in liberating Taiwan, lest it risk an open clash with the United States. Mao thus proposed "volunteer pilots" or "secret military detachments" as a way to keep the Soviet Union in the background but still get its actual support. Seeking to dodge a direct refusal of Mao's request, Stalin suggested that, "Assistance has not been ruled out, though one ought to consider the form of such assistance. What is most important here is not to give the Americans a pretext to intervene." But, continued Stalin, "With regard to headquarters staff and instructors, we can give them to you anytime. The rest we will have to think about." Practically speaking, this silenced Mao on the issue of Soviet assistance in the liberation of Taiwan.

Mao was very unhappy with this first meeting.[17] Kovalev observed that over the next few days, Mao "stayed holed up, moody and dejected, in the guest house." To make his case clearer, on December 22, after joining in the celebration of Stalin's 70th birthday, Mao summoned Kovalev, asking that a record of their conversation be reported to Stalin.

Mao asked to see Stalin on December 23 or 24, proposed two alternative agendas for the meeting and pressed for Stalin to decide between these two agendas. Mao's first proposed agenda foresaw the two leaders reaching consensus on a new, revised Sino-Soviet treaty, a loan agreement, a trade treaty and an air agreement. If Stalin agreed to the first agenda, said Mao, Zhou Enlai would need to come immediately to Moscow to oversee preparations for signing these agreements. Mao's second notional agenda merely envisioned the two leaders exchanging views on the issues outlined in the first agenda. If the second agenda were adopted, there would be no agreements to sign, and Zhou would not need to rush to Moscow. Mao reiterated that Stalin should make the call.[18] Despite Mao's prompting via Kovalev, in meeting with Mao on December 24, Stalin did not raise the treaty issue, leaving Mao profoundly disappointed.[19]

Years later, Mao was still nursing a deep sense of grievance over how he was treated by Stalin. In his March 30, 1956 conversation with Soviet Ambassador Pavel Yudin, Mao complained that Stalin's silence in their second (December 24, 1949) meeting had betrayed his lack of trust in the Chinese Communist Party.

> One of the most important goals of our trip to Moscow was to conclude a Sino-Soviet Treaty of Friendship, Cooperation, and Mutual Assistance.... The Chinese people had asked us whether the USSR would sign a treaty with New China, and why the treaty with the Nationalists remained in juridical force. The question of signing a treaty was very important for us, since it would decide the perspective for the future development of the People's Republic of China. In my first meeting with Stalin, I posed the question of signing a treaty, but Stalin dodged the question. In my second meeting, I returned to this issue, showing him a CCP CC telegram containing a detailed request for a treaty. I proposed summoning Zhou Enlai to Moscow to sign the treaty, since he was Foreign Minister. Stalin, however, used this proposal as a pretext for refusal, saying, 'It wouldn't be appropriate, since the bourgeois press would say that the whole Chinese government had come to Moscow.' Afterwards, Stalin avoided me. I phoned his apartment, but was told that Stalin was out, with the recommendation that I see Mikoyan. This treatment made me quite angry.... I decided it was best to stay in the guest house and do nothing.[20]

At this point, Stalin was still clearly reluctant to sign a new bilateral treaty. On the one hand, Stalin feared losing the economic rights in Northeast

China that he had wrested from Chiang Kai-shek in 1945; on the other hand, he feared that if he forfeited these rights, the West might throw into question the entire Yalta system, putting the Soviet Union in an awkward international position. However, compared with the Soviet position at the time of Mikoyan's early 1949 visit to Xibaibo and Liu's mid-summer 1949 visit to Moscow, the position articulated by Stalin in his first meeting with Mao was an advance. He was now willing to "modify" provisions of the 1945 treaty and subsidiary agreements, as long as there was no change in their form.

Stalin no doubt thought that the Soviet Union had already made a huge concession, but he didn't realize that Mao put more emphasis precisely on the form. Mao wanted to abrogate the existing Sino-Soviet treaty to enhance the prestige of China's new Communist leadership and to pressure Western countries into sweeping away all unequal treaties.

As Mao put it,

> Once Sino-Soviet relations are established in a new treaty, China's workers, peasants, and intellectuals, as well as the left wing of the national bourgeoisie, will feel elated, and we will be able to isolate the right wing of the national bourgeoisie; internationally, we will have greater political capital to deal with the imperialist countries, and to evaluate the treaties formerly concluded between China and individual imperialist countries. [This] will put the People's Republic in a more advantageous position, will force various capitalist countries to make accommodations with us, and will be helpful in forcing various countries to unconditionally recognize China, abolish old treaties, conclude new treaties, and restrain various capitalist countries from taking rash actions.[21]

The outcome of the December 24 meeting seemed to show that Stalin was waiting for Mao to compromise. After his second meeting with Stalin, Mao sulked out of dissatisfaction and pique, and proposed merely to rest and return home early.

A new year

On January 1, 1950 Ambassador Roshchin called on Mao at Foreign Minister Andrei Vyshinsky's direction. Since he still was not feeling well, said Mao, he wanted to rest and recuperate for another week. During this period he asked to see a number of Soviet leaders, one a day in the late afternoons, for short, simple conversations, without any discussion of substantive issues. "In this period," said Mao, "I want to discuss substantive issues with Stalin personally." Noting that he had originally planned to travel extensively in the Soviet Union, Mao said that now, out of consideration for his health and the long journey back home, he wanted to forego factory visits, reports and speeches, and planned to leave Moscow early, by the end of January.[22] It seems that except for discussing "substantive questions" with Stalin, Mao did not want to do much else.

Faced with an uncompromising Mao, Stalin had to make a choice.

In this period the Western press unexpectedly pressured Stalin. Since Mao had not been mentioned in the Soviet press after his participation in Stalin's 70th birthday celebration, Moscow diplomats were asking about his whereabouts. This fueled Western press speculation, including that Mao had been placed under house arrest. This, in turn, put the Chinese and the Soviets in an awkward position. Chinese Ambassador Wang Jiaxiang proposed getting out of this predicament by having Mao submit to a TASS interview during which he could explain the goals of his Moscow visit.[23]

On January 2, *Pravda* carried out a TASS interview with Mao. Mao said that his primary goal in coming to Moscow was to decide what to do about the Sino-Soviet Treaty of Friendship and Alliance and related issues. He indicated that the amount of time he would spend in the Soviet Union would "depend in part on the time needed to resolve issues related to the interests of the People's Republic of China." Mao added that he "planned to visit a few places and cities in the Soviet Union."[24]

Mao's display of starkly different public and private faces was designed to pressure Stalin into discussing a new treaty. Stalin's decision to approve of Mao's use of the Soviet press to express his views was, in fact, an early indication that the Soviet leader was now inclined toward compromise. Mao later claimed that his *Pravda* interview "constituted a big step forward."[25]

In this period Mao also used another set of events to bring Stalin around. Mao told Ambassador Roshchin on January 1 that he had recently "received a report from Beijing that the governments of Burma and India had expressed their readiness to recognize the People's Republic of China." The Chinese government would advise the Burmese and Indian governments that, if they really wanted to improve relations with the People's Republic of China, they should first break relations with Chiang Kai-shek and announce that they would categorically refuse to help the Chiang Kai-shek regime. If the Burmese and Indians accepted this proposal, they could dispatch delegations to Beijing for talks. Mao told Roshchin another piece of news: "In the near future, England (*sic*) and other British Commonwealth members would take steps toward recognition of the People's Republic of China."[26]

Mao had a tactical motive for telling the Soviets that Burma, India, Britain and the British Commonwealth countries would be establishing diplomatic relations with China. As Mao later noted, "It's possible the change in Stalin's position was helped along by the Indians and British, who recognized the PRC in January 1950."[27] Historian Sergei Goncharov and others, for example, believe that Britain's recognition of China was a big shock to Stalin, who would have seen it as a harbinger of Sino-U.S. rapprochement.[28] In any case, at a time when Sino-Soviet talks were stalemated, the prospect of the rapid establishment of relations between China and a number of countries, especially Western countries, doubtless encouraged Stalin to more seriously consider concessions to China.

Based on his reading of the Russian archival record, Professor Arne Westad has argued that Mao changed Stalin's calculus by acting through the Soviet leader's subordinates. As Westad has noted, while staying in Moscow over the New Year holiday, Mao worked hard on First Deputy Prime Minister Molotov, Vice Chairman of the Council of Ministers Mikoyan, Ambassador Roshchin and others, leading these important Soviet figures to believe that if Mao left Moscow without signing a new treaty, his personal position and the Chinese Communist Party's position in China would suffer. Therefore, the Soviet Union had a responsibility to support its new Communist neighbor. Among these Soviet figures, Mikoyan took the lead, proposing to Stalin that he find a way to conclude a new Sino-Soviet treaty on terms that would not damage Soviet interests.[29]

A new dawn

The stalemate broke on January 2; Stalin conceded. At 8 p.m. on the evening of January 2, Molotov and Mikoyan went to Mao's villa and asked his views on concluding a Sino-Soviet treaty and other issues. Mao proposed three options: (1) signing a new Sino-Soviet treaty; (2) issuing a simple statement through the two countries' press services that the two countries were exchanging views on the old Sino-Soviet Treaty of Friendship and Alliance, while actually deferring the issue; or (3) signing a general statement on the essentials of bilateral relations. Molotov immediately expressed his support for the first option. Mao followed up: "Would this replace the old treaty with a new treaty?" Molotov answered clearly: "Yes." On the spot Mao described how he proposed to proceed:

> My telegram will reach Beijing on January 3. Zhou Enlai will take five days to prepare, will leave from Beijing on January 9, and, after eleven days on the train, will get to Moscow on January 19. From January 20 through the end of the month, for about ten days, we will negotiate and conclude various treaties, and, at the beginning of February, I will return to China with Zhou.[30]

Mao and Stalin now worked hard to foster the appearance of friendly cooperation, smoothing over the differences that had cropped up between China and the Soviet Union. On January 6, Foreign Minister Vyshinsky called on Mao, with I. V. Kovalev and Chinese Ambassador Wang in attendance. Vyshinsky brought news that China's request for help in restoring the disastrous condition of the Jilin hydroelectric generating station had been approved. The Soviet government would send four experts to China within five days, and within a month, these experts would draft a report and suggest measures to restore the Jilin hydroelectric station. Mao voiced his gratitude, calling this Soviet assistance "of great significance to China's entire national economy."[31]

Vyshinsky also reported that in response to China's request for fuel for aeronautical training, and in accord with Soviet aeronautical standards and its experts' calculations, the Soviet Union would provide the requisite fuel immediately, with repayment conditions to be decided during bilateral trade talks in 1950. Mao also expressed his appreciation for this Soviet assistance.

The Soviet Foreign Minister made another proposal that piqued Mao's interest, namely that (Communist) China challenge the Nationalist claim to China's seat in the United Nations and seek to expel the Nationalist representative from the UN Security Council. The Soviet Union would support both steps. Moreover, the Soviet representative would declare that, "he will not participate in the work done by the [UN Security] Council so long as the [Nationalist Chinese] representative will be participating in it." Mao quickly indicated "100 per cent agreement with this proposal."

After this exchange, Mao further explained China's position, indicating that he would consider Soviet interests in concluding a new treaty. Mao argued that a new treaty was necessary since two fundamentals of the old bilateral treaty had ceased to exist. The Nationalists had been replaced and Japan no longer constituted an armed force. As a consequence, many Chinese were no longer content with the old treaty.

Vyshinsky still cautiously told Mao that, "the question of a new treaty ... seems to be a complicated matter, since the signing of a new treaty or reviewing of the existing treaty and the introduction of any kind of corrections may be used as an excuse" by the Americans and the British to harm Soviet and Chinese interests. "This is not desirable and must not be allowed to occur," said Vyshinsky. Mao replied that, "[T]his circumstance must be taken into consideration when creating a formula for solving the given problem."

Mao reiterated to I. V. Kovalev on January 9 that China would respect the decisions that were endorsed by the Soviet Union at Tehran, Yalta and Potsdam. And, pledged Mao, in renegotiating all existing treaties with the capitalist countries signed by the Chiang Kai-shek government, China's starting point would be the agreements under discussion with the Soviet Union.[32]

To further demonstrate solidarity with the Soviet Union, Mao ordered the closure of all U.S. consular, military and economic assistance facilities in China. On January 13, he contacted Liu Shaoqi, who was then in charge in Beijing, agreeing with his proposal to requisition U.S. and other foreign military facilities in China, including U.S. consulates and property occupied by the U.S. Agency for Economic Assistance in Shanghai. On January 17, Mao told the Soviets what he had done, explaining that he was "forcing" American consular representatives from China and would seek to delay diplomatic recognition by the United States, since "the later the Americans receive legal rights in China, the better it is for the People's Republic of China."[33]

In the midst of this positive movement between Mao and Stalin, however, the Soviets were unhappy over a serious misunderstanding between Mao and Stalin regarding a planned joint reaction to U.S. Secretary of State Dean Acheson's January 12 National Press Club speech.

Shi Zhe recalls that Stalin was irritated by Acheson's attempt to sow discord between China and the Soviet Union (by claiming in his speech that the USSR intended to annex Manchuria). Acting through Molotov and Vyshinsky, Stalin asked Mao to join the Soviet Union and Mongolia in issuing similarly worded official statements condemning Acheson's speech. Mao, however, apparently "did not sufficiently understand what was meant by an 'official' statement." As a result, the Soviet Union and Mongolia issued statements in the name of their foreign ministers, while the director of the Chinese official news agency issued China's statement. An unhappy Stalin rebuked Mao for not implementing the originally agreed upon plan, messing things up and providing the United States with an opening. He added tartly that, "We all should keep our promises, coordinate closely, march together, and, in this way, increase our strength." Mao was filled with pent-up anger, but said not a word.[34]

Shi's description of the incident as yet another "misunderstanding" is contradicted by recently released documentary material. When Molotov and Mao met on January 17, the Soviet First Deputy Premier clearly proposed that the statement be issued in the name of the Chinese government. Mao agreed to issue the statement, but asked "if it would not be better for Xinhua [the Chinese News Agency] to make this kind of declaration." Molotov replied that, since the issue involved a speech by the U.S. Secretary of State, a declaration should come from China's foreign ministry, not a news agency. Mao then agreed, promising that he would have a statement drafted and shown to the Soviet side in Moscow before it was cabled to Beijing, where the Chinese Vice Foreign Minister, who was acting for the Foreign Minister, would issue the statement.[35] Clearly, this event cannot be passed off as a "misunderstanding." There is no way to know now why Mao insisted on issuing the statement in the name of the Chinese official news agency. But Mao held to his own view and was quite unhappy over Stalin's rebuke.

Zhou arrives, hard bargaining begins

In contrast to this contretemps, negotiations on the new Sino-Soviet treaty started off in an atmosphere of friendship and geniality. Zhou Enlai got to Moscow on January 20. On January 22, Stalin and Mao, together with

Zhou, began discussing how to revise the 1945 bilateral treaty. Stalin came armed with twelve documents related to a new treaty and side agreements, all prepared for him by Soviet officials.[36] While Stalin was well prepared, in contrast, Mao and Zhou appear to have been a little passive in their first meeting with Stalin.[37]

Mao noted vaguely that, "The new treaty must include questions of political, economic, cultural and military cooperation. Of most importance will be the question of economic cooperation." But he expressed no specific views. Stalin proposed and Mao agreed that the Soviet Union would declare that the 1945 agreement on the Lushun naval base would remain in force until a peace treaty with Japan was signed, after which Soviet forces would withdraw. Stalin indicated that the Soviet Union did not plan to retain any rights with respect to Dalian, but pointed out that should Dalian remain a free port, this would serve the Anglo-American "Open Door" policy. Mao agreed, and proposed that the Lushun could serve as a base for joint Sino-Soviet military cooperation, while Dalian "could serve as a base for Sino-Soviet economic collaboration."

Mao proposed that a new treaty should stipulate that the Changchun Railroad would continue to be jointly operated and managed; however, the Chinese should take the lead in railroad management. At the same time, both sides should study shortening the duration of the railroad agreement and specifying the amount of the investment held by each side. Molotov replied that,

> The conditions governing the cooperation and joint administration of an enterprise by two interested countries usually provide for equal participation by both sides, as well as for alternation in the appointment of replacements for management positions. In the old agreement, the administration of the railroad belonged to the Soviets; however, in the future we think it necessary to alternate in the creation of management functions. Let's say that such an alternation could take place every two–three years.

Zhou countered that,

> Our comrades believe that the existing management of the Changchun Railroad and the office of the director ought to be abolished and a railroad administration commission set up in their place, and that the offices of the commission chairman and of the director should be replaced by Chinese officials. However, given Comrade Molotov's proposals, this question requires more thought.

Supporting Molotov, Stalin pointed out that, "If we are talking about joint administration, it is important for the managing position to be alternated [between the Soviet Union and China]. As for the duration of the agreement, we would not be against shortening it." Molotov argued that Zhou's request to increase China's investment ratio to 51 percent "would go against the existing provision for parity." Stalin added that, "Since we already have a joint administration, we might as well have equal participation." Mao acted at this point to smooth things over, but, throughout the negotiations, the issue of how to manage the Changchun Railway proved to be the main sticking point.

This meeting set the basic principles for the treaty negotiations. After some haggling, the two sides reached agreement. In comparing the 1950 treaty and side agreements with those reached in 1945, the main changes were: the return of Lushun Port and the Changchun Railroad to China, set at 30 years from 1945 in the earlier treaty, was now set to coincide with the signing of a peace treaty with Japan, or no later than the end of 1952; the administration of Dalian, formerly subject to Soviet restrictions, was now under complete Chinese control; and the posts of Changchun Railroad director and executive board chairman, and Lushun Port Joint Military Commission chairman, formerly all selected by the Soviet Union, now were to be filled in rotation by the Soviet Union and China. On specific issues, especially China's ownership and management rights over the Changchun Railroad, the Soviet Union at the outset leaned toward maintaining the substance of the 1945 agreement, and China's draft aimed to replace the 1945 agreement with new content. As it turned out, Stalin made repeated concessions, for the most part accepting the revised draft proposed by Zhou Enlai on January 26, 1950.[38]

In at least two cases of sharp disagreements between China and the Soviet Union, the texts of the side agreements reached in Moscow remain secret to the present day. In a February 13, 1950 discussion with Foreign Minister Vyshinsky, Zhou said that he and Mao believed all the agreements signed in Moscow should be made public. Zhou explained that the Chinese texts of these agreements had been sent to Beijing and reported to China's Government Administrative Council. "If there is anything in the signed agreements that cannot be made public," Zhou pointed out, "we need to explain this to the Government Administrative Council members." Zhou stressed that from China's perspective, publication of all the signed agreements would be helpful since it would raise the global prestige of both China and the Soviet Union. Vyshinsky indicated that although Zhou's view was very clear, there was no arrangement between the two countries that all the agreements should be made public. Therefore, the question of publishing these documents needed to be discussed, and he would report to Stalin on this issue.[39] No documents have been found regarding the continued discussion of this question, but the final outcome was, in fact, that some of the agreements were not published. Among the unpublished agreements, according to declassified Russian material, are two issues worthy of scholarly attention.

Bones of contention

One of these issues concerned Soviet military use of the Changchun Railway.[40]

In agreeing to the earlier return of the Changchun Railway to Chinese control, the Soviet Union proposed that the Soviet Army should retain the right to move on this rail line from Siberia through Manchuria to Vladivostok. In discussions held between January 31 and February 2, China and the Soviet Union set out very different views. Zhou agreed that the Soviet Army should be able to move along with Changchun Railway under the threat of war, but argued that the new agreement should also stipulate that the Chinese Army and its equipment could be transported from Manchuria to Yining in Xinjiang on the Soviet-controlled rail line linking Chita, New Siberia and Alma Ata, and that the transport fee paid by the Chinese Army should be set according to the fee then currently in force for the Soviet Army.

On February 1, Mikoyan replied that, to accommodate Chinese wishes, they could change the text "to stipulate that army movement on the Changchun Railway could occur were the Soviet Far East under threat of war." Mikoyan explained that, for the Soviet Army, the distance could be cut in half by military movement along the rail line through Manchuria to Vladivostok (i.e., compared with the Trans-Siberian Railway route), and, further, that this would provide two lines for Soviet Army movement in time of war. This was quite natural and understandable, claimed Mikoyan, since this stipulation was aimed at an emergency situation, when the Soviet Union was under actual threat of war in the Far East.

However, argued Mikoyan,

> The Chinese proposal to have the right to move its army and military equipment on the rail line between Manchuria and Xinjiang is incorrect.... The Soviet side believes this proposal is totally unacceptable. It is not that we oppose the movement of the Chinese army along our rail line, but because we believe that this is a counterproposal to the Soviet proposal to move the Soviet army on the Changchun rail line between Manchuria and Suifenhe. This is a form of covert opposition to the Soviet proposal.

Mikoyan and Vyshinsky continued that,

> [The Soviet side] is very surprised to have such an issue raised, since Zhou Enlai himself confirmed that, if the Soviet Union returned the Changchun Railway to China, the Chinese Government would agree to allow the Soviet Union to move its army on the Changchun Railway in any direction.... Now, when we have agreed to give the Changchun Railway back to China, the Chinese view has changed, and they oppose

moving our military on the Changchun Railway between Manchuria and Suifenhe.

In offering a detailed explanation of the Chinese proposal, Zhou "did the utmost to prove that this was not at all a counterproposal or antagonistic proposal." He noted that the Chinese delegation had not started out with the idea that the protocol would have an article stipulating military movement by both sides. Logically speaking, said Zhou, this kind of movement would flow naturally as a consequence of the Treaty of Friendship, Alliance and Mutual Assistance. It should be easy to reach agreement regarding the issue at any time as needed. If the draft agreement were to stipulate that the Soviet military could move its forces on the Chinese Changchun Railway, and, at the same time, China did not gain the right to move its forces on Soviet territory, China would not be able to understand this clause. Therefore, the Chinese delegation thought it needed to add a provision that the Chinese side could move its military on the Soviet railway between Northeast China and Xinjiang. Besides this, said Zhou, the Chinese government proposed to use these rail lines to move grain and other goods from Northeast China to provision its army in Xinjiang, since this would save a lot of time and expense.

Since both sides held their ground, Mikoyan finally suggested that if the Chinese remained opposed to the Soviet proposal, then it could be taken off the table, while keeping the existing protocol, and merely shortening the period of validity from thirty to ten years. This implied that, as long as the Soviet Union and China jointly owned the Changchun Railway, on the basis of the already agreed upon 1952 expiration date, the 1945 agreement could just be extended another three years (i.e., until the end of 1955).

Naturally, Zhou could not agree to reopen the question of the period of validity of the Changchun Railway agreement. Therefore, he could only agree to the Soviet view on revision, which was that if the Soviet Far East came under threat of war, the Soviet military could use the Changchun Railway to move its troops. Still Zhou maneuvered. He noted that while there might be no stipulation in the document, perhaps in a situation of need, China could move its troops from Northeast China to Xinjiang over the Siberian rail trunk lines. Mikoyan said that the fact that China's proposal to have the right to move its troops across Soviet territory had been rejected did not exclude the possibility that, in a time of actual need, under the alliance treaty, it could use the Soviet railways to move Chinese troops. This concluded the discussion.

However, this issue made a strong impression on the Soviets. As Mikoyan said,

> As allies, the Soviet Union transferred without recompense property of immense value: the Changchun Railway, Dalian, Lushun port, and

all the rights that we held in these areas, and the Chinese side didn't even want to agree to the Soviet Union moving its military on only one rail line. If the Chinese couldn't even make this concession, what kind of allies were we?

This is how things stood. The Soviet impression was to a certain extent reasonable. However, based on the principle of equality, the Chinese view on revision of the railway agreement is also beyond criticism. Moreover, China's leaders, taking a long view, were clearly worried about the suggestion that the Soviet Army had a right to move its troops on Chinese territory.

The second issue concerns the still secret Sino-Soviet "Additional Agreement."[41]

Based on currently available Chinese material, albeit not archival material, the Soviets insisted during negotiations that in addition to the new Sino-Soviet treaty, the two sides should conclude and sign a secret "Additional Agreement." This would stipulate that in the Soviet Far East and Central Asia, and in China's Northeast and Xinjiang, "no leasehold rights are to be granted to foreigners, and, furthermore, no industrial, financial, commercial, or other enterprise, organization, society, or group activities in which third-country capital or citizens participate directly or indirectly are permitted." Mao was unhappy, but was forced to concede on this principle. Chinese material reveals that during negotiations, on January 22, Mao expressed reservations and was unwilling to sign this agreement. However, after Stalin's repeated insistence, "out of consideration of the overall situation of Sino-Soviet unity, it was necessary to concede this issue."

The Russian record of the January 22 Stalin–Mao meeting does not touch on the "Additional Agreement" issue.[42] There is need for caution, however, since Chinese material on this issue does not consist of archival documentation. Only publication of contemporary Chinese documents may resolve this issue.

It is a fact, however, that Mao later voiced great unhappiness over the secret "Additional Agreement." Many times in discussions Mao referred to Northeast China and Xinjiang as two Soviet "colonies" or "spheres of influence."[43] Objectively, there was some basis for Chinese leaders to express such unhappiness. The "Additional Agreement" on the surface seemed fair, but, in fact, at the time, there were no "third-country" commercial interests or foreign citizens engaged in commerce and industry in the Soviet Far East or in Soviet Central Asia. The clause, therefore, restricted China's exercise of sovereignty in Northeast China and Xinjiang without any real concession on the Soviet Union's part. Concerning the separate agreement at the time regarding joint stock companies, a subject on which Mao later also railed,[44] it is, in fact, unfair to blame the Soviets. As recounted earlier, Chinese leaders had invited the Soviets to manage leased and joint stock companies in China during Mikoyan's 1949 secret visit to Xibaibo, an invitation that Mao had repeated in Moscow with specific reference to Xinjiang.[45]

Lingering Soviet dissatisfaction?

The new Sino-Soviet alliance benefited China and the Soviet Union politically, militarily, diplomatically and economically. Chinese and Soviet understandings differed, however. The Sino-Soviet Treaty of Friendship, Alliance and Mutual Assistance signed on February 14, 1950 generally accorded with China's wishes. While not all its provisions were satisfactory from China's point of view, the sovereignty and interests that China had lost in 1945 would soon be recovered. As for Stalin, the outcome of the treaty negotiations meant that Soviet strategic gains in the Far East, including an ice-free port on the Pacific – secured in the Yalta Agreement and the 1945 Sino-Soviet treaty – would be forfeited by the end of 1952, if not earlier. Perhaps it was for this reason, to make up as much as possible for this impending loss, that Stalin insisted on signing the secret "Additional Agreement," hoping thereby to counter American, British and Japanese infiltration and influence in Northeast and Northwest China, two regions that bordered on the Soviet Union.

Stalin almost certainly did not believe that the outcome of his negotiations with Mao and Zhou had fully satisfied Soviet requirements in the Far East. The regional strategic goal Stalin had set out and implemented in 1945 matched Russia's historical and traditional strategy in the Far East. After World War II, comparing Soviet gains as a result of its (short) 1945 war with Japan to Czarist Russia's losses in the Russo-Japanese War, Stalin said that,

> [T]he defeat of the Russian troops in 1904 during the Russo-Japanese War left bitter memories in the minds of our people. It lay like a black stain upon our country ... We of the older generation waited for this day for forty years, and now this day has arrived.[46]

When Stalin realized after his meetings with Mao that the Soviet Union would soon be forced to give up its only recently acquired ice-free port on the Pacific, he was bound to search for a compensatory measure to foster this traditional Russian strategic aspiration. As a result, the Korean issue found its way onto Moscow's agenda and Stalin's map. At this time, only the Korean peninsula could in some measure satisfy the Soviet Union's desire for a suitable base for its Pacific fleet, an ice-free port on the Pacific Ocean that could be linked with the shortest possible rail link to the eastern part of the Soviet Union. As a consequence, at this time, Stalin changed his strategy toward the tense situation on the Korean peninsula. Moscow turned abruptly then from its long-maintained defensive posture in the Far East to a strategic offensive.

6   Stalin reverses his Korea policy

Scholars the world over have noted that documents in the Russian archives show that Stalin changed his Korea policy in January 1950, that is, during the time when he was negotiating the new Sino-Soviet treaty. Throughout 1949, though the standoff between North and South Korea had been very tense, and arguably had teetered on the brink of civil war, Moscow steadfastly had resisted Kim Il-sung's entreaties to unify Korea through military force. Yet, in the early months of 1950, Stalin abruptly changed course. What caused him to change his mind?

The only direct, though vague reference to the rationale for the Soviet policy change is captured in the phrase "in light of the changed international situation." Stalin employed this phrase in his May 14, 1950 telegram to Mao, when Mao questioned the message that Kim had brought to him. In his reply to Mao, Stalin for the first time acknowledged his agreement in principle with Kim's proposal to "move toward reunification."[1] What did Stalin mean by "the changed international situation" and what was the main reason for Stalin's change of mind?

Multiple plausible causes

In the decades since the war, including in recent years, Russian and other scholars around the world have advanced several theories about what led Stalin to support a North Korean invasion of South Korea in June 1950, all plausible, none mutually contradictory.[2]

A. V. Torkunov and E. P. Ufimtsev, two Russian scholars of the Korean conflict, have argued that the phrase "the changed international situation" refers above all to the Communist victory in China. As they see it, Stalin assessed that the United States could now only concern itself with Chiang Kai-shek's fate on Taiwan, and would not want to be drawn into a conflict on the Korean peninsula. Like others, they argue that another key factor was the Soviet Union's breakout from the American nuclear monopoly. This meant that America could no longer use the nuclear threat against the Soviet Union.[3]

Russian scholar E. P. Bajanov has argued that by 1950 the maturation of the Cold War led the Soviet Union to embrace the outbreak of war on the

Korean peninsula. Stalin, in Bajanov's view, regarded the newly established NATO as a threat to the Soviet Union. As a counter strategy, Soviet control of Korea would weaken U.S. control of Japan. And, the Communist victory in China seemed to ensure success in Korea, especially at a time when Stalin was also influenced by his recent acquisition of nuclear weapons and the American loss of China.

Russian–American scholar Sergei Goncharov has disputed that the Soviet acquisition of nuclear weapons and the establishment of NATO heavily influenced Stalin's new Korea strategy. He points instead to the impact on Soviet calculations to President Truman's January 5, 1950 statement and, above all, to Secretary of State Acheson's January 12, 1950 National Press Club speech, which placed Korea outside the American defensive perimeter. However, this was not the only factor, argues Goncharov. The situation in Germany and Europe, and concern about Japan, also played a role.

The American scholar John Garver has pointed to Japan as the main reason for the change in Stalin's formerly cautious approach, arguing that Moscow believed that by 1950 the U.S. was intent on turning Japan into a forward U.S. military base, something that the Soviet Union could not tolerate.[4]

In a different context, Goncharov, John Lewis and Xue Litai in their joint book, *Uncertain Partners*, have concluded that Stalin changed his Korea policy with several objectives in mind: to expand the Soviet Union's buffer zone in Asia, to gain a springboard for an attack on Japan in a future global war, to test American will, to intensify Sino-American antagonism and, most importantly, to draw American power away from Europe.[5]

The issues adduced by these scholars all help elucidate the factors or considerations behind Stalin's changed Korea policy. But they are not all of equal weight, and they influenced Stalin's decision at different levels. Among these possible factors, the most important were the motives for the change in policy, and next important were the conditions for carrying out the new policy. Importantly, in implementing this important policy shift, Stalin would be impinging on Soviet relations with the United States (here including Japan), Korea and China. These relationships were not all of equal weight. Most important was the impact on relations with China. Next in importance was Stalin's calculation of the U.S. policy response.

Korea: a place of Stalin's choosing

Stalin's agreement with Kim Il-sung's strategy of unifying Korea by force implies that he had decided to face a war in Northeast Asia. There were two central premises behind this decision. First, the Soviet Union, already in a hostile confrontation with the United States, had now decided on a major rupture with Washington. With the outbreak of war in Korea, it would face an indirect – and, in an extreme situation, even the possibility of a direct – conflict with the United States. Second, the long-standing, tense military standoff on the Korean peninsula had forced North Korea – still under Soviet control – into making mental and material preparations to cope with a war situation. Yet, this latter, Korea-specific predicate was in place by the end of 1949, but then Stalin was still unwilling to change the basic strategy toward Korea he had adopted in 1945. What had changed?

After the Soviet Union adopted a fiercely antagonistic response to the Marshall Plan, two great opposing blocs appeared on the international scene. Conflict between the Soviet Union and the United States occurred primarily in Europe, with the Cold War structure crystallizing between June 1948 and May 1949. In the first Cold War crisis between the Soviet Union and the West, the Berlin crisis, the Soviet Union flinched in the face of an unyielding U.S. and Western position. Stalin had decided to express Moscow's determination and antagonistic attitude toward the United States on the most sensitive East–West issue, the German question, but he had not correctly calculated that Washington would start from a policy of strength and adopt a tit-for-tat response. Moscow especially misjudged America's economic power to resolve the Berlin question. Since the balance of power was not favorable to the Soviet Union, in the end, Stalin had to abandon his resort to open conflict with the United States in Europe.[6]

However, while Stalin now became more cautious about confrontation in Europe, he had not abandoned his strategy of confronting the United States. He just had to find the right conditions – a suitable time and place of his choosing.

The 38th parallel: a high tension line

Even before the Berlin crisis, in Northeast Asia, the Korean peninsula was in a very tense situation verging on war. From the drawing in 1945 of the 38th parallel as a supposedly temporary line of Soviet and American occupation onward through 1950, Moscow-backed North Korea and Washington-backed South Korea were in constant conflict. The situation worsened after the authorities in the North and the South established separate, independent governments in late 1948. Syngman Rhee in the South and Kim Il-sung in the North both wanted to unify Korea, by military means if necessary. There was constant friction between the two states, including live fire exchanges near the 38th parallel. And, especially after Soviet occupation troops withdrew from North Korea, the Syngman Rhee regime repeatedly threatened war and launched frequent, provocative border incursions. But, throughout 1949, Stalin restrained Kim Il-sung from overreacting.

Soviet Army Chief of General Staff Sergei Shtemenko and Defense Minister Alexander Vasilevsky reported to Stalin on April 20, 1949 that after the withdrawal of Soviet troops, South Korean armed forces had repeatedly violated the 38th parallel provisions, with 37 violations between January 1 and April 15, of which 24 occurred between March 15 and April 15.

> Incidents ... consisted of small-scale clashes between security troops, usually at the company or battalion level, using light machine gun and mortar fire.... In all instances of violation, the initiative for opening fire lay with the "Southerners."
>
> [D]uring March and April, the "Southerners" have brought a portion of their field army up to the 38th parallel. We cannot exclude the possibility [they] may undertake new provocative acts against North Korea government troops and may employ ... greater troop strength than we have seen to date. [We] recommend the North Korean government Army Command take appropriate measures to prepare [for] possibly stronger provocative "Southerner" actions.[7]

On May 2, Soviet Ambassador to Pyongyang T. F. Shtykov reported to Moscow that,

> The South Korean authorities have enlarged the size of their "National Defense Army" to carry out their plan to incur into the North. According to intelligence, the "National Defense Army" grew from 53,600 on January 1 this year to 70,000 men at the end of the first quarter. At the same time, [the South Koreans] are emphasizing technical, mechanized, and special forces, with troops of these types growing [in number] one to three times.

Shtykov reported that the South Korean authorities had concentrated more than 41,000 troops near the 38th parallel. "The war plan for the attack on the North has been set and, in the First Brigade, has been communicated down to battalion commanders. It is assessed that it will be activated in June."[8]

Tension increased in June and July 1949. On June 18, Ambassador Shtykov told Moscow that South Korean leaders were advocating "using military means to resolve the issue of national unification ... only with different opinions on timing." He reported that the South Korean army and police had openly crossed the 38th parallel many times in the Ongjin region, that fighting was ongoing in this area and that the number of South Korean troops along the border had increased. South Korean troops on one occasion reportedly incurred 10 km into the North, retreating back across the 38th parallel only after a North Korean police brigade was deployed. North Korean troops had occupied two tactically important heights, but the two sides were still fighting for control of high ground. Shtymenko also reported that Rhee, in reaction to the Ongjin incident, stated on June 11 that, "We are drawing up an attack plan to inflict serious damage on the Communists. This plan will be implemented in the next two or three weeks."[9]

On July 13, Shtykov again cabled Foreign Minister Vyshinsky, reporting on statements made by South Korean soldiers from the 2nd battalion of the 18th regiment captured on the Ongjin peninsula:

> Their unit commander held several meetings in July at which he stated that the North Korean army planned to attack the South, and, therefore, the South Korean army must forestall the North, deliver a sudden attack on the North Korean army, and occupy North Korea before August 15 (Korean Liberation Day).

Shtykov noted further that,

> The [South Korean] 12th regiment's task is to attack and capture the [heights] thirty kilometers west of Haeju. The 18th regiment's task is to set off from Ongjin, and, together with the 13th regiment, which, according to our intelligence, is based near Kaesong, to attack north, envelop Haeju, annihilate the North Korean army group north of that city, and, within a week, occupy Haeju Province.

According to Shtykov, there was intelligence that Syngman Rhee had stated that he would gain the initiative by "launching an attack on the northern armed forces in July."[10]

By this time, U.S. occupation troops (but not U.S. military advisers) had been withdrawn from Korea. As described by Professor Niu Jun, U.S. military withdrawals from China (in May 1949) and South Korea (in June 1949) "indicated that the United States, by shrinking its force level and defensive line, had fundamentally completed its strategic realignment in Asia."[11]

Soviet "defensive" military assistance to the DPRK in 1949

In the face of the U.S. pullout of its occupation troops, the South Korean authorities stepped up their provocations and offensive preparations. As seen by Moscow, the U.S. military withdrawal from South Korea was meant "to give the South Korean military the freedom to act [and] loosen restraints on the reactionary movement in South Korea."[12] As tension grew on the peninsula, in June 1949, Moscow agreed to Kim's request for military assistance, supplying 100 military aircraft, 87 tanks, 57 armored vehicles, 102 self-propelled cannons, 44 collapsible landing craft and small rubber boats, ammunition and other military equipment.[13]

But, at this point in 1949, Soviet assistance was intended to strengthen the North's defensive capability, not to encourage the North to go on the attack.[14] While some Soviet military figures advocated military action,

Stalin's policy sought to relax the situation on the peninsula and do everything possible to avoid direct involvement in the (the low-level) Korean conflict. In line with this policy, Moscow approved Ambassador Shtykov's proposal that, in view of the U.S. troop withdrawal from South Korea, Soviet forces should vacate their naval base at Seishin and military airfields in Pyongyang and elsewhere in the North. Since these facilities might be used by the Korean People's Army, this put the Soviet Union in a passive position.[15] But, in this period, Moscow curbed Kim Il-sung from adopting military measures that might lead to an escalation in conflict.

While implementing its plan to unify Korea peacefully (i.e., through political agitation in the South),[16] Pyongyang was also strengthening its military preparations. In the face of the southern threat, Kim Il-sung urged that the time was right to unify Korea by military means.

Divided counsel on unleashing Kim

On September 3 Soviet Charge d'Affairs G. I. Tunkin reported that Mun Il, Kim Il-sung's private secretary, had reported that the North had reliable information that South Korea would soon try to seize the portion of the Ongjin peninsula above the 38th parallel and shell the cement plant in Haiju city. Kim asked permission to begin military operations against the South, aiming to seize the Ongjin peninsula and South Korean territory east of the Ongjin peninsula, approximately to Kaesong, thereby shortening North Korea's defensive line. If "the international situation permits," Kim was prepared to move further south. "Kim Il-sung is convinced that they are in a position to seize South Korea in the course of two weeks, maximum two months." Tunkin assured Moscow that North Korea had intercepted a South Korean order to begin shelling the Haiju cement plant, "which the Southerners consider [a] military [objective]." Tunkin noted, however, that "the time set ... for the shelling had passed, and nothing had happened."[17]

Then Soviet First Deputy Foreign Minister Andrei Gromyko, in reply, instructed Tunkin on September 11 to see Kim as soon as possible to get a clearer reading on the South Korean army, its numbers, arms and fighting strength; the condition of the communist partisan movement in the South; how the public would react if the North initiated an attack; what kind of support the people in the South would give the northern army; and how the North judged its own military strength. Gromyko also asked Tunkin for his independent assessment of the situation and the advisability of the North Korean proposal.[18]

After meetings with Kim Il-sung and Pak Hon-yong, on September 14, Charge Tunkin reported in detail on the military strength of South and North Korea, Kim's views and his own views. Tunkin reported that, "Kim considers that the northern army is superior to the southern army in its technical equipment (tanks, artillery, planes), its discipline, the training of its officers and troops, and also morale." But Kim wavered in his assessment of how the Korean population would react if the North began a civil war. At his most pessimistic, Kim felt that, "[I]f a civil war were drawn out, [North Korea] will be in a politically disadvantageous position." Therefore, "[H]e does not propose to begin a civil war, but only to secure the Ongjin peninsula and a portion of the territory of South Korea to the east of this peninsula, for example to Kaesong." If the Ongjin campaign succeeded, Kim hoped that it would be possible to "organize a number of uprisings in South Korea," and, should the southern army become demoralized, it might be possible to move further south. Kim and Pak believed the United States would not send troops to intervene directly in a Korean civil war.

Charge Tunkin disagreed with Kim's analysis, judging that, "The partial operation outlined by Kim Il-sung can and probably will turn into a civil war between north and south." However, "the northern army is not strong enough to carry out successful and rapid operations against the South." Moreover, "a drawn out civil war would be militarily and politically disadvantageous for the North." Tunkin concluded that "under the indicated conditions it is inadvisable to begin the partial operation conceived by Kim Il-sung."[19]

On his return to post, Ambassador Shtykov disagreed with (his deputy) Minister-Counselor Tunkin. In a long telegram to Stalin on September 15, Shtykov supported Kim's plan. The Soviet ambassador echoed Kim's basic idea, that the Korean people wanted unification, but if it were not possible to unify Korea peacefully, without resort to force, "the issue of unification could drag on for many years." Given the time and opportunity, argued Shtykov, South Korean reactionaries would "suppress the democratic movement in the South ... establish a more formidable military force in order to attack northern Korea [and] destroy everything that has been established in recent years in the North."

Shtykov analyzed the economic and political situation in North and South Korea in detail, arguing that "the South Korean government's political footing [is] shaky," and conditions on the peninsula were favorable to the North. The Soviet ambassador did not exclude the possibility that the Americans would intervene and vigorously support South Korea, and admitted that the North Korean People's Army was still not strong enough in numbers or materiel to guarantee a complete annihilation of the southern army and occupation of South Korea. Nevertheless, he believed that, "it was both possible and appropriate to develop and provide assistance and leadership to the guerilla movement" in South Korea. And, "under favorable conditions," it would be possible to use South Korean provocations on the 38th parallel to punish its violation of the 38th parallel and occupy the Ongjin peninsula, Kaesong city and the surrounding area. Appended to Shtykov's telegram was a detailed comparison of North and South Korean military strength.[20]

At the time, developments in Asia were all favorable to the Soviet policy of global confrontation with the United States: the Chinese Communist revolution was on the verge of victory; the U.S. military (with the exception of a military advisory group) had withdrawn from South Korea; there were many indications of revolutionary fervor among the South Korean people; and the political and economic situation in South Korea was extremely unstable. Still Stalin refused to authorize the initiation of military moves on the Korean peninsula.

Moscow tells Shtykov: just say Nyet

On September 24, the CPSU Politburo discussed the Korean situation and instructed Ambassador Shtykov to tell Kim Il-sung and Foreign Minister Pak Hon-yong that the Soviet Union could not sanction starting a war on the Korean peninsula: "Since North Korea does not have the necessary superiority of military forces in comparison with South Korea ... a military attack on the South is now completely unprepared for and therefore ... is not allowed."

To drive home the point, Shtykov warned the North Koreans leaders that "a partial operation to seize the Ongjin peninsula and the region of Kaesong," by moving the North Korean border "almost to Seoul itself," would mean the "beginning of a war between North and South Korea, for which North Korea is not prepared either militarily or politically [and] give the Americans cause for any kind of interference in Korean affairs." Instead, Moscow directed North Korea to develop the partisan movement in the South, create liberated areas and prepare for a general uprising in the South.[21]

Moscow's instruction to Kim Il-sung through Shtykov shows that Soviet policy in the fall of 1949 supported the unification of Korea only through partisan and political struggle in the South rather than through overt resort to military force by the North. Kim Il-sung and other North Korean leaders accepted Moscow's advice, albeit cooly,[22] but did not stop their military preparations.

On October 14, another fierce fight broke out near the 38th parallel when the North's 3rd Police Guards Brigade attacked South Korean forces that had occupied two points of high ground 1.5 km north of the 38th parallel. Stalin was not happy to learn that his ambassador – against instructions and without notice to Moscow – had given his tacit consent, had helped plan the action and had then not reported to Moscow after the fact. Gromyko severely rebuked Ambassador Shtykov both for acting against his instructions and for not filing timely reports "on all actions which are being planned and events which are occurring along the 38th parallel," and forbade him "to recommend to the government of North Korea that it carry out active operations against South Korea absent approval from the Central Committee."[23] Russian documents indicate that from this point through to the end of 1949, Stalin upheld this policy of restraint on the Korean peninsula.

Despite thin evidence, consisting mainly of Khrushchev's stream-of-consciousness recollections, (not based on a diary or other records), some present-day scholars still wonder whether Stalin and Kim held secret talks in late 1949 and, if so, what they discussed. According to Khrushchev, Kim came to Moscow in late 1949 wanting "to prod South Korea with the point of a bayonet [and] touch off an internal explosion in the South."[24]

In a 1992 interview, M. C. Kapitsa, a former-ranking Soviet Foreign Ministry official, also claimed that Kim, encouraged by the Communist victory in China, during a late 1949 Moscow visit, proposed "a full-scale conventional attack against the South." But, according to a high-ranking Russian Foreign Ministry official with access to Soviet-era archives, there is no record of any such Stalin–Kim meeting in late 1949. As Goncharov, Lewis and Xue have concluded,

> It seems likely that the active flow of communication between Moscow and Pyongyang at this time has been misinterpreted as Kim–Stalin meetings. [But] what matters is the evolution of the exchanges, not whether specific visits did or did not occur.[25]

To take a step back then, even if there had been a late 1949 Kim visit to Moscow, as remembered by Khrushchev and Kapitsa, Stalin did not agree with Kim's proposal to launch a conventional war for a reunified Korea.

The global antagonistic relationship between the Soviet Union and the United States, and the high state of tension between the two Korean states on the peninsula were the main predicates behind Stalin's early 1950 decision to go to war. Why did Stalin not agree in late 1949 to use military means to unify Korea? The Soviet archival material described above indicates that Stalin had two concerns: that the United States might be drawn into a Korean conflict, and that Pyongyang was not sufficiently prepared.[26]

1950: a new year, a new Soviet calculus

In the early months of 1950, Stalin fundamentally changed his policy toward Korea.

The issue of whether the United States might intervene in a Korean conflict naturally played a very important role in Stalin's decision-making. But, logically speaking, Stalin would not decide to sanction starting a war in Korea merely because the U.S. would not intervene. Rather, if he were motivated to launch a war, the probable U.S. response would be a critical factor in deciding whether or not to actually carry out a war plan. As will be discussed below, when Moscow later judged that the U.S. would not intervene and agreed to Kim's military action, Stalin still carefully avoided giving the United States a pretext to intervene. This concern about a possible U.S. reaction was therefore based mainly on tactical, not strategic, considerations.

Stalin's decision in early 1950 was not based on whether or not Pyongyang was in a good position to launch a military action against the South – as had been laid out in the September 24, 1949 Politburo directive to Kim. In fact, by the time Stalin changed his mind, the preparatory work that had been suggested by the CPSU Politburo directive, namely a ramp-up in partisan and political activity in the South, was further behind than had been the case during most of 1949.[27]

Stalin, true to form, never revealed his real thoughts and calculations concerning the Korean question. But, if the overarching goal of Soviet foreign policy was to further its national security interests, we should analyze Stalin's shift on Korea in light of the Soviet Union's strategic goals in the Far East.

On January 19, shortly after Stalin agreed to negotiate a new treaty with China, Ambassador Shtykov reported to Moscow on Kim Il-sung's state of mind as reflected during a small lunch held two days earlier at the North Korean Foreign Ministry. The January 17 lunch was held to send off North Korea's ambassador to the China, Li Juyeon. After lunch, Kim excitedly told two Soviet embassy counselors that with China now liberated, the next issue was how to liberate South Korea:

> The people of the southern part of Korea trust me and rely on our armed might. Partisans will not resolve the question. The people of the South know that we have a good army. Lately I cannot sleep at night, thinking about how to resolve the question of the unification of the whole country. If the matter of the liberation of the people of the southern part of Korea and the unification of the country is drawn out, then I can lose the trust of the people of Korea.

Kim told one of the Soviet embassy counselors that, when he was in Moscow,

> Comrade Stalin said to him that it was not necessary to attack the South; in case of an attack on the North by Syngman Rhee's army, it is possible to go on the counteroffensive to the southern part of Korea. But since Syngman Rhee is still not instigating an attack … the liberation of the people of the southern portion of Korea and the unification of the country are being drawn out [and] he thinks that he needs to visit Comrade Stalin and receive an order and permission for offensive action by the People's Army for the purpose of the liberation of the people of southern Korea.

The Soviet Embassy counselors sidestepped Kim's feeler. Kim then took Ambassador Shtykov aside, reiterating that he wanted to see Stalin to discuss the situation in South Korea and the issue of launching an attack on the South, claiming that the North Korean People's Army was now much stronger than Syngman Rhee's army. If he could not meet Stalin, said Kim, then he wanted to meet with Mao Zedong, after Mao's return from Moscow. Kim pressed Shtykov as to why he was not allowed to attack the South on the Ongjin peninsula, which, he said, his army could take in three days, with a general attack on Seoul following in several more days. Shtykov reported to Moscow that Kim "was in a mood of some intoxication." But, "[i]t was obvious that he began this conversation not accidentally, but had thought it out earlier, with the goal of laying out his frame of mind and elucidating our attitude toward these questions."[28]

As he had been instructed in the September 24, 1949 Politburo instruction, Shtykov held the line in his discussion with Kim: "On the question of an attack on the Ongjin peninsula, I answered him that it is impossible to do this."

Unexpectedly, however, after receiving Ambassador Shtykov's report, Stalin changed his attitude. On January 30, less than two weeks after Stalin had been forced to accept the Chinese draft agreement on the Changchun Railway, Lushun and Dalian, he adopted a new position on Korea, personally cabling Ambassador Shtykov that:

> I understand the dissatisfaction of Comrade Kim Il-sung, but he must understand that such a large matter in regard to South Korea such as he wants to undertake needs large preparation. The matter must be organized so that there would not be too great a risk. If he wants to discuss this matter with me, then I will always be ready to receive him and discuss it with him. Transmit this to Kim Il-sung and tell him that I am ready to help him in this matter.[29]

According to documents that have thus far come to light, Stalin's January 30 cable to Shtykov is the first indication that Stalin was considering giving a green light to Kim's military plan. Afterwards, events moved fairly smoothly in the new policy direction.

Excited by Stalin's reply, Kim started to prepare to travel to Moscow. He proposed organizing three more infantry divisions to raise total North Korean army strength to ten divisions. To purchase equipment for the three new infantry divisions, he wanted to use in 1950 a loan the Soviet Union had allocated for use in 1951. Moscow replied immediately, totally satisfying Kim's request, and began to provide weapons on a large scale.[30]

In late February 1950, Moscow sent Lt. General Alexandre Vasiliev to North Korea to be the principal military adviser to Korean People's Army, with the task of strengthening the North Korean army's organization and command and control functions. As chief military adviser, Vasiliev replaced Ambassador Shtykov, who had been double-hatted in this role after the withdrawal of Soviet troops from North Korea.[31]

On March 9, Ambassador Shtykov reported to Moscow that, "to strengthen the People's Army and to fully equip it with arms, ammunition and technical equipment," North Korea wanted Moscow to provide 120–150 million rubles worth of military-technical equipment as outlined in a list provided to the Soviet government. In return, North Korea promised to send more than 133 million rubles worth of gold, silver and monazite concentrate to the Soviet Union in 1950. On March 18, Stalin agreed to fully satisfy the North Korea request for arms, ammunition and technical equipment.[32]

On March 20, Kim Il-sung asked to pay an unofficial visit to Moscow in early April to discuss "ways and means of unifying the north and south of the country ... economic development prospects," and other questions. After Moscow quickly approved, Ambassador Shtykov reported on March 24 that he had finished arranging Kim's trip. On March 29, Foreign Minister Vyshinsky informed Stalin that, "Kim Il-sung and [North] Korean Foreign Minister Pak Hon-yong will depart Pyongyang for Moscow on March 30. Soviet Ambassador to [North] Korea General Shtykov will accompany them; they will arrival in Moscow on April 8."[33]

No documents have yet been found in the Russian archives regarding the content of the April 1950 secret talks between Stalin and Kim; versions of what happened in scholarly works are based on the recollections of involved parties.[34] However, an August 9, 1966 "Background Report on the Korean War" drafted by the Soviet Foreign Ministry for CPSU General Secretary Leonid Brezhnev and other Soviet leaders acknowledged that Stalin gave his final approval of North Korea's draft plan during Kim Il-sung's March–April (*sic*) 1950 visit to Moscow.[35] Thus, while Stalin decided to change his Korea policy in principle in January 1950, he gave his final approval of Kim's invasion of the South in April 1950.

What happened to prompt Stalin to change his mind at this time? The most important event at the time in Asia was the new strategic situation that followed the Communist victory in China, namely, the new Sino-Soviet alliance and a Treaty of Friendship, Alliance and Mutual Assistance.

The role of the Chinese revolution and the Sino-Soviet alliance in spurring changes in Stalin's Korean and Far Eastern policies, however, is not necessarily as thought by some scholars, namely, that since the Soviet Union felt its position in the Far East was now stronger, it follows that Moscow was more confident it could confront and defeat U.S. power on the Korean peninsula.

Actually, the opposite was true. The change in the political regime in China and the signing of the new Sino-Soviet treaty made Stalin wonder if Soviet interests in the Far East were threatened or, possibly, even lost. Therefore, he felt compelled to change his policies to guarantee enduring Soviet strategic goals in the Far East. As far as Moscow was concerned, the establishment of New China was like a dual-edged sword. On the one hand, it constituted a new Soviet security shield in Asia that surely strengthened Soviet rights and interests in this region. On the other hand, if this neighboring country should ever become big and powerful, it would possibly become a threat to Soviet security and interests. In the same way, the signing of the new Sino-Soviet treaty carried dual significance. The new alliance surely strengthened Soviet political power in Asia. But, in establishing the alliance, Stalin was forced to give up most of the political and economic rights and interests that he had wrested from Chiang Kai-shek in 1945. It is therefore possible to conclude that Stalin's motive for changing his Korean policy in early 1950 was based on a desire to maintain and protect Soviet political and economic interests in Asia, especially in Northeast Asia. This was the crux of the issue for Stalin.

As noted in the last chapter, in a certain sense, Stalin had no choice but to sign the Sino-Soviet Treaty of Friendship, Alliance and Mutual Assistance of February 1950. Yet, as a result of that treaty, in two or three years, the Soviet Union would lose the significant rights and interests in the Far East it had gained at Yalta and in the 1945 Sino-Soviet treaty with Chiang Kai-shek. Therefore, if Stalin wished to maintain Soviet postwar aims in the Far East, to make up for the rights and interests that would be lost by signing the new bilateral treaty, he would have to do this outside of China. In this context, the change in his Korea policy arguably was an opportunistic response to new realities in Soviet relations with China.

It would be obvious to Stalin that if war broke out on the Korean peninsula, whatever the result, the Soviet strategic goal in the Far East – acquisition of an outlet on the ocean and an ice-free port – would be guaranteed.

If the war ended in victory, the Soviet Union would control the whole Korean peninsula, and Inchon and Pusan would replace Lushun and Dalian, which he had pledged to return to China. When Kim Il-sung met Stalin in March 1949, the North Korean leader had proposed building a short, direct rail link between Kraskino in the Soviet Far East and Aoji in North Korea.[36] Though this potential line was somewhat longer compared to the Soviet rail link to North Korea via the Changchun Railway, the Soviet railway system could be linked directly with the two major Pacific Ocean ports of Inchon and Pusan, both south of the 38th parallel.

Even if the war went poorly, the Soviet Union would achieve what it wished if the resultant tense situation in Northeast Asia forced China to ask Soviet forces to stay on in Lushun and Dalian. Moreover, based on the new Sino-Soviet agreement, in the event of war, the Soviet Army had the right to use the Changchun Railway, and, if this happened, the Changchun Railway would effectively remain under Soviet control.

Admittedly, speculating on what Stalin thought at this time about the Korean issue is based on inference, but some facts can be adduced. As World War II ended, Moscow focused on the Korean peninsula's strategic value in guaranteeing the security of the Soviet Far East. A June 1945 report by the Soviet Foreign Ministry Second Far East Division pointed out the significance of expanding Soviet influence in Korea, noting that

Czarist Russia's struggle to oppose Japan in Korea had been "an histori-cally justified act." In the wake of World War II, "Japan must be forever excluded from Korea, since a Korea under Japanese rule would be a con-stant threat to the Soviet Far East." The report advocated that Korea be independent enough to keep it from again becoming a base for invasion into continental Asia, whether by Japan or any other country intending to pressure the Soviet Union in the Far East.[37]

This report shows that in mid-1945 the Soviet Union regarded Japan as its main threat in the Far East, but was not proposing then to control Korea unilaterally. However, the Soviet government was even then keenly aware of the possible resurgence of great power rivalry in Northeast Asia, and thus wanted to prevent the Korean peninsula from becoming a spring-board for expansion into continental Asia.

The Soviet Union at this point paid especially close attention to three strategic positions in the southern part of the Korean peninsula – Pusan, Cheju Island and Inchon – linking these strategic positions conceptually with the Lushun in Northeast China.

A September 1945 report in the Russian Foreign Ministry archives entitled "Notes on the Question of Former Japanese Colonies and Trust Territories" argued that after two years of Soviet–American joint occupa-tion of Korea, Moscow should urge transition to a four-nation (Soviet, U.S., China and British) trusteeship, with three strategic areas, Pusan, Cheju Island and Inchon, all south of the 38th parallel, under direct Soviet military control. The Foreign Ministry hoped to gain these three strategic positions in exchange for the U.S. desire to acquire trusteeships over strategic islands in the Pacific. If this Soviet attempt encountered opposition, the Foreign Ministry proposed that the Soviet Union appeal to (then Nationalist) China, proposing joint Soviet–Chinese control of these strategic positions in Korea.[38]

A second Soviet Foreign Ministry report in September 1945 proposed that, in any agreement on a four-nation trusteeship under United Nations Charter Article 82 rules, Pusan, Cheju Island and Inchon should be identified as strategic areas. The Soviet Foreign Ministry deemed these three places essential for guaranteeing dependable sea lines of approach to the joint Soviet–Chinese Lushun Naval Base, and argued that, under UN Charter Article 82, they should be put under Soviet military administration.[39]

From all this, it is clear that, from the start of the postwar period, the Korean peninsula occupied an important place in Soviet strategic thinking in the Far East. As World War II ended, the Soviet Union gained its basic strategic aims in the Far East under the Sino-Soviet Treaty of Friendship and Alliance concluded with Chiang Kai-shek, even as it jointly occupied Korea with the United States. Soon afterwards, when the U.S. and the Soviet Union came into conflict, Stalin's attention was first drawn to Europe. By 1947, after the Soviet Union parted ways with the U.S., it basically abandoned any residual strategic pretensions with respect to South Korea and contented itself with control over North Korea, turning the North into a security buffer for the Soviet Far East region.

Right up to Mao Zedong's visit to Moscow in the winter of 1949–50, Stalin's intention was to maintain the existing 1945 Sino-Soviet treaty. In this way, he could preserve existing Soviet extraterritorial rights and interests in the Far East, and could avoid a crisis that might lead to a confrontation with the United States. However, after talks with Mao in early 1950, Stalin realized that the Soviet Union's existing rights and interests in the Far East would be lost. Therefore, Stalin then placed control of strategic objectives on the Korean peninsula on his agenda.

Dating back to Czarist Russia, there is a long Russian diplomatic tradition of "exchanging" spheres of influence. Stalin's practice of exchanging spheres of influence or occupied territory with the West in order to promote Soviet security interests was thus not without precedent. Stalin had done this not only in Europe – for instance on the Greek question – but he also tried to do this out in the Far East with respect to the Korean peninsula. As described in Chapter 2, when it came to drawing the 38th parallel, Stalin tried to trade the American occupation of the southern part of the Korean peninsula for Soviet occupation of a portion of Japanese home island territory north of the 38th parallel. Owing to the American hard-line position, Stalin's plan was frustrated, but his method and intention of exchanging spheres of influence to attain other foreign strategic objectives is clear.

Naturally, as the leader of the world Communist movement, Stalin also had to be concerned about his reputation as a revolutionary. Moscow could not repeatedly block the revolutionary demands of Asian countries, especially after facts proved that the Soviet Union had made this error with respect to the Chinese revolution, and Stalin did not want to be criticized on the issue of the Korean revolution as well. However, Stalin, above all, was a Great Russian chauvinist, and his concern over personal reputation took second place to national interests. It can be said, therefore, that Stalin's concern over Soviet strategic interests in the Far East drove his decision to resort to military means on the Korean peninsula. In implementing this policy, however, there were essential conditions that he could not ignore.

America and China factors in Stalin's eyes

In implementing his new policy of support for Kim Il-sung's plan to reunify Korea by resort to a military attack against South Korea, Stalin had to calculate and manage correctly relations with both the United States and China.

According to available documentation, in managing relations with the United States, Stalin had three considerations.

First, to the extent possible, he wanted to avoid direct military conflict with the United States.

With the Soviet Union already in a global confrontation with the United States, Stalin knew that conflict and perhaps even war with the United States could not be avoided, but he also knew that the Soviet Union did not have sufficient strength to face this reality in the short term. The outcome of the Berlin crisis made him especially uncertain of military victory over his opponent, and, therefore, a hasty action that would place the Soviet Union in conflict with the United States would be dangerous. As a result, even while agreeing to support Kim Il-sung's military plan, Stalin provided only covert direction and behind-the-scenes military assistance. At the very least, by avoiding overt Soviet involvement, Stalin intended to gain plausible deniability vis-à-vis the United States.

On June 20, when North Korea was stepping up its war preparations, Ambassador Shtykov sent an urgent telegram to Moscow:

> Kim Il-sung asks [for] naval vessels to use in attacks and landings. Two vessels have arrived, but naval crews have not yet completed preparations. He requests dispatch of ten Soviet advisers to employ on these vessels. I believe this request should be satisfied.

On June 22, Gromyko replied that, "We cannot accept your proposal. This would give a pretext for [foreign] intervention."[40] As will be seen in some detail, after the war broke out, Soviet actions were even more cautious.

Based on Stalin's care to avoid giving the United States a pretext for intervening in Korea, we can make the following judgment: Stalin's determination to take military action in Korea was not in any important sense taken to confront the United States over its Japan policy. Though the U.S. unilateral occupation of Japan had stirred strong Soviet dissatisfaction, by 1949 U.S. policy in Asia was mainly characterized by retrenchment of American forces and defense lines. America's return of sovereignty and independence to Japan and the legalization of the U.S. force presence in Japan both occurred after the start of the Korean War.[41]

Soviet control over the Korean peninsula would of course help to prevent the advance of Japanese militarism on the Asian continent, but, with respect to Stalin's motivation in backing the North Korean plan, he certainly did not want to spur the United States to change its retrenchment policy. Unless the Soviet Union was determined to turn control over the Korean peninsula into a springboard for attacking Japan, there was no real significance to making this decision based on calculations about Japan. And to attack Japan would, of course, bring on direct military conflict with the United States, which was against existing Moscow policy. Put another way, if Stalin had thought the Soviet decision would lead to U.S. intervention in Korea, things likely would have turned out completely differently.

Second, Stalin gradually moved toward the judgment that the United States would not directly intervene should a military crisis develop in Korea.

During the summer and fall of 1949, when the Korean peninsula was in a tense state, and Stalin was concerned about how the United States would react, he asked Kim Il-sung and his Ambassador in Pyongyang for their assessments. At that time, the North Korean leadership judged that, in case of "a civil war in Korea," the United States would not intervene directly, but could assist the South from the sea and air, with American military instructors helping to organize South Korean military resistance.[42]

If Stalin had reservations about this North Korean assessment, high-level statements by U.S. officials in early 1950 made a deep impression on him. Moscow took note that the January 12 speech by Secretary of State Dean Acheson had excluded Korea from the U.S. security sphere in the western Pacific. According to V. P. Tkachenko, a former CPSU Central Committee Korea expert, Stalin carefully studied the Acheson speech and this had a major impact on his thinking.[43]

When Kim visited Moscow in April 1950, Stalin again raised the issue of possible U.S. involvement. On this occasion, Kim's answer was quite firm. According to his interpreter, Mun Il, Kim adduced four reasons to assure Stalin that the United States would not join a war on the Korean peninsula:

1   North Korea would gain a military victory within three days;
2   In South Korea, 200,000 Communist Party members would rise in revolt;
3   South Korean partisans would help the People's Army in their fight; and
4   The United States would have no time to prepare.[44]

Stalin clearly accepted Kim's assessment. Just after this secret meeting, Stalin agreed to Kim's plan to attack South Korea.

Lt. General Yu Song-chol, who served as Chief of the Operations Directorate of the North Korean forces at the start of the war, worked directly on the invasion plan. (A North Korean "dissident" long exiled in the former Soviet Union), in 1990, Yu visited Seoul where he was interviewed by a South Korean paper. Yu recalled that the Soviet military advisory group, judging that North Korea's war plan would not succeed, drafted its own plan, envisioning military exercises to prepare for a counterattack following an invasion of the North by the South. The Soviet-drafted war plan included routes of march, combat orders for different units and directions for different types of forces to coordinate their operations. Under the plan, North Korea advancing units were divided into two routes, with the First Front Army commanded by Kim Woong serving as the primary attack force on Seoul, and the Second Front Army commanded by Mu Chong acting as a flanking force, enveloping Seoul from the south. The aim of the plan was to take Seoul, since, at the time, the consensus was that military action would end if Seoul was taken and there was an uprising in the South, as was then expected.[45] In actual fact, after the North Korean People's Army took Seoul, its military advance stalled for some time.

As indicated, Moscow assessed that after war broke out on the Korean peninsula the United States would not directly intervene, or at least would not do so before it was too late. With this condition of surety, Stalin agreed to support North Korea's military action against the South.

Third, if America intervened, as Stalin saw it, China would have to get involved and take control of the situation.

Stalin always managed international affairs with great caution, so he naturally would have considered how the Soviet Union would react if the United States unexpectedly intervened. In this eventuality, Stalin expected China to take responsibility, with the Chinese military directly confronting the U.S. Based on this calculation, while he gave his "tacit but conditional" approval to the North's resort to military action, Stalin stressed that the North Korean leader had to seek Mao's views.

According to M. C. Kapitsa, at Stalin's last meeting with Kim in April 1950, the Soviet leader again urged Kim to consult Mao, reportedly warning that, "If you should get kicked in the teeth, I shall not lift a finger. You have to ask Mao for all the help."[46]

After Kim accepted Stalin's directive and secretly visited Beijing to seek Mao's advice, the North Korean leader ran into Chinese doubts. In response to Chinese questioning, on May 14, Stalin informed Mao that he and his Soviet colleagues had taken the position that, "in light of the changed international situation, they agreed with the Koreans regarding the plan to move toward reunification." However, Stalin added that, "the question should be decided finally by the Chinese and Korean comrades together, and in case of disagreement by the Chinese comrades the decision ... should be postponed pending further discussion."[47] In effect, by forcing Mao to accept an established fact, Stalin's basic intent was to fob off all responsibility on China should the U.S. unexpectedly intervene. This was Stalin's method of managing relations with the United States.

However, from Stalin's point of view, managing relations with China was more important and thornier than managing the U.S. factor.

Faced with a tense situation in Northeast Asia, in relations with China, Stalin had two mutually related and, it seems, also mutually contradictory intentions.

First, Stalin could not and would not allow the Soviet Union to get bogged down in a possible conflict between China and the United States; on the other hand, Stalin needed China as an ally and vanguard in the Soviet Union's confrontation with the United States in Asia.

Second, in early 1950, Stalin faced demands from two directions: Kim needed Soviet agreement and assistance to unify the Korean peninsula, and, though Mao did not need Moscow's approval to launch a campaign to liberate Taiwan, he also needed Soviet military assistance to assure success. Put differently, when Stalin was considering the issue of Korean unification, he also had to confront the issue of the planned Chinese Communist liberation of Taiwan. Comparing the two, Stalin naturally thought it more beneficial to the Soviet Union to first resolve the Korean issue. His reasoning was:

1   In considering possible U.S. interventions, Soviet assistance to Communist China in a Taiwan campaign would more likely involve the Soviet Union in a direct conflict with the U.S., since while the superbly confident Kim only asked for Soviet arms, Mao had asked for Soviet air and naval assistance to attack across the Taiwan Strait. After the People's Liberation Army's attack on Jinmen (Quemoy) failed in October 1949, Soviet help seemed even more vital. On January 11, 1950, Liu Shaoqi reported to Mao in Moscow that,

> I have transmitted to you all the operational war material with regard to Zhoushan, Taiwan, Jinmen, and Hainan Island. According to [PLA Commander] Su Yu's report, if there is neither air support nor some measure of needed naval support, cross-sea amphibious offensive warfare [against Taiwan] is impossible, and recent reports regarding Hainan Island and Jinmen bear this out.[48]

However, Stalin feared that if the Soviet Union sent its air force into an action against Taiwan this could lead the United States to intervene to protect Taiwan, a point he made clearly in his meetings with Liu in summer 1949 and Mao in winter 1949–50.

2   In considering Soviet bilateral relations with Pyongyang and Beijing, actions by North Korea, which depended entirely on Soviet aid and support, could be controlled by Moscow.[49] Though the Soviet Union had an alliance with China, Stalin still neither trusted nor felt at ease with Mao.
3   In considering Soviet strategic interests in Asia, unification of the Korean peninsula by Kim at this time clearly accorded with Stalin's strategic objectives. But Stalin had no assurance how Mao would behave if China strengthened its position as a result of the liberation of Taiwan. In that event, China might constitute a future potential threat to the Soviet Union.

As Stalin would see it, based on these factors, he should give his support to military action on the Korean peninsula, while Mao's actions should help serve Soviet strategic objectives. In fact, the outbreak of the Korean War actually achieved this effect: on the one hand, it stopped

Mao from launching a military campaign to liberate Taiwan, and, on the other hand, it brought Chinese force and actions within the orbit of Soviet strategy.

Did Mao understand and support Kim's plan to unify the Korean nation? Was China's position on the Korean peninsula issue in contradiction with the Soviet position? Was Stalin clear about Mao's attitude regarding Korea? These questions, which still require answers based on further research, are essential for understanding the measures taken by Stalin to manage Beijing in the context of what was about to occur in Korea. Available material shows that in mid-1949, before the Communist victory in the Chinese civil war, Mao did not want to see the rise of tension and a slide to war on China's border. At that point, Stalin was very clear about the Chinese Communist leadership's attitude on the Korean issue.

Communist Chinese–North Korean talks in 1949

As early as May 1949, Mao and other Chinese leaders understood the tense situation that had arisen on the Korean peninsula and the circumstances under which the Korean Democratic People's Republic required assistance. Mao agreed to help, but did not support the initiation of war preparations by Kim.

In late April 1949, at Kim Il-sung's behest, Kim Il, head of Korean People's Army Political Department, paid a secret visit to China. During a stopover in Shenyang, Kim Il met Gao Gang, as noted, then a leading CCP figure in Northeast China. In Peiping (later Beijing), Kim Il met four times with Zhu De and Zhou Enlai, and once with Mao, discussing the Korean situation, the repatriation of Korean divisions in the People's Liberation Army, and the possible creation of an Eastern Cominform. There are two reports in the Russian archives on the Kim Il visit to China, one from Kim Il-sung to Soviet Foreign Minister Vyshinsky via Ambassador Shtykov, the other from Mao to Stalin via I. V. Kovalev. There are differences in these two reports concerning Kim Il's meeting with Mao.

According to Kim Il-sung's report to Vyshinsky, Mao noted that of the three Korean divisions in the People's Liberation Army, two were deployed in Shenyang and Changchun, in China's Northeast, and the other was still engaged in combat. China was ready at any time to repatriate to North Korea the two divisions garrisoned in Northeast China along with their equipment. However, the other division could only be repatriated after the end of hostilities in China, and at least one month beyond the end of hostilities would be needed to arrange the repatriation of these troops. Kim Il asked if China could supply ammunition for the three divisions, and Mao replied that China could supply ammunition, and the Koreans could have as much as they needed.

Mao and Zhu asked probing questions about the Korean situation. Mao said there could be military action in Korea at any time, so Kim Il-sung should pay attention to the situation and thoroughly prepare. In Korea, war might be either very fast or protracted. Mao said:

> Protracted war would not be good for you, since Japan then might get involved and help the South Korean 'government'. You shouldn't worry. The Soviet Union is at your side, and we are in the Northeast. If the need arises, we can quietly send Chinese troops; we all have black hair, no one can tell the difference.

Mao wanted to know if a recent North Korean delegation to Moscow had discussed the idea of creating an Eastern Cominform, and what the Korean Worker's Party Central Committee thought about the issue. Kim Il said he knew nothing about the issue. Mao advised that it was too early to set up an Eastern Cominform, since fighting was still going on in China and Indochina, and the Korean situation was tense. If an Eastern Cominform were formed, this could be viewed as a military alliance.[50]

On the issues of establishing an Eastern Cominform and assisting the North Korean army with troops and arms, Mao's report to Stalin basically paralleled Kim Il-sung's report. But Mao's report of his discussion of the Korean situation with Kim Il differed significantly from Kim Il-sung's report. According to Mao, he told Kim Il that if war occurred in Korea, China would do all in its power, especially in providing arms to the repatriated Korean divisions discussed above. When Kim Il said that after the U.S. army's withdrawal from the South, the South might launch an attack on North Korea with Japanese help, Mao urged North Korea to counterattack, but to be careful if Japanese troops joined in. In that case, said Mao, the enemy might be in a superior position.

Most importantly, according to Mao's account, he stressed to Kim Il that,

> If the Americans leave, and the Japanese do not come in, in this situation, we urge the Korean comrades not to launch an offensive on the South, but rather to wait for a more favorable situation, since, during such an offensive, [General] MacArthur can quickly send Japanese troops and arms to [South] Korea. And, we cannot quickly and forcefully come to your aid, since all of our main force has been deployed south of the Yangtze River... Should the Japanese invade Korea, we can quickly dispatch our crack troops to annihilate the Japanese army... [But we] can only take these steps after coordination with Moscow.[51]

As is evident from these two reports, Mao was concerned in mid-1949 that North Korea might come under attack from the South. But, while Kim Il-sung's report to Foreign Minister Vyshinsky did not mention Mao's opposition to launching a preemptive attack on the South, Mao's report to Stalin clearly indicated that he had urged the North not to initiate such an attack. As to which of these two reports is more accurate, the formula used by Kim Il-sung in his September 12, 1949 meeting with Soviet Embassy Charge Tunkin can serve as a touchstone. According to Tunkin, when Kim discussed the military situation on the Korean peninsula, he mentioned that,

> [I]n the spring of this year Mao stated that in his opinion the north-erners should not begin military action now, since, in the first place, it is politically disadvantageous and, in the second place, the Chinese friends are occupied at home and cannot give them serious help. [52]

In sum, in the spring of 1949, Mao clearly did not support military action against the South by North Korea, and held that this possibility should only be considered after the end of the Chinese civil war and consultations with the Soviet Union.

China repatriates Korean soldiers in the PLA

But what about Communist China's repatriation to North Korea in 1949 and 1950 of ethnic Koreans in the People's Liberation Army? Does this action indicate that the Chinese Communist Party actually supported an early North Korean military action against South Korea? Some scholars have argued that China's repatriation of Koreans from the People's Liberation Army is strong evidence of Communist China's "collusion" in North Korea's invasion of South Korea.[53] This theory, however, is baseless.

There is, in fact, a long history behind the repatriation of Korean troops who served in the Chinese Communist army. During the Anti-Japanese War (World War II) and the later civil war between the Communists and the Nationalists, many Koreans entered Northeast China and joined the Chinese Communist army. When the Anti-Japanese War ended, Mu Chong, a North Korean military leader, led a regiment of 1,000 Korean soldiers back to North Korea. During the Chinese civil war, other Korean troops continually returned to Korea.[54]

A large-scale repatriation of Korean troops then occurred after Kim Il met with Chinese Communist leaders in April–May 1949. There have been various earlier accounts of the number and timing of the repatriation at this time.[55] Based on documents in the archives and recollections of contemporaries, a more up-to-date assessment can now be made. After the meeting between Mao and Kim Il, about 37,000 Korean officers and soldiers comprising three divisions returned to Korea, first two divisions in July 1949 and then the "third" (actually a composite) division in April 1950.

After Mao met with Kim Il, he instructed Gao Gang to arrange for the two Korean divisions garrisoned in Shenyang and Changchun to return to North Korea in July and August 1949. These two divisions, the 164th and the 166th, until then part of China's Northeast Military Region, began to enter Korea in July 1949. When they arrived in Korea, the 164th comprised 10,821 officers and soldiers, and the 166th comprised of 10,320 officers and soldiers.[56]

The issue of repatriating the "third division" to Korea was raised in early January 1950. At that time, Lin Biao informed Mao, then in Moscow, that there were still more than 16,000 Korean troops in various all-Korean formations in the People's Liberation Army. Now that the Chinese Communist army had entered south China, Korean morale was deteriorating, and some Koreans were asking to be sent home to Korea. With the civil war now drawing to a close, Lin Biao proposed to repatriate these troops as one division or as four or five regiments.

The Chinese government then informed Kim Il-sung that, "owing to the end of war operations, Korean troops now serving in the Chinese People's Liberation Army have less to do, and, if the Korean government wishes, can be repatriated." Kim approved, proposing that before repatriation, most of the Korean troops still in the People's Liberation Army should be formed into a "Korean infantry division" comprised of two infantry regiments, with the rest, officers and regular soldiers, filling out a full-strength motorized regiment and a mechanized brigade. The North Korean leader sent representatives to China for consultations. Given problems stationing these troops in Korea, North Korea wanted them repatriated in four months time. This force finally reached Wonsan on April 18, 1950.[57]

There is no evidence that the Chinese leadership repatriated Korean troops because it agreed to and supported military action to unify Korea. Perhaps the 1949 repatriation to some degree reflected Mao's fear that North Korea might come under attack from South Korea, and thereby demonstrated "internationalist" sympathy and support for the North Korean revolutionary regime. More concretely, however, the repatriation of the Korean divisions – especially the "third" division in 1950 – was due, on the one hand, to the desire of the Korean troops to return home, and, on the other, to the fact that with the Chinese civil war virtually over, China's leaders were grappling with cost cutting and demobilization.[58] The explanation made long ago by Professor Allen Whiting remains persuasive: "Chinese Communist concern over military expenditures and preparations for a cutback in its armed forces during 1950 made such a transfer expedient from Peking's point of view."[59]

As discussed above, the Soviet leadership surely understood the Chinese position regarding conflict in Korea in 1949. From reports by both Pyongyang and Beijing, Stalin knew about the April 1949 exchange between Mao and Kim Il-sung's representative, Kim Il. Importantly, moreover, throughout 1949 Chinese and Soviet leaders held the same view: they did not support military action against South Korea by North Korea.

Russian Professor Andrei Ledovsky found (in the Russian Presidential archives) two telegrams that were exchanged between Mao and Stalin in mid-October 1949 on the Korean issue. Mao reportedly told Stalin that the North Koreans wanted to use military force to resolve the issue of South Korea, but Chinese leaders had urged them not to do so. Stalin, in reply, said that he agreed completely with the Chinese view that a war should not be started in Korea, and military means should not be used to unify Korea. For the time being, North Korea was not well prepared, and the best way ahead would be for it to organize guerrilla forces in South Korea.[60]

Whether or not Mao and Stalin decided to support military action in Korea during their winter 1949–50 meetings in Moscow has long been the subject of great controversy. Now, a large amount of material and the results of research confirm that in Moscow, in addition to a banquet and a celebratory event, Stalin and Mao held three official meetings (December 16, 1949; December 24, 1949; and January 22, 1950) and a small meeting (in late January) in which they discussed Secretary of State Dean Acheson's January 12 National Press Club speech. So far as is known, however, none of these meetings touched on military action by North Korea against the South. In the December 24 meeting, though Mao and Stalin may have discussed the Korean situation, they certainly did not discuss taking military action on the Korean peninsula. And, from all we now know, it appears that in January 1950, when Stalin and Kim Il-sung had just begun to bruit possible military action in their exchanges through the Soviet Embassy in Pyongyang, Stalin did not mention a word to Mao about his decision (then only in principle) to support military action and to invite Kim Il-sung to Moscow for consultation.

Some may suspect, of course, that Stalin and Mao held secret meetings that touched on using military force in Korea. The author has discussed this issue with Professor Odd Arne Westad, who spent six years in Moscow exploring Russian archives and interviewing many knowledgeable former Soviet officials. According to M. C. Kapitsa, Stalin invited Mao to his private dacha twice for meetings, with no officials present, and with Stalin inviting only a personal friend in (Soviet) military intelligence to interpret. In the second private meeting, on February 15, 1950, Stalin and Mao reportedly discussed the Korean issue, but Kapitsa has provided no details. However, as shown by the events following Stalin's meeting with Kim in April 1950, even if there was a secret meeting (or two) with Mao in Moscow, Stalin likely did not discuss his decision regarding a North Korean attack with Mao in Moscow.[61]

After Kim returned to Pyongyang from his April trip to Moscow, on May 3, Stalin sent a telegram telling Mao that, "The Korean comrades have been here. I will send you a special report on the results of the discussions with them in a couple days."[62] In fact, however, Stalin did not then report directly to Mao. Rather, based on Stalin's request, Kim confirmed to Ambassador Shtykov on May 12 that he had decided to make a secret trip to Beijing. His purpose would be to inform China "of their intentions to unify [Korea] through military means and … the results of their discussions … in

Moscow." Kim also told Stalin that he did not need to ask for Chinese assistance, "since all his requests were satisfied in Moscow and the necessary and sufficient assistance was given him there."[63]

Kim informs Mao of war plans

Kim and his party arrived by air in Beijing on May 13, and met that evening with Mao and Zhou. No documentary material has been found on this meeting. However, based on Soviet Ambassador Roshchin's report to Moscow, it seems the first Mao–Kim meeting did not go smoothly, and broke off early. Roshchin reported that Zhou Enlai came to see him at 11:30 p.m. on May 13, asking that he send an immediate message to Stalin on behalf of Mao. Zhou told Roshchin that,

> In the conversation with Comrade Mao Zedong, the Korean comrade informed him about the directives from Comrade Filippov [Stalin] that the present situation has changed ... and that North Korea can [now] move toward actions; however, this question should be discussed with China and personally with Comrade Mao.

In reporting Zhou's visit, Ambassador Roshchin noted that, "Comrade Mao Zedong would like to have personal clarifications from Comrade Filippov [Stalin] on this question." He added in closing that, "The Chinese comrades are requesting an urgent answer."[64]

Clearly not trusting Kim's explanation of the situation, Mao broke off his meeting with Kim and asked for Stalin's clarification overnight. This event provides circumstantial evidence that Stalin had not raised this issue (i.e., of supporting Kim's desire to launch his forces into the South) while Mao was still in Moscow. Only now, through the medium of Kim's secret visit to Beijing, did Stalin, it appears for the first time, inform Mao that his attitude on the Korean issue had changed.

On May 14, Foreign Minister Vyshinsky sent a message of reply from Stalin to Mao:

> In a conversation with the Korean comrades Filippov [Stalin] and his friends expressed the opinion that, in light of the changed international situation, they agreed with the proposal of the Koreans to move toward reunification. In this regard a qualification was made, that the question should be decided finally by the Chinese and Korean comrades together, and in case of disagreement by the Chinese comrades the decision ... should be postponed pending further discussion. The Korean comrades can tell you the details of the conversation.[65]

In this circumstance, it was hard for Mao Zedong to suggest an opposing view.[66]

To summarize, Stalin clearly understood that:

First, China was accelerating its preparations to liberate Taiwan. Soviet experts were training the first group of "fast-track" pilots to graduate from a Chinese air force school, and China was continually pushing the Soviet Union to speed up its provision of air and naval arms.[67] In April 1950, Zhou Enlai had sent Deputy Prime Minister Bulganin a list of "urgently needed" naval vessels, aircraft and coastal artillery, asking that this equipment be sent to China by the summer of 1950, or, at the latest, before spring 1951.[68]

Second, China did not want a military crisis or tension on China's northeastern border at this time,[69] since the bulk of China's military forces were then concentrated in south China, opposite Taiwan. At this time, there were fewer than 200,000 troops in China's Northeast, including the 42nd Army, which had been assigned the task of opening virgin land. Meanwhile, 16 armies had been concentrated on the southeast China coast opposite Taiwan.[70]

In view of these conditions, in reaching his decision on Korea, Stalin took three related steps to manage the China factor in his Korean decision.

1 Judging that at a time when China itself was asking for Soviet help in the liberation of Taiwan, it would be hard in Moscow to get Mao to agree to military action in Korea, Stalin was not in a position to seek Mao's opinion until after he (Stalin) had reached final agreement with Kim.
2 In view of Communist China's position in the Asian revolutionary movement, and hoping that China would take on future responsibility on the Korean question (if it became necessary), Stalin, after deciding the issue with Kim, still had to convey this decision to Mao and seek China's approval.
3 Considering that China was then intensifying preparations to invade Taiwan, and that it appeared that China's involvement was not then needed in Korea, since the U.S. would not intervene militarily in Korea, Stalin did not in the slightest way reveal details of the war plan on the Korean peninsula to Mao.[71]

The Korean War was the first great international issue faced after the formation of the Sino-Soviet alliance, and also the greatest test of this relationship. In handling this issue, Stalin showed a (residual) lack of trust in Mao, revealing, albeit not to the outside world, fissures in the relationship.

In considering changing policy toward the Korean peninsula, Stalin had two fundamental concerns about his new alliance with China: first, that Mao would oppose Moscow's Korea decision beforehand, and second, that if the situation in Korea became difficult, Mao would refuse to be drawn in, and would not follow Soviet direction. Therefore, Stalin, in managing his relations with China, operated from detailed considerations as described above. In this way, he sought to gain Chinese acceptance of his policy and assure the achievement of Soviet strategic objectives. If the war in Korea went smoothly, even though the Soviet Union would soon lose its special rights in Northeast China, its losses would be offset and its overall strategic interests in the Far East would still be guaranteed. If, on the other hand, there were unexpected difficulties in Korea, China, as a Soviet ally, would take responsibility, and the result would be the same, achievement of Soviet strategic aims.

In a nutshell, the starting point in Stalin's strategy toward war in Korea was to guarantee Soviet political and economic interests in the Far East, while avoiding any direct, armed clash with the United States in the region.[72]

7   North Korean forces cross the 38th parallel

On June 25, 1950, the Korean People's Army of North Korea crossed the 38th parallel and quickly advanced south. Against the expectations of Mao, Kim or Stalin, within days the United States intervened militarily, sending air, naval and land forces to and toward Korea, while simultaneously deploying the 7th fleet to the Taiwan Strait. Soon thereafter, the armed forces of more than a dozen nations joined the international "police action" to defend South Korea under the United Nations flag. Four months later, as the North Korean army started to collapse and U.S. forces approached Korea's northern border, an army of tens of thousands of Chinese – the so-called Chinese People's Volunteers – crossed the Yalu River into North Korea. From that point on, the Korean War involved the largest number of countries and the largest military forces deployed in war between World War II and the Vietnam War. "It was not so much a local war as a localized general war."[1]

In its essence, the Korean War reflected the clash of the world's two great camps, with newly allied China and the Soviet Union playing major roles in the war. China and the Soviet Union had their respective war goals, strategies and tactics. The cooperation and discord between the two affected the outcome of the war, greatly testing their alliance.

Between the start of the war on June 25, 1950 and the entry of Chinese troops on October 25, 1950, the policies and tactics adopted by China and the Soviet Union toward the Korean War evolved along diametrically different lines: As North Korea's war situation changed from good to bad, Soviet policy moved from close participation in planning and preparation for the initial military advance to studious avoidance of over-involvement as the situation spiraled downward, at one point approaching a Soviet decision to abandon North Korea.

In contrast, Chinese policy and tactics transitioned from arguably rather peripheral attention to the conflict as it began to an active defensive strategy as the North began to collapse and China's own border came under threat, with China in the end deciding to send troops to help North Korea under extremely unfavorable conditions.

Soviet support for North Korea's war plan

By spring 1950, Soviet policy began to reflect a strategy of military confrontation with the United States, missing no opportunity to strengthen Soviet influence and control in Asia. However, the Soviet Union itself was not prepared for open conflict, and thus sought to avoid a direct military clash with the United States. Chinese policy, by contrast, was based on nurturing the nascent "New China," but China did not hesitate to cross swords with the world's greatest superpower when it felt driven into a corner. At this point, China's leaders mobilized public opinion and troops under the slogan "Resist America and Assist Korea, Defend our Homes and Protect our Nation."

The opening phase of the war went as well as the North Koreans and their Soviet sponsors and advisers could have wished. A June 26, 1950 report from Soviet Ambassador Shtykov to General M. V. Zakharov, Deputy Chief of Staff of the Soviet Red Army, described in detail the situation at the start of the war:

> The planning of the operation at the divisional level and the reconnaissance of the area was carried out with the participation of Soviet advisers.
>
> All preparatory measures for the operation were completed by June 24th.
>
> ... The political order of the Minister of Defense was read to the troops, which explained that the South Korean army had provoked a military attack by violating the 38th parallel and that the government of the DPRK had given an order to the Korean People's Army to go over to the counterattack.
>
> The troops went to their starting positions by 24:00 hours on June 24th. Military operations began at 4 hours 40 minutes local time. Artillery preparation was accompanied in the course of 20–40 minutes by direct fire and a ten-minute artillery barrage. The infantry rose and went on the attack in good spirits. In the first three hours individual units and formations advanced three to five kilometers.
>
> The attack of the troops of the People's Army took the enemy completely by surprise.
>
> ... On the very first day the DPRK navy made two landings on the coast of the Sea of Japan. The first landing party was in the Kangnung area, and consisted of two battalions of naval infantry and around a thousand partisans. The second landing was in the Ulchin area, consisting of 600 partisans.
>
> ... On June 26 troops of the People's Army continued the attack and ... advanced deep into the territory of South Korea. During June 26 ... the Ongjin peninsula and the area around Kaesong were completely cleared and units of the 6th division made a forced landing ... taking the populated area near Kimpo airport.

Near Seoul, the 1st and 4th divisions have taken the cities of Munsan and Tongduchon and the 2nd division has taken the provincial capital of Chunchon. On the coast of the Sea of Japan the advance has continued. The port of Chuminjin has been captured.

During the course of the day there has been no communication with the 12th Infantry Division, moving in the direction of Hongchon, or with the 3rd Infantry Division and the mechanized brigade attacking through Songuri toward Uijongbu.[2]

U.S. intervention: a surprise

But, in stark contrast to Soviet and North Korean expectations, the United States immediately decided to enter the war and then steadily increased the scope of its involvement. In American eyes, the North Korean People's Army's crossing of the 38th parallel was viewed as the opening of a global advance by the Communist bloc, and even perhaps the start of World War III. The U.S. government therefore was determined to make a swift and strong response.[3]

The U.S. intervention took Stalin by surprise, and thereafter caused him great concern throughout the war. On July 1, three days after the U.S. Congress authorized a full-scale intervention in the Korean War, an agitated Stalin cabled Ambassador Shtykov in Pyongyang:

1   You do not report anything about what kind of plans the Korean command has. Does it intend to push on? Or has it decided to stop the advance? In our opinion, the attack must continue and the sooner South Korea is liberated the less chance there is for intervention.

2   Communicate also how the Korean leaders regard the attacks on North Korean territory by American planes. Are they not frightened or do they continue to hold firm? Does the Korean government plan to make an open statement of protest against the attacks and the armed intervention? In our opinion, this should be done.

3   We have decided to fulfill fully by July 10 the Koreans' requests for the delivery of ammunition and other military equipment.[4]

Moscow received reports from Ambassador Shtykov on July 2 and 4. He reported general elation in Pyongyang over the capture of Seoul, but that the U.S. entry in the war, especially the U.S. bombings, was starting to affect popular morale and to raise doubts about final victory. Some of the North Korean leadership thought it would be difficult to fight the United States and wanted to know what the Soviet Union thought. In addition to forwarding Kim Il-sung's request for the expedited delivery of more arms, Shtykov asked Stalin for permission to allow two Soviet military advisers to accompany each North Korean army group, and for a group of Soviet officers, including Lt. General Vasiliev, the chief Soviet military adviser to the North Korean army, to be permanently stationed at the Korean People's Army frontline command in Seoul.[5]

On July 6, Stalin approved Kim's request for more arms[6] but responded laconically to his ambassador's request to attach Soviet military advisers to the North Korean front armies, noting simply that, "Concerning the location of the chief military adviser Vasiliev, we consider it more useful for him to be in Pyongyang."[7]

Though Stalin clearly wanted Pyongyang to achieve rapid victory, and toward that end pledged ample military equipment and arms, he did not want the outside world to know about the level of Soviet support for Kim. Meanwhile, Moscow stalled and, as it had earlier promised Mao, did not allow the Soviet representative to return to the UN Security Council.

Soviet advisers and "Kim's affair"

At the start of the Korean War, there were more than 3,000 Soviet advisers attached to the Korean People's Army, one Soviet military adviser for every forty-five Korean officers and soldiers. Soviet military advisers were responsible for training North Korean troops and coordinating command of the war. Even the Korean People's Army war plan was formulated with participation of the Soviet advisers.[8] When the Korean People's Army had moved south of the 38th parallel, however, Stalin ordered the withdrawal of all Soviet advisers attached to the North Korean army's frontline units. When Khrushchev asked Stalin why he did this, Stalin reportedly "snapped" that there was a danger Soviet advisers might be taken prisoner, and "We don't want there to be evidence for accusing us of taking part in this business. It's Kim Il-sung's affair."[9]

This was the Moscow backdrop against which Ambassador Shtykov asked Stalin to allow Soviet military advisers to accompany frontline North Korean forces south of the 38th parallel. Receiving no (favorable) reply from Moscow, he conveyed to Stalin an imploring personal letter from Kim Il-sung:

> Being confident of your desire to help the Korean people rid themselves of the American imperialists, I am obliged to appeal to you with a request to allow the use of 25–35 Soviet military advisers in the frontline staff of the Korean Army and the staff of the 2nd Army Group, since [Korean] military cadres have not yet sufficiently mastered the art of commanding modern troops.[10]

Stalin could no longer avoid a decision, but he was extremely unhappy with his ambassador's handling of this issue. In reply, Stalin's criticized Shtykov for "incorrectly ... promising the Koreans to send advisers without asking us." He sharply reminded Shtykov that, "You should remember that you represent the USSR, not [North] Korea." However, since Kim had made a direct request and the situation was dire, Stalin caved, but still with considerable reluctance. Soviet military advisers, he cautioned Shtykov, should be sent to frontline headquarters and army group staffs in the guise of *Pravda* reporters, not as military personnel. Stalin warned that Shtykov was "personally responsible to the Soviet government for seeing that [they] are not taken prisoner."[11] Stalin's caution was clearly written all over this exchange.

At the same time, faced with the American military intervention in Korea, Stalin began to explore how to use his new ally, China, to get out of this difficult situation. On July 2, Soviet Ambassador Roshchin reported to Moscow on a conversation he had held with Zhou Enlai. Zhou complained that the North Koreans had ignored China's warning and had underestimated the possibility of a U.S. military intervention. (In what turned out to be a prescient warning,) Zhou told Roshchin of Mao's recommendation to the North Koreans: Since American forces might land at Inchon, they should set up a strong defense line behind Inchon. Zhou assured Roshchin that three Chinese armies comprised of 120,000 soldiers were deployed in the Shenyang area, and confirmed that if U.S. forces crossed the 38th parallel, the Chinese military would join in resistance disguised as North Koreans. He asked if the Soviet Air Force could provide cover for these Chinese forces.[12]

This exchange represented Stalin's effort to have Roshchin test China's attitude on a possible intervention. However, as will be discussed below, the Chinese leadership as a whole had still not considered the question of dispatching troops to Korea, and had not even officially decided to mass three armies in Northeast China. Zhou's formulation, to a certain degree, represented an attempt to manage as well as to test Stalin.

Stalin reacted conscientiously, on July 5 sending Ambassador Roshchin a message for Zhou: "We consider it correct to concentrate nine Chinese divisions on the Chinese–Korean border for volunteer actions in North Korea in case the enemy crosses the 38th parallel." Stalin added that, "We will do our best to provide air cover for these units."[13]

To urge China to pay closer attention to Korea, on July 8, Stalin again instructed Roshchin:

> Communicate to Mao Zedong that the Koreans are complaining that there is no representative of China in Korea. A representative should be sent soon, so it will be possible to communicate and resolve questions more quickly, if, of course, Mao Zedong considers it necessary to have communications with [North] Korea.[14]

After mid-August, the Korean War entered a period of stalemate. At this point Stalin showed both greater anxiety and greater caution. Besides offering military guidance and equipment to the North Koreans, he began to provide greater moral support. On August 28, he instructed Ambassador Shtykov to

> Verbally transmit the following to Kim Il-sung. If he demands it in written form – give it to him in written form, but without my signature.
>
> The [CPSU] Central Committee salutes Comrade Kim Il-sung and his friends for the great liberation struggle … which Comrade Kim Il-sung is leading with brilliant success. …
>
> Comrade Kim Il-sung should not be embarrassed by the fact that he does not have solid successes in the war against the interventionists, that the successes are sometimes interrupted by delays in the advance or even by some local setbacks. In such a war continuous successes do not occur. The Russians also did not have continuous successes during the civil war and even more so during the war with Germany … Comrade Kim Il-sung should not forget that Korea is not alone now, that it has allies, who are rendering and will render it aid. The position of the Russians during the Anglo-French–American intervention of 1919 was several times worse than the position of the Korean comrades at the present time.
>
> Advise Comrade Kim Il-sung not to scatter the air force, but to concentrate it on the front. It is necessary that each attack by the People's Army on any portion of the front begin with a number of decisive blows by attack planes on the troops of the enemy, that the fighter planes defend the troops of the People's Army from the blows of the enemy planes as much as possible. If it is necessary, we can throw in additional assault aircraft and fighter aircraft for the Korean air force.[15]

In sum, prior to the U.S. landing at Inchon, Soviet Union policy toward the Korean War was constructive, but cautious. Stalin supported the North Korean military offensive, but with the stipulation that the Soviet Union would not openly or directly engage in the conflict. This was especially the case after the U.S. entered the war. At this point, Stalin began to consider bringing China into the war.

China's early reaction to the war

In contrast to Soviet actions leading up to and during the early phase of the war, the Chinese leadership was surprised by the sudden outbreak of the Korean War. With no access to the war preparations taking place between North Korea and its Soviet advisers, Chinese leaders lacked sufficient mental and military preparation,[16] and were therefore slow to adjust their own domestic agenda in reaction to the outbreak of the war.

On June 30, the same day the U.S. decided to enter the Korean War, China promulgated a land reform law and kicked off a nationwide mass land reform movement. Also on June 30, the CCP Central Committee Demobilization Commission, in accord with an existing plan, promulgated "The Decision of the Military Commission and the Government Administrative Council on Demobilization Work in 1950." Mao Zedong and Zhou Enlai signed this decision, which launched China's largest military post-civil war demobilization. Although some questioned whether demobilization should be stopped and war preparations should be made owing to the outbreak of the Korean War, Zhou directed that, "the General Staff and the Foreign Ministry will closely follow the Korean War [but will] continue to carry out demobilization work according to plan."[17]

Even China's military plan to liberate Taiwan was not completely abandoned after the U.S. 7th Fleet entered the Taiwan Strait. In a meeting with Chinese Navy Commander Xiao Jingguang on June 30, Zhou noted that changed circumstances had heightened difficulties with respect to Taiwan planning, since the United States was now blocking Taiwan. But, said Zhou, while China would censure American interference with respect to Taiwan, "The army's plan will be to continue to demobilize, while stepping up naval and air force preparations and pushing back the date for the liberation of Taiwan."[18] It seems that in the days right after the outbreak of the Korean War, Chinese leaders were not yet fully focused on the war and its possible ramifications.

Yet the Chinese government paid enough attention to show some measure of support for North Korea. When the Korean War broke out, China's Ambassador to Pyongyang, Ni Zhiliang, was recuperating in Wuhan. Consequently, on June 30, Zhou Enlai ordered Chai Junwu (also known as Chai Chengwen), who had been posted to East Berlin, to proceed instead to Pyongyang. There, as Charge and Political Counselor, he was to maintain liaison with the North Koreans. Zhou told Chai before he left a week later that,

> American land forces have now joined the Korean War and the U.S. imperialists will surely get more countries to send forces. It will, therefore, be very hard to avoid a lengthy war in Korea. ... We need to show our support for the Korean comrades; if there is some way we can help, have them make a request, and we will do all we can. The main tasks of the embassy now are to maintain liaison between the two parties and armies, and understand changes on the battlefield.[19]

In early July, to strengthen the officer corps of the North Korean army, China agreed to send 200 ethnic Korean officers from the PLA's Northeast China Military District to North Korea. In the same period, China also agreed to Moscow's request to ship military materiel bound for North Korea over the Changchun Railway and through its air space. China also agreed to an expedited procedure to route rail traffic from the Sino-Soviet border to Andong (Dandong) across the Yalu River from North Korea.[20]

In the second week in July, about ten days after the U.S. entered the Korean War, the Chinese leadership (as a whole) finally focused on the battlefield situation in Korea, deciding (as Zhou had foreshadowed to the Soviet Ambassador days earlier) on a large military deployment to Northeast China as a precaution in the face of the U.S. intervention. At Mao's suggestion, Zhou convened the Central Military Commission on July 7 and 10 to discuss defensive preparations in the Northeast. The Commission issued a "Decision Regarding Protection of the Northeastern Border," and ordered the deployment prior to August 5 of 255,000 troops (comprised of four armies, three artillery divisions and three air corps) to form the Northeast Border Defense Army.[21] By mid-July, the 38th, 39th, 40th and 42nd armies, under 13th Army Corps Commander Deng Hua, had organized the defense in the Northeast. Until this point, Northeast China had hosted the smallest military presence of all China's strategic regions, with only 1/27th of all troops deployed throughout China.[22]

The standing up of the Northeast Border Defense Army and its assigned task – to strengthen Chinese defensive force in the region – shows that Northeast China had now become a more important Chinese military concern. Importantly, when Zhou Enlai discussed the question of sending Chinese troops to assist Korea during his early July meeting with Soviet Ambassador Roshchin, he had stipulated that this could happen only if American forces crossed the 38th parallel. At that time, with the Korean People's Army still advancing south, and with no prospect of the U.S. military crossing the 38th parallel, the question of possibly deploying Chinese forces still seemed remote.

Increasing the "China factor"

Chinese leadership concerns, however, soon deepened in response to the changing situation in Korea. When the Chinese Communist Party Politburo met on August 4, the North Korean advance had ground to a halt and United Nations forces had stabilized a perimeter around Pusan. At the August 4 Politburo meeting, Mao argued that,

> If the American imperialists are victorious, they will become dizzy with success, and then be in a position to threaten us. We have to help [North] Korea; we have to assist them. This can be in the form a volunteer force, and be at a time of our choosing, but we must start to prepare.

Zhou added that:

> If the American imperialists crush North Korea, they will be swollen with arrogance, and peace will be threatened. If we want to assure

victory, we must increase the China factor; this may produce a change in the international situation. We must take a long-range view.[23]

On August 5, Mao sent a telegram to Northeast Military District Commander Gao Gang with the following instruction:

> All units of the Border Defense Army have now massed. They likely will have no combat mission in August, but need to prepare for possible combat in early September.... All units should complete preparations ... and await an order to deploy into battle.

On August 18, he told Gao that,

> The time for the Border Defense Army to complete training and other preparatory work can be extended until the end of September. Please tighten oversight work, so that all preparations are completed before the end of September.

As conditions on the Korean front continued to worsen daily between late August and early September, China made major changes in its strategic dispositions, and Mao considered adding another eight armies to the four that had already been deployed in the Northeast.[24]

On August 25, at the 47th Session of the State Administrative Council, Zhou Enlai commented that "the likelihood the Korean War will be prolonged has increased ... the Korean people will have to fight a long war. We have to support them...." He relayed Mao's directives to create a three-year military development plan; increase air, artillery and armored troop training; and prepare for war in the spring of 1951.

On August 26, at the Second National Military Conference, Zhou declared that help to North Korea was important for the (anti-imperialist) struggle, and China should be prepared for a long, drawn-out fight:

> This time we are facing the American imperialists ... not merely the Syngman Rhee puppet army.... This requires us to strengthen our preparatory work. We need to be fully prepared, and cannot 'make last minute changes under the duress of battle,' but must be ready to achieve victory.

On August 27, Mao instructed local officials to consider the relationship between the political situation and the three-year military development plan, and to be prepared to discuss the issue at the Fourth Plenum of the Seventh Congress of the CCP and the National Political Consultative Conference meeting planned for that November or December.[25]

All this activity indicates that Chinese leaders were becoming increasingly concerned over the deteriorating situation in Korea, and were more engaged with the issue with each passing day. However, as illustrated by moves toward a "three year military development plan" and talk of avoiding "[making] last minute changes under the duress of battle," dispatching actual forces was still not on the agenda. At the time, Chinese leaders were considering the situation mainly from the perspective of how to prepare for all contingencies, rather than acting on a strategic plan.

Stalin reacts to the U.S. Inchon landing

On September 15, after U.S. (and South Korean) forces landed at Inchon, the Korean situation changed rapidly, bringing Soviet and Chinese countermeasures and attitudes into sharper focus.

Stalin's first reaction to the turnabout in the Korean situation was to express irritation and misgivings. On September 18, he instructed Soviet military adviser General Vasiliev and Ambassador Shtykov to tell Kim Il-sung to redeploy four divisions of the Korean People's Army from the Naktong River frontline (near Pusan) to the vicinity of Seoul. On the same day, Stalin ordered Soviet Defense Minister Marshal A. M. Vasilevsky to urgently formulate a plan for the Soviet air defense of Pyongyang. This was to include the deployment of several Soviet fighter squadrons with radar and air defense battalions from the Soviet maritime region, including Vladivostok, to airfields around Pyongyang. Stalin then urgently dispatched a special mission led by Soviet Army Deputy Chief of Staff General M. V. Zhakharov (under the alias Matveev) with orders to halt the North Korean advance on the defensive perimeter around Pusan, withdraw all North Korean forces from the frontline along the Naktong River, and redeploy these forces to the eastern and northeastern fronts to guard Seoul. Stalin also repeatedly urged Vasilevsky to do all he could to provide air protection to the Korean People's Army and to establish an anti-air system around Pyongyang and its environs.[26]

The urgent measures set in motion by Stalin, had they been implemented, would have inserted the Soviet Air Force into the war, sharply departing from Stalin's earlier consistent avoidance of a direct military clash with the United States. In these desperate straits, maybe Stalin really was thinking in new terms, since these new Korean developments directly affected Soviet strategic interests in Northeast Asia. But, after weighing the pros and cons, Stalin abandoned this plan.

On September 23, responding to Stalin's instructions, Vasilevsky reported that the Soviet Air Force was preparing to deploy 40 fighter aircraft from the Soviet Maritime region to airfields near Pyongyang, arriving on October 1 and 2, to be operational on October 3. Vasilevsky warned, however, that since air combat commands would have to be given by radio in Russian, the U.S. military would realize after the first air engagement that Soviet pilots were in action in the air over Pyongyang.[27] Vasilevsky's warning apparently had its effect. As the military situation worsened and the Americans crossed the 38th parallel, when North Korea urgently needed Moscow's direct military assistance, Stalin deployed neither his land nor air forces to protect Pyongyang. Rather, he tossed the hot potato to Mao.

By September 26, the situation was extremely serious. Matveyev (General Zakharov) reported from Pyongyang that,

> With their unhindered air dominance, which has caused aircraft-fright in the ranks of the People's Army and in the rear areas, U.S. troops have managed to move from Suwon eastward and southeastward for 25 to 30 kilometers and some of their troops have taken Sangju and Anto to the north and northeast of Taegu.... [T]ank units of the enemy's Seoul group continue to advance toward Chongju, threatening to encircle the KPA's First Front Army.... [KPA troops,] having lost almost all their tanks and much artillery, are engaged in difficult battles to hold their positions.... [KPA] command and control is poor [and its communications work] intermittently....[28]

Now, a restless and anxious Stalin sharply criticized both the North Korean Army and its Soviet advisers. In a September 27 cable, he first excoriated "the series of grave mistakes" in command and control, and tactics made by the North Korean Army. Then he turned on the Soviet advisers, citing them as "even more to blame for these mistakes." He criticized their failure to implement the timely withdrawal of four divisions from the central front (near Pusan) to the area near Seoul, "erroneous and absolutely inadmissible" tank tactics, and "incompetence in intelligence matters."

Stalin stressed the failure of Ambassador Shtykov and the Soviet military advisers in Korea "to grasp the strategic importance of the enemy's assault landing in Inchon." Shtykov, noted Stalin, "even suggested that we bring to trial the author of an article in *Pravda* about the U.S. assault landing." "This blindness" caused them to question the need to redeploy forces from the south to the Seoul area, asserted Stalin, delaying the movement of troops and thereby "losing a week to the enemy's enjoyment." Stalin believed that had "they pulled out these divisions on time, this could have changed the military situation around Seoul considerably."[29]

Stalin may have conveniently forgotten that Chinese leaders had suggested in early July that he remind the North Koreans of the danger that the U.S. military could land at Inchon or elsewhere behind the lines of the Korean People's Army. Kim Il-sung, anxious to wrap up victory, had ignored China's warning.[30] In fact, before the U.S. landing at Inchon, Stalin had also disregarded this possibility.

In an October 1 telegram, Stalin complained that Ambassador Shtykov had not provided his assessment and recommendations to the North Koreans, "fostering the rocky mood of the North Korean leadership." Stalin further complained that,

[Matveev] still has not sent Moscow his own thorough evaluation of the military situation in Korea, not to mention the fact that he has failed to offer any proposals or advice relevant to the situation, thus making it difficult for us to make decisions concerning Korea.

This failure, complained Stalin, meant that the North Korean leadership "to this day has no plan of defense ... at and to the north of the 38th parallel, and has no plan for withdrawing its troops from South Korea."[31]

Stalin may have also forgotten that it was his own orders that severely limited the activities of the Soviet military advisers in Korea. Soviet advisers were under orders not to cross the 38th parallel under any circumstances, sharply constraining their understanding of the battlefield situation and their ability to exercise influence.

After U.S. forces landed at Inchon on September 15, Stalin almost immediately considered asking China to send troops. According to Shi Zhe, within two days after the Inchon landing, Stalin cabled Mao, inquiring whether China's military deployments in the Northeast made it possible for it to send troops to Korea.[32]

China's response as the North Koreans fall back

In fact, the worsening situation in Korea put China under pressure similar to that faced by the Soviet Union; by this point, Mao was already thinking about sending troops to come to North Korea's aid. Given the desperate situation, Chinese leaders began to prepare for war.

On September 20, Zhou Enlai cabled Ambassador Ni Zhiliang in Pyongyang with instructions to share the following with Kim Il-sung:

1   Your thoughts about a lengthy war are correct.
2   [The key task now is] to preserve your main force.... If the enemy takes Seoul, there is danger that the People's Army's route of retreat will be cut off.
3   The main force of the People's Army should concentrate a mobile reserve to identify the enemy's weak points, then carve them up and annihilate them.
4   ... [D]ivide and pin down large numbers of the enemy [troops], using the overwhelming superiority of large troop numbers (three to five times) and fire power (more than two times) to surround small numbers of enemy troops that [have been] cut off (for instance, a regiment).
5   Under the principle of protracted warfare ... think long-term and forestall the tendency of the lower ranks to risk everything on a single engagement. The enemy wants a quick resolution and fears a drawn-out fight, but, for the Korean people, a quick resolution is impossible; victory can come only through protracted war.

Kim cabled back his agreement with this Chinese advice.[33]

On the evening of October 1, Zhou sent Ambassador Ni another message for Kim:

> With eight divisions [of the Korean People's Army] already cut off, please consider whether or not it is possible to divide these eight divisions into two forces: with four divisions destroying their heavy weapons, breaking into a number of small detachments, and withdrawing north of the 38th parallel through gaps in the enemy's lines; and with [the remaining] four divisions in South Korea dividing into a number of small detachments, engaging in guerilla warfare behind enemy lines with the help of the people, and tying up a large force of the enemy, so that they cannot advance north.... Your military forces must quickly withdraw north, the sooner, the better.

The next day, in another cable to Ni, Zhou emphasized that, beyond the gist of his last telegram, Ni should tell Kim that,

> [T]o the maximum extent possible, he should divide up and withdraw to the north by various routes the military forces that have been surrounded by the enemy, while those military forces that cannot be withdrawn engage in guerilla warfare where they are.... [I]n this way, there is hope, and victory is possible.[34]

The issue of sending its own troops to Korea was now a pressing matter before the Chinese leadership. On September 17, two days after the Inchon landing, the Central Military Commission decided to dispatch immediately to Korea a five-man advance group (accompanied by Chinese Embassy officer Chai Chengwen) to get a handle on the situation, reconnoiter the terrain and prepare the battlefield. When the group passed through Shenyang, Chai passed a letter to Gao Gang from Mao, telling Gao that, "It looks like it will be impossible not to send troops, so you should do all you can to prepare."[35]

A last-minute (unheard) message to the Americans

On September 25, Acting Chief of the General Staff, General Nie Rongzhen, told Indian Ambassador Pannikar that, "China cannot stand idly by if the Americans cross the 38th parallel." Even if war inflicts great harm on China, said Nie, it "has to make whatever sacrifice is necessary to stop an aggressive American advance."[36]

In a September 30 speech (published October 1), Zhou reiterated a warning aimed at the U.S. government: "The Chinese people certainly cannot tolerate foreign aggression, and also cannot sit idly by while the imperialists wantonly aggress against their neighbor." The last half of this sentence was added to the draft[37] with the intent of focusing U.S. attention on the possibility that China would enter the war. But, at this time, with General MacArthur determined to cross the 38th parallel, and the White House and the Pentagon dizzy with success, Washington simply did not hear China's warning.

Kim asks for direct assistance

At this point, Kim Il-sung was forced to ask the Soviet Union and China for direct military help. On September 28, the Korean Workers' Party Politburo discussed and approved a letter to Stalin asking the Soviets to deploy their air force to help Korea. The Politburo also approved sending a letter to Mao that "hinted about aid."

On September 29, Kim summoned Soviet Ambassador Shtykov, explaining the situation facing his frontline troops: "[B]ecause of [our forces'] poor discipline and failure to follow orders, the enemy has managed to cut off the First Army Group and is moving to cut off the Second Army Group." Kim said that he had lost contact with Choe Yong-gon in Seoul, and was worried the enemy would cross the 38th parallel. Noting that the North Koreans had thought they could unify Korea on their own, Kim admitted that now, "[S]hould the enemy cross the 38th parallel, [we] simply cannot organize new forces, and cannot effectively resist the enemy."

Shtykov reported to Moscow that,

> The military situation lately has worsened dramatically. The enemy has managed to cut off the entire First Army Group's six divisions and two brigades [and] the Second Army Group's seven divisions. Seoul has fallen. There are no reserve forces ready to provide any serious resistance to the enemy advancing to the 38th parallel.... The political situation is also getting more and more complicated. The enemy has stepped up the insertion of paratroops into North Korean territory to gather intelligence on deliveries shipped from the Soviet Union and to organize subversive activities. Counter-revolutionary forces are cropping up in North Korea.

Kim, reported the Soviet ambassador, had wanted to ask his advice about the letter to be sent to Stalin, but he had "dodged" the question.[38]

In their September 29 letter to Stalin, Kim and North Korean Foreign Minister Pak Hon-yong reported on their severe military losses in the wake of the Inchon landing, and, anticipating the imminent fall of Seoul, pleaded for Soviet military assistance or, failing that, Soviet pressure on China to provide assistance.

In some detail, Kim and Pak outlined the "perilous" military situation, acknowledging street fighting in Seoul. Ominously, they reported that the

U.S. Air Force "totally dominate[s] the air space and perform[s] air raids at the front and in the rear day and night." Under this air cover, "On all fronts ... the enemy engage[s] us in combat at its free will and inflict[s] great losses to our manpower and destroy[s] our armaments," cutting off communications and logistical supply and isolating North Korean forces in the South.

After pledging to fight to "the last drop of blood," they pleaded that,

> at the moment when the enemy troops cross over the 38th parallel we will badly need direct military assistance from the Soviet Union.... If for any reason this is impossible, please help us by forming international volunteer forces in China and other people's democracies to assist in our struggle.[39]

The North Korean letter, received as "a very urgent" cable at 23:30 on the evening of September 30 in the Soviet Armed Forces General Staff, was decoded at 00:35 on October 1, typed up at 01:45, and sent to Stalin's dacha in the south at 02:50.[40] Stalin's response to Kim Il-sung's request for military assistance was reflected in messages he sent to Shtykov and Matveev in Pyongyang and to Mao in Beijing.

In his message to Shtykov and Matveev (Zakharov), Stalin instructed that the North Koreans "must immediately mobilize all forces to prevent the enemy from crossing the 38th parallel [but must also be prepared] to fight the enemy north of the 38th parallel." He appended several concrete recommendations. Above all, however, he repeatedly stressed that North Korea had the capacity to do all this on its own. Stalin warned his advisers and North Korean leaders not to "underestimate the forces and capabilities of the Korean Republic [the DPRK] in organizing defenses."

Responding to Kim's plea for direct Soviet military assistance, Stalin without any hesitation pushed this off to China, telling Kim that, "[C]oncerning the question of providing [Soviet] military assistance ... we consider formation of volunteer units to be a more acceptable form of assistance. We must first consult with our Chinese comrades on this issue."[41]

Stalin raised the issue of China sending troops to help Korea in an October 1 message to Mao and Zhou. The Soviet leader's tone was respectful, but left no room for discussion: "I am far away from Moscow on vacation and somewhat detached from events in Korea. However, judging by the information that I have received from Moscow today, I see that the situation of our Korean friends is getting desperate."

After recounting the Korean situation in broad strokes, Stalin recommended that,

> [I]f in the current situation you consider it possible to send troops to assist the Koreans, then you should move at least five–six divisions toward the 38th parallel at once so as to give our Korean comrades an

opportunity to organize combat reserves north of the 38th parallel under the cover of your troops. The Chinese divisions could be considered as volunteers, with Chinese in command at the head, of course.

Stalin obviously did not want Mao to know that North Korea had made the same request of the Soviet Union and had been turned down. Therefore, as a final point, he added that, "I have not informed and am not going to inform our Korean friends about this idea, but I have no doubt in my mind that they will be glad when they learn of it."[42]

At this critical juncture, with North Korean troops reeling in the wake of the Inchon landing, the responsibility for assisting North Korea landed on Mao's shoulders.

8   China decides

"Whatever the sacrifice necessary"

Only months into the new Sino-Soviet alliance, whether or not China would send its troops to assist Korea became the most important issue between Stalin and Mao. This decision was the first great test of that alliance and, from the record, it is clear many subtle considerations came into play between the two leaders.

As we saw, in forming their new alliance relationship, both leaders tried first to figure out their opposite number's psychology, then probed their intentions, and only then took cautious steps. Stalin took this approach on issues involving China. And, as will be explained below, Mao also took this approach in considering issues in relations with the Soviet Union. Deeply rooted historical factors engendered mutual suspicions between Mao and Stalin; both were prone to misunderstandings.

How did Mao react to Stalin's proposal that China deploy its force to Korea to assist North Korea? What did he think? There has been a lot of international academic debate on this issue, all based on the discovery of two separate, apparently contradictory October 2, 1950 messages from Mao to Stalin on the issue of sending Chinese troops to Korea. The differences have excited great interest and attention among scholars of Sino-Soviet relations and Korean War historians.

When the first volume of *Mao Zedong Documents after the Establishment of the State* was published by China in 1987, it contained (what was then portrayed as) an October 2 message from Mao to Stalin spelling out China's decision to send a volunteer force into the Korean conflict, and specifying the number of troops to be sent, the deployment date and the initial battle plan.

For many years, scholars relied widely on this document in their research. It was generally believed that on October 2, 1950, China had conveyed to Moscow its agreement to send troops to Korea. At an academic symposium on the Cold War held in Washington in 1995, however, a Russian scholar reported that another, quite different October 2, 1950 message from Mao to Stalin had been found in the Russian Presidential Archives. In this message, sent in an October 3 telegram from Soviet Ambassador Roshchin to Moscow, Mao rebuffed Stalin's request, and enumerated several reasons why China could not in the short term send troops to fight in the Korean War.

At a January 1996 international scholarly symposium on the "Cold War in Asia," the issue of these two conflicting messages and what they indicate was again a hot topic of conversation. Based on the message found in the Russian archives, Russian scholars held that Mao's reply to Stalin, in sharp contrast to the version earlier published by China, showed "doubt and lack of confidence" on the part of the Chinese leader and "an unexpected twist in the Chinese position." Russian scholars, in fact, questioned the validity or authenticity of the other October 2 message published by China.

Comparing the two messages, similarly dated but with different content, Russian scholars argued that the document in the Russian archives could not possibly be "an elaborately concocted forgery," while the document published by China "was unreliable [and] perhaps was inaccurate, unsent, or wrongly dated." They also suggested that it was possible that "Chinese authorities altered or distorted the Chinese document's content to fit an historical narrative they regarded as more ideologically or politically correct."

Furthermore, some scholars believed that the discovery of the message in the Russian archives "raised the question of whether the Mao Zedong October 2 through 14 telegraphed messages that had appeared in officially sanctioned Chinese document collections and later in scholarly works were reliable or even authentic." On this basis, they warned that people "should handle with extreme caution Chinese documents concerning Mao Zedong's decision to join the Korean War."[1]

These mutually contradictory documents, which had uniquely been published and publicized separately by Beijing and Moscow, stand in stark contrast with each other and demand to be somehow reconciled.[2] The reason for focusing on these divergent October 2 messages is that the outcome of this discussion is important to understanding the timing, content and process behind China's decision to send troops to Korea.

The content of the October 3, 1950 telegram sent from the Soviet Embassy in Beijing as well as other telegrams in the Russian archives from this period are similar in logic and diction. Based on textual analysis, therefore, the Russian-published October 2 message does not appear to be a forgery. As for the October 2 message published by China in its collection of Mao Zedong manuscripts, the author understands from discussions with Chinese authorities that the original is actually a draft telegram in Mao's hand. While a portion of this manuscript has been redacted, the excised part is principally a list of military items China was seeking from the Soviet Union. The redactions reportedly do not track with the October 2 Mao message to Stalin published by Russia.

Nevertheless, according to Chinese authorities, the published portion of the Chinese version (except for redactions) is the same as the original version in the archive. Thus, the document published by China is also authentic, at least in the sense that it reflects a draft in Mao's hand. This document helps clarify what Mao and the Chinese leadership as a whole thought about deploying troops and how they (ultimately) made their decision at this time of greatest tension in the Korean War. Therefore, to understand the issue, it is necessary to scrutinize and analyze the content of these documents.

Mao's October 2 message published by China

The October 2 telegram as published by China is from Mao to Stalin and states:

1 We have decided to send a portion of our army in the guise of a Volunteer Force to Korea to fight the military forces of the United States and its running dog, Syngman Rhee, and to assist [our] Korean comrades. We believe it is necessary to do this. If all of Korea is occupied by the Americans, Korean revolutionary forces will be basically defeated, and the American aggressors will run even more rampant, bringing great harm throughout the East.

2 We think that since we have decided to dispatch Chinese military forces to Korea to battle the Americans, first, in order to be able to solve the issue, we have to prepare to annihilate and drive from Korea the aggressor armies of the United States and other countries; second, since Chinese forces will fight with the Americans in Korea (though we will be doing this in the guise of a Volunteer Force), we have to prepare for the United States to declare that it is in a state of war with China, and to prepare for the possibility that the United States, at the very least, may use its air force to bomb many Chinese large cities and industrial areas, and its navy to attack coastal areas.

3 … It would be most unfavorable if the Chinese forces in Korea were unable to annihilate en masse the American army, the two armies became stalemated, and the United States, having already openly entered into a state of war with China, then destroys the economic reconstruction plan that China has launched, and stirs up dissatisfaction against us on the part of the [Chinese] national bourgeoisie and some other elements of the people. (They are very afraid of war.)

4 In the present situation, we have decided to start to [re]deploy on October 15th the twelve divisions that we have already deployed in southern Manchuria to an appropriate place in North Korea (not necessarily to the 38th parallel). On the one hand, it would engage any enemy [forces] that dare to advance north of the 38th parallel, in the first period, only fighting defensively, annihilating small enemy groups, and clarifying conditions. On the other

hand, it would await the arrival of Soviet military materiel, and the arming of our forces, and then, in coordination with Korean comrades, counter-attack and annihilate the American aggressor forces.

5   ... The enemy has air superiority, and, of the air forces we have started to train, by February 1951, we will be able to employ only 300 or so aircraft in battle....[3]

Mao's October 2 message from the Russian archives

The telegram available to scholars by Russia (after dissolution of the Soviet Union and the opening of Soviet-era archives) is an October 3 telegram from Ambassador Roshchin that transmits an October 2 message from Mao to Stalin together with Roshchin's analysis. The content and tone of Mao's message here is quite different from the October 2 message or "draft telegram" released by China in 1987 as a purportedly sent telegram.

> I received your telegram of 1 October 1950. We originally planned to move several volunteer divisions to North Korea to assist the Korean comrades when the enemy advanced north of the 38th parallel.
>
> However, having thought this over thoroughly, we now consider that such actions may entail extremely serious consequences.
>
> First, it would be very difficult to resolve the Korean question with a few divisions (our forces are extremely poorly equipped, there is no confidence in the success of military operations against American troops), and the enemy can force us to retreat.
>
> Second, it is most likely that this will provoke an open conflict between China and the United States, as a consequence of which the Soviet Union can also be dragged into war, and the question would thus become extremely large.
>
> Many comrades in the Chinese Communist Party Central Committee judge that caution is necessary.
>
> Or course, not to send troops to provide assistance is very bad for the Korean comrades, who are now in such difficulty, and we feel this keenly; but if we advance several divisions and the enemy forces us to retreat; and this moreover provokes an open conflict between the United States and China, then our entire plan for peaceful construction will be completely ruined, and many people in [China] will be dissatisfied (the wounds inflicted on the people by war have not yet been healed, we need peace).
>
> Therefore, it is better to act with restraint now, not dispatch forces, [and] actively prepare our forces to be in a better position to fight the enemy at the time of war with the enemy.
>
> Korea, while temporarily suffering defeat, will change the form of struggle to partisan war.

We will convene a Central Committee meeting, with the main comrades of various bureaus of the Central Committee in attendance. A final decision has not been taken on this question. This is our preliminary telegram. We want to consult with you. If you agree, we are ready immediately to send Comrades Zhou Enlai and Lin Biao by plane to your sanatorium to report on the Chinese and Korean situations and discuss this issue.

We await your reply. Mao Zedong

The personal views appended by Ambassador Roshchin probably had a great impact on Stalin's thinking and decision.

1   In our view, Mao Zedong's answer is indicative of a change in the original position of the Chinese leadership on the Korean question. It contradicts the earlier appraisal, which was repeatedly expressed in Mao Zedong's conversations of with Yudin, Konov, and Kotov [and] Liu Shaoqi with me, which were reported at the time. In these conversation, it was noted by them that the people and the PLA [People's Liberation Army] are ready to help the Korean people, the fighting spirit of the PLA is high, and it is able, if necessary, to defeat the American troops, regarding them as weaker than the Japanese.

2   The Chinese government undoubtedly could send to Korea not only five–six battle-ready divisions but even more. It goes without saying that Chinese troops need to be equipped with antitank and artillery weapons.

   The reasons for the changes in the position of the Chinese are not yet clear to me. It is possible to suppose that it has been influenced by the international situation, the worsening situation in Korea [and] the intrigues of the Anglo-American bloc working through [Indian Prime Minister] Nehru, who has urged the Chinese toward patience and abstention [from intervening] in order to avoid catastrophe. Roshchin.[4]

It is fairly easy to understand why this telegram – declassified and released by Russian archivists – is not in the Chinese archives. This telegram was not sent directly from Mao to Stalin, but rather was a reply from Mao to Stalin conveyed by way of the Soviet Ambassador in Beijing. Quite possibly, Mao's reply was made orally in a meeting with Ambassador Roshchin, and then sent to Moscow with Mao's approval after drafting and editing by the Soviet ambassador. This would explain why no copy of this document exists in the Chinese archives.

If that is the case, however, then why is the "telegram" published by China not in the Russian archives? As far as can be determined, the document published by China is simply a draft that was not sent at the time.

According to a Chinese official with access, the original copy in the Chinese archives has no time stamp or record of the sender. By contrast, an October 2 telegram sent by Mao to Gao Gang and Deng Hua features a time of transmission and a record that it was signed out for release by Yang Shangkun. This only shows, of course, that there is no basis or evidence that this document was ever actually transmitted. Two related questions are why Mao did not send a message that he had clearly drafted, and why he discussed another message on the same subject which was then sent by Soviet Ambassador Roshchin.

The principal reason Mao's personal (draft) telegram was not sent is that differences of opinion had arisen within the Chinese leadership, even though Mao himself had long thought about this issue and, on several occasions, had aired his views on sending troops to Korea with other Chinese leaders. Mao's mind appears to have been firmly set after the American landing at Inchon. But based on presently available material, the Chinese leadership before October 1 had not formally discussed the issue of sending troops to Korea and had not yet reached consensus about sending troops to Korea.

Based on what is known, on October 1, after receiving Stalin's message asking that China dispatch troops to Korea, Mao convened an all-night urgent session of the Central Committee Secretariat to discuss the Korean situation and how to deal with it. Attending the meeting were Mao, Zhu De, Zhou Enlai and Liu Shaoqi (Ren Bishi did not attend due to illness). There were differences over whether or not to send troops, but, with Zhou's support, Mao's proposal to send troops prevailed. The meeting then decided to call an expanded meeting of the Central Committee Secretariat the next day, to invite senior military leaders in Beijing to attend and to discuss the issue again. After the meeting, Mao sent an urgent telegram to Gao Gang to come to Beijing and ordered the Northeast Border Defense Army to prepare for orders to deploy.[5]

Also after the October 1 meeting, Mao drafted a telegram to Stalin, though this draft telegram, while later published in China as if it had been sent, was, in fact, not sent owing to questions that arose at the October 2 expanded Central Committee Secretariat meeting. According to (unpublished) material still only available in China, and the reminiscences of people involved in the October 2 expanded Central Committee Secretariat meeting, Mao argued at the October 2 meeting that it was extremely urgent to send troops to Korea. The meeting decided to put Peng Dehuai in command of Chinese troops (after Lin Biao, Mao's first choice, declined), and to hold further discussions at an expanded Politburo meeting on October 4. Mao then instructed Zhou to send a plane to Xi'an to bring Peng Dehuai to Beijing to attend the October 4 Politburo meeting.[6]

The author has not seen detailed material on these discussions, but based on the results of the meeting and an analysis of the tone of what

Mao told Ambassador Roshchin, Central Committee Secretariat members in attendance were cautious about sending troops to Korea.[7]

Although the Korean situation was critical, Mao likely felt constrained by internal Chinese leadership disagreement to tell Stalin that China at that point could not dispatch troops in the short term. Clearly, when Mao told Roshchin that, "Many Chinese Communist Party Central Committee comrades believe it is necessary to be cautious about this," he was indicating internal differences on the issue of sending troops. The discussion between Mao and Roshchin naturally reflected the discussion at the October 2 meeting, but what actually occurred during the process of drafting the two divergent October 2 Mao messages (one unsent and one sent) awaits the further release of documents from the Chinese archives.

Was Mao's signal that the time was not yet right to send Chinese troops to Korea, as understood by Ambassador Roshchin and Stalin, and later by Russian scholars, an indication of Chinese "indecision" over sending troops to assist Korea and a "change in [China's] initial position on the Korean issue"? We need to analyze these two messages together with Mao's statements and actions before and after the date of these two conflicting "messages."

Based on the recollection of participants in the October 4 expanded Politburo meeting, the decision to send Chinese troops into war in Korea was extraordinarily difficult. Many of those present, citing existing hardships, did not support sending troops, or argued in favor of putting off a decision. The prevailing sentiment at the meeting was, "Unless there is no alternative, this is a battle best not fought."[8]

At the same time, by all accounts, Mao conveyed the sense that the decision to send troops to Korea was forced on him. He understood the enormous hardships that China would face after entering the Korean War. On this point, he agreed with the thoughts of other party leaders who were against sending troops to Korea or argued in favor of putting off a decision.

After more than 20 years of war with Japan, followed by a brutal civil war, China's economy was exhausted. Inflation was skyrocketing, unemployment rising, enterprises underutilized, agriculture in a perilous state and modern transportation facilities largely destroyed. Industrial output was running only at 30 percent of prewar highs; light manufacturing and agricultural output were less than 70 percent of prewar levels.[9] In 1950, the rate of industrial machinery utilization was only about 45 percent. With production in decline, unemployment was rising. On top of all this, China had been hit with widespread flooding in 1949, leaving millions dependent on public welfare.

In Shanghai, China's industrial center, unemployment was especially acute owing to the Nationalist blockade and bombing. An April 14, 1950 Central Committee directive on unemployment relief revealed that, in the most recent quarter, about 120,000 Shanghai workers had been newly laid

off. Life for unemployed workers was very hard, leading to a string of sui-
cides. U.S. and Nationalist agents were reportedly fanning discontent
among urban workers. Mismanagement of the crisis, the April 14 directive
concluded, could lead to great difficulties in the CCP's urban work, "even
shaking the basis of people's state power in the cities."[10]

Under these conditions, it was difficult to conceive of China sending
troops against the world's greatest power, the United States. In this
context, a careful comparison of the October 2 messages published by
China and Russia is in order.

Two messages compared

In the October 2 message published by Russia, Mao laid out the reasons
for not sending troops at that time, including that Chinese military equipment was inferior, that open conflict with the U.S. would lead to an escalation of the issue, and that the disruption of China's economy would foster
domestic discontent. These factors were also all indirectly or obliquely
referred to in the (draft) message published as a telegram by China.

The difference was in the way the divergent documents posed these
questions. When in the first message (published by China) Mao talked
about how the war might unfold ("the two armies become stalemated") or
about the basis for the initial war strategy ("only fighting defensively"), he
was revealing his concerns about a difficult situation.

In the second message (declassified by Russia), Mao also indicated that,
"many comrades in the Chinese Communist Party Central Committee"
shared great concern about going to war in Korea. However, this does not
indicate that Mao had changed his own decision to send troops to Korea,
and also does not show indecisiveness on the issue (though many other
Chinese leaders waffled at the time).

A rigorous side-by-side comparison and analysis of the two messages
shows that in the message published by Moscow, Mao had not changed his
objectives. He had merely changed his tactics for getting to them. He did
not directly and immediately respond to Stalin's request, but rather
approached the issue in a roundabout way. Mao still personally advocated
sending troops, so he took pains to remind Stalin that, "We have not made
a final decision on this issue," that he had called a Central Committee
meeting to discuss the question and that he wanted to send Zhou Enlai to
the Soviet Union to confer on the issue.

There is, moreover, no basic contradiction between Mao's statement
that, for the time being, he would not dispatch troops to Korea and the
Chinese leadership's former agreement (in principle) to send troops.
Perhaps Russian scholars have not noticed, but on the occasions when
Chinese leaders talked about China sending troops, they always specified a
precondition for making this move, i.e., that the enemy had crossed the
38th parallel. When Mao and other Chinese leaders discussed this issue,

they always referred to this precondition. For instance, and importantly, in (Prime Minister and Foreign Minister) Zhou Enlai's October 3 1 a.m. meeting with Indian Ambassador Panikkar, Zhou stressed that if American troops (he did not include South Korean troops in his warning) crossed the 38th parallel, China "would get involved."[11] At the time of the Zhou–Panikkar meeting this precondition had not been met, at least according to intelligence then in the hands of the Chinese leadership. [12]

Stalin's October 1 telegram asking China to send troops to Korea was set in the context of helping Korea to establish a defensive line to protect the area north of the 38th parallel, but he did not clearly analyze the seriousness of the situation. Therefore, when Mao conveyed his opinion that the time was not yet ripe to deploy troops, he had a basis for doing so. Mao thought that delaying a decision, while still preparing to intervene, would allow China to confront the enemy with greater confidence once the decision was made to fight.

Mao was not then in a position to give Stalin a positive answer because he needed time to build consensus within the Chinese Communist Party leadership. While Mao had given very careful consideration to the issue and had made his own decision in favor of assisting North Korea militarily, China, in fact, faced many difficulties, and it was reasonable for Mao's peers to object to sending troops on hardship grounds. With most of the Chinese leadership either opposed to sending troops or advocating putting off a decision,[13] it was clearly impossible at this stage for Mao to provide a guarantee to the Soviet Union. Therefore, Mao called a number of high-level meetings, working hard to bring his peers on board a decision to send troops to Korea.

At this key juncture, Peng Dehuai played a crucial role in forging Chinese leadership consensus. On the afternoon of October 4, after he was summoned to Beijing to attend an ongoing expanded Politburo meeting, about which he had no advance knowledge, he found "the atmosphere of the meeting … quite unusual," with large differences of opinion. He did not express an opinion at this time. On the morning of October 5, at Mao's request, Deng Xiaoping brought Peng to Mao's office in the Zhongnanhai central leadership compound. After determining that Peng favored Chinese intervention, Mao asked Peng to command the Chinese People's Volunteers. Later, at the Politburo meeting on October 5, Peng turned the situation around through his impassioned statement in favor of sending troops.[14]

Once the decision was made, China took immediate action. After the Politburo meeting ended on October 5, Mao asked Zhou Enlai, Gao Gang and Peng Dehuai to dinner to continue discussing the deployment of Chinese troops to Korea. Mao emphasized that Chinese forces needed to enter Korea as quickly as possible; he feared any delay could bring serious consequences. Mao asked Gao and Peng to convey the party center's decision to commanders above the division level as soon as they arrived back in Shenyang, and to prepare to deploy Chinese forces to Korea on October 15. On October 6, Zhou chaired an enlarged meeting of the Central Military Commission to decide logistical issues and personnel assignments in preparation for the deployment to Korea.[15]

While the Chinese leadership was finally on board, however, Mao was not in a hurry to give Stalin a clear answer. At this point, Stalin was not as sober and steady as Mao. After he received Mao's cautious (October 2) message through Ambassador Roshchin on October 3, Stalin decided to evacuate Soviet personnel from North Korea.

Soviets prepare to withdraw

A few days earlier, on September 30, Deputy Foreign Minister Andrei Gromyko reported to Stalin that Ambassador Shtykov in Pyongyang had asked for authority to send some Soviet experts and non-essential personnel back home pending consultations with the North Korean government and other Soviet government organizations. The Soviet Foreign Ministry agreed in principle, but told Shtykov that, "You should not display any initiative in raising the issue of the evacuation of Soviet specialists before the Koreans do." He was, however, authorized to repatriate personnel of Soviet organizations after consultations via the Foreign Ministry with their home ministries and agencies.[16]

On October 5, the Soviet Foreign Ministry informed Ambassador Shtykov that the CPSU Politburo (also on October 5) had authorized him to evacuate Soviet experts after consultation with the North Korean government, as well as to approach other Soviet organizations concerning their personnel in North Korea. This time no conditions were attached.[17] Also on October 5, Shtykov sent another telegram recommending the evacuation from North Korea of Soviet specialists and personnel, families of Soviet citizens of Korean nationality (i.e., ethnicity), staff of the Soviet air commandant's office and, in *extremis*, all Soviet citizens. In reply, Moscow authorized Shtykov to use his discretion regarding "the evacuation of families of Soviet citizens of Korean nationality … the Soviet personnel of the air commandant's office and families of Soviet military advisers [and] in case of emergency, all Soviet citizens … to the territory of the USSR and China."[18]

This exchange makes it appear that Stalin was very worried, and had lost hope in the Korean situation. The onus of turning the situation around was left now to China. Though Stalin was resigned to evacuating Soviet personnel and citizens from North Korea, he turned again to China, twice asking Mao to send troops immediately. Stalin's tone was increasingly determined and his arguments more insistent.

Stalin to Kim: it's all up to Mao

In an October 8 message to Kim Il-sung, Stalin conveyed for the North Korea leader's enlightenment two messages he had sent to Mao pleading for the dispatch of Chinese troops to Korea. Stalin's intention clearly was to place all responsibility for North Korea's fate on Chinese shoulders. Ambassador Shtykov was instructed to read the message and allow Kim to copy it, but not to leave it, "because of its extreme confidentiality."

Comrade Kim Il-sung!
My reply has been delayed because of my consultations with the Chinese comrades, which took several days. On 1 October, I sent a letter to Mao Zedong, inquiring whether he could dispatch to Korea immediately at least five or six divisions under the cover of which our Korean comrades could form reserve troops. Mao Zedong refused, saying that he did not want to draw the USSR into the war, that China's army was ill-equipped technically, and that the war would cause great dissatisfaction in China. I replied to him with the following letter:

'I considered it possible to turn to you with the question of five–six Chinese volunteer divisions because I was well aware of a number of statements by leading Chinese comrades regarding their readiness to move several armies in support of the Korean comrades if the enemy were to cross the 38th parallel. I explained the readiness of the Chinese comrades to send troops to Korea by the fact that China was interested in preventing the danger of the transformation of Korea into a USA springboard or a bridgehead for a future militaristic Japan against China. While raising before you the question of dispatching troops to Korea, I considered five–six divisions a minimum, not a maximum, and I was proceeding from the following considerations of an international character:

1 The USA, as the Korean events showed, is not ready now for a big war;

2 Japan, whose militaristic potential has not yet been restored, is not capable of rendering military assistance to the Americans;

3 The USA will be compelled to yield on the Korean question to China, behind which stands its ally, the USSR, and [the U.S.] will have to agree to such terms of the settlement of the Korean question that would be favorable to [North] Korea and that would not give the enemies a possibility of transforming Korea into their springboard;

4 For the same reasons, the USA will not only have to abandon Taiwan, but also to reject the idea of a separate peace with the Japanese reactionaries, as well as to abandon their (*sic*) plans for

revitalizing Japanese imperialism and converting Japan into their springboard in the Far East.

In this regard, I proceeded from the assumption that China could not extract these concessions if it were to adopt a passive wait-and-see policy, and that, without serious struggle and an imposing display of force, not only would China fail to obtain all these concessions but it would not be able to get back even Taiwan which at present the United States clings to as its springboard not for Chiang Kai-shek, who has no chance to succeed, but for themselves or for a militaristic Japan of tomorrow.

Of course, I took into account also that the USA, despite its unreadiness for a big war, could still be drawn into a big war out of [consideration of] prestige, which, in turn, would drag China into the war, and along with this draw into the war the USSR, which is bound with China by the Mutual Assistance Pact. Should we fear this? In my opinion, we should not, because together we will be stronger than the USA and England, while the other European capitalist states (with the exception of Germany which is unable to provide any assistance to the United States now) do not present serious military forces. If a war is inevitable, then let it be now, and not in a few years when Japanese militarism will be restored as an ally of the USA and when the USA and Japan will have a ready-made bridgehead in a form of the entire Korea run by Syngman Rhee.

Such were the considerations and prospects of an international nature that I proceeded from when I was requesting a minimum of five–six divisions from you.'

In response to this, on October 7, I received a letter from Mao, in which he expresses solidarity with the fundamental positions discussed in my letter and declares that he will dispatch to Korea nine, not six, divisions. But he will not send them now, but after some time. He also requested that I receive his representatives and discuss some details of the mission with them. Of course, I agreed to receive his representatives and to discuss with them a detailed plan of military assistance to Korea.[19]

Stalin's strong advice to Mao was clearly intended to pressure China into making a quick decision. Actually, at the time, not only had Mao already made a decision, he had also conveyed China's decision to Kim. On October 8, Mao issued an order organizing the Chinese Volunteers force, appointing Peng Dehuai as commander and political commissar of the 13th Army Group (comprised of four armies) and the Border Artillery Command (comprised of three artillery divisions), and instructing Peng to await a further order to go into action. Gao Gang was placed in command of logistical arrangements. On October 8, Mao also advised Kim by telegram of this decision.[20]

Based on Kim Il-sung's letter to Stalin, sent by Ambassador Shtykov to Moscow on October 9, and from the similar tenor of Gromyko's October 10 meeting in Moscow with North Korean Ambassador Chu Yong-ha, Kim was well aware of China's preparations to send troops to Korea. The North Koreans were no longer urgently requesting (all-out Soviet) assistance, rather they were now merely requesting Soviet training for their pilots, radio operators and other technical personnel.[21]

As revealed in an only recently released document from Russian archives, on October 8, the same day he informed Kim, Mao also told Moscow of his decision to send troops to Korea, including details of China's concrete arrangements:

> It was with pleasure that I received your reply telegram. The Central Committee of our party is in full agreement with your opinion. I have appointed Peng Dehuai as commander and political commissar of the Chinese People's Volunteers Army.
>
> Comrade Gao Gang will take charge of guaranteeing logistics for the Volunteers Army. They flew this morning (October 8) from Beijing to Mukden (Shenyang).
>
> On or about October 15, the army will start to move into Korean territory.
>
> I have already conveyed the decision concerning the dispatch of the Chinese People's Volunteers Army to Comrade Kim Il-sung.
>
> Comrade Zhou Enlai and Comrade Lin Biao boarded an airplane at eight this morning to fly to where you are. Please keep their mission secret.[22]

Zhou's mission to the USSR

The purpose of the secret mission of Zhou Enlai and Lin Biao was to determine how Stalin would carry out his commitment to provide military equipment and air support to the Chinese Army. This was one of China's main conditions for sending troops to Korea to fight with the United States.

Both of the purported October 2 messages from Mao make clear that Mao's decision to deploy troops to Korea was premised on a sure and quick victory. Only this outcome would resolve China's concerns and difficulties. And, as an ally, the Soviet Union was obligated, in the view of Chinese leaders, to provide massive military assistance to China, especially air support.[23]

China's top military leaders, in particular, were insisting on Soviet air support. As early as August 31, Generals Deng Hua, Hong Xuezhi and Xie Fang, all commanders in the Chinese People's Volunteers, had recommended to PLA Commander-in-Chief Zhu De that to achieve the plan for a "quick war and a quick decision," the first step was "to do everything possible to organize massive air force involvement in the war." They continued hopefully that,

> If the Soviet Army is able to give us more air [support] and greater technical assistance, the implementation of our plan will have a better material guarantee [of success]. If our air force requirements are not ready, then we will be forced to delay the timing of deployment.[24]

Testing time for the new alliance

With no clear agreement from the Soviet Union on the key issue of air support, Mao delayed giving a direct answer to Stalin's request. He only conveyed China's decision after Zhou was in the Soviet Union, in fact, after Zhou's initial meeting with Stalin. If, for Stalin, China's decision on whether or not to send troops to Korea constituted a test of the Sino-Soviet alliance, for Mao, whether or not the Soviet Union would guarantee needed military assistance was an even greater test of the Sino-Soviet alliance relationship.

Accounts and opinions vary widely about what happened in the meeting between Zhou Enlai and Stalin at the Soviet leader's Black Sea villa, at least in part, because, even to this day, no documents or records about this meeting have been made public. Therefore, we can only speculate on what happened based on the recollections of those present or at least involved. When recollections differ and primary material is lacking, we cannot determine historical facts, but merely make deductive judgments based on collateral material and logic. Therefore, we can delineate, albeit speculatively, only the main objectives and results of Zhou's talks in the Soviet Union.

First of all, there are totally divergent explanations[25] regarding the very reasons for Zhou's trip, not to speak of disagreement over the dates of the Black Sea meeting.

One stream of opinion is based on the memoirs of Shi Zhe, the Chinese interpreter for the talks. Shi believes that the CCP Politburo had not yet reached consensus before Zhou left Beijing and that Zhou arrived in the Soviet Union carrying a brief against sending troops. From Shi's vantage, Zhou only discussed the issue of Soviet military assistance with Stalin after receiving a telegram from Mao stating that a majority in the Chinese leadership favored sending troops.[26]

Another stream of opinion, based on the recollection of Kang Yimin, also a member of Zhou's party (albeit one who did not attend Zhou's talks with Stalin), holds that the objective of Zhou's trip, in fact, was to tell Stalin that China had decided to send troops, to discuss the reequipping of the Chinese People's Volunteers with Soviet arms and to arrange for the Soviet Union to deploy its air assets in coordination with Chinese ground forces.[27]

Russian scholars, based on the memoir of Soviet interpreter N. T. Fedorenko, believe that "Zhou Enlai and Lin Biao went to see Stalin with a strong belief that China could not and should not intervene in Korea."[28]

The basis for Shi's view is that at the outset of his meeting with Stalin, Zhou laid out all the reasons for China not to send troops to Korea. On this point, the Shi and Fedorenko memoirs agree. The basis for Kang's view is the final result of Zhou's Soviet visit, specifically that there was agreement in the end that China would send troops to Korea while the Soviet Union would provide military assistance to China. Fedorenko's view is based principally on his firm belief that Zhou's original intention was to advocate forcefully that China not send troops to Korea.

Zhou addressed this issue head-on on two later occasions. He told a CCP Central Committee meeting in 1960 and then Kim Il-sung in 1971 that he had carried two options to Stalin, to send or not to send Chinese forces, but that in offering this choice, China's intention was to secure Soviet air support for China's entry into the Korean War.[29]

Actually, before Zhou left China, the Chinese leadership had already arranged to send troops. The October 6 Military Commission meeting over which Zhou had presided did not discuss the question of whether or not to dispatch Chinese troops, but rather how to deploy and supply them. Zhou, therefore, knew before he left for the Soviet Union that China had decided to deploy troops to Korea.

When Zhou met with Stalin, however, he indeed first laid out the reasons why it would be difficult for China to deploy troops to Korea. And, as will be seen below, the initial outcome of the Black Sea meeting was that China would not send troops. It can thus be deduced that Zhou indeed carried two views to the Soviet Union, for and against sending troops, but that the crux of the question was whether or not the Soviet Union would employ its air force in coordination with China's Volunteers when they entered Korea. It is thus easy to see why Zhou first laid out all the reasons why China should not send troops, though it had already decided to send troops. This was a negotiating tactic, aimed at securing more Soviet weaponry and a guarantee that Soviet air assets would cover China's Volunteers.

One Russian scholar believes that Zhou was one of "the chief opponents within the CCP Central Committee Politburo of China's entry into the war," and that Zhou "viewed his visit to Stalin as the last opportunity to prevent China from entering the Korean War and to shift the burden of saving Kim's regime onto Stalin's broad shoulders." This interpretation is baseless.[30]

Though there had been differing views among Chinese leaders over sending troops to Korea, they reached consensus to do so at the October 5 Politburo meeting. As described above, Zhou had always supported this policy, and, after the Politburo reached consensus, he vigorously implemented the decision. While chairing the October 6 Military Commission meeting that reviewed preparations for sending in troops to Korea, Zhou sought to convince the doubters:

> We don't want to fight, but the enemy has forced this on us. He will soon be at the Yalu River. We can't look on idly at impending danger. This is both helping Korea and defending ourselves. If one falls, the other will be in immediate danger.[31]

Still, compared with Mao's idealism, Zhou, in his capacity as both Prime Minister and Foreign Minister, was more of a pragmatist. If Mao put relatively greater emphasis on China's resolution and heroic spirit in sending troops, Zhou put greater emphasis on the practical hardships and the necessary conditions for deploying troops to Korea. In this way, in his discussion with Stalin, Zhou first stressed the hardships China faced in sending troops, and when Stalin said that in the immediate future the Soviet Union was not ready to deploy sufficient air assets in support of the war, Zhou then proposed that China also delay sending in its troops.

There are, however, differing versions of the outcome of the meeting between Zhou and Stalin.

According to Kang Yimin's memoir,

> Stalin agreed initially to equip ten Chinese divisions, and also to deploy his air force to Northeast China to defend the areas around Andong [Dandong], and China's large coastal cities. Consequently, during their talks, China and the Soviet Union reached total agreement on resisting America and aiding Korea....

Some scholarly works have adopted this view.[32]

Based on Fedorenko's memoir, the Russian-American scholar Alexandre Mansourov maintains that the talks between Stalin and Zhou went on for two days, with no agreement. At this point, Zhou said he needed to get new instructions from Beijing. Mansourov stoutly maintains that in the talks, Stalin agreed without hesitation to the Chinese request for air cover, and "never reneged on his promise to Mao to provide the CPV [Chinese People's Volunteers] with Soviet air cover."[33]

Most evidence indicates, however, that the Stalin–Zhou talks initially agreed that, for the time being, the Soviet Union would not deploy its air force, that neither the Soviets nor China would immediately deploy their forces, and that they would both propose that North Korea withdraw as soon as possible.

In Shi Zhe's memoir, he recounts Stalin's proposal that, "China can send a certain amount of its military force," with the Soviet Union "providing weapons," and "a certain portion of its air force to provide cover," but "this will be limited to the rear and along the forward positions, and cannot penetrate to the enemy's rear." Later, as recounted by Shi, as a result of their first meeting, Stalin and Zhou agreed to postpone any decision on sending troops to Korea and to tell the North Koreans "to prepare as soon as possible to retreat."[34]

According to Nikita Khrushchev, after the talks ended and Stalin returned to Moscow, the Soviet leader said that Zhou had come on instructions from Mao to ask Stalin whether Chinese forces should be sent in to stop the American and South Korean advance in the wake of the collapse of the North Korean army. At first, Stalin and Zhou thought that it would be fruitless for China to intervene. On the eve of Zhou's return to China, however, they decided that China should vigorously assist North Korea, and Chinese troops then began massing on the border with North Korea.[35]

Based on research by Chinese scholars Li Haiwen and Zhang Xi, Stalin and Zhou sent a joint telegram (on October 11 at 7 p.m.) to the CCP Central Committee reporting the result of their first meeting. They noted that the Soviet Air Force had not yet made any preparations, and there was no way for it to mobilize on short notice. Therefore, they had decided that, for the time being, neither China nor the Soviet Union would deploy forces, and they wanted Kim Il-sung to withdraw north of the Yalu River. The principal basis for the recommendation by Stalin and Zhou was that the Soviet Air Force "needs two to two-and-a-half months before it can deploy to assist the [Chinese] Volunteers to fight in Korea."[36]

Mao and Zhou later referred to this issue. Mao said that, "We only wanted assistance from their air force, but they wouldn't do it." Zhou also said:

> In sending in [Chinese] troops what we wanted was for their air force to assist us.... We asked, 'Can you help with your air force?' [Stalin] vacillated, saying that if China had difficulty, then it was better not to send troops, that if North Korea was lost, we would still be socialist, and China would still exist.... We just wanted the Soviet Union to send some of their air force, and then we could go in, but without the air force, we would be in trouble. Stalin said he could not send [his] air force.[37]

Thus it is clear that the initial result of the Black Sea meeting between Stalin and Zhou Enlai was that China would delay deploying troops to fight in Korea, and, at the same time, both China and the Soviet Union would propose that Kim withdraw his main forces from North Korea to China.

The long-bruited and long-sought joint Stalin–Zhou telegram of October 11, 1950 reporting this consensus was finally published in Russia in 2005. Fortunately, the published text is consistent with information provided in earlier, second-hand sources:

Soviet Embassy in Beijing for immediate transmittal to Comrade Mao Zedong.

Your representatives arrived today, and leading comrades of the [CPSU] and your representatives have had an opportunity to discuss the issue that is known to you.

After exchanging opinions, the following has become clear:

Chinese forces that are intended to render assistance are ill prepared, poorly armed, and short of artillery and tanks. It will be at least two months before it will be possible to provide air cover. And it will take at least six months to equip and train the designated army.

If a sizable, well-equipped force does not render direct help within a month, in view of the instability in the part of Korea north of the 38th parallel, Korea will be occupied by the Americans.

Consequently, serious armed assistance can be provided to the Koreans only after half a year, that is, after the occupation of Korea by the Americans, or after it will no longer be needed.

Taking into consideration the unfavorable domestic situation in China that, according Comrade Zhou Enlai's report, will occur subsequent to China's participation in the war, we have arrived unanimously at the following conclusions:

Despite favorable international conditions, the Chinese force, owing to its unpreparedness at the present time, should not cross the Korean border, so as to avoid falling into a disadvantageous situation.

If the force has already crossed the border, it should not advance beyond the mountainous region along the Chinese border.

An appropriate portion of the Korean army should occupy and defend the mountainous area north of Pyongyang and Wonsan, and a portion of the army should switch to a partisan role in the enemy's rear.

Superior elements of Koreans under arms and commanding cadres should be slowly and quietly brought out to Manchuria, where they will be formed into Korean divisions.

Pyongyang and other strong points south of the mountainous region of North Korea should be evacuated at the earliest possible time.

The USSR will do all that it can to satisfy the needs of the Chinese comrades for tanks, artillery, and airplanes to re-equip the Chinese Army.

We await your decision.

Signed: Filippov [Stalin]
Zhou Enlai
October 11, 1950[38]

In the event, however, neither the prospect of receiving arms half a year in the future nor the difficulties confronting China internally proved to be stumbling blocks to sending Chinese troops. Mao had decided on October 5 to send troops and had fixed the date of deployment on October 15. So he had already considered these conditions. But Mao was counting on the Soviet Air Force to coordinate with and to help Chinese forces in the fight. He had not thought that Stalin would be unwilling to mobilize his air force to assist Chinese forces as they entered Korea. This is the nub of the issue.

Yet, in the end, in response to Stalin's urging, and despite the mounting danger and hardships to China, Mao decided to send Chinese troops into the Korean War.[39]

Stalin clearly was not inclined to recommend that China not deploy its troops to come to the aid of North Korea. However, he was forced to agree to postpone a decision after Zhou laid out the difficulties that China would face if it did send troops. Mao's main objective in sending Zhou to talk with Stalin was to request Soviet air cover. Zhou, in representing Mao in the talks with Stalin, without further instructions from Mao, certainly had sufficient reason on the spot to indicate that China could not dispatch troops. Before leaving Beijing, he had discussed with Mao having Stalin guarantee the condition under which China would send troops. During the talks, however, this condition was not met. The condition was that the Soviet Union would provide sufficient air assistance, i.e., that the Soviet Air Force would assist the Chinese People's Volunteers entering the fight in Korea. But Stalin did not satisfy China's condition, that is, he did not agree to the request that he send his air force to assist the Chinese forces as they entered the Korean fight.

Had the Soviet Union previously agreed to send its air force to assist China, and had Stalin reneged on this commitment? This was the main issue in the Black Sea talks between the Chinese and Soviet leaderships, and it was a critical juncture in the bilateral alliance relationship that had only been established in February 1950.

In the Chinese Army's entrance into Korea and its engagement with the U.S. army, its most unfavorable military condition was its lack of an air force. According to Russian documents, China had raised the air issue as early as July 1950, and the two sides had exchanged views on the subject. Zhou, in a meeting with Ambassador Roshchin on July 2, asked whether the Soviet Air Force would be able to provide cover to Chinese forces that entered Korea to fight.[40]

As already noted, in response, Stalin directed his ambassador on July 5 to convey to Zhou that, "we will do our best to provide the air cover" for Chinese divisions that might fight in Korea if the enemy crosses the 38th parallel.[41]

On July 13, Stalin sent a message to Mao and Zhou through Roshchin noting that:

> It is not known to us whether you have decided to deploy nine Chinese divisions on the border with Korea. If you have made such a decision, then we are ready to send you a division of jet fighter planes – 124 aircraft for covering these troops. We intend to train Chinese pilots for two to three months with the help of our pilots and then transfer all equipment to your pilots. We intend to do the same thing with the [Soviet] air divisions in Shanghai.[42]

On July 22, Soviet Ambassador Roshchin sent a cable on behalf of Mao regarding this issue that said in part:

> We plan to deploy the [Soviet] jet fighter division that you are using to cover our forces near Shenyang, with two regiments at Anshan, and one regiment at Liaoyang. In coordination with the fighter regiments of our mixed air brigade stationed in the Andong [Dandong] region, this would help provide air cover for our military forces as well as the Shenyang, Andong, and Fushun industrial areas.

Mao added that China "would be able to [accept] the turnover of all weapons and equipment" from two Soviet air divisions before March or April 1951.[43]

On July 25, Soviet Foreign Minister Vyshinsky cabled instructions to Roshchin that, "On the authorization of Filippov [Stalin], convey to Mao Zedong or Zhou Enlai that we agree with the proposed procedure and timeline for training Chinese pilots on jet planes." Stalin sent another message for Zhou on August 27:

> The Soviet government has satisfied your request [for] Soviet military advisers – specialists in [anti-aircraft defense] and [aviation] to the eastern and northeastern [Chinese] military districts. 38 advisers will be sent to China, of which ten will be [anti-aircraft] and 28 will be [aviation] specialists.[44]

Certainly, based on the telegrams cited above, the Chinese and Soviet sides had fairly detailed discussions about Soviet assistance in setting up and training the new Chinese air force. But, while both Chinese and Soviet leaders paid a lot of attention to air issues, whether in Mao's or Stalin's messages, the issue of providing air cover for the Chinese Army's possible engagement in the Korean War was only touched on in passing and in principle.

However judged, the task of the Soviet fighter division provided to China appears to have been primarily to help guarantee air defense over Northeast China. At the time, however, the Chinese and Soviets had not clearly discussed two important points: First was the timing for the deployment of the Soviet Air Force. Would it deploy simultaneously with the Chinese military move into North Korea or let the Chinese ground forces move first? Second was the form of the Soviet Air Force assistance. Would it be coordinated with Chinese ground forces entering Korea? Would it be responsible only for the air defense of Chinese territory? Or, would it possibly also be responsible for the defense of the Chinese rear-area supply line (even inside Korea) as well?

Embodying the Soviet strategic principle of avoiding to the maximum extent possible direct military conflict with the United States, Stalin clearly preferred to put his energy into arming the Chinese air force and letting it take on the job of doing battle in Korea. Furthermore, he wanted to avoid, so far as he could, making a firm pledge on the issue of using the Soviet Air Force. China's request for Soviet air assistance was unequivocal, however, since Soviet air coordination with Chinese ground forces entering Korea was critical for China. At the time, China still did not have a substantial air force, and it realized that once the fighting started, it would be highly dependent on Soviet air power.[45]

Once the decision was made to deploy troops to Korea, Chinese commanders were again seized with the need for air cover. At an October 9 meeting of top commanders of the Chinese People's Volunteers called by Peng, many of these officers pressed the issue. As a result, while the meeting was still in session, Peng and Gao sent an urgent telegram to Mao posing some serious questions: "When our army goes abroad to fight, how many fighters and bombers can the [Central] Military Commission deploy to provide cover? When can they deploy and who will be in command?"

Many top commanders in the Chinese People's Volunteers General Headquarters argued that if Chinese troops were sent in without coordinated air support, they would be sitting ducks. At one point, Chinese commanders even proposed that,

> [T]he original plan should be implemented only if there is an assurance that, within two to three months, there will be new equipment (and especially that the air force can be deployed). Otherwise, the idea of postponing the troop deployment is well-worth considering.[46]

The air force referred to here is the Soviet Air Force – China simply didn't have an air force worthy of the name. As a result of the October 11 meeting between Stalin and Zhou, however, it was now established that the Soviet Air Force would postpone its deployment, and it was still not clear what form Soviet air assistance would take. Consequently, the initial result of the meeting between Stalin and Zhou was that, for the time being, China would not send troops to Korea.

Mao's first response was to agree with the position taken in the joint cable sent by Stalin and Zhou. On October 12, Ambassador Roshchin sent two telegrams in succession, telling Stalin that Mao had agreed not to send troops for the time being, and had already ordered the Chinese Army to "cease implementation of the plan to move into Korea."[47]

At this point, Stalin received the news of another disaster. On the morning of October 13, the Chief of the General Staff of the Soviet Navy reported that in the early hours of that day in the Far East, a massive U.S. naval flotilla comprised of a battleship, three heavy aircraft carriers, two aircraft carrier escorts, three heavy cruisers, three cruisers, 12 destroyers, a squadron of minesweepers and assault landing groups had been discovered off the northeast coast of North Korea near Chongjin, which was then under heavy bombardment from air and sea.[48]

Given the strategic importance of the Chongjin area, Stalin quickly calculated that the American military was set to carry out yet another amphibious assault. This time it was not on the Inchon–Seoul line in the southern part of Korea, but on the Pyongyang–Wonson line in northern Korea. The rear of the Korean People's Army was totally defenseless, and United Nations forces could now advance without encountering any resistance toward the Yalu and Tumen rivers on the Korean–Chinese and Korean–Soviet borders. This for Stalin was indeed a decisive turn of events.

Without the prospect of Chinese reinforcements and with the military situation now so critical, Stalin had to make a quick decision. On the afternoon of October 13, he sent a cable to Ambassador Shtykov for transmittal to Kim Il-sung, reporting on his meeting with Zhou Enlai and Lin Biao, apologetically informing Kim that Zhou had indicated that China was not yet ready to enter the war. Stalin recommended that Kim's best course would be to withdraw his remaining forces to China and the Soviet Union. Stalin instructed Shtykov to help Kim formulate the evacuation order.[49]

With Stalin's instructions in hand, Shtykov met that evening with Kim and Pak Hon-yong, reporting that, "The content of the telegram caught Kim Il-sung and Pak Hon-yong by surprise. Kim Il-sung stated that it was very hard for them [to accept] but since there is such advice they will fulfill it." Kim asked Shtykov for Soviet help in drafting a withdrawal plan. Arrangements for a withdrawal were made that evening.[50]

Moscow took another important initiative on October 13. Foreign Minister Andrei Vyshinsky, then representing the Soviet Union at the United Nations, urged the United States in a meeting at Lake Success to abandon its "get tough" policy and return to its wartime cooperation with the Soviet Union. Vyskinsky pledged that the Soviet Union would be willing to meet the United States "halfway."[51]

Just when it seemed Stalin had decided to abandon North Korea, China then came to the opposite decision.

When the October 11 joint telegram from Stalin and Zhou reached Beijing, the situation there became tense. Given the five-hour time difference between the two capitals, the telegram arrived in Beijing in the early hours of October 12. After the Soviet Embassy sent the cable to the CCP Central Committee, it reached Mao in the mid-afternoon of October 12.[52]

When Mao learned that the Soviet Union had decided not to send its air force in the near term (to support China's intervention), he sent two urgent telegrams on October 12. Mao instructed Peng Dehuai and Gao Gang in the Northeast, and Rao Shushi and Chen Yi in East China: "[F]or the time being, do not carry out the order of October 9 ... units of the 13th Army Group should remain in place and carry on with training; do not go into action...." Mao ordered Gao and Peng to Beijing for consultations.[53]

Fearing that Mao's instruction would be delayed in transmission, Acting Chief of the General Staff Nie Rongzhen hurried to the Central Military Commission War Room at 7p.m. to track down Peng Dehuai. Told by the duty officer that Peng was inspecting the Andong (Dandong) river crossing on the Yalu, Nie reached Peng by phone, telling him that the situation had changed and that he must return to Beijing for a face-to-face meeting.[54]

Peng and Gao arrived in Beijing at noon on October 13. Mao convened an emergency Politburo meeting that afternoon to discuss once again the pros and cons of sending troops to Korea. Taking the lead, Mao worked to persuade Peng and others that although the Soviet Union could not provide air support over Korea in the early stage after China's entrance into the war, Stalin had agreed to provide air cover over Chinese territory and massive amounts of military materiel to China.

The final decision of the October 13 Politburo meeting was that even without Soviet air cover in Korea in the foreseeable future, massive U.S. Army advances meant that China must send troops immediately to help North Korea, no matter what the hardships might be. The next day, Mao, Peng and Gao made a detailed study of the battle plan for the Chinese People's Volunteers once they entered Korea.[55]

Following the Politburo decision, Mao informed Zhou by telegram on October 13 that,

> As a result of discussions with Politburo comrades, we unanimously agree that it is still to our advantage to send our forces to Korea.... If we do not deploy troops, and allow the enemy to push on to the Yalu River border, domestic and international reactionary arrogance will swell, and this will be harmful on all fronts.

Since the Chinese Volunteers would not have Soviet air cover over Korea, said Mao, in the early stage of their intervention, they would only fight against South Korean forces.[56]

Mao directed Zhou to "stay in Moscow for a few days" to discuss with Soviet leaders what form the Soviet provision of military equipment would take, as well as the timing and form of any Soviet air deployment. Mao proposed that,

> If we can use the lend lease method to maintain a budget of U.S.$200 million for [domestic] economic and cultural projects and ordinary

military needs, our forces [will] go into Korea with our minds at rest, and carry out a lengthy war while we maintain the unity of most people at home. Only if the Soviet Union is able within two to two-and-a-half months to provide air assistance to our Volunteers in Korea, and also to mobilize air cover over Beijing, Tianjin, Shanghai, Ningbo, and Qingdao, can we then be free of the fear of comprehensive bombing. But, if we are hit with American bombing within those two or two-and-a-half months, we will have to endure some losses.[57]

On October 14, Mao sent another cable to Zhou, reporting on plans for the Chinese deployment to Korea, telling Zhou that the Chinese People's Volunteers would start to cross the Yalu on October 19, with all 260,000 Chinese troops scheduled to be in Korea by October 28.[58]

A day earlier, on October 13, Mao had informed Soviet Ambassador Roshchin of China's decision to send troops to Korea, again stressing their crucial need for air cover: "Past hesitations by our comrades occurred because questions about the international situation, Soviet assistance, and air cover were not clear to them." But, said Mao, the Chinese Communist leadership had decided China had "the absolute obligation to send troops into Korea." It would start with a "first echelon composed of nine divisions [which] though poorly armed, could fight against the troops of Syngman Rhee," while China prepared a second echelon.

Mao reiterated to Roshchin that, "The main thing that we need is air power which will provide us with air cover. We hope to see it arrive as soon as possible, but not later than within two months." Mao said China could not pay cash for armaments delivered and hoped to get arms on credit. Zhou Enlai, said Mao, would have to meet again with Stalin to discuss this matter.[59]

Stalin's last-minute surprise

The Chinese leaders' unilateral decision took Stalin by surprise. After receiving Mao's message, Stalin immediately instructed Ambassador Shtykov to inform Kim that,

> I have just received a telegram from Mao Zedong in which he reports that the [Chinese Communist Party Central Committee] discussed the situation [in Korea] again and decided after all to render military assistance to the Korean comrades, regardless of the insufficient armament of the Chinese troops. I am awaiting detailed reports … from Mao Zedong. In connection with this new decision … I ask you to postpone temporarily the implementation of the telegram sent to you yesterday about the evacuation of North Korea and the retreat of Korean troops to the north.[60]

After receiving another report from Roshchin, Stalin sent yet another cable to Kim noting that, "After vacillations and a series of temporary decisions, the Chinese comrades have at last made a final decision to render assistance to Korea with troops." Therefore, said Stalin, the recommendations of the Chinese–Soviet leading comrades meeting (i.e., Stalin's meeting with Zhou) were annulled. The USSR would provide armaments to China, but North Korea should work jointly with China to resolve concrete issues with respect to the entry of Chinese troops into Korea.[61]

China had taken the decision to send troops to Korea, but the issue of Soviet air cover remained under discussion. When Mao asked Stalin "to provide air assistance to our Volunteers in Korea," he was requesting Soviet Air Force coordination with Chinese ground forces entering the fight in Korea. That is to say, while Mao accepted that the deployment of the Soviet Air Force would be delayed, he explicitly raised the issue of the form that Soviet Air Force help would take when it arrived. Stalin, after getting the news that China had decided to deploy troops, clearly and carefully indicated that the Soviet Air Force would be deployed only to protect Chinese territory and the Chinese Army's rear area, and that this assistance would not be directly coordinated with the Chinese Army as it fought in Korea.

After Zhou received Mao's October 13 telegram, he met the same evening with Soviet First Deputy Premier Molotov, conveying Mao's message, and requesting it be reported immediately to Stalin. On October 14, he received two more telegrams from Mao. The first presented the latest information on the situation along both sides of the front line, and initial thoughts about what would happen after China deployed the Volunteers into Korea. Mao indicated that once the Chinese People's Volunteers reached Korea, they would organize defense of the mountains north of a line from Pyongyang to Wonson,

> to raise concern among the American and puppet armies, and then stop the forward advance.... In this way, our army will be able to avoid fighting and gain time to arm and train, to await the arrival of the Soviet air force, and only then to fight.

This telegram also again raised the issue of the need for a clear Soviet response regarding the timing and form of Soviet Air Force assistance.

Mao's next telegram, on October 14, reported on the timing and disposition of the Chinese deployment, explaining that the Chinese People's Volunteers would wait six months before advancing on Pyongyang and Wonsan. Zhou relayed the content of these two cables at once to Stalin, and Stalin had Molotov immediately inform Zhou that the Soviet Union would send its air force only to protect Chinese territory, but would not be prepared to enter the fight in Korea for at least two to two-and-a-half months.[62] It seems Stalin wanted to make sure that China's leaders were absolutely clear that Chinese forces should not count on Soviet air cover as they launched their advance. In response to the emerging situation, on October 17, Mao sent an urgent telegram ordering Peng Dehuai and Gao Gang to Beijing for talks on October 18, and to await an official order before deploying to Korea.[63]

Clearly the degree to which the Soviet Union would provide air cover and arms was an important factor in the strategic calculation of China's leaders as they decided to deploy troops to Korea. It was, therefore, a great disappointment for Chinese leaders, including military leaders about to go into a difficult fight, to learn that even after China had decided to enter the conflict, the Soviet Union had limited its air force to covering China's rear area and would not coordinate directly with Chinese forces entering the conflict.

Therefore, when we refer to Mao's and Zhou's later complaints about Soviet reluctance to deploy its air force, what we are really referring to is the fact that the Soviet Air Force would not coordinate with the Chinese ground forces entering the Korean fight. The constraints on Soviet Air Force participation in the Korean War, when it did come, meant that Soviet air cover would be limited only to protecting Chinese territory and the rear area of the Chinese and North Korean supply lines.

Thus, though Stalin had earlier indicated his willingness to provide air assistance to Chinese forces, he decided at a critical juncture to delay deployment of the Soviet Air Force, and, throughout the war, he precluded the Soviet Air Force from coordinating with the Chinese ground forces fighting U.S. forces.

To be fair, however, it would be a stretch to say that Stalin went back completely on his earlier commitment to provide air assistance to the Chinese forces. Stalin never said that he would not provide air assistance to China, but merely clarified at the last minute that this assistance would be limited to covering the Chinese rear area. This ability to walk a fine line illustrates Stalin's brilliant diplomatic tactics and slick and sly diplomatic language. On this front, the Chinese leadership clearly lacked experience. Until October 13, they had hoped for Soviet air cover. The principal aim of Zhou's last-minute visit to the Soviet Union was none other than to underscore China's central precondition for sending troops to Korea, that the Soviet Air Force support and cover Chinese ground forces entering the Korean fight. Only now, after China had decided to send troops to Korea, was the Soviet Union indicating that the type of support China desired was not on the cards. It is therefore understandable that Mao would in later years express frustration and resentment toward Stalin on this issue.

Notwithstanding the lack of forward air cover, the main force of the Chinese People's Volunteers crossed the Yalu River on October 19. On October 25, the Volunteers fought their first battle in China's "War to Resist U.S. Aggression and Assist Korea."

The push and pull of assistance

As far as assisting North Korea, Stalin asked China to send troops while Mao asked the Soviet Union to provide air support. If this can be called a behind-the-scenes contest of wills between two allies, Stalin came out ahead. At a time of great domestic economic hardship, and in an unfavorable military situation that precluded assured victory, Mao's decision to send troops into battle in Korea was not based solely on Stalin's request, but was rooted in Mao's own deep calculations. Stalin wanted at all costs to keep the Soviet Union from being drawn into an open conflict with the United States, and, at the point of danger, asked China to confront the United States in Korea. Why did Mao bend all efforts to send Chinese troops to Korea under conditions of extreme hardship?

Historians have long debated this question and deduced various theories, of which two are compelling. The first is that Mao proceeded primarily from considerations of national security.[64] To protect China's industrial base in the Northeast and to prevent the emergence of reactionary threats to its security, China was forced into a battle to keep the enemy outside China's gates. Various statements by Mao and other Chinese leaders can be adduced as evidence to support this view. The second holds that Mao, in fact, proceeded from revolutionary conviction, stoked with a strong desire and sense of responsibility to defeat the American imperialists, wanting thereby to promote revolution and raise China's international standing.[65]

These theories flow from an analysis of Sino-U.S. relations. But the issue can also be seen through the lens of Sino-Soviet relations. Though China's deployment of troops to Korea was not done merely to satisfy Stalin's request, Mao had to consider the Soviet factor.

If Kim were defeated, the threat of war would likely loom over Northeast China. Moscow's planned arrangements in the face of the worsening situation actually increased this possibility. M. V. Zakharov (Matveev), head of the Soviet military delegation in Korea, had recommended that Kim move his remaining military forces across the Yalu to Northeast China, and reorganize them there with the intent of reentering Korea. When Stalin met Zhou, he accordingly proposed that the North Koreans make an organized withdrawal, taking their main forces, arms, materiel and officials into Northeast China so they could more easily reenter Korea. Stalin even told the CCP Central Committee that he wanted Kim to organize a government-in-exile in Northeast China.[66]

If the war expanded, Northeast China would become a battleground between China and the United States. Mao would of course calculate that if the United States invaded China, the Sino-Soviet Treaty of Friendship, Alliance and Mutual Assistance would require that Stalin send several hundred thousand troops from the Soviet Far East into Northeast China to help China fight off the invaders.

Stalin, in the October 1 telegram to Mao quoted above, had made it quite clear that if the war expanded, based on the Sino-Soviet alliance, the Soviet Union would join in the war. Mao could not forget that in 1945, Stalin had used the excuse of fighting Japan to send troops into Northeast China, and thereby had forced Chiang Kai-shek under duress to sign a treaty that injured China's interests. Mao also could not forget that the leaders of New China (the People's Republic of China) had carried out very difficult negotiations with the Soviet Union concerning Northeast China, with the return of the Changchun Railway, Lushun and Dalian as stipulated in the new Sino-Soviet treaty having been gained only with great effort on China's part, like "taking meat out of a tiger's mouth." If the war spread to China, and the Soviet Union again sent troops into the Northeast, this region would either be occupied by the United States or controlled by the Soviet Union. That is to say, whether the war resulted in victory or defeat, China would not be able to prevent the compromise of its sovereignty in the Northeast. The only way to prevent this eventuality was to stop the war outside of China's borders.[67]

Based on an analysis of China's strategy in deploying troops to Korea, in the early stages of the Korean War, Sino-Soviet alliance relations clearly were complex and delicate, reflecting the respective national security and economic needs of the two countries. After the Soviet Union entered the Cold War and fixed on a basic strategy of all-out contention with the United States and the West, it needed an Eastern power like China to provide a security screen in the Far East, and to act as a proxy to test U.S. policy and strength. Therefore, Stalin was not forced to accept China's prerequisite (and, as it turned out, maximum) demand for sending troops to Korea. On the contrary, at a time when Stalin thought that Soviet strength was insufficient to engage the United States in an open and direct military conflict, this is precisely when he needed China to take the lead in opposing the United States, to draw in and exhaust the United States in Asia. As Moscow saw it, this was China's duty as an ally.

China on its side faced serious disadvantages. The country, just (re)established by the Chinese Communist Party, was poor and backward. Facing imperialist hostility and pressure, China had to rely on the strength of the socialist Soviet Union. It was on this basis that Mao decided to establish an alliance with the Soviet Union. Now, in a situation in which American troops were closing in on China's northeastern border, China could rely only on Soviet military and economic assistance to resist U.S. encroachment and defend its national security interest.

Mao's precondition for sending forces to Korea to fight against the United States was that he had to receive a Soviet guarantee of military assistance. However, Stalin's objectives and strategy during the war made it impossible for him to fully satisfy China's requests for military aid, especially for air support in the fight with the U.S. Thus, while there was a unity of interest on the issue of the Korean War between Beijing and

Moscow, there were clear differences and contradictions regarding their objectives and demands.

Mao's final decision to send forces to Korea resolved a crisis in the just formed Sino-Soviet alliance, and gained China the initiative in relations with the Soviet Union. Still, though Sino-Soviet disagreements and contradictions remained, once China sent its forces to fight in Korea, harmony and cooperation were the main trends in Sino-Soviet alliance relations.

9   A new stage in Sino-Soviet cooperation

Stalin long had strong doubts about Mao Zedong and the Chinese revolution, as is well known. He thought Mao was not a real Marxist, suspected China had ulterior motives for aligning with the Soviet Union and feared it might take the "Titoist" road. These doubts influenced Stalin's behavior when faced with the question of whether China would send troops to Korea. Mao in his turn had to make a very tough call, as Stalin's reaction signaled that the Chinese Army would go into Korea without Soviet air cover over its fighting front. In the end, Mao's decision to send the Chinese People's Volunteers into Korea had a significant impact on Stalin's thinking.

Chinese leaders understood what was on Stalin's mind. Zhou Enlai once said that, "[Stalin] changed his views at the time of the War to Resist America and Assist Korea."[1] Mao also thought that, "one of the main reasons Stalin came in some measure to trust the CCP" was "the outbreak of the Korean War and the participation of the Chinese People's Volunteers."[2] Genuine cooperation between the Soviet Union and China as allies started only after China deployed its forces to Korea. During the Korean War, the Soviet Union and China increased their mutual trust and understanding – at the very least at the level of Stalin and Mao. Russian historian D. Volkogonov has concluded that, "The Korean War undoubtedly strengthened Stalin's confidence in Mao, thereby putting Sino-Soviet relations on a positive footing as a whole."[3]

Soviet air cover arrives earlier than promised

Stalin reacted unexpectedly after Mao decided to send Chinese troops into Korea, ordering the Soviet Air Force to cover the Chinese forces' rear area and transport routes, rather than delay for another two months. There are still no documents available bearing directly on Soviet air deployments, but it appears that in early November 1950, less than two weeks after the Chinese Army entered Korea, elements of the Soviet Air Force joined the fight in the sky over the Chinese–Korean border. Based on interviews with Soviet personnel who participated in the Korean air war, British journalist Jon Halliday has described in some detail the Soviet Air Force entrance into the war and its engagement with the U.S. Air Force.

According to Halliday, "MiG-15s piloted by Russians apparently first entered the Korean theater in early November 1950," though sources "do not agree whether they first entered combat in early November 1950 [the predominant view] or mid-January 1951." However, one "well-informed" source told Halliday that, "The first MiG appeared over Korea on 1 November 1950; the first all-jet air battle was on November 8." Another source claimed that the first jet air battle occurred in late November, without giving an exact date. Lt. Gen. G. A. Lobov, Commander of the Soviet 303rd Air Defense Division, stated in his memoir that he went to Sinuiju, in North Korea, "literally the day after a huge U.S. air raid." There was a huge air raid on Sinuiju (across the Yalu River from China) on November 8, so it appears that Lobov was in China by the first week in November.[4]

A newly declassified report sheds some further light on the issue. According to a November 2 war situation report to Stalin from Col. General S. E. Zakharov, the Soviet military adviser in China, the first air clash in the Korean War occurred on November 1, 1950. On that day, eight Yak-9s of the North Korean air group "went into battle for the first time" in the Anju region, reportedly downing two U.S. B-29s and a Mustang. Two Yak-9s did not return from their mission. Soviet planes joined the fight in the Andong–Sinuiju (Dandong–Sinuiju) area.

> Two F-82 planes were downed by our pilots in Mig-15s and two planes were brought down by antiaircraft artillery. In all, four planes [were downed]. We had no [Soviet] losses in the air battle … MiG-15s of Comrade [General] Belov flew from airbases at Shenyang and Anshan. In all, eight sorties were made from each airport.[5]

For Stalin, the issue of air support was extremely sensitive. But by engaging Soviet air assets in combat a week after the Chinese People's Volunteers officially entered the war on October 25, albeit only in the rear area, Stalin showed he was determined to support China. Later, as the war developed, in response to China's request, the Soviet air contingent was strengthened. One week after the outbreak of the air war in Korea, Stalin decided to send 120 MiG-15 fighter jets to China to reinforce General Belov's air force. Mao was very grateful, noting that "over the last twelve days" Soviet pilots had "downed 23 invading American planes."[6]

Since Chinese rear-area supply lines were severely disrupted by enemy aircraft, logistics for the Volunteers became very difficult. On February 23, 1951, Zhou Enlai, Nie Rongzhen and Peng Dehuai asked Soviet military adviser General S. E. Zakharov to redeploy two air divisions from north of the Yalu River to cover Chinese transport lines north of the 38th parallel.

When Zakharov refused, Peng was extremely unhappy; on February 25 and 28, he approached Mao, asking him to appeal directly to Stalin.[7]

As a result, on March 1, Mao sent a long, brutally frank telegram to Stalin arguing that,

> The difficulty we are facing now in the Korean War is that the enemy holds an advantage in fire power, and our transportation capability is weak. Since we have no air cover, under enemy bombing we are losing 30–40 percent of the materiel shipped to the front.... In Comrade Peng Dehuai's opinion, it would be advisable if Soviet airmen took responsibility for covering airfields north of a line between Pyongyang and Wonsan. At the same time, it would be advisable if Soviet airmen were redeployed from their current airfields to airfields in Korea.... If this is not done, it will be impossible to repair the airfields on the territory of Korea, Chinese airmen will not be able to join the battle in Korea, and it will be extremely difficult to move tanks and guns. The resolution of this issue, however, needs to be decided with a view to the overall international situation. Therefore, we do not know if this is possible.[8]

Stalin, now not as irresolute as he had been, immediately cabled back that,

> If you are able to leave two Chinese air force divisions in the Andong [now Dandong] area to cover the electric power station and the supply line there, we agree to transfer the 151st and the 324th fighter divisions under the command of General Belov to Korean territory to cover the Chinese and Korean rear area. If the Koreans have a metal runway, we can supply two more runways from the Soviet Union.... If you agree, we can supply you with anti-aircraft guns and ammunition to protect the airfields.[9]

On March 15, Stalin, via S. E. Zakharov, reminded Mao and Zhou that he had agreed earlier to deploy two Soviet Air Force divisions to Korea "in the rear of your troops, but with the condition that two Chinese fighter divisions be placed in the Andong [Dandong] region to cover this area." However, said Stalin,

> [W]e now see that in view of forthcoming major operations, you will need the largest possible aviation force at the front. We have therefore decided to send to Andong from the USSR an additional fighter division so that the two Chinese fighter divisions designated to cover Andong can be sent to the front for use in operations there.[10]

Yet, with work to restore North Korean airfields repeatedly disrupted, Soviet Air Force units that fought in rear areas of the Korean theater never had the option of garrisoning in North Korea. At first, Soviet air units were garrisoned in China at Andong, across the Yalu River from North Korea, but, in July 1951, these units moved to Miaogou, about 20 km west of Andong. Then, since both Andong and Miaogou (in China) were vulnerable to American attack, Dapu airfield, situated further inland in China, was built and Soviet units moved there in 1952.[11] Clearly, however, Stalin's views with respect to use of Soviet air power had gone far beyond his initial caution, a step that would not have been possible without trust and confidence in Mao and the Chinese Army.

During the Korean War, Lobov's 64th Air Defense Corps rotated twelve divisions through the conflict, with the number of planes rising to about 150 by late spring 1951. About 75 percent of these planes were operational at any one time. Also attached to the 64th Air Defense Corps in theater were two anti-aircraft divisions, including fixed units along the Yalu River and mobile units inside North Korea. Altogether, 72,000 Soviet airmen cycled through combat tours during the Korean War, with 26,000 participating in the peak year of 1952.[12]

Of the 1,600 to 1,700 U.S. and allied planes reported lost to "enemy action" or "combat," Russia claims credibly to have downed over 1,300 in aerial combat and by ground fire and anti-aircraft artillery, while China claims only 330 aerial combat "kills." However, as pointed out by Halliday, there are problems with these numbers, as there are with American estimates of total Communist losses. If Russian claims that they lost only 345 planes in aerial combat and to a few other hostile acts are correct, then the vast majority of "Red" planes lost in combat were Chinese and North Korean.[13] The scope and results attained by the Soviet Air Force in aerial combat indicate that the Soviet Union participated strongly throughout the Korean War. However, in a curious case of double deniability, the Soviet Union and the United States both remained silent about Soviet involvement in the air war over Korea.[14]

Despite Stalin's actions to cover the Chinese and North Korean rear areas, he made it clear to his military advisers in China that he was committed to not deploying the Soviet Air Force on the front lines in Korea. He chided another Soviet military adviser in China, Marshal Krasovsky, as well as General Belov about the slow training of Chinese pilots: "You and General Belov apparently intend to make professors rather than battle pilots out of the Chinese pilots." Noting that Chinese troops would not fight without air cover, Stalin instructed his generals to:

[C]reate more quickly a group of eight Chinese fighter divisions and send them to the front. This is now your main task.... It is necessary to arrange matters so that the Chinese rely only on their own aviation at the front.[15]

Soviet Air Force officers who participated in the Korean War have confirmed that, "there was no coordination between their air units and

Sino-Korean ground forces," let alone with the joint Chinese–North Korean air command. One Soviet pilot recounted that, "[T]he Chinese, who had no experience in aerial combat, asked [us] to 'protect' them on their first missions [but] we declined." General Lobov asserted in an interview that, "We did not have one bomber. Nor did we have even one bomb [with which] to bomb U.S. ships. Not that it was our task." Ace Soviet aviator Pepelyayev, another Korean War veteran, confirmed that, "the Russians did not fly bombers in combat – and did not intend to."[16]

The Chinese air force: trouble getting off the ground

Chinese documents also show that most air combat during the Korean War occurred in the border areas between the Yalu and Chongju Rivers and the Yalu and the Taedong Rivers. The main task of the nascent Chinese air force as well as the Soviet Air Force was to cover transportation corridors and restoration work on airfields, along with hydroelectric generation facilities, the Yalu River bridges, transportation lines to the front and the area north of the Chongju River. Uniquely, the Chinese Eighth Air Division flew two bombing runs in November 1951 to support a ground operation against U.S. and South Korean forces manning an intelligence station on Taehwado Island off the Korean west coast. (Soviet advisers to the Eighth Division had returned home before this air action.)[17]

Despite Chinese actions, Stalin never satisfied Beijing's initial (pre-intervention) request, that the Soviet Air Force and the Chinese Army coordinate their actions. However, Chinese leaders later expressed their understanding and never raised the issue again. In every post-intervention cable Mao sent asking for Soviet Air Force assistance, he was always careful to note only that he needed Soviet air cover for Chinese rear-area communications and transportation. His cautious wording in the introduction to these cables indicates his wariness of raising this issue, showing that he truly understood the difficult position in which Stalin found himself. This indicates that the two allies, China and the Soviet Union, had a tacit understanding that, in actual combat, there could be no military cooperation between their forces.

This is of course not to say there were no differences of opinion between China and the Soviet Union during the Korean War. Differences arose over specific orders in the course of military campaigns and over the use of specific tactics, but Stalin and Mao were able to exchange opinions candidly, fostering the resolution of issues between them.

Mao's obsession: mobile warfare

Mao's experience in the Chinese civil war left him with the *idée fixe*, that, when it came to issuing military orders, mobile warfare could overwhelm an enemy's combat strength. Results in the early stage of the Korean War strengthened Mao's belief in the efficacy of mobile warfare and, even as the war stalemated, he still advocated strongly for mobile warfare.

On May 26, 1951, Mao sent a message to Chinese People's Volunteers Commander Peng Dehuai. After noting that it was proving difficult to annihilate a U.S. division or even a regiment by outflanking and surrounding it, Mao advised that, "You should not be overly ambitious in every battle. It is enough to ask every Chinese division to annihilate one or two whole U.S. or British battalions in each battle." "In the past, fighting against Chiang Kai-shek's New First Army, New Sixth Army, Fifth Army, Eighteenth Army, and the Guangxi Seventh Army, we proceeded in stages from this kind of small-scale to large-scale annihilation of the enemy." Mao at the same time advocated mobile warfare tactics to lure the enemy into a trap: "[A]s for the place of battle, if the enemy is willing to advance, the farther north the better, as long as the enemy does not go beyond the Pyongyang–Wonsan line."[18]

Stalin's warning: the Americans are not foolish

When Mao shared this view with Stalin, Stalin suggested a different idea, telling Mao,

> In my view, the plan you outlined in your cable is risky and can only be successfully employed once or twice.... The British and Americans will easily guess at such a plan, and will therefore change their tactics; you will not be able every time to draw their main force north without suffering losses.... Besides this, you need to consider that when the British and the Americans push north, they will establish new defense lines, one by one. Therefore, whenever you need to go on the offensive, it will be hard to break through the British and American defense lines without incurring massive losses, which, of course, is not desirable.... It is not convincing to argue by analogy to Chiang Kai-shek's army. First, you are now facing a different army, and, second, there is no basis to believe that the British and American armies are as foolish as Chiang Kai-shek, and that they will allow you your choice of annihilating their whole army one battalion at a time.

Finally, Stalin reminded Mao that, "If Pyongyang should fall again into enemy hands, not only would the morale of the Korean people and the [North] Korean army plummet, this would also raise British and American morale."[19]

Mao accepted this advice, and from then on the fighting settled into a pattern of positional warfare. Until this point, exchanges between Stalin and Mao were cautious, indirect or tentative, reflecting the lingering suspicion and lack of mutual understanding that still existed between them.

But, on this one occasion, Stalin was able candidly to advance a contrary point of view, indicating a turnabout in his view of Mao, a shift toward enhanced confidence.

Mao also showed growing trust in and respect for Stalin. Russian documents reveal that throughout the war, from the fighting to the peace talks, from military strategy to operational instructions, and even on specific tactical and logistical issues, Mao sought and respected Stalin's advice.

Chinese and Soviet leaders put special emphasis on firming up Sino-Soviet friendship and bilateral relations. For instance, in a January 4, 1951 message to all party bureaus and military districts, Mao praised the CCP Northeast China Bureau's December 29, 1950 telegram instructing its branches to promote good relations with Soviet Army personnel stationed in the Northeast. Mao advised that, "All places with Soviet Army personnel should adopt this attitude."[20]

As PLA General Ye Jianying told A. M. Malukhin, the Soviet Consul in Guangzhou:

> Our Chinese Communist Party Central Committee has no secrets from the [CPSU] CC. I have worked in Shanghai, Yan'an and other places in north China, and I know this is the only view among the CCP leadership. I often take part in meetings of the CCP CC Politburo, so I know that the Politburo never adopts any resolutions behind the back of the Bolshevik [Soviet] Party Central Committee. Only the [CPSU] and the Soviet Union can and right now are providing friendly assistance to China. Naturally, therefore, the CCP and the PRC leadership must report on the true conditions in China to the Soviet party and government. Correct policies and friendly actions on the part of the Chinese are most important for the Chinese people and for Soviet friendship. This is Mao Zedong's viewpoint.

Ye Jianying then cited this anecdote:

> In 1950, a leading comrade in the Chinese leadership complained to Mao Zedong about friction with a Soviet comrade in Beijing. In reaction, Mao Zedong reminded the Chinese leader that if relations with the Soviet side suffered a downturn, whatever the situation, the Chinese Communist Party Central Committee would in the first instance regard this as the fault of the Chinese leader.[21]

This is not to say that bilateral relations were without friction during the Korean War. The two sides diverged on issues of national interest, especially evident, for example, with regard to rubber cultivation. Rubber, which Stalin termed "liquid gold," was a vitally needed strategic material in the Soviet Union. Owing to the economic embargo imposed by the Western powers, Stalin repeatedly proposed that China, on its own or in cooperation with the Soviet Union, cultivate rubber in southern China through a Sino-Soviet joint stock company. Mao was adamantly opposed. He told Stalin that,

> After repeated investigation into this issue, we have concluded that we urgently need Soviet specialist and technical assistance, but, under present Chinese conditions, it would be inappropriate to form a Sino-Soviet joint stock company to develop rubber.

Mao suggested that the Soviet Union provide a loan and that China could repay the loan in the form of more than 50 percent of the rubber produced, with the price set below the world market price.[22]

In September 1952, when Zhou Enlai went to Moscow to sign an agreement on the Chinese supply of rubber, Stalin said in their meeting that,

> We would like to receive from you 15 to 20 thousand tons of natural rubber each year. You, it seems, object, citing difficulties. The fact is that we have a tremendous need for natural rubber, since automobiles and trucks, which are also being sent to you, require large amounts of rubber.

When Zhou indicated that he was unable to guarantee such a large request, Stalin said that, as long as China supplied the maximum amount that it could, the language of the agreement could be softened. However, if China were not able to supply this amount of rubber, the Soviet Union would have to cut the Chinese truck order.[23]

Nevertheless, there were few conflicts of this period, since China depended predominantly on its Soviet ally for wartime military and economic assistance, and Stalin actually provided a huge amount of assistance to China.

Massive Soviet military assistance to China

In a significant way, China's simple act of sending troops to Korea bolstered the Soviet Union's strategic objectives and interests in the Far East. Stalin was very clear on this point. However one looked at it, the Soviet Union had a duty to support Chinese troops engaged in a life-and-death struggle on the battlefield. Stalin indeed carried out this duty.

And China needed the help. In weaponry alone, it was impossible for China to meet the needs of this kind of modern war solely on its own. China was not even up to the task of supplying enough ammunition. In the first quarter of 1951, for instance, Korean battlefields required more than 14,100 tons of ammunition; China's own arsenals could produce only about 1,500 tons. Only the Soviet Union was capable of meeting China's gaping need.[24] Stalin basically satisfied the battlefield needs of Chinese forces, and, especially before the start of armistice talks, he supplied virtually everything China requested. Documents in the Russian archives reflect this situation.

On October 28, 1950, shortly after entering the conflict, Mao asked the Soviet Union to supply various naval weapons, including high-speed torpedo boats, floating mines, armored ships, small patrol boats, minesweeping equipment and coastal artillery, and proposed that PLA Navy Commander Xiao Jingguang travel to Moscow for talks on supply of these arms, as well as plans to create the future Chinese navy. Stalin cabled his agreement the next day.[25]

On November 17, Zhou Enlai reported to Stalin that, "A new operation will begin soon. Railroad bridges across the Yalu are under daily enemy air bombardment." In view of this situation, as well as the critical loss of Chinese vehicles to bombing, Zhou asked Stalin to order the Soviet Army on the Liaodong Peninsula to transfer immediately 500 automobiles for Chinese Army use. Stalin answered on the same day:

> In order to speed up the transfer of the automobiles to you, orders have been given to our military command not to give you old automobiles from Lushun, but to send new automobiles to the Manzhouli [border] railroad station, transferring to Chinese representatives 140 automobiles on November 20 and 355 automobiles on November 25–26.

He promised that another 1,000 automobiles would reach Manzhouli before December 5.[26] Within days of Zhou's request for 15 Soviet military advisers to help establish a PLA air force group being formed to take part in Korean operations, the Soviet leader informed Zhou on February 16, 1951 that he would be sending military aviation advisers "who know China and are familiar with the air war in Korea."[27]

To strengthen the air combat capability of the Chinese People's Volunteers, Stalin also proposed to provide gratis a large number of new-type aircraft. In a May 22, 1951 message he informed Mao that

> The air war along the Manchuria–North Korea border has finally convinced us that if MiG-15 jet fighters are put in the hands of outstanding aviators, they are completely capable of going up against the best American and British jet fighters, and, especially bombers.
>
> Up until now, you have received ten fighter aircraft divisions from the Soviet Union, six of which are MiG-9 fighter divisions and four of which are MiG-15 fighter divisions. In order for Chinese fighter aviation to become more militarily capable, you should replace the MiG-9 fighters with MiG-15 fighters. To do this, we have to send you 372 MiG-15s from the Soviet Union. Since we do not have enough aircraft, until now, it has not been possible to do so, but now we can do this.

We plan to provide these 372 MiG-15s to you free of charge, with payment only for the cost of shipping from the Soviet Union, which can be paid by military credit. As for the MiG-9s that you have, you can keep them for your large-scale training of jet aircraft aviators, or you can use them in combat against bombers and other not very modern fighters. Your pilots who already know how to fly MiG-9s can easily learn to master MiG-15s; it takes ten days or less for us to do this in the Soviet Union.

We have made the following plan to send these 372 planes to China: the first batch of 72 planes will be provided to you before June 20; other batches will arrive in succession, so that by early August you will have all 372 aircraft.[28]

Several days later, Stalin further explained this decision to the Chinese:

We Russians made a mistake: Originally we thought that the MiG-9 fighter would be more than competitive against the best Anglo-American jet fighters. Now, after air combat over North Korea, everything has become clear. The significance of this error is that, if we do not correct it, this will harm the air defense of China. Since the responsibility for this error rests entirely with us – the Russians – we must remedy this error, replacing the MiG-9 fighters with MiG-15 fighters at our expense, that is, with no cost to China. Since we believe strengthening the air defense of our ally, China, is our goal, we cannot do otherwise. As for the MiG-9 fighters you now have, we originally were going to bring them back to the Soviet Union. But since you now need them much more than we do, we have decided to leave them at your disposal. Let this reciprocate the help you gave us in purchasing natural rubber.[29]

This move by Stalin showed the sincerity of the Soviet Union in its capacity as ally, and Mao was appreciative. Judging by the exchange of telegrams between the Chinese and Soviet leaders, alliance relations were clearly strengthened through mutual assistance and cooperation.

Of course, negotiations between China and the Soviet Union over military assistance were not without conflicts and differences. Especially after the war entered the stalemate stage of "fighting while talking," and Mao was still asking the Soviet Union for large-scale provision of equipment, Stalin seemed to believe that Chinese military assistance requests were no longer totally necessary or urgent.

On May 25, 1951, during the latter stage of the fifth Chinese battle campaign of the Korean War, Mao sent a delegation to Moscow co-led by Gao Gang and PLA Chief of the General Staff Xu Xiangqian to negotiate the purchase of Soviet arms for 60 divisions. According to the telegram sent after the initial discussions between Xu and the Soviet General Staff, the

Soviets maintained that, of the quantity of arms needed for these 60 divisions, they could provide arms for only 16 divisions (including arms for three Korean divisions) in 1951; the arms for the remaining 44 divisions would be provided during 1952 and 1953.

Mao, extremely unhappy with this news, sent a message to Stalin on June 21, 1951 stating that,

> Our troops' eight months of experience in conducting war in Korea has clearly shown the great difference in the equipment of our troops and the troops of the enemy, and the extreme necessity of improving the equipment of our troops. This is why we commissioned Comrade Gao Gang to appeal to you with a request for delivery to us of arms for sixty divisions, to which you had agreed. This is the minimum requirement for our troops in Korea for the present year.

After spelling out his sharp disappointment with the message conveyed by the Soviet General Staff in talks with Chinese representative, Mao implored Stalin to reconsider:

> [To satisfy] the urgent needs of the Korean theater of military operations, I ask you to study the applications transmitted by Comrade Gang ... and explore the possibility of fulfilling all deliveries of rifles, artillery, tanks, airplanes, automobiles ... and other military equipment, at 1/6th [of the total] monthly, from July to the end of the year, so that the various military units in the Korean theater ... receive replenishment ... for the conduct of military operations.[30]

In response, Stalin told Mao that,

> As concerns arms for 60 division then I must say to you directly that to fulfill this application in the course of a single year is physically impossible and altogether unthinkable. Our production and military specialists consider it completely impossible to provide arms for more than ten divisions in the course of 1951. The fulfillment of the application is possible, and that with great difficulty, only in the course of 1951, '52, '53, and the first half of '54, that is, over three years. Such is the final opinion of our production and military specialists. I have tried in every way to shorten these periods even if by half a year, but unfortunately, upon examination it has turned out that this is impossible.[31]

Negotiations started in early June and stretched through the end of October. Under the agreement, the Soviet Union agreed to supply equipment for 16 divisions during 1951, with the Soviet Union to supply equipment for the remaining 44 divisions only by 1954, at the rate of one-third of the remaining 44 divisions equipped every year.[32] Through April 1952, however, the Soviet Union actually supplied equipment for only four divisions, most of which would go to the Korean People's Army. Objectively speaking, however, when Stalin cited Soviet production difficulties, he was telling the truth, while Mao's insistence on the urgent need for this equipment was designed to modernize China's military.

During the Korean War, Chinese forces were rotated into the Korean battle reequipped and redeployed with complete sets of Soviet equipment. Wang Yazhi, an adviser in the War Bureau of the Central Military Commission and a secretary to Peng Dehuai, has recounted the situation in considerable detail.[33] In the early 1950s, according to Wang, China had 106 army divisions, of which 56 were equipped according to Soviet Army strength, that is, the equipment that was discussed for 60 divisions during the war, (including equipment for three divisions that was donated to the Korean People's Army and equipment for one division that was distributed to Chinese military schools for training purposes). Another 50 Chinese divisions were outfitted with domestically produced copies of Soviet military equipment.

As for the 56 divisions outfitted completely according to the Soviet Army's organizational table, every division (14,963 men) had three infantry regiments, an artillery regiment, a tank and self-propelled cannon regiment, an independent anti-aircraft artillery battalion and an independent 57 mm anti-tank battalion. Each of the 12 battalions of the artillery regiments was equipped with a 122 mm howitzer, a 76.2 mm field gun, and a 120 mm mortar; the tank and self-propelled cannon regiment received 24 T-34 tanks and 16 76 mm self-propelled artillery pieces; the independent anti-aircraft artillery regiment equipment consisted of 12 37 mm artillery pieces; and the independent anti-tank battalion equipment consisted of 12 57 mm anti-tank guns. Each division had 13,938 infantry weapons, 303 guns, 261 cars, 84 special vehicles, 517 horse wagons and 1,136 horses. These forces were garrisoned principally in China; only three of these Soviet-rearmed divisions made it to the Korean front. The main reason was that the equipment arrived late, and, by the time all of the 56 Chinese divisions were reequipped with Soviet arms, the war was almost over. The second reason was that Soviet military equipment was not well suited to the mountainous battle conditions in Korea.

As for armor, once the Chinese People's Volunteers entered the Korean War, in November 1950, the Soviet Army honored a Sino-Soviet agreement by dispatching ten Soviet tank and self-propelled cannon regiments to China to establish and train Chinese tank and armored units. A force of ten regiments established by China received Soviet equipment and training from its Soviet counterparts; its equipment consisted of 300 T-34 light tanks, 60 IC-2 heavy tanks and 40 ICU-122 self-propelled artillery pieces. China used this equipment to organize three tank divisions each with two regiments (along with an additional motorized infantry regiment and an artillery regiment), three independent tank regiments and a base training regiment.

And, as for anti-aircraft artillery, China used 37 mm guns provided by the Soviet Union to organize 101 independent anti-aircraft artillery battalions, of which 53 battalions engaged in combat in Korea; 40 more battalions were placed in air defense artillery divisions and regiments protecting various large Chinese cities; four battalions were placed in tank divisions; and four battalions were placed on naval bases. Additionally, there were five field anti-aircraft artillery divisions and one urban defense anti-aircraft artillery division. Twenty-four regiments were equipped with 85 mm anti-aircraft artillery guns, and 14 regiments were equipped with 76.2 mm anti-aircraft artillery guns. All of these forces saw service in the Korean War.

The Chinese Army in the 1950s also used Soviet artillery equipment to arm two rocket divisions (nine regiments), fourteen howitzer divisions, two anti-tank artillery divisions, thirty-three anti-aircraft artillery regiments, four searchlight regiments, one radar regiment and eight independent radar battalions.

Chinese engineering troops used Soviet construction equipment and floating bridges to equip 28 engineering regiments, of which 13 fought in Korea. Ten Chinese railroad divisions served in Korea. Along with other railway personnel, they totaled over 150,000 men. Their engineering equipment was basically all purchased from the Soviet Union.

Communication and anti-chemical weapons equipment was also purchased from the Soviet Union and used in communication and anti-chemical weapons elements throughout the Chinese Army.

Through early 1954, China stood up 28 air divisions and five independent air regiments with over 3,000 airplanes, all purchased from the Soviet Union.

Sino-Soviet discussions regarding Soviet assistance to China's navy were plagued by financial and technical issues, and went very slowly. The Korean War was almost over before the first bilateral naval agreement, "The Agreement on Providing Naval Equipment and Technical Assistance in the Construction of Military Vessels," was signed.

Not all arms provided by the Soviet Union were modern and advanced. Some arms were surplus American lend lease materiel given to the Soviet Union during World War II. Soviet-provided naval ammunition, for instance, was limited to U.S.-made 76.2 mm coastal guns.

In May 1952, the Chinese Military Arms Industrial Commission decided to produce 18 types of standard weapons. Three were to copy American designs and fifteen were to be produced using Soviet blueprints. Later that year, the Soviet Union sent experts to China with blueprints, but it later came out that the Soviet blueprints were for weapons no longer in Soviet production.

In August 1952, Peng Dehuai went to Moscow to discuss strengthening Chinese air forces. When Peng asked the Soviet Union to provide modern

Ilyushin-28 bombers, Stalin enthusiastically agreed, but with the condition that China also buy 120 of the older Tu-4 bombers, enough to equip four air divisions. Because it lacked sufficient funds to do so, China bought only ten of the TU-4s, which, it turned out, were about to be phased out in favor of the newly developed Tu-16 bombers.

China used U.S.$20 million of a U.S.$3 billion Soviet loan to buy a fleet of fast torpedo boats. However, the life of their overhauled main engines was less than half that of new engines. Similarly, two submarines and four destroyers later purchased for the Chinese Navy were also second-hand. In the end, however, the Soviet Union was the only country able to provide military assistance to China, and Soviet assistance undeniably enabled the Chinese Army to achieve the results it did on the Korean battlefield.

Sino-Soviet economic relations take off

Sino-Soviet economic relations took off during the Korean War, even as China's engagement in the conflict exacerbated its already difficult economic conditions. In September 1952, Zhou Enlai informed Stalin that China's military expenditures as a percentage of the total state budget had risen from 44 percent in 1950 to 52 percent in 1951.[34] The U.S. and Western economic embargo of China had also greatly harmed China's economic development. Between the end of 1950 and July 1951, for instance, the prices of imported raw materials and equipment generally doubled, with some prices quadrupling, while China's exports plummeted.[35] As Zhou laid out to Soviet Ambassador Roshchin, China's state finances were extremely tight, and China remained hobbled by a severe shortage of technical personnel.[36]

The Soviet Union provided massive assistance to China, playing a major role in China's economic revival. In 1950, China asked the Soviet Union for more than 280 million U.S. dollars worth of equipment related to metallurgy, mining, transportation, energy production, and metal rolling and milling, all needed to revive China's economy, and available only from the Soviet Union. The Soviet Council of Ministers approved the shipment of over U.S.$135 million worth of these goods to China, simultaneously importing over U.S.$150 million worth of goods from China.[37]

The volume of Sino-Soviet trade, valued in 1949 at U.S.$26,300,000, increased nine-fold to U.S.$241,900,000 in 1950. Sino-Soviet trade, which was ranked third in China's overall trade volume in 1949, jumped to first place in 1950.[38] The Soviet Union sold China vital industrial inputs, including machinery, tools, petroleum and steel, all at prices below international market prices.

In this period, the Soviet Union sent a large number of economic experts and technicians to China, and hosted a large number of Chinese personnel for study in the Soviet Union. At the outset of the Korean War, the Chinese government asked the Soviet Union to extend for another year the term of 126 Soviet experts then working in China. At the same time, it asked the Soviet Union to host a group of 133 Chinese economic specialists (along with 33 interpreters) for a three- to six-month study tour. Both Chinese requests were granted. By March 1952, there were 332 Soviet advisers and instructors and 471 Soviet technical experts in China. When some of these experts went back to the Soviet Union, on September 21, 1952, Zhou Enlai asked Soviet Deputy Prime Minister Molotov to send 239 more to China in 1952 and 1953.[39] These Soviet experts played important roles in China's economic development.[40]

In sum, the Korean War did not merely strengthen Sino-Soviet military cooperation, it also strengthened and increased bilateral economic cooperation. As noted by Professor Arne Westad, China's performance in the war deeply impressed Stalin, leading him in his waning years to think seriously about taking the Sino-Soviet alliance to a higher level through economic and technical cooperation.[41]

Fighting without break: "Politics demand we break through the 38th parallel"

From the day the Chinese People's Volunteers crossed the Yalu River until the armistice was signed, Mao and Stalin shared a fundamental common understanding of the war situation and strategic policy. As a result, though they may have started from different vantages, they readily reached common views on some of the most significant wartime questions.

Shortly after the Chinese People's Volunteers entered Korea, they carried out two very successful mobile warfare campaigns, not only liberating Pyongyang, but also pushing the front lines near to the 38th parallel. At this point, sharp differences arose on the Chinese side over whether immediately to launch a third campaign to advance south of the 38th parallel. As the Commander in Chief at the front, Peng Dehuai argued that his army was exhausted after two campaigns, with a rising number of sick personnel and an urgent need for rest and replenishment. Logistical supply was intermittent, most of the army lacked winter clothes, and ammunition and grain were not getting through in sufficient quantities. As the Chinese forces advanced, moreover, these problems would worsen. As a consequence, Peng recommended delaying a third campaign until February–March 1951.[42]

When the Chief of the PLA General Staff, General Nie Rongzhen, read Peng's December 8 telegram conveying his request to rest his troops, Nie agreed that after more than two months of continuous fighting, the Chinese Army was exhausted, the loss of materiel and equipment was enormous, and the need for rest and replenishment was urgent. Moreover, in terms of the number of troops on the front line, the Chinese Army no longer outnumbered its foes. Therefore, Nie asked Mao to delay the next campaign for two months.[43]

Mao disagreed, however, and strongly advocated a third campaign immediately to break through the 38th parallel. In a December 13 telegram to Peng, Mao argued that,

> At present, the United States, Britain, and other countries are demanding that our army stop north of the 38th parallel, in order to put all their forces in a better position to continue fighting. Therefore, our army must cross the 38th parallel. If it stops north of the 38th parallel, this will be politically extremely disadvantageous.[44]

After he received Mao's telegram, Peng and the Chinese People's Volunteers headquarters staff agreed to discard their original plan to rest and reorganize over the winter. Instead, they resolved to confront and overcome their soldiers' extreme fatigue, their lack of sufficient troops and supplies, and other difficulties, and to launch a third campaign to fight across the 38th parallel. As Peng summed up the situation,

> Now, since the political situation demands that we fight, and since Chairman Mao Zedong has ordered that we fight, and since we really will face a lot of hardships when we fight, therefore we must be extremely prudent and know when and where to stop. Politics demands that we break through the 38th parallel. Therefore, we will resolutely push forward. Afterwards, we will adopt a policy of steady advance.[45]

On December 19, Peng replied to Mao:

> As I see it, the Korean War will be relatively long and hard. The enemy has turned from offense to defense, and the United Nations' combat forces have an advantage as the battlefront has shrunk, their armed forces are concentrated, and they have developed in depth. While American and puppet army morale is lower than it was before, they still have 260,000 men under arms. Looked at politically, it would be very bad for its camp if the enemy were to leave Korea precipitously. If two or three more of their divisions are annihilated, maybe they will withdraw and defend a few bridgehead positions, but they cannot immediately withdraw completely from Korea. Our army now should still advance steadily, so as not to undermine the vitality of our forces. My telegram to you of the 8th proposed, for the time being, we not fight across the '38th parallel,' in order to replenish our equipment and get ready to resume fighting next spring. After receiving your reply cable of the 13th, I have obeyed your instruction to fight across 'the 38th parallel.' Barring some unforeseen event, we cannot be defeated, but there exists the possibility that our attack will be blunted or our victory limited.[46]

Just before Mao's exchange with Peng, Stalin and Mao had come to a tacit understanding on whether or not to cross the 38th parallel. On December 4, the Soviet Union offered its own somewhat tendentious view. In a conversation with Deputy Foreign Minister Gromyko, Chinese Ambassador Wang Jiaxiang probed Soviet views about whether the Americans, under then existing conditions, might engage in talks on the Korean question with China and the Soviet Union. Gromyko replied that, at the time, the U.S. had had not proposed to settle the Korean situation peacefully. Following up, Wang Jiaxiang asked: "Looked at from a political viewpoint, if it can continue to advance successfully, should the Chinese military cross the 38th parallel?" Gromyko replied that, "In the present situation in Korea, the old adage 'strike while the iron is hot' is quite apt." Wang indicated he shared that opinion. Though Wang and Gromyko had both stated at the outset that their conversation was unofficial and merely reflected their personal views, they were clearly feeling each other out on the suggestions and reactions of their leaders.[47]

On December 5, 11 Asian and African countries, including Burma, Egypt and India, urged Chinese and North Korean military forces not to cross the 38th parallel; the United Nations, led by Britain, India and other countries, was simultaneously probing China's conditions for a ceasefire. In order to keep the initiative and appear positive, the Chinese government drew up five conditions for an armistice: All foreign military forces should withdraw from Korea; the U.S. military should withdraw from the Taiwan Strait and Taiwan; the Korean issue should be resolved by the Korean people themselves; the representative of the People's Republic of China should join the United Nations, replacing Chiang Kai-shek's representative; and the foreign ministers of the four great powers should convene a conference to prepare a peace treaty with Japan. Mao did not forget to check with the Soviets before issuing these conditions. Mid-afternoon on December 7, Zhou Enlai called in Ambassador Roshchin, handed him the Chinese conditions for ceasefire talks and said:

> [B]efore we send the present conditions for a cessation of military operations in Korea, the Chinese government wishes that Wu Xiuquan [the head of China's special delegation to the UN] consult with the government of the USSR and asks the Soviet government to express its opinion on this question.

Zhou asked to receive a Soviet answer the same day.[48]

The Soviet government replied immediately, indicating it "completely agree[d] with [China's] conditions for a ceasefire in Korea," adding that, "without the satisfaction of these conditions military action cannot be ceased." At the same time, the Soviet Union cautioned that, "while Seoul is still not liberated the time has not arrived for China to show all its cards," but rather that China should insist that the United Nations and the

United States first put forward their conditions.[49] Also on December 7, in order to coordinate the Soviet position with the Chinese proposal, the CPSU Politburo instructed the Soviet UN delegation to add two conditions to the Soviet ceasefire proposal, drawing on the Chinese conditions, namely, "The immediate withdrawal of all foreign troops from Korea" and "The resolution of the Korean question must be left to the Korean people."[50]

Against this background, Mao could not agree to Peng's recommendation to temporarily halt the Chinese advance. Clearly, when Mao referred to "politics" in his telegram, he was not only speaking of Britain and the United States, he was also referring to preserving the interests of the Soviet Union, North Korea and other socialist countries. As Mao said in a December 29 cable,

> [If] our army spends the whole winter resting and reorganizing without acting, this will spur a lot of speculation in the capitalist countries, and, in the countries in the democratic front, some will disapprove, leading to a lot of debate.[51]

China's volunteers run out of steam

While the third campaign ultimately achieved a degree of success, the Chinese People's Volunteers were by then a spent force. During the fighting, there was a planned withdrawal of United Nations forces. Thus, while Chinese and North Korean military forces occupied some territory, they inflicted no great damage to the enemy's combat strength.[52] Since there was no letup in the difficulties facing Chinese forces, after they broke through the 38th parallel and captured Seoul on January 8, Peng ordered that the People's Volunteers, which had been fighting continuously since entering Korea three months earlier, stop, rest and reequip. This time Mao and Stalin supported Peng's decision.

The North Koreans and Soviet advisers in China, however, all strongly opposed Peng's order to stop the advance. On the afternoon of January 9, the chief Soviet military adviser in China, Col. General Zakharov, came to the war room of the PLA General Staff. When he learned that the campaign had been ended and the forces in Korea had halted their advance, he expressed dissatisfaction and incomprehension, saying that it was unheard-of for victorious forces not to pursue the enemy and exploit the fruits of victory. Peng's order gave the enemy breathing space and forfeited the chance to achieve a decisive victory, complained Zakharov. Even after hearing PLA Chief of Staff Nie Rongzhen's painstakingly detailed description of the hardships faced by the Chinese People's Volunteers, Zakharov held to his opinion.

In Pyongyang, Kim Il-sung, together with the new Soviet Ambassador, Lt. General V. N. Razuvaev, also vigorously advocated that the Chinese

People's Volunteers continue to advance south. Kim and DPRK Foreign Minister Pak Hon-yong sought an immediate meeting with Peng, at which they expressed strong unhappiness with his decision to halt the advance of the Volunteers. They then complained directly about Peng to Mao and Stalin. But when these differences reached the top levels in China and the Soviet Union, the dispute was smoothed over by Mao and Stalin; Stalin said Peng was correct.[53]

At the same time, however, Stalin also recommended that to avoid international censure, the Chinese People's Volunteers could stay north of the 38th parallel and let the Korean People's Army advance south. When Kim again demanded that time for rest and reorganization be shortened and the southward advance continued, Mao cabled Peng suggesting that the Korean People's Army be put on the front line south of the Han River, while the Chinese Volunteers withdrew to Inchon and north of the Han River to rest and regroup. Mao noted that the Korean People's Army's advance south could be commanded by the North Korean government, while the Chinese People's Volunteers took the responsibility of defending Inchon, Seoul and the area north of the 38th parallel.[54]

Since North Korea's army was not able to penetrate deeply into enemy territory on its own, Kim in the end had to accept Peng's position. On January 14, Mao cabled instructions to Peng and Kim (with a copy to Stalin) ordering a two–three month period of rest and reorganization in preparation for launching a new spring campaign (April–May) to finally resolve "the South Korean question." Without such preparations, warned Mao, "[W]e can repeat the mistakes committed by [North] Korean troops in the period from June to September 1950."[55]

Only the concerted efforts of the Chinese and Soviet leaders resolved the difference in views between the Chinese and North Korean frontline commanders and forged unity of purpose. Nevertheless, Mao and Stalin agreed only to a temporary rest and reorganization period; they did not advocate a complete halt in the advance. Their joint strategic goal was to drive the American army out of South Korea, though realization of this goal was actually no longer within their grasp.[56] Thus, when the United Nations Tripartite Korean Ceasefire Committee plan was adopted by the United Nations General Assembly on January 13, 1951, the Chinese government rejected it outright.

UN ceasefire proposal: U.S. reluctantly agrees, China says no

The UN Tripartite Korean Ceasefire Committee proposed a five-step process: a ceasefire; a political conference to restore peace; a multi-stage withdrawal of foreign armed forces and the election by the Korean people of a unified government through appropriate mechanisms; arrangements for management of a unified Korea; and a quadripartite post-ceasefire conference of Britain, the United States, the Soviet Union and Communist

China to resolve a basket of Far Eastern questions, including Chinese representation in the United Nations and the status of Taiwan.

This new UN plan, shared only a few hours in advance with the United States, put Washington in a bind. As Secretary of State Acheson put it:

> The choice whether to support or oppose this plan was a murderous one, threatening on one side, the loss of the [South] Koreans and the fury of Congress and press and, on the other, the loss of our majority in the United Nations.

In deciding to support the UN proposal, the State Department "did so in the fervent hope and belief that the Chinese would reject it (as they did) ...."[57] Put in the position opposite to that of the United States, had China accepted this proposal, it would have come out ahead one way or the other. As Korean War historian Chen Jian has put it, an immediate ceasefire would have allowed the Chinese People's Volunteers to remain legally in all the areas they had occupied to the south of the 38th parallel, and, even if the ceasefire had failed, they would have had precious time to rebuild their potential for advance.[58]

Pressure grows on Chinese and North Korean Forces

Just as Chinese and North Korean forces entered a period of rest and reorganization, the new Commander of United Nations Forces, General Matthew Ridgeway, launched a large-scale advance, putting the Chinese People's Volunteers and the Korean People's Army in a very difficult position. While not surprised by the enemy advance, Chinese People's Volunteers Commander Peng was caught off balance by the speed of the enemy's quick turnaround after its hasty retreat in the face of his earlier advance.

Top Chinese and North Korean commanders met to analyze the situation. They decided that Chinese and North Korean forces still urgently needed to rest, recuperate and reequip before continuing the fight. After consultation with the North Koreans, Peng cabled Mao on January 27 proposing that, in reaction to the UN Tripartite Ceasefire Commission plan,

> [T]o increase dissension among the imperialist countries, perhaps news could be spread that the Chinese and [North] Korean armies support a limited ceasefire, and the [Korean] People's Army and the [Chinese] Volunteers have withdrawn 15 to 20 kilometers north of a line between Osan, Taepyongri, and Tangu. If you agree, please spread this news from Beijing.[59]

But Mao was still fairly optimistic. On January 28, he ordered Peng to halt rest and reorganization and continue to push southward. Mao demanded that,

Our troops must immediately prepare for the fourth campaign, with the goal of destroying 20,000–30,000 American and [South Korean] puppet soldiers and occupying the area to the north of a line between Taejon and Anto. In preparing for this campaign, it is necessary to hold Inchon, the bridgehead position on the south side of the Han River, and Seoul, and lure enemy's forces into the Suwon–Inchon area. After the campaign starts, North Korean and Chinese forces must break through the enemy's defensive line near Wonju, and advance toward Yongsong and Anto.

Continuing, Mao stressed that,

The withdrawal of Chinese and North Korean troops 15–30 kilometers to the north and release of a statement in support of a temporary ceasefire would be disadvantageous, since the enemy clearly wants to cease military operations only when our troops withdraw some distance to the north and he can blockade the Han River.

Mao instructed Peng to explain this strategy at a commanders meeting, in preparation for a fourth campaign. Mao then reported his decision to Stalin, seeking his reassurance that "this is advisable from the point of view of the international situation." Stalin backed up Mao, assuring him that, "From the international point of view it is undoubtedly advisable that Inchon and Seoul not be seized by the enemy."[60] Later facts show that, under the conditions at the time, there was absolutely no way to achieve the goal of a fourth campaign as envisioned by Mao.

Stalemate: the war that wouldn't end

Ultimately, after fighting near the 38th parallel stalemated, efforts by Mao and Stalin led to a proposal for an immediate ceasefire by Soviet United Nations representative Jacob Malik.

Mao grasped the tremendous hardships faced by the Chinese People's Volunteers only after an early 1951 face-to-face meeting with Peng. After the meeting, Mao told Stalin that,

Unless the enemy suffers massive losses, it will not withdraw from Korea, and to inflict massive losses on the enemy will take time. Therefore, the Korean War will likely be prolonged.... Under these circumstances, our army is planning to let the enemy advance to the area south and north of the 38th parallel, and proceed with a new, powerful campaign only after the arrival of our second echelon of nine armies of the Volunteers.

Mao continued:

[A]s long as the United States continues to fight, and the U.S. Army continues to receive massive supplies and prepare for a long war of attrition against our forces, our forces must be ready for a long war. In several years, and only after our forces eliminate hundreds of thousands of Americans, will they know real pain and withdraw. Only then will we resolve the Korean question.

Stalin responded to Mao's assessment, with the two coming to a common understanding.[61] In the fighting after this point, the Chinese People's Volunteers stopped the American advance near the 38th parallel, but only at the cost of huge sacrifices in dead, wounded, captured and missing in action.[62]

At the end of May 1951, at Mao's direction, the Chinese Communist Party Central Committee undertook a thorough review of China's strategic position in Korea. Nie Rongzhen summed up the process and results in his memoir:

After the Fifth Campaign, the Central Committee met to consider what the next step should be. Most of the comrades present at the meeting felt that our forces should stop in the vicinity of the 38th parallel, continue fighting [in place] during the armistice talks, and strive to settle the issue through negotiations. I, too, agreed with this. In my opinion, by driving the enemy out of northern Korea, we had achieved our political objective. Stopping at the 38th parallel, which meant a return to the 'status quo ante,' would be easily acceptable to all quarters.

After discussion, the meeting fixed on the policy advocated by Nie and most of his Central Committee "comrades."[63]

"Talking and fighting"

On June 3, 1951, Kim Il-sung arrived in Beijing. Following talks between the Chinese Communist Party Central Committee and the North Koreans, the two sides reached broad strategic agreement. The agreed strategy was to end the war through negotiations while preparing to fight a longer war.[64] However, in deciding how to implement this strategy, hard questions remained concerning how to finance frontline operations and how to confront "a possible enemy landing on the sea coast in our rear." To resolve these issues, Mao asked Stalin to receive Kim and Gao Gang, along with Lin Biao, who was then recuperating in the Soviet Union. With Stalin's agreement, Kim and Gao flew to Moscow for these discussions.[65]

Stalin had already begun to think about peace talks. In early May 1951, Soviet Representative at the United Nations Malik and Deputy Representative Semyon Tsarapkin contacted some Americans and revealed the Soviet desire to hold peace talks. On May 18, George Kennan, a U.S. diplomat and Soviet expert then teaching at Princeton, was called to Washington to meet with Secretary of State Acheson, where he was given the task of meeting with Malik. In a June 5 (second) meeting with Kennan, Malik said that the Soviet Union wanted a peaceful resolution of the Korean question as rapidly as possible, but it could not properly take part in ceasefire talks. If Kennan wanted his personal opinion, said Malik, he thought the United States should contact the North Korean and Chinese governments. Kennan noted that Malik did not refer at all to any wider Far Eastern international issues, such as Taiwan or a Japanese peace treaty. While the U.S. State Department apparently had trouble fathoming Moscow's intentions, Malik's formulation clearly indicated that the Soviet Union was promoting peace talks without the conditions earlier advanced by China.[66]

After their talks with Stalin, Kim and Gao reported to Mao on June 13.[67] The same day, Stalin told Mao that, "We [three] agreed that an armistice is now to our advantage."[68] Mao immediately (on June 13) conveyed to Gao and Kim several thorny political questions related to armistice negotiations. The two shared Mao's observations with Stalin on June 14:

> Concerning how to raise the question of negotiations about an armistice, we consider it inadvisable for Korea and China ... to advance this question at this time since the Korean army and the Chinese volunteer troops must occupy a defensive position for the next two months.
>   It is better to act in this way:
>
> 1   Wait for the enemy to make an appeal.
> 2   It is hoped that on the basis of what was said by Kennan, the Soviet government would make an inquiry to the American government about an armistice.
>   It is possible to bring this about in two ways simultaneously, namely that from one side the Soviet government makes an inquiry, and from the other – if the enemy puts forth the question of an armistice, then Korea and China will express their agreement to this. We ask you to share opinions about which is more advisable and decide with Comrade Filippov [Stalin].
> 3   Conditions for the armistice: restoration of the border at the 38th parallel; apportion from both North Korea and South Korea an insignificant strip [to serve] as a neutral zone. A proposal that the neutral zone come only from the territory of North Korea will by no means be accepted. North and South Korea [should not] interfere with one another.
>   As concerns the question of the entrance of China into the UN, we consider it is possible not to raise this question as a condition, since China can refer to the fact that the UN has in fact become

an instrument of aggression, and therefore China does not at the present time attach a special significance to the question of entrance into the UN.

You must think about whether it is worth raising the question of Taiwan as a condition. In order to bargain with them, we consider that this question should be raised.

If America firmly insists that the question of Taiwan be resolved separately, then we will make a corresponding concession.[69]

As noted above, Soviet Representative Malik had told the Americans through Kennan that the Soviet Union was not in a position to propose truce talks. However, since the United States and China were both unwilling to take the initiative to start peace talks, Stalin finally decided that the Soviet Union, after all, had to make a proposal. On June 23, in a radio address at the United Nations, Soviet representative Malik proposed that both sides to the Korean conflict agree to an immediate ceasefire. The U.S. confirmed that Malik's statement represented the official Soviet position in a June 27 meeting between U.S. Ambassador to Moscow Alan Kirk and Soviet Deputy Foreign Minister Andrei Gromyko. On June 30, the United Nations Military Commander, General Ridgeway, made a ceasefire proposal in a radio broadcast.[70] On July 1, China and North Korea responded positively to Ridgeway's proposal. From this point on, the Korean War entered a long and bitter stage of "talking and fighting."

If there had not been this kind of tacit cooperation between Stalin and Mao, that is, if Stalin had maintained the firm position that the Soviet Union could not make a proposal on the question of peace talks, the stalemated war would have gone on, and the conditions facing the North Korean and Chinese armies would have become even more difficult.

On June 24, the day after Malik's radio address, Stalin sent a message to Mao to make it clear that the new Soviet position was a positive move that respected China's views: "You must already know from Malik's speech that we have fulfilled our promise to raise the question of an armistice."[71]

In a June 30 message to Stalin, Mao acknowledged that, "Malik's statement secured us the initiative in the matter of conducting peace negotiations." At the same time, while accepting the U.S. proposal that two military representatives from each side should participate in ceasefire negotiations, Mao proposed to Stalin that, "If negotiations begin, it is extremely necessary that you personally lead them, so that we do not find ourselves in a disadvantageous position."[72] Later, in fact, though Stalin did not directly coordinate the Chinese and North Korean sides during the ceasefire talks, it is obvious from Russian documents that cables flew back and forth between Moscow and Beijing during the negotiation process, and that Stalin approved every concrete measure adopted and every plan decided.

There are two important examples of this dynamic. In January 1952, when the peace talks fell into stalemate, North Korean Foreign Minister Pak Hon-yong told Chinese Commander Peng that, "the Korean people throughout the country demand peace and do not want to continue the war." At this point, however, Mao held that it would be impossible to yield under then unfavorable conditions. Stalin supported Mao and worked with him to convince Kim Il-sung.[73]

Later, ceasefire negotiations dragged on over the prisoners-of-war exchange issue, which was of more concern to China than to North Korea. On July 14, 1952, Kim wrote to Mao arguing that they should accept American conditions in order to achieve a quick ceasefire. Mao replied on July 15 that,

> [A]fter two days study ... our comrades unanimously consider that, at present, when the enemy is subjecting us to furious bombardment, accepting a provocative and fraudulent proposal from the enemy, which does not signify in fact any kind of concession, is highly disadvantageous for us.

Rejecting the enemy proposal, argued Mao, "will bring only one harmful consequence – further losses for the Korean people and the Chinese People's Volunteers." However, "the people of China and Korea, especially their armed forces, have [been] tempered ... in the struggle against American imperialism." Meanwhile, argued Mao, the war was sucking American strength in Asia, giving the Soviet Union time to build the world revolutionary movement, and delaying "a new world war."

Mao pledged to do all in the power of the Chinese people "to overcome the difficulties of the Korean people," and told Kim that, "If we are not able to resolve your questions, then we will together with you appeal to Filippov [Stalin] with a request to render assistance for the resolution of these questions." Kim accepted China's view in a July 16 reply cable to Mao, telling Stalin the same day that,

> In Kaesong, we must ... work to speed up the signing of an armistice, implement a ceasefire, and exchange prisoners of war based on the Geneva Convention. This demand will be supported by all peace-loving people, and will get us out of the passive position in which we find ourselves in Kaesong.[74]

In a July 17 message to Mao, Stalin threw his support behind Mao's position: "We believe your position in the negotiations on an armistice to be completely correct. Today we received a report from Pyongyang that Comrade Kim Il-sung also agrees with your position."[75] On August 20, in talks between Stalin and Zhou, when Zhou reviewed the differences between China and North Korea on the prisoners-of-war issue, Stalin indicated again that,

Mao Zedong is right. This war is getting on America's nerves. The North Koreans have lost nothing, except for casualties that have suffered during the war. Of course, one needs to understand Korea – they have suffered many casualties. But we have to explain to them that this is an important matter. They need patience and lots of endurance.[76]

The Korean endgame and beyond

In sum, from the entrance of Chinese troops into Korea until Stalin's death in March 1953, Chinese and Soviet leaders, especially Mao and Stalin, closely coordinated their steps and views on all the important issues regarding the war in Korea.

Stalin died while the military conflict and the peace talks in Korea dragged on. If Stalin's decision to take military action in Korea was the last major decision of international consequence in his life, then Mao's decision to send the Chinese military to Korea was the first major decision of the new Chinese republic that he had proclaimed on October 1, 1949.

Cooperation between the Mao and Stalin on the Korean War established a foundation for the further broad development of Sino-Soviet alliance relations in the early years after the founding of New China. At the same time, several factors – the Soviet Union's political and economic strength, Stalin's prestige in the international communist movement and within the Chinese Communist Party itself, and Stalin's rapier-like diplomatic skills – put Mao in a passive, subordinate position. In time, these looming factors played a subtle role in the ultimate decline of the Sino-Soviet alliance relationship.

After Stalin's death, the Soviet Union's new leaders changed its foreign policies to favor more accommodation and détente with the West. Although Mao probably favored a harder line, he had to follow the changing views of the new Soviet Union leaders[77] and, in July 1953, the protracted and difficult Panmunjom armistice talks finally concluded, ending the Korean War. Sino-Soviet relations entered a new stage, characterized at first by apparent harmony, but over the course of the 1950s, by growing sub-surface tension and finally open discord.

Notes

The endnotes to this edition are based on the endnotes in the first Chinese edition (2003) and additional footnotes in the second Chinese edition (2007) of this work, but there are several changes that should benefit readers of this English-language edition.

When the author cited Chinese translations of English-language primary sources or secondary material, the translator has found and cited the primary source or secondary material in English. Thus, for instance, citations from the *Foreign Relations of the United States* (*FRUS*) series, a compilation of U.S. diplomatic records, appear as they are in the *FRUS* series. Similarly, whenever possible, the translator has found and cited Russian primary source and secondary material when the author cited Chinese translations of such material.

The author placed copies of Russian primary source documents used in his first edition in the Peking University Contemporary History Research Centre, the Chinese University Research Service Centre in Hong Kong, and the Academia Sinica Modern History Research Institute in Taipei.

The vast majority of these documents are available abroad in English translation or as copies of the original Russian archive documents. Most are accessible on the Wilson Center's Cold War International History Project (CWIHP) digital archive website (www.wilsoncenter.org/program/cold-war-international-history-project). These documents are indicated by the abbreviation "CWIHP," as are CWHIP Working Papers that are also available on this site. The translator has often adapted CWIHP translations. The abbreviation "NSA" indicates referenced Russian documents that are available at the National Security Archive in Washington, D.C.

A number of other Russian documents cited by Shen were published in Russian journals, sometimes in English translation in *Far Eastern Affairs*, the sister publication of *Problemy dal'nego vostoka*, both then published by the Institute of the Far East in Moscow, and sometimes in Russian in *Problemy dal'nego vostoka* or other Russian journals. When English translations of such documents were available, the translator cited these translations, sometimes adapting them slightly for orthographic or other reasons.

Note abbreviations

APRF   *Arkhiv prezidenta Rossiskoi Federatsii* (Russian Presidential Archive).

AVPRF   *Arkhiv vneshneii politiki Rossiskoi Federatsii* (Russian Foreign Policy Archive).

CWIHP   Cold War International History Project at the Woodrow Wilson Center for International Scholars, Washington, D.C.

FRUS   *Foreign Relations of the United States*, Washington, D.C.: U.S. Government Printing Office, various years.

NSA   National Security Archive at the Gelman Library of The George Washington University, Washington, D.C.

RGASPI   Rossiiskii gosudarstvennyi arkhiv sotsial'no-politicheskoi istorii (Russian State Archive of Socio-Political History). Including former RTsKhIDNI (Russian Centre for the Preservation and Study of Documents of Recent History) and TsPA (CPSU Central Committee Archive).

Introduction

1 Adapted with permission from Yang Kuisong, "Sidalin weishenme zhichi Chaoxian zhanzheng – du Shen Zhihua zhu *Mao Zedong, Sidalin yu Chaoxian zhanzheng*" (Why Did Stalin Back the Korean War? On Reading Shen Zhihua's *Mao Zedong, Stalin and the Korean War*), *Ershiyi shiji* (Twenty-first Century), February 2004. Yang's review critiques the 2003 edition of Shen's book. Yang is professor of history at Peking University and Shanghai's East China Normal University, where he is also Director of the Institute of Contemporary Studies. He is the author of *Mao Zedong yu Mosike de enen yuanyuan* (Mao Zedong and Moscow – Gratitude and Enmity), Jiangxi renmin chubanshe, 1999.

2 Shen Zhihua first published the results of his research on the Korean War outside mainland China. Shen Zhihua, *Chaoxian zhanzheng jiemi* (Unveiling the Secrets of the Korean War), Hong Kong: Tiandi tushu youxian gongsi, 1995.

3 Khrushchev's Talk with a Chinese Party Delegation, June 22, 1960, in "Mao Zedong yu waibin de tanhua huibian" (Compendium of Discussions between Mao Zedong and Foreign Guests). (Unpublished manuscript held by Yang Kuisong).

4 Telegram from Stalin to Mao, May 14, 1950. APRF, fond 45, opis 1, delo 331. list 55.

5 See Chapter 2, p. 41.

6 See Chapter 6, pp. 117–18.

7 See Chapter 6, p. 118.

8 In an extensive untranslated appendix to this book, Shen adduces mountains of information on Soviet military and economic assistance to China during and after the Korean War. Other extensive appendices, none of which are translated here, describe the clash of interests during negotiation of the 1950 bilateral treaty between China and the Soviet Union, Soviet air cover during the war and political considerations of both countries during the process of reaching a ceasefire in Korea.

9 The major exception, of course, was North Korea (see below), where the Soviets had nurtured the Korean Workers' Party and the North Korean regime in the occupation period, and over which Moscow continued to exercise unique influence and ultimate control.

10 The Eurocentric Cominform (Communist Information Bureau) was set up by Stalin in September 1947 after the U.S. announcement of the Marshall Plan in May 1947 revealed fissures between Moscow and some Eastern European capitals. The Cominform was an instrument of Soviet control over Eastern European communist parties and regimes and influence over key Western European communist parties.

11 Report in *Renmin ribao* (People's Daily), January 11, 1950, p. 1.

12 "Ribenren jiefangbde daolu" (The Road to Japanese Liberation), *Renmin ribao*, January 17, 1950.

13 Conversation between Stalin and Mao, Moscow, December 16, 1949. APRF, fond 45, opis 1, delo 329, listy 9–17. CWIHP. See Chapter 5, p. 92.

14 See Chapter 6, p. 116.

15 Telegram from Shtykov to Vyshinsky regarding meeting with Kim, May 12, 1950. AVPRF, fond 059a, opis 5a, delo 3, papka 11, listy 100–3. CWIHP.

16 For an account of Soviet suspicions of possible sensitive leaks from within the Chinese Communist Party leadership, see "Mikoyan's Secret Mission to China in January and February 1949," *Far Eastern Affairs*, 1995, no. 3, pp. 75–6.

17 I. V. Kovalev, "Dialog Stalin s Mao Tsedunom" (Stalin's Dialogue with Mao Zedong), *Problemy dal'nego vostoka* (Problems of the Far East), 1991, no. 6.

18 Telegram from Shtykov to Vyshinsky, May 15, 1949. NSA. See Chapter 6, p. 126.

19 Telegram from Shtykov to Vyshinsky regarding meeting with Kim, May 12, 1950. AVPRF, fond 059a, opis 5a, delo 3, papka 11, listy 100–3. CWIHP.

1 Stalin: from Yalta to the Far East

1 Robert Conquest, *Stalin, Breaker of Nations*, New York: Viking Penguin, 1991, pp. 278–81. R. C. Raack, *Stalin's Drive to the West, 1938–1945: The Origins of the Cold War*, Stanford, CA: Stanford University Press, 1995, pp. 165–7.

2 Odd Arne Westad, *Cold War and Revolution: Soviet–American Rivalry and the Origins of the Chinese Civil War, 1944–46*, New York: Columbia University Press, 1993, p. 118. Vladislav Zubok, "Stalin's Goals in the Far East: From Yalta to the Sino-Soviet Treaty of 1950," Paper for the International Conference on "The Cold War in Asia," Hong Kong, January 1996.

3 Elliot Roosevelt, "A Personal Interview with Stalin," *LOOK*, vol. 11, no. 3 (February 4, 1947), p. 22.

4 Felix Chuev, *Molotov Remembers: Inside Kremlin Politics*, ed. by Albert Resis, Chicago: Ivan R. Dee, 1993, p. 8.

5 J. V. Stalin, *Works*, Moscow: Foreign Language Publishing House, 1952–55, vol. 12, pp. 261–2. Quoted from "Political report of the Central Committee to the Sixteenth Congress of the C.P. S. U. (B.), June 27, 1930," which appears on pp. 242–385.

6 Speech delivered by J. V. Stalin at an election meeting in the Stalin Election District, Moscow, February 9, 1946, in *THIRTY YEARS OF THE SOVIET STATE: CALENDAR: 1917–1947*, Moscow: Foreign Languages Publishing House, 1947. In February section (pages unnumbered).

7 J. Stalin, *Economic problems of socialism in the U.S.S.R.*, Moscow: Foreign Language Publishing House, 1952, p. 39.

8 Bruce Kuniholm, *The Origins of the Cold War in the Near East: Great Power Conflict and Diplomacy in Iran, Turkey, and Greece*, Princeton, NJ: Princeton University Press, 1980. Natalia I. Yegorova, "The 'Iranian Crisis' of 1945–1946: A View from the Russian Archives," CWIHP Working Paper no. 15 (1996).

9 Stalin explained the reason for the Soviet withdrawal from Iran in a letter to Ja'afar Pishevari, head of the Democratic Party of Azerbaijan. While using a lot

of high-sounding language, Stalin indicated that he hoped to trade Soviet withdrawal from Iran for American (and British) withdrawal from other world areas, thereby preserving Soviet–U.S. parity and cooperation. AVPRF, fond 06, opis 7, papka 34, delo 544, listy 8–9. Cited in Yegorova, "The 'Iranian Crisis,'" pp. 23–5.

10 L. Ia. Gibianskii, "Kak voznik kominform: po novim arkhivnim materialam" (How the Cominform Emerged: According to New Archival Material), *Novaia i noveishaia istoriia* (Modern and Contemporary History), 1993, no. 4, pp. 134–8.

11 This report was actually written at the direction of Foreign Minister Vyacheslav Molotov. According to Ambassador N. V. Novikov's memoir, "This report can only be regarded as written by me in a qualified sense," and Molotov was the unnamed co-author. See N. V. Novikov, *Vospominaniia diplomata: zapiski, 1938–1947* (Reminiscences of a Diplomat: A Memoir, 1938–1947), Moscow, Izdatel'tsvo politicheskoi literatury, 1989, p. 353. For an English translation, see "The Novikov Telegram: Washington, September 27, 1946," *Diplomatic History*, 1991, vol. 15, no. 4, pp. 527–37. (This translation includes Molotov's underlinings and marginal notes on what was likely a pouched report, rather than a telegram. This issue of *Diplomatic History* includes commentaries by George Kennan and others on the origin of this analysis. Kennan speculates that Novikov's report possibly was drafted to share with and to influence governments under Soviet control in Eastern and Central Europe as well as to strengthen Molotov's hand in foreign policy debates in Moscow. See pp. 539–63, and especially 539–40).

12 Soviet press reaction to the Truman Doctrine was relatively mild. While *Novoe Vremia* (New Times; no date given) criticized the speech and its support for the "fascist" Greek and Turkish regimes, accusing the U.S. of seeking world hegemony, it predicted that "more far-sighted and circumspect people" in the U.S. would not support the Truman Doctrine. The Soviet Consul in New York claimed that the Truman Doctrine "provoked a serious wave of dissatisfaction among the populace." He estimated that "70–80 per cent of the American people are opposed to granting aid to Greece and Turkey for the reasons given by Truman," since they feared the Truman plan "could lead to war between the Soviet Union and the United States." AVPRF, fond 0129, opis 31, papka 192, delo 12, list 19. Cited in Scott D. Parrish and Mikhail M. Narinsky, "New Evidence on the Soviet Rejection of the Marshall Plan, 1947: Two Reports," CWIHP Working Paper no. 9 (1994), p. 12.

13 Parrish and Narinsky, "New Evidence: Two Reports."

14 Parrish and Narinsky, "New Evidence: Two Reports," pp. 25–32, 49–51.

15 Gibianskii, "Kak voznik kominform," p. 142. For an analysis of the Soviet–Yugoslav conflict, see Shen Zhihua, *Sidalin yu Tietuo: Su Nan chongtu de qiyin ji qi jieguo* (Stalin and Tito: The Origin and Consequences of the Soviet–Yugoslav Conflict), Guangxi shifan daxue chubanshe, 2002.

16 RGASPI (TsPa), fond 77, opis 3, delo 90, list 11. Cited in Gibianskii, "Kak voznik kominform," p. 139.

17 See Shen Zhihua: "Gongchandang qingbaoju de jianli ji qi mubiao" (The Founding of the Cominform and its Goals), *Zhongguo shehui kexue* (Social Sciences in China), 1992, no. 3, pp. 172–87. See also Gibianskii, "Kak voznik kominform," and Parrish and Narinsky, "New Evidence: Two Reports," esp. pp. 4–5.

2 Korea – the evolution of Soviet postwar policy

1 For a discussion of this process, see Shen Zhihua, "Sulian chubing Zhongguo dongbei: mubiao he jieguo" (The Soviet Armed Intervention in Northeast China: Aims and Consequences), *Lishi yanjiu* (Historical Research), 1994, no. 5.

2 For more on the origin of the 38th parallel, see Shen Zhihua, "Sanbaxian de youlai ji qi zhengzhi zuoyong" (The Origin and Political Function of the 38th Parallel), *Shanghai shifan daxue xuebao* (Journal of Shanghai Teachers University), 1997, no. 4.

3 Message from Truman to Stalin, August 15, 1945; Message from Stalin to Truman, August 16, 1945; and Message from Truman to Stalin, August 18, 1945, in Ministry of Foreign Affairs of the USSR, *Stalin's Correspondence with Roosevelt and Truman 1941–1945*, New York: Capricorn Books, 1965, pp. 261–7.

4 Joseph C. Goulden, *Korea: The Untold Story of the War*, New York: Times Books, 1982, p. 20.

5 FRUS, *1945*, vol. 6, p. 1039.

6 Lee Chong-sik, "Why Did Stalin Accept the 38th Parallel?" *Journal of Northeast Asian Studies*, Winter 1985, vol. 4, no. 4.

7 Milovan Djilas, *Conversations with Stalin*, translated by Michael B. Petrovich, New York: Harcourt Brace and World, 1962, p. 114.

8 Message from Stalin to Truman, August 16, 1945, in *Stalin's Correspondence*, p. 266.

9 Message from Truman to Stalin, August 18, 1945, in *Stalin's Correspondence*, p. 267.

10 Message from Stalin to Truman, August 22, 1945, in *Stalin's Correspondence*, pp. 267–8. Douglas MacArthur, *Reminiscences*, New York: McGraw-Hill, 1964, pp. 326–7.

11 FRUS, *Conferences at Malta and Yalta, 1945*, pp. 770, 858.

12 Harry S. Truman, *Memoirs of Harry S. Truman: Volume One, Years of Decision*, Garden City, NY: Doubleday and Company, 1955, p. 265.

13 In reading hundreds of pages of Soviet documents in the Russian archives, Korean War scholar Kathryn Weathersby found no documents suggesting or reflecting policy debate, indicating that there was no free flow of opinion within the Soviet government at this time. Soviet Foreign Ministry documents of the type mentioned here thus reflect top–down views. If not approved in principle, a proposal would not have been drafted and submitted. See Kathryn Weathersby, "Soviet Aims in Korea and the Outbreak of the Korean War, 1945–1950: New Evidence from the Russian Archives," CWIHP Working Paper no. 8 (1993), p. 11, footnote 18.

14 Zhukov and Zabrodin, Korea, Short Report, June 29, 1945. AVPRF, fond 0430, opis 2, papka 18, delo 5, listy 18–30. Cited in ibid., pp. 11–12.

15 Soviet Foreign Ministry, Notes on the Question of Former Japanese Colonies and Mandated Territories and Proposal on Korea, September 1945. AVPRF, fond 0431I, opis 1, papka 52, delo 8, listy 40–43. Cited in ibid., pp. 14–15.

16 In 1945, Stalin's Korea policy was not as imagined by some South Korean scholars, namely, that the Soviet Union aimed from the beginning to divide Korea as part of its plan to implement global Communist domination. See Henry H. Em, "'Overcoming' Korea's Division: Narrative Strategies in Recent South Korean Historiography," *Positions*, 1993, vol. 1, no. 2, p. 453.

17 Report by Malik on Establishing a Unified Provision Korean Government, December 10, 1945. AVPRF, fond 0102, opis 1, papka 1, delo 15, listy 18–21. CWIHP unpublished.

18 Report from the Political Directorate of the Primorsky Military Region to the Central Committee, November 5, 1945. TsPA (RGASPI), fond 17, opis 128, delo 47, listy 19–21. Cited in Weathersby, "Soviet Aims in Korea", p. 16.

19 Report by Suzdalev Concerning Japanese Military and Heavy Industries in Korea, December 1945. AVPRF, fond 0102, opis 1, papka 1, delo 15, listy 22–9.

20 Lee In Ho, "The Soviet Military Government in North Korea," *Korea Observer*, 1992, vol. 23, no. 4, pp. 525–7.

21 Intelligence Summary, North Korea, no. 1, December 1, 1945, p. 6. Cited in ibid., p. 525.
22 Zabrodin, The Question of a Single Provisional Government for Korea, December 1945. AVPRF, fond 0102, opis 1, papka 1, delo 15, listy 11–17. Cited in Weathersby, "Soviet Aims in Korea," pp. 18–19.
23 For details, see Lee, "The Soviet Military Government," pp. 529–31.
24 For details regarding the Soviet civil administration in North Korea, see ibid., pp. 534–8.
25 Sergei Goncharov, John Lewis and Xue Litai, *Uncertain Partners: Stalin, Mao, and the Korean War*, Stanford, CA: Stanford University Press, 1993, pp. 132, 326–7.
26 RGASPI (TsPA/RTsKhIDNI), fond, 17, opis 128, delo 1119. Cited in Weathersby, "Soviet Aims in Korea," p. 22.
27 Intelligence Summary: North Korea", July 15–31, 1947, p. 6. Cited in Lee, "The Soviet Military Government," p. 545.
28 Ibid., p. 546.
29 These three letters are quoted in Weathersby, "Soviet Aims in Korea," pp. 23–4. As pointed out by Weathersby, "The flaw in Soviet policy was that while Stalin was not interested in extending Soviet control into southern Korea [i.e., in the early postwar period], the highly nationalist communists whom Soviet occupation officials placed in power in North Korea were quite determined to extend their authority over the rest of the country.... Stalin was therefore caught in his own rhetoric." Ibid., pp. 23–4.
30 Telegram from Meretskov and Shtykov to Stalin, May 12, 1947. APRF, fond 45, opis 1, delo 346, listy 4–6. NSA.
31 See Paik Nak-chung, "From the Korean War to a Unified Korea, An Interview with Bruce Cummings," *Korea Journal*, Winter 1992, vol. 32, no. 4, p. 10. Also Em, "'Overcoming' Korea's Division"; Weathersby, "Soviet Aims in Korea," pp. 17–19; and Lee, "The Soviet Military Government," p. 542.
32 Telegram from Stalin to Kim, October 12, 1948. APRF, fond 45, opis 1, delo 346, list 10. NSA.
33 Telegram from Shtykov concerning a North Korean delegation visit to the Soviet Union, January 19, 1949. NSA.
34 Evgueni Bajanov, "Assessing the Politics of the Korean War, 1949–1951," *CWIHP Bulletin*, 1995/1996, nos. 6–7, p. 54. A. V. Torkunov and E. P. Ufimtsev, *Koreiskaia problema: novyi vzgliad* (The Korean Problem: New Views), Moscow: Ankil, 1995, p. 15. The record of the March 5, 1949 discussion between Stalin and Kim does not support the conclusion that Kim pressed Stalin at this time to approve military action against the South. AVPRF, fond 59a, papka 11, delo 3, listy 10–20. CWIHP. Of course, despite this record and Kapitsa's recollection, it is possible there were other secret discussions between Stalin and Kim that have not been revealed.
35 Kim Hakjoon, "North Korean Leaders and the Origins of the Korean War," Paper for the International Conference on "The Cold War in Asia," Hong Kong, January 1996.
36 While some scholars believe the Soviet Union and North Korea signed a secret military agreement in March 1949, no documents have surfaced in support of this thesis.
37 For analyses of postwar American Korea policy, see Niu Jun, "Zhanhou Meiguo dui Chaoxian zhengce de qiyuan" (The Origin of American Postwar Korea Policy), *Meiguo yanjiu*, 1991, vol. 2; and Shen Zhihua, *Chaoxian zhanzheng jiemi* (Unveiling the Secrets of the Korean War), Hong Kong: Tiandi tushu youxian gongsi, 1995.

3 China – twists and turns of Soviet postwar policy

1 For a discussion of this process, see Shen Zhihua, "Sulian chubing Zhongguo dongbei: mubiao he jieguo" (The Soviet Armed Intervention in Northeast China: Aims and Consequences), *Lishi yanjiu* (Historical Research), 1994, no. 5.

2 For a detailed treatment of the 1945 Sino-Soviet treaty negotiations, see Liang Jingchun, "1945 nian Zhong su youhao tongmeng tiaoyue qianding neimu" (Behind the Scenes of the 1945 Sino-Soviet Treaty of Friendship and Alliance), in Zhonggong zhongyang dangshi yanjiushi keyanju bianyichu bian (Chinese Communist Party Central Committee History Research Bureau Scientific Research Office transl. and ed.), *Guowai Zhonggong dangshi Zhongguo gemingshi yanjiu yiwen ji* (Compendium of Translated Documents on the Revolutionary History of the Chinese Communist Party Abroad), Beijing: Zhonggong dangshi chubanshe, 1991, pp. 223–43.

3 For the Sino-Soviet treaty and agreements of August 14, 1945, see Wang Tieya ed., *Zhongwai jiuyuezhang huibian* (Compilation of Old Chinese Treaties), Beijing: Sanlian shudian, 1962, vol. 3, pp. 1327–38.

4 Zhang Baijia, "Dui Chongqing tanpan yixie wenti de tantao" (An Inquiry into Some Questions Regarding the Chongqing Talks), *Jindaishi yanjiu* (Modern Chinese History Studies), 1993, no. 5, pp. 3–4. While analytically insightful, Zhang's conclusion that the Chinese Communist Party advocated "Nationalist–Communist cooperation to implement peaceful reconstruction [of China] as a long-term policy and not a short-term tactic" is probably incorrect. It may be more accurate to say that the Chinese Communists implemented the two approaches of cooperation and preparation for armed struggle alternately based on changing circumstances.

5 Qin Xiaoyi ed., *Zhonghua Minguo zhongyao shiliao chubian – duiRi kangzhan shiqi, disanbian, zhanshi waijiao* (Draft of Important Historical Material of the Republic of China – The War Against Japan, Collection Three, Wartime Diplomacy), Taipei: Zhongguo guomindang zhongyang weiyuanhui dangshi weiyuanhui, 1981, vol. 2, pp. 596, 594.

6 Ibid., vol. 2, pp. 588, 602, and 609.

7 Hu Qiaomu, *Hu Qiaomu huiyi Mao Zedong* (Hu Qiaomu Recalls Mao Zedong), Beijing: Renmin chubanshe, 1994, pp. 87–8.

8 In 1973, at the depth of the long freeze in Sino-Soviet relations, Moscow published the diary of Stalin's wartime personal representative in Yan'an, P. Vladimirov. Though strongly imbued with Vladimirov's own anti-Mao sentiment, Stalin's antipathy toward Mao is also quite clear in this diary. For an English edition, see Peter Vladimirov, *The Vladimirov Diaries, Yenan, China: 1942–1945*, Garden City, NY: Doubleday, 1975.

9 Stalin's unhappiness with Mao is evident in then Comintern General Secretary and Stalin confidant Georgi Dimitrov's stark "private advice" to Mao regarding "unease" in Moscow over CCP internal politics. See Dimitrov's letter to Mao, December 22, 1943. For a Chinese translation of this letter held in the CCP archives, see *Zhonggong dangshi yanjiu* (Chinese Communist Party Historical Studies), 1988, no. 3, pp. 88 and 61.

10 *FRUS, 1944*, vol. 6, pp. 799–800.

11 Mao Zedong: Concluding Remarks to the Chinese Communist Party Seventh Congress, 31 May 1945. In *Mao Zedong zai qida de baogao he jianghua ji* (Compilation of Mao Zedong's Report and remarks at the Seventh Congress), Beijing: Zhongyang wenxian chubanshe, 1995, pp. 197, 199.

12 Central Committee Decision Concerning Our Party's Task Following the Japanese Surrender, August 11, 1945. In Zhongyang dang'anguan bian (Central

Committee Archives, ed.): *Zhonggong zhongyang wenxian xuanji* (Selection of Chinese Communist Party Central Committee Documents), Beijing: Zhonggong zhongyang dangxiao chubanshe, 1991, vol. 15, pp. 228–9.

13 Zhonggong zhongyang wenxian yanjiushi bian (Chinese Communist Party Central Committee Document Research Office, ed.), *Liu Shaoqi nianpu (1898–1969)* (Liu Shaoqi Chronology (1898–1969)), Beijing: Zhonggong zhongyang chubanshe, 1996, vol. 1, pp. 476–7. The former provinces of Chahar, Jehol and Suiyuan, created late in the Nationalist-era generally on the borderlands between Northeast China and Inner Mongolia, had complicated inter-war histories and, at war's end, were heavily controlled by the Chinese Communists.

14 Zhonggong zhongyang wenxian yanjiushi bian (Chinese Communist Party Central Committee Documentary Research Office, ed.): *Mao Zedong nianpu (1893–1949)* (Mao Zedong Chronology (1893–1949)), Beijing: Renmin chubanshe he Zhongyang wenxian chubanshe, 1993, vol. 3, p. 9. When the Nationalists moved the capital from Peking (Beijing) to Nanking (Nanjing; Southern Capital) in 1927, they changed the name of the former capital to Peiping (Northern Peace). When the Communists took power in 1949, they returned the capital to the north and restored its previous name, Peking (Beijing).

15 For an exploration of the reason for and process behind Chiang Kai-shek's proposal for Chongqing talks with the Communists, see Zhang, "Dui Chongqing tanpan."

16 Shi Zhe, *Zai lishi jüren shenbian: Shi Zhe huiyilu* (Together with Historical Giants: Memoirs of Shi Zhe), Beijing: Zhongyang wenxian chubanshe, 1991, p. 308. The date of the telegrams from Stalin are in dispute, and the originals have not been found, but Mao and Zhou Enlai later both spoke about this issue, and what they said accords with Shi Zhe's recollection. See also Hu, *Hu Qiaomu huiyi Mao*, pp. 401–2. P. Iudin, "Zapis besedi s tovarishchem Mao Tszedunom" (Record of Meetings with Comrade Mao Zedong), *Problemy dal'nego vostoka* (Problems of the Far East), 1994, no. 5, p. 105.

17 *Mao Zedong nianpu*, vol. 3, pp. 9–10.

18 Mao Zedong's Speech to the Enlarged Meeting of the CCP Central Committee, August 23, 1945. Cited in Jin Chongji ed., *Mao Zedong zhuan (1893–1949)* (Biography of Mao Zedong (1893–1949)), Beijing: Zhongyang wenxian chubanshe, 1996, pp. 727–9.

19 Mao Zedong's Speech to the CCP Central Committee Politburo, August 26, 1945. Cited in ibid., p. 730.

20 Comrade Wang Ruofei's Report, August 3, 1945, available in Zhongguo renmin daxue zhonggong dangshi ziliaoshi (Chinese People's University Chinese Communist Party History Material Office), no. 6442/1. Cited in Niu Jun, "Zhong Su tongmen de qiyuan" (The Origin of the Sino-Soviet Alliance), Paper for the Hong Kong International Conference on "The Cold War in Asia," January 1996.

21 Central Committee Instruction on Quickly Entering the Northeast and Controlling the Broad Countryside and Medium-sized and Small Cities, August 29, 1945. In *Zhonggong zhongyang wenjian xuanji*, vol. 15, p. 257.

22 Central Committee Directive Regarding Issues that Need Attention in Proceeding to the Northeast, August 29, 1945. Cited in Yang Kuisong, *Zhongjian didai de geming – Zhongguo geming de celue zai guoji beijingxia de yanbian* (The Revolution in the Middle Zone – Chinese Revolutionary Tactics Seen Against the Background of the Evolution of the International Environment), Beijing: Zhonggong zhongyang dangxiao chubanshe, 1992, p. 405.

23 *FRUS, 1945*, vol. 7, p. 1026.

24 For this reason, many Chinese Communist memoirs understandably promote the view that relations between the Chinese Communist Party and the Soviet Red Army were severely strained during the Soviet occupation of Northeast China.

25 *Liu Shaoqi nianpu*, vol. 1, p. 489.

26 See Yang, *Zhongjian didai*, pp. 405–6.

27 RGASP [TsPA], fond 17, opis 128, delo 46, listy 19–21, 22–3. Cited in Brian Murray, "Stalin, the Cold War, and the Division of China: A Multi-Archival Mystery," Cold War International History Project Working Paper no. 12, 1995, pp. 3–4. CWIHP.

28 *Liu Shaoqi nianpu*, vol. 1, p. 490. Telegram from the CCP Central Committee to the CCP Chongqing delegation, September 14, 1945. Document held by Shen.

29 Central Military Commission Directive on the Strategic Policy and Specific Deployments for Taking the Northeast, September, 28 1945, in *Zhonggong zhongyang wenjian xuanji*, vol. 15, p. 300.

30 Donald Gillin and Ramon Myers eds, *Last Chance in Manchuria: The Diary of Chang Kia-ngau*, Stanford, CA: Hoover, 1989, pp. 97–8, 105–6.

31 Document held by Shen.

32 Central Committee Instruction to Peng Zhen, Chen Yun and others on the Question of Preventing the Nationalist Party from Entering the Northeast, October 16, 1945; Central Committee Instruction to the Northeast Bureau on Concentrating its Main Force to Prevent the Chiang Army from Landing, October 19, 1945; Central Military Commission Instruction on War Deployments, November 1, 1945. In *Zhonggong zhongyang wenxian xuanji*, vol. 15, pp. 351, 364–6, 394–6.

33 Document held by Shen.

34 For details on the negotiations, see Xue Xiantian, ed., *Zhong Su guojia guanxi shiliao huibian (1945–1949)* (Collection of Historical Material on Sino-Soviet State Relations (1945–1949)), Beijing: Shehui kexue wenxian chubanshe, 1996, pp. 1–103.

35 Gillin and Myers, *Last Chance in Manchuria*, pp. 132–6.

36 Chen Yun, Some Opinions on Work in Manchuria, November 30, 1945. In Zhonggong zhongyang wenxian bianji weiyuanhui (Chinese Communist Party Central Committee Document Editorial Commission): *Chen Yun wenxuan (1926–1949)* (Selected Works of Chen Yun (1926–49)), Beijing: Renmin chubanshe, 1984, p. 221. See also *Liu Shaoqi nianpu*, vol. 1, pp. 529–31. Document held by Shen.

37 Molotov to Marshal Meretskov, no date, but early December 1945, AVPRF, fond 06, opis 7, delo 524, listy 16–17. Cited in Murray, "Stalin, the Cold War," p. 5.

38 Central Committee Instruction to the Northeast Bureau on the Main Task After the Withdrawal from Large Cities, November 20, 1945; Central Committee Instruction to the Northeast Bureau on the Development Strategy After the Withdrawal from Large Cities and the Main Rail Lines, November 28, 1945. In *Zhonggong zhongyang wenjian xuanji*, vol. 15, pp. 433–4, 447–8.

39 Chen Yun, Some Opinions on Work in Manchuria, November 30, 1945. Cited in *Chen Yun wenxuan*, pp. 221, 223.

40 For material on the Moscow Conference of Foreign Ministers, see Xue, *ZhongSu guojia guanxi*, pp. 196–209.

41 Memorandum of Conversation between Stalin and Chiang Ching-kuo, December 30, 1945. Cited in A. M. Ledovskii, "Stalin i Chan Kaishi: Sekretnaia Missiia Syna Chan Kaishi v Moskvy, Dekabr' 1945 – Yanvar' 1946" (Stalin and Chiang Kai-shek: The Secret Mission of the Son of Chang Kai-shek to Moscow, December 1945–January 1946), *Novaia i noveishaia istoria* (Modern and Contemporary History), 1996, no. 4, pp. 109–18.

42 Telegram from Zhou Enlai to the Chinese Communist Party Central Committee, July 17, 1946; Telegram from Peng Zhen Regarding a Friend's Warning Not to Fight in the Northeast, January 26, 1946. Cited in Niu Jun, *Cong Yan'an zouxiang shijie – Zhongguo gongchandang duiwai guanxi de qiyuan* (From Yan'an to the World – The Origin of Chinese Communist Party Foreign Relations), Fujian renmin chubanshe, 1992, p. 228.

43 Hu, *Hu Qiaomu huiyi*, p. 88.

44 Mao Zedong, Build Stable Base Areas in the Northeast, December 28, 1945. In *Selected Works of Mao Tse-tung*, Beijing: Foreign Languages Press, 1961, vol. 4, pp. 81–4. Telegram from Liu Shaoqi to Peng Zhen on the Need to Use (Your) Main Force to Establish Bases in East, West, and North Manchuria, December 24, 1945. In *Zhonggong zhongyang wenjian xuanji*, vol. 15, pp. 512–13.

45 See Gillin and Myers, *Last Chance in Manchuria*, pp. 208, 243.

46 The 1945 Sino-Soviet treaty stipulated that Soviet troops were to be withdrawn from Northeast China by December 3, 1945, but after discussions between the Soviets and the Nationalist Chinese government, the withdrawal date was pushed back to February 1, 1946.

47 *FRUS, 1946*, vol. 9, pp. 427–8.

48 For related historical material, see Xue, *ZhongSu guojia guanxi*, pp. 168–95.

49 Gillin and Myers, *Last Chance in Manchuria*, pp. 207–8.

50 Ibid., p. 197.

51 Ledovskii, "Stalin i Chan Kaishi," p. 119.

52 Yang, *Zhongjian didai*, pp. 429–30.

53 I. Kovtun-Stankevich: "Shenyang weishu siling" (Shenyang Garrison Commander), *Zhong'E guanxi wenti* (Issues in Chinese–Russian Relations), no. 28, October 1990, p. 43. (Not available outside China.)

54 Central Committee Instruction to the Northeast Bureau and the Chinese Communist Delegation to the Chongqing Talks, March 13, 1946. In *Zhonggong zhongyang wenjian xuanj*, vol. 16, p. 90. Before World War II, the "Chinese Eastern Railway" was the name commonly used in English works for the northern line of what is now called the Chinese Changchun Railroad. After the Russo-Japanese War of 1904–05, the southern section of (the formerly unified) Chinese Eastern Railway, i.e., the portion from Changchun to Lushun (Port Arthur), was given to Japan by the Treaty of Portsmouth of 1905. This section was called the South Manchurian Railway. After the defeat of Japan in World War II, the South Manchurian Railway and the Chinese Eastern Railway came under joint Soviet–Chinese administration, through the Sino-Soviet Treaty of August 14, 1945, and the administratively reunited line was renamed the Chinese Changchun Railway. In accord with a new Sino-Soviet agreement on the railway on February 14, 1950, the Soviet government transferred to the People's Republic of China, without compensation, all its rights in the joint administration of the railway, along with all railway properties, on December 31, 1952.

55 Documents held by Shen.

56 I. Lyudnikov: "Chuanyue daxing'anling" (Crossing Daxing'anling); Bo Yike: "Jiefang Shiming" (A mission for liberation), *Zhong'E guanxi wenti*, no. 28, October 1990, pp. 13, 30. (Not available outside China.)

57 CCP Central Committee Instruction to the Northeast Bureau, 5 March 1946. Document held by Shen. Also see *Liu Shaoqi nianpu*, vol. 2, p. 24.

58 *Mao Zedong nianpu*, vol. 3, pp. 60, 62. As early as mid-February 1946, when Nationalist–Communist negotiations turned to the question of Northeast China, the CCP Central Committee understood that the Soviet Union, to show its even-handedness, "may want [us] to make more concessions to the Nationalists." See the CCP Central Committee telegram to the Northeast Bureau

concerning the status of the ceasefire negotiations in the Northeast, February 12, 1946. Cited in Niu, *Cong Yan'an zouxing shijie*, pp. 231–2.

59 CCP Central Committee Instruction to the Northeast (Bureau) on Controlling Changchun, Harbin and the Changchun Railway, and Defending Northern Manchuria, March 24, 1946; CCP Central Committee Instruction to Lin Biao, Peng Zhen and others on Resolutely Defending Strategic Points in the Northeast in Advance of a Ceasefire, March 25, 1946. In *Zhonggong zhongyang wenjian xuanji*, vol. 16, pp. 100–2.

60 *Mao Zedong nianpu*, vol. 3, pp. 70–1. The People's Front organized by the Spanish Communist Party and other leftist parties won the February 1936 election and established a coalition Spanish Republican government. On 18 July, General Franco attacked the Spanish Republican government, gaining the open assistance of Nazi Germany and Italy. In support of the Spanish Republican government, the Comintern and the Soviet Union organized a 50,000 man international corps that fought with the Spanish Republican People's Army under the slogan "Defend Madrid."

61 For details see Deng Ye, "Dongbei wenti yu Siping juezhan" (The Northeast Question and the Decisive battle of Siping), *Lishi yanjiu*, 2001, no. 4, pp. 57–71.

62 *Mao Zedong nianpu*, vol. 3, pp. 84–6.

63 Elliot Roosevelt, A Personal Interview with Stalin, p. 23. LOOK, vol. 11, no. 3 (February 4, 1947).

64 A. S. Anikin, *Istoriia diplomatii tom V (v dvukh knigakh) kniga pervaia* (Diplomatic History Volume 5 (in two books) Book One), Moscow: Izdatel'stvo politicheskoi literatury, 1974), p. 156.

65 For details see Wang Peiping and Sun Baoyun, eds, *Sulian hongjun zai Luda* (The Soviet Red Army in Lushun and Dalian), Dalianshi shizhi bangongshi 1995 nian bianyin (Dalian City Historical Annals Office 1995 Compilation) (unpublished).

66 Petrov to Guan Naiguang, March 7, 1947; Petrov-Wang Shijie meeting minutes, March 7 and 31, 1947; Petrov to Wang Shijie aide-memoire, April 16, 1947; Petrov to Wang Shijie aide-memoire, May 4, 1947; and Wang Shijie to Petrov aide-memoire, May 12, 1947. See ROC-MFA, 119.13/320.25. Cited in Murray, "Stalin, the Cold War," p. 5.

67 Telegram from Ambassador Zheng Yitong in Tehran to the Foreign Ministry in Nanjing, October 19, 1947. See ROC-MFA, 112.1/61.11. Cited in Murray, "Stalin, the Cold War," pp. 7–8.

68 Ambassador Leighton Stuart to the Secretary of State, February 24, 1948; Stuart to the Secretary, February 26, 1948; Stuart to the Secretary, March 8, 1948. For these telegrams, see *John Leighton Stuart, The Forgotten Ambassador: The Reports of Leighton Stuart*, ed. by Kenneth W. Rea and John C. Brewer, Boulder, CO: Westview Press, 1981, pp. 176–9, 185–8.

69 Report by the Defense Ministry Second Department to the Foreign Ministry, June 4, 1948. ROC-MFA 112.2/319.13. Cited in Murray, "Stalin, the Cold War," p. 8.

70 Record of the Discussion between Foreign Minister Wang Shijie and Soviet Ambassador Roshchin, August 25, 1948. ROC-MFA 112.3/314.57. Cited in Murray, "Stalin, the Cold War," pp. 8–9. Reportedly, Chiang Kai-shek's visit to Moscow was cancelled at the last minute, but before he changed his mind the Soviet Union had sent an airplane for him.

71 An Opinion Regarding Adjustments in Our (ROC) Foreign Policy, September 26, 1948. ROC-MFA 112.1/314.14. Cited in Murray, "Stalin, the Cold War," p. 7. See also Stuart's messages to the Secretary, July 15 and 30, 1948; December 14 and 16, 1948, and June 6, 1948. In *FRUS*, 1948, vol. 7, pp. 360–1, 387–8; 644, 655–6, 281–2.

72 In April 1946, Mao wrote a short article later translated and published as, "Some Points in Appraisal of the Present International Situation." In *Selected Works of Mao*, vol. 4, pp. 87–8. Originally shown only to top Chinese Communist Party leaders, Mao's article was later disseminated at a December 1947 Central Committee meeting. Cited in Hu, *Hu Qiaomu huiyi*, pp. 432–3.

73 CCP Central Committee Telegram to Luo Ronghuan, July 30, 1946. Cited in Jin, *Mao Zedong zhuan*, p. 772.

74 Shi, *Zai lishi jüren shenbian*, p. 351.

75 April 1948 Foreign Ministry Political Instruction to the (Soviet) Ambassador to China (draft), AVPRF, fond 018, opis 10, papka 24, delo 21, listy 11–14. NSA.

76 I. V. Kovalev, "Dialog Stalina s Mao Tszedunom" (Stalin's Dialogue with Mao Zedong), *Problemy dal'nego vostoka*, 1992, nos. 1–3, p. 77.

77 S. L. Tikhvinskii, *Put Kitaia k obedineniiu i nezavisimosti* 1898–1949 (China's Road to Unification and Independence 1898–1949), Moscow: Vostochnaia literatura, 1996, p. 420.

78 Murray, "Stalin, the Cold War," p. 13.

79 O. B. Borisov and B. T. Koloskov, *Sovetsko-Kitaiskie Otnosheniiia 1945–1980*, (Soviet–Chinese Relations 1945–80), Moscow: Mysl, 1980, pp. 35–6.

80 For details see Shen Zhihua, *Sidalin yu Tietuo: Su Nan chongtu de qiyin ji qi jieguo* (Stalin and Tito: The Origin and Consequences of the Soviet–Yugoslav Conflict), Guangxi shifan daxue chubanshe, pp. 29–40.

81 CCP Central Committee Resolution on the Question of the Yugoslav Communist Party, July 1, 1948. (This resolution is not easy to find. For instance, it has not been published in the multi-volume collection of party documents, *Zhonggong zhongyang wenjian xuanji*.)

82 *Renmin ribao* (People's Daily), November 7, 1948. *Dongbei ribao* (Northeast Daily), November, 8 1948.

83 APRF, fond 39, opis 1, delo 31, listy 30–1, 34. Cited in Andrei Ledovsky, "Mikoyan's Secret Mission to China in January and February 1949," *Far Eastern Affairs*, 1995, no. 2, pp. 74–5.

84 APRF, fond 39, opis 1, delo 31, listy 33, 34. Ibid., p. 75.

85 APRF, fond 39, opis 1, delo 31, listy 37, 38. Ibid., pp. 75–6.

86 APRF, fond 39, opis 1, delo 31, list 42. Ibid., p. 77.

87 APRF, fond 39, opis 1, delo 31, list 44 and Memorandum of A. I. Mikoyan to the Presidium of the CPSU Central Committee on His Visit to China in January and February 1949, September 22, 1960. Ibid., p. 77, 79–80.

4 Paving Mao's road to Moscow

1 Cited in Sergei Goncharov, John Lewis and Xue Litai, *Uncertain Partners: Stalin, Mao, and the Korean War*, Stanford, CA: Stanford University Press, 1993, p. 32. Filippov was Stalin's code name in ciphered telegrams to China.

2 For details on Mao's discussions with Mikoyan, see Shi Zhe, *Zai lishi jüren shenbian: Shi Zhe huiyilu* (Together with Historical Giants: Memoirs of Shi Zhe), Beijing: Zhongyang wenxian chubanshe, 1991, pp. 375–86.

3 Memorandum of A. I. Mikoyan to the Presidium of the CPSU Central Committee on His Visit to China in January and February 1949, September 22, 1960. Cited in Andrei Ledovsky, "Mikoyan's Secret Mission to China in January and February 1949, *Far Eastern Affairs*, 1995, no. 2, pp. 88–9.

4 Ibid., pp. 87–8.

5 For a discussion of the Soviet Union's complicated relations with and shifting policies toward Xinjiang, and how this played out in postwar Sino-Soviet relations, see Shen Zhihua, "ZhongSu jiemeng yu Sulian dui Xinjiang zhengce de

bianhua" (The Sino-Soviet Alliance and the Evolution of Soviet Policy toward Xinjiang), *Jindaishi yanjiu* (Modern Chinese History Studies), 1999, no. 3.

6 See Li Sheng, *Xinjiang duiSu(E) maoyishi, 1600–1990* (History of Xinjiang–Soviet (Russian) Trade, 1600–1990), Xinjiang renmin chubanshe, 1993, Chapter 9.

7 Shen Zhihua and Li Danhui have gathered information on the local "overseas Soviet" presence Xinjiang and its influence in the Ili region of Xinjiang in local archives and interviews. See Li Danhui, "Xinjiang Sulian qiaomin wenti de lishi kaocha, 1945–1965" (Historical Investigation Concerning Soviet Nationals in Xinjiang: 1945–1965), *Lishi yanjiu* (Historical Studies), 2003, no. 3.

8 Cited in Ledovsky, "Mikoyan's Secret Mission," 1995, no. 2, p. 87. Also Ledovsky, "Mikoyan's Secret Mission," 1995, no. 3, pp. 83–4. The latter is the second part of Ledovsky's article.

9 Cited in I. V. Kovalev, "Dialog Stalina s Mao Tszedunom" (Stalin's Dialogue with Mao Zedong), *Problemy dal'nego vostoka* (Problems of the Far East), 1992, nos. 1–3, p. 86.

10 APRF, fond 39, opis 1, delo 39, listy 78–9. Cited in Ledovsky, "Mikoyan's Secret Mission," 1995, no. 3, pp. 83–4.

11 For details on military and economic assistance issues raised by the Chinese side at the Xibaibo discussions, see APRF, fond 39, opis 1, delo 39, listy 29, 37, 44. Cited in Ledovsky, "Mikoyan's Secret Mission," 1995, no. 3, pp. 78–82. Also see Pei Jianzhuang, *Zhonghua renmin gongheguo waijiaoshi (1949–1956)* (A diplomatic history of the People's Republic of China (1949–1956)), Beijing: Shijie zhishi chubanshe, 1994, p. 11.

12 Ledovsky, "Mikoyan's Secret Mission," 1995, no. 3, pp. 78–9, 82–3.

13 Ledovsky, "Mikoyan's Secret Mission," 1995, no. 2, pp. 85–6, 89, and 1995; no. 3, pp. 85–7.

14 Hu Qiaomu, *Hu Qiaomu huiyi Mao Zedong* (Hu Qiaomu Recalls Mao Zedong), Beijing: Renmin chubanshe, 1994, p. 548.

15 In an April 1949 cable, Stalin said that he was prepared to engage in barter trade, but was not in a position immediately to satisfy Mao's request for a loan, since this needed the approval of the Supreme Soviet. Stalin said he was not opposed to an immediate loan, but it could not be approved before all details were worked out. From Kovalev's unpublished memoirs. Cited in Goncharov *et al.*, *Uncertain Partners*, p. 63.

16 APRF, fond 45, opis 1, delo 331, listy 16–19. Cited in Sergei Tikhvinsky, "New Facts About Zhou Enlai's 'Secret Demarche' and the CPC's Informal Negotiations with the Americans in June 1949," *Far Eastern Affairs*, 1994, no. 1, pp. 50–1.

17 APRF, fond 45, opis 1, delo 331, listy 24–5. Ibid., p. 51.

18 Kovalev, "Dialog Stalina s Mao," 1992, nos. 1–3, pp. 83–4.

19 APRF, fond 45, opis 1, delo 331, listy 66–9. Cited in Tikhvinsky, "New Facts about Zhou," pp. 51–2.

20 Hu, *Hu Qiaomu huiyi*, p. 88.

21 *FRUS, 1949*, vol. 8, pp. 217–18.

22 For details on the *Amethyst* Incident, see Kang Maozhao, "Yingjian *Zishiying* hao shijian" (The HMS *Amethyst* incident), in Waijiaobu waijiaoshi bianjishi (Foreign Ministry Diplomatic History Editorial Office): *Xin Zhongguo waijiao fengyun – Zhongguo waijiaoshi huiyilu* (New China's Stormy Diplomacy: Reminiscences of Chinese Diplomatic History), Beijing: Shijie zhishi chubanshe, 1990, pp. 33–47.

23 Kovalev, "Dialog Stalina s Mao," 1991, no. 6, p. 87.

24 APRF, fond 45, opis 1, delo 331, listy 73–5. Cited in Tikhvinsky, "New Facts about Zhou," p. 52. As Tikhvinsky notes, the Chinese and Soviet press gave only low-key coverage to the July 17, 1949 meeting at which the Sino-Soviet Friendship Association was established, with the Soviet press failing to mention Zhou Enlai's speech at the meeting and Chinese English-language radio cutting any reference to Zhou's praise for Lenin and Stalin.

25 APRF, fond 45, opis 1, delo 329, list 7. See A. M. Ledovskii, "Vizit v Moskvu delegatsii kommiunisticheskoi partii Kitaia v iiune – avguste 1949" (The Moscow Visit of a Delegation of the Communist Party of China in June–August 1949), *Problemy dal'nego vostoka*, 1996, no. 4, p. 70. (This information is not contained in the translation of this article cited below in *Far Eastern Affairs*, the English-language journal of Moscow's Institute of the Far East that publishes many, but far from all, of the articles first published in *Problemy dal'nego vostoka*.)

26 Many authors formerly placed Liu Shaoqi's departure for Moscow in early July, based on Shi Zhe's incorrect recollection; see Shi, *Zai lishi jüren shenbian*, p. 396. The importance of this issue is that if Liu's trip to the Soviet Union started in early July, then Mao's June 30 declaration that China was now "leaning to one side" was uttered to pave the road for Liu's visit. But, in fact, Liu came to substantial agreement in his talks with Stalin on the nights of June 26–27 (see below), and only then did Mao make it clear where he stood. This shows that Mao regarded Liu's achievement as significant. Mao's pro-Soviet "leaning to one side" statement put China in a precarious position between the Soviet Union and the United States.

27 Report from Liu Shaoqi to the CPSU Central Committee and Stalin, July 4, 1949. APRF, fond 45, opis 1, delo 328, listy 11–50. Cited in Andrei Ledovsky, "The Moscow Visit of a Delegation of the Communist Party of China in June to August 1949," *Far Eastern Affairs*, 1996, no. 4, pp. 70–85.

28 Ibid., pp. 82, 84.

29 Telegram from Liu Shaoqi to the Central Committee Secretariat, July 27, 1949. (Hand-copied from Chinese archives and held by Shen.) Pei, *Zhonghua waijiaoshi*, p. 13. Shi, *Zai lishi jüren shenbian*, pp. 414–15.

30 Telegram from Liu to the Central Committee Secretariat, July 27, 1949. Ibid., p. 412.

31 Telegram from Liu to the Central Committee Secretariat, July 27, 1949. Cited in Kovalev, "Dialog Stalina s Mao," 1992, nos. 1–3, pp. 78–9.

32 Memorandum of Conversation between Stalin and a Chinese Communist Party Central Committee Delegation, June 27, 1949. APRF, fond 45, opis 1, delo 329, listy 1–7. CWIHP.

33 Shi, *Zai lishi jüren shenbian*, p. 408.

34 Lu Liping, "Fu Su canyu tanpan yuanjian kongjun de huiyi" (Reminiscences of Traveling to the Soviet Union for Air Force Assistance Talks), *Junshi shilin* (Military Histories), 1994, no. 1, p. 25.

35 Cited in Goncharov *et al.*, *Uncertain Partners*, p. 74. Goncharov *et al.* state that Stalin ordered Soviet Air Force units from Lushun to Shanghai to end Nationalist air attacks, while Shen says that Stalin ordered Soviet Air Force units to organize air defenses around Lunshun and Dalian.

36 AVPRF, fond 07, opis 23a, papka 236, delo 18, listy 32–3, 126. Cited in B. Kulik, "Kitaiskaia narodnaia respublika v period stanovleniia, 1949–1952" (The People's Republic of China in the Founding Period, 1949–1952), *Problemy dal'nego vostoka*, 1994, no. 6, p. 75.

37 Memorandum of Conversation between Stalin and a Chinese Communist Party Central Committee Delegation, June 27, 1949. APRF, fond 45, opis 1, delo 329, listy 1–7. CWIHP.

38 Letter from Liu to Stalin, July 6, 1949. APRF, fond 45, opis 1, delo 328, listy 51–5. Cited in Andrei Ledovsky, "The Moscow Visit," 1996, no. 5, p. 87.

39 Telegram from Mao to Liu, July 25, 1949. APRF, fond 45, opis 1, delo 328, listy 137–40. Cited in Andrei Ledovskii, Raisa Mirovitskaia and Vladimir Miasnikov, Russko-Kitaiskie otnosheniia v XX veke: materialy i dokumenty, tom V, kniga 2 (Soviet–Chinese Relations in the 20th Century: Materials and Documents, Volume 5, Book 2), Moscow: Pamiatniki Istoricheskoi Mysli, 2005, pp. 170–1.

Telegram from Peng Dehuai to Mao on Preparations to Occupy Xinjiang, in *Zhonggong dangsi ziliao* (Chinese Communist Party History Material), 1990, no. 36, p. 2. See also Zhonggong zhongyang wenxian yanjiushi bian (Chinese Communist Party Central Committee Documentary Research Office, ed.): *Mao Zedong nianpu (1893–1949)* (Mao Zedong Chronology (1893–1949)), Beijing: Renmin chubanshe, Zhongyang wenxian chubanshe, 1993, vol. 3, p. 541.

40 For details on Deng Liqun's actitivies in Xinjiang and the Soviet role, see Deng Liqun, "Xinjiang heping jiefang qianhou – Zhong Su guanxi zhi yiye" (The Peaceful Liberation of Xinjiang – From Start to Finish – A Page in Sino-Soviet relations), *Jindaishi yanjiu* (Modern Chinese History Studies), 1989, no. 5, pp. 143–50.

41 Soviet diplomat M. C. Kapitsa recalled in a 1992 interview that, "One of the most serious reasons for Stalin's distrust of Mao was Lushun, Dalian, and the Chinese Changchun Railroad." Cited in Goncharov *et al.*, *Uncertain Partners*, p. 67.

42 Zhou Enlai: "Report on Problems Concerning the Peace Talks," April 17, 1949. In *Selected Works of Zhou Enlai*, Beijing: Foreign Languages Press, 1989, vol. 1, p. 360.

43 Xu Zehao, *Wang Jiaxiang zhuan* (Biography of Wang Jiaxiang), Beijing: Dangdai Zhongguo chubanshe, 1996, pp. 298–9.

44 Report from Liu to the CPSU Central Committee, July 4, 1949. APRF, fond 45, opis 1, delo 328, listy 11–50. Cited in Ledovsky, "The Moscow Visit," 1996, no. 4, p. 83.

45 Kovalev, "Dialog Stalina s Mao," 1992, nos. 1–3, p. 86. Document from Kovalev's private archive cited in Goncharov *et al.*, *Uncertain Partners*, pp. 63–4.

46 *Hu Qiaomu huiyi*, pp. 550–1. Pei, *Zhonghua renmin gongheguo waijiaoshi*, pp. 12–13.

47 See Shi, *Zai lishi jüren shenbian*, pp. 406–7. Pei, *Zhonghua waijiaoshi*, pp. 12–13.

48 Report from Liu to the CPSU Central Committee, July 4, 1949. APRF, fond 45, opis 1, delo 328, listy 11–50. Cited in Ledovsky, "The Moscow Visit," 1996, no. 4, p. 71.

49 Letter from Mao to Zhou, July 10, 1949. Cited in Jin Chongji ed., *Mao Zedong zhuan (1893–1949)* (Biography of Mao Zedong (1893–1949)), Beijing: Zhongyang wenxian chubanshe, 1996, p. 924.

50 *Mao Zedong nianpu*, vol. 3, p. 529.

51 Telegram from Mao to Liu, July 25, 1949. APRF, fond 45, opis 1, delo 328, listy 137–40. Cited in Ledovsky, "The Moscow Visit," 1996, no. 5, p. 91.

52 Kovalev, "Dialog Stalina s Mao," 1991, no. 6, p. 88. Goncharov *et al.*, *Uncertain Partners*, pp. 69–70.

53 Chen Jian, "The Sino-Soviet Alliance and China's Entry into the Korean War," Cold War International History Project Working Paper, no. 1 (1992), p. 17. CWIHP.

5 Mao's trip to Moscow

1 Odd Arne Westad, "The Sino-Soviet Alliance and the United States: Wars, Policies, and Perceptions, 1950–1961," Paper for the International Conference on "The Cold War in Asia," Hong Kong, January 1996.

2 Memorandum of Roshchin's Discussion with Chen Yun, October 28, 1949. AVPRF, fond 0100, opis 42, papka 288, delo 19, listy 58–62.

3 AVPRF, fond 0100, opis 43, papka 132, delo 313, listy 2–4. Cited in B. Kulik, "Kitaiskaia narodnaia respublika v period stanovleniia, 1949–1952" (The People's Republic of China in the Founding Period, 1949–1952), *Problemy dal'nego vostoka* (Problems of the Far East), no. 5, p. 115.

4 Liu Shaoqi's Report at the Meeting on the Foundation of the Sino-Soviet Society for Friendship and Cooperation, October 5, 1949. Cited in *Remin ribao* (People's Daily), October 8, 1949.
5 Memorandum of Roshchin's Discussion with Li Kenong, November 17, 1949. ARPRF, fond 07, opis 22, delo 220, listy 67–73.
6 *FRUS, 1949*, vol. 8, pp. 537–8.
7 I. V. Kovalev, "Dialog Stalina s Mao Tsezdunom" (Stalin's Dialogue with Mao Zedong), *Problemy dal'nego vostoka*, 1992, p. 89.
8 Memorandum of Roshchin's Discussion with Zhou Enlai, November 10, 1949. ARPRF, fond 0100, opis 42, papka 288, delo 19, listy 81–5. Cited in Andrei Ledovskii, Raisa Mirovitskaia and Vladimir Miasnikov, Russko-Kitaiskie otnosheniia v XX veke: materialy i dokumenty, tom V, kniga 2 (Soviet–Chinese Relations in the 20th Century: Materials and Documents, Volume 5, Book 2), Moscow: Pamiatniki Istoricheskoi Mysli, 2005, pp. 218–19.
9 Zhonggong zhongyang wenxian yanjiushi bian (Chinese Communist Party Central Committee Document Research Office, ed.): *Jianguo yilai Mao Zedong wengao* (Mao Zedong Documents Since the Founding of the State), Beijing: Zhongyang wenxian chubanshe, 1987, vol. 1, p. 131.
10 Memorandum on Lavrentiev's Discussion with Wang Jiaxiang, November 10, 1949. AVPRF, fond 100, opis 42, papka 288, delo 17, listy 27–9. Cited in Andrei Ledovskii *et al.*, Russko-Kitaiskie otnosheniia, pp. 216–17.
11 Request for Instructions from Gromyko to Stalin, November 12, 1949. AVPRF, fond 07, opis 22a, papka 13, delo 198, listy 29–30.
12 Kovalev, "Dialog Stalina s Mao," 1992, nos.1–3, p. 88.
13 Shi Zhe, *Zai lishi jüren shenbian: Shi Zhe huiyilu* (Together with Historical Giants: Memoirs of Shi Zhe), Zhongyang wenxian chubanshe, 1991, pp. 435–7.
14 N. T. Fedorenko, "Stalin i Mao Tszedun" (Stalin and Mao Zedong), *Novaia i noveishaia istoriia* (Modern and Contemporary History),1992, no. 5, p. 100.
15 Ledovsky has incorporated this view in his writings. See A. M. Ledovskii, "Peregovori I. V. Stalina s Mao Tszedunom b dekabre 1949–fevrale 1950" (Talks of I. V. Stalin with Mao Zedong in December 1949–February 1950), *Novaia i noveishaia istoriia*, 1991, no. 1, p. 25.
16 Information below is cited from the record of the Stalin–Mao discussion on December 16, 1949. Conversation between Stalin and Mao, Moscow, December 16, 1949. APRF, fond 45, opis 1, delo 329, listy 9–17. CWIHP.
17 According to Chinese material, Mao reported to Liu Shaoqi in a December 18, 1950 telegram that he had told Stalin that, "There is the view in Chinese public opinion that because the original treaty was concluded with the Chinese Nationalist Party, and since the Nationalist Party has fallen, the original treaty has lost its significance." According to Mao, Stalin replied that, "The original treaty should be revised, [but] in about two years, and, moreover, there should be a relatively large revision." Cited in Pei, *Zhonghua waijiaoshi* (Diplomatic History of the People's Republic of China (1949–1956)), Beijing: Shijie zhishi chubanshe, 1994, p. 18.
18 Kovalev, "Dialog Stalina s Mao," 1992, nos. 1–3, pp. 88–9.
19 Pei, *Zhonghua waijiaoshi*, p. 18. Unfortunately, to date, no documents concerning this conversation have been opened to the public in either the Chinese or the Russian archives. Stalin and Mao reportedly discussed principally Vietnam, Japan and India issues in this meeting.
20 P. Iudin, "Zapis besedi s tovarishchem Mao Tszedunom" (Record of Meetings with Comrade Mao Zedong), *Problemy dal'nego vostoka*, 1994, no. 5, pp. 105–6.
21 *Mao Zedong wengao*, vol. 1, pp. 211, 213.
22 Summary of Mao's Meeting with Roshchin, January 1, 1950. AVPRF, fond 0100, opis 43, papka 10, delo 302, list 2. NSA.

23 Wang Dongxing, *Wang Dongxing riji* (Diary of Wang Dongxing), Beijing: Zhong-guo shehui kexue chubanshe, 1993, pp. 169–72. Shi, *Zai lishi jüren shenbian*, pp. 438–9.

24 *Mao Zedong wengao*, vol. 1, p. 206.

25 Iudin, "Zapis besedi s Mao," p. 106. Mao complained to Iudin (Yudin) in March 1956 that the draft reply for his *Pravda* interview was actually written by Stalin, a charge Shen doubts based, among other factors, on Mao's character. Whatever the facts, Mao got his message out.

26 Summary of Mao's Meeting with Roshchin, January 1, 1950. AVPRF, fond 0100, opis 43, papka 10, delo 302, list 1. NSA.

27 Pei, *Zhonghua waijiashi*, p. 96. On January 5, 1950, British Foreign Secretary Bevin sent a cable to Zhou Enlai communicating Britain's desire to recognize the People's Republic of China, but Sino-British talks on diplomatic relations were later suspended over the Korean War. China established relations with India in April 1950 and with Burma in June 1950. In June 1954, China and Britain established diplomatic relations at the Chargé level.

28 Sergei Goncharov, John Lewis and Xue Litai, *Uncertain Partners: Stalin, Mao, and the Korean War*, Stanford, CA: Stanford University Press, 1993, p. 211.

29 Westad, "The Sino-Soviet Alliance."

30 *Mao Zedong wengao*, vol. 1, p. 212.

31 Information below is cited from the record of the Mao–Vyshinsky discussion on January 6, 1950. Conversation between Vyshinsky and Mao, Moscow, January 6, 1950. AVPRF, fond 0100, opis 43, delo 43, papka 302, listy 1–5. CWIHP.

32 Goncharov *et al.*, *Uncertain Partners*, p. 248.

33 Zhongyang wenxian yanjiushi he Zhonghua remin gongheguo waijiaobu (Central Committee Archives Research Office and the Foreign Ministry of the PRC): Mao Zedong waijiao wenxuan (Selected Diplomatic Documents of Mao Zedong), Beijing: Shijie zhishi chubanshe, 1994, p. 125. Record of Discussion between Molotov, Vyshinsky and Mao, January 17, 1950. AVPRF, fond 07, opic 23a, papka 18, delo 234, listy 1–7. CWIHP.

34 Shi, *Zai lishi jüren shenbian*, pp. 454–7.

35 Conversation of Molotov, Vyshinsky and Mao, January 17, 1950, AVPRF, fond 07, opis 23a, delo 234, papka 18, listy 1–7. CWIHP.

36 See Report from Molotov *et al.* to Stalin, January 22, 1950. AVPRF, fond 07, opis 23a, papka 18, delo 235, listy 42–50.

37 Information below is cited from the discussion of Stalin, Mao and others on January 22, 1950. Minutes of Conversation between Stalin and Mao, Moscow, January 22, 1950. APRF, fond 45, opis 1, delo 329, listy 29–38. CWIHP.

38 Text of the 28 January 1950 Soviet Revision of the Chinese Draft. AVPRF, fond 07, opis 23a, papka 20, delo 248, listy 74–9. For the texts of the 1950 treaty and related agreements, see Qi Shirong, *Dangdai shijieshi ziliao xuanji* (Selected contemporary historical material), Beijing: Beijing shifan xueyuan chubanshe, 1990, vol. 1, pp. 518–23. For more on the negotiation process, see Shen Zhihua and S. Goncharov, "Zhong Su tiaoyue tanpan: yuanwang he jieguo" (Sino-Soviet Treaty Talks: Expectations and Results), *Zhonggong dangshi yanjiu* (Chinese Communist Party Historical Studies), 1998, nos. 2, 3. Also, see Pei, *Zhonghua waijiaosji*, pp. 23–5; Goncharov *et al.*, *Uncertain Partners*, pp. 126–7; and Wu Xiuquan, *Zai waijiabu banian de jingli* (My Eight Years in the Ministry of Foreign Affairs), Beijing: Shijie zhishi chubanshe, 1983, pp. 11–12, 17–18.

39 Summary of the Vishinsky's Discussion with Zhou, February 13, 1950. AVPRF, fond 07, opis 23a, papka 18, delo 234, listy 75–6. Cited in Andrei Ledovskii *et al.*, *Russko-Kitaiskie otnosheniia*, pp. 295–6.

40 Information below is cited from Vishinsky's reports to Stalin. Vishinsky's Reports to Stalin, February 1–3, 1950. AVPRF, fond 07, opis 23a, papka 18, delo 234, listy 8–13, 29–34, 50–5. Ibid., pp. 271–80, 281–3, 287–90.

41 Information below is sourced to Pei, *Zhonghua waijiaoshi*, p. 25, and Shi, *Zai lishi jüren shenbian*, p. 446.

42 Minutes of Conversation between Stalin and Mao, January 22, 1950. APRF, fond 45, opis 1, delo 329, listy 29–38. CWIHP.

43 See Mao Zedong's Concluding Remarks at a January 1957 Meeting of Provincial and Municipal Party Secretaries, and His Remarks at the March 1958 Chengdu Conference. Cited in Dennis Twitchett and John K. Fairbank, *The Cambridge History of China, Volume 14, The People's Republic of China, Part I*, Cambridge: Cambridge University Press, 1987, pp. 268–9. The speeches cited in this work are from the book *Mao Zedong sixiang wansui* (Long live Mao Zedong thought) published during the Cultural Revolution. Cited in Iudin, "Zapis besedi s Mao," p. 106.

44 Mao expressed his resentment on this score in his July 21–2, 1958 discussions with Soviet Ambassador Iudin. Ibid. See also Wu Lengxi, *Shinian lunzhan (1956–1966): Zhong Su guanxi huiyilu* (Ten years of Polemics: Recollections of Sino-Soviet relations (1956–1966)), Beijing: Zhongyang wenxian chubanshe, 1999, pp. 157–60. *Mao Zedong waijiao wenxuan*, pp. 322–33, especially p. 323.

45 Wang Yan *et al.*, ed., *Peng Dehuai zhuan* (Biography of Peng Dehuai), Beijing: Dangdai Zhongguo chubanshe, 1993, p. 390. Zhonggong zhongyang wenxian yanjiushi bian (Chinese Communist Party Central Committee Document Research Office, ed.), *Liu Shaoqi nianpu (1898–1969)* (Liu Shaoqi Chronology (1898–1969)), Beijing: Zhonggong zhongyang chubanshe, 1996, vol. 2, p. 237.

46 Stalin's address to the people, September 2, 1945, in *THIRTY YEARS OF THE SOVIET STATE: CALENDAR: 1917–1947*, "September" section (pages are unnumbered). These remarks were first published in *Pravda* on September 3, 1945. Ironically, "older generation" Bolsheviks and Mensheviks, at least at the time, claimed to be encouraged by the Czarist defeat in the Russo-Japanese War. See V. I. Lenin, "The Fall of Port Arthur." In *Collected Works*, Moscow: Foreign Languages Publishing House, 1962, vol. 8, pp. 47–55.

6 Stalin reverses his Korea policy

1 Telegram from Stalin to Mao, May 14, 1950. APRF, fond 45, opis 1, delo 331, list 55. NSA.

2 The views reported below were expressed during a July 24–25, 1995 conference on the Korean War held in Washington. The author benefited from Kathryn Weathersby's conference report. See Kathryn Weathersby, "Conference Report: The Korean War, An Assessment of the Historical Record, Korea–America Society," Georgetown University, July 1995.

3 See also A. V. Torkunov and E. P. Ufimtsev, *Koreiskaia problema: noveii vzgliad* (The Korean Problem: New Views), Moscow: Ankil, 1995, p. 32.

4 See also John Garver, "Polemics, Paradigms, Responsibility, and the Origins of the U.S.–PRC Confrontation in the 1950s," *The Journal of American–East Asian Relations*, 1994, vol. 3, no. 1, pp. 27–8.

5 Sergei Goncharov, John Lewis and Xue Litai, *Uncertain Partners: Stalin, Mao, and the Korean War*, Stanford, CA: Stanford University Press, 1993, p. 152.

6 See A. M. Narinsky, "Berlinskii krisis 1948–1949: Novye dokumenty iz rossiiskikh arkhivov" (The 1948–1949 Berlin Crisis: New Material from the Russian Archives), *Novaia i noveishaia istoriia* (Modern and Contemporary History), 1995, no. 3, pp. 16–29.

7 Telegram from Vasilevsky and Shtemenko to Stalin, April 20, 1949. NSA.

8 Telegram from Shtykov from Pyongyang, May 2, 1949. NSA.

9 Telegram from Shtykov to Vyshinsky, June 18, 1949. NSA.

10 Telegram from Shtykov to Vyshinsky, July 13, 1949. For details on the small-scale engagements that occurred along the 38th parallel in spring and summer 1949, see John Merrill, *Korea: The Peninsula Origins of the War*, Newark, DE: University of Delaware Press, 1989, pp. 130–51. (Translator's note: Low-level armed conflict between South Korean and North Korean military forces began from 1948 after the Republic of Korea was formed in the South and the Democratic People's Republic was formed in the North. There were many military clashes along the 38th parallel, then just a line on the map, totally unlike the present Korean War armistice Demilitarized Zone.)

11 Niu Jun, "Zhanhou Meiguo dui Chaoxian zhengce de qiyuan" (The Origin of American Postwar Policy toward Korea), *Meiguo yanjiu* (American Studies), 1991, vol. 2, p. 64.

12 Telegram from Vyshinsky to Shtykov, April 17, 1949. NSA.

13 Telegram from Shtykov to Stalin, May 1, 1949. APRF, fond 6, opis 9, delo 14, list 57. NSA. Telegram from Menshchikov and Shtemenko to Shtykov, June 4, 1949. APRF, fond 6, opis 9, delo 14, listy 57–62. NSA. On Soviet military assistance also see Park Mun Su, "Stalin's Foreign Policy and the Korean War: History Revisited," *Korea Observer*, 1994, vol. 25, no. 3, p. 348; and Torkunov and Ufimtsev, *Koreiskaia problema*, p. 20.

14 Shtykov repeatedly told Moscow that the Korean People's Army lacked military materiel, "had no power to put up [battle] resistance," and "had important deficiencies in preparation for war." Telegram from Shtykov to Molotov, February 4, 1949; Telegram from Shtykov to Vyshinsky, April 20, 1949. APRF, fond 3, opis 65, delo 839, listi 13–14. NSA. On June 25, 1949, Shtykov's report contended that the prerequisite for strengthening the North Korean Army's war-fighting potential was to be faced with a "threat from the South." See Torkunov and Ufimtsev, *Koreiskaia problema*, pp. 20–1.

15 Telegram from Shtykov to Vyshinsky, July 2, 1949. NSA.

16 For documents on this plan and its implementation, see telegrams from Shtykov to Vyshinsky, June 5 and 28, 1949. NSA.

17 Telegram from Tunkin to Vyshinsky, September 3, 1949, AVPRF, fond 059a, opis 5a, papka 11, delo 4, listy 136–8. CWIHP. CWIHP virtual archive incorrectly ascribes this telegram to Shtykov vice Tunkin.

18 Telegram from Gromyko to Tunkin, September 11, 1949, AVPRF, fond 059a, opis 5a, papka 11, delo 3, list 45. CWIHP.

19 Telegram from Tunkin to Soviet Foreign Ministry, in reply to September 11, 1949 telegram, September 14, 1949. AVPRF, fond 059a, opis 5a, papka 11, delo 3, listy 46–53. CWIHP.

20 Telegram from Shtykov to Stalin, September 15, 1949. APRF, fond 3, opis 65, delo 776, listy 1–21. NSA.

21 Politburo's decision to confirm the attached instructions to the Soviet ambassador in Pyongyang, September 24, 1949. AVPRF, fond 059a, opis 5a, delo 3, papka 11, listy 75–7. CWIHP.

22 Telegram from Shtykov to Vyshinsky, October 14, 1950. NSA.

23 Telegram from Gromyko to Shtykov, October 26, 1949. Telegram from Shtykov to Gromyko, October 31, 1949. NSA.

24 Nikita Khrushchev, *Khrushchev Remembers*, transl. and ed. by Strobe Talbott, Boston: Little, Brown and Company, 1970, pp. 367–8.

25 Goncharov *et al.*, *Uncertain Partners*, pp. 137–8.

26 For a review of scholarly views on this issue, see Shen Zhihua, "Chaoxian zhanzheng yanjiu zongshu: xin cailiao he xin kanfa" (Korean War Research Appraised: New Material and Views), *Zhonggong dangshi yanjiu* (Chinese Communist Party Historical Studies), 1996, no. 6.

27 When the North Korean-controlled guerillas in the South were at their strongest, in fall 1949, they were able to attack cities, and could match Republic of Korea forces in terms of armament. Despite several attempts to reinforce them with well-trained partisan units from the North, by spring 1950, the Republic of Korea government had suppressed this guerilla activity. See the Japanese history of land warfare in Korea (Rikusenshi kenkyu fukyukai, ed.) in Chinese, translation, *Chaoxian zhanzheng* (The Korean War), transl. by Gao Pei *et al.*, Beijing: Guofang daxue chubanshe, 1990, vol. 1, p. 4.

28 Telegram from Shtykov to Vyshinsky, January 19, 1950. AVPRF, fond 059a, opis 5a, delo 3, papka 11, listy 87–91. CWIHP. (Translator's note: Before the North Korean invasion of June 25, 1950, especially during 1949, there was tremendous violence in Korea, mainly in the South, with bloody guerilla fighting that cost tens of thousands of lives. Most, but not all, guerilla operations in the South were supported by North Korea. The Rhee regime's successful suppression of these uprisings was extremely brutal, but its very success, along with regimental-sized border clashes, probably was an impetus for Kim Il-sung to approach Stalin again, having been politely turned down on a visit to Moscow in March 1949, for a green light to invade the South.)

29 Telegram from Stalin to Shtykov, January 30, 1950. AVPRF, fond 059a, opis 5a, delo 3, papka 11, list 92. CWIHP.

30 Telegram from Shtykov to Stalin, January 31, 1950. AVPRF, fond 059a, opis 5a, papka 11, delo 3, listy 92–3. Telegram from Shtykov to Vyshinsky, February 7, 1950. AVPRF, fond 059a, opis 5a, delo 4, papka 11, listy 145–6. January 31 and February 7, 1950 telegrams. CWIHP. Telegram from Vyshinsky to Shtykov, February 9, 1950. APRF, fond 45, opis 1, delo 346, list 76. February 9, 1950 telegram. CWIHP unpublished.

31 Telegram from Shtykov to Maj. General A. M. Vasilevsky, February 23, 1950. AVPRF, fond 059a, opis 5a, papka 11, delo 4, list 148. CWIHP.

32 Telegram from Shtykov to Vyshinsky, March 9, 1950. AVPRF, fond 059a, opis 5a, papka 11, delo 4, listy 149–50. CWIHP. Telegram from Stalin to Shtykov, with message for Kim Il-sung, March 18, 1950. AVPRF, fond 059a, opis 5a, papka 11, delo 4, list 142. CWIHP virtual archive provides a document from another Russian archive that, from all appearances, is the same as this second telegram.

33 Telegram from Shtykov to Vyshinsky, March 21, 1950. AVPRF, fond 059a, opis 5a, papka 11, delo 3, listy 94–5. Telegram from Shtykov to Vyshinsky, March 24, 1950. AVPRF, fond 059a, opis 5a, papka 11, delo 4, listy 96–7. CWIHP. Kathryn Weathersby, "The Soviet Role in the Early Phase of the Korean War: New Documentary Evidence," *Journal of American–East Asian Relations*, Winter 1993, vol. 2, no. 4, p. 441. Kim Chullbaum ed., "The Truth about the Korean War, Testimony 40 Years Later," Seoul, 1991, pp. 3, 8. According to Russian historian Dmitri Volkogonov, prior to Kim Il-sung's April 1950 Moscow visit, he held highly restricted talks with Stalin in Moscow in February 1950. Volkogonov's claim, however, is not supported by Soviet documents declassified to date. Volkogonov – while claiming that Stalin "almost never kept records of important matters" – also noted that he had checked and found no documents on the alleged February 1950 meeting in Russian Foreign Ministry archives.

34 Weathersby, "The Soviet Role," p. 433. Kim, "The Truth," pp. 105–6.

35 RGASPI (TsPa), fond 5, opis 58, delo 266, listy 122–31. Cited in Weathersby, "The Soviet Role," p. 441.

36 Stalin's meeting with Kim, March 5, 1949. AVPRF, fond 059a, opis 5a, delo 3, papka 11, listy 10–20. CWIHP.

37 Zhukov and Zabrodin: "Korea, Short Report," June 29, 1945. AVPRF, fond 0430, opis 2, delo 18, papka 5, listy 18–30. Cited in Kathryn Weathersby, "Soviet

Aims in Korea and the Outbreak of the Korean War, 1945–1950: New Evidence from the Russian Archives," CWIHP Working Paper no. 8, 1993, pp. 11–12. CWIHP.

38 Soviet Foreign Ministry Notes on the Question of Former Japanese Colonies and Mandated Territories, September 1945. AVPRF, fond 0431I, opis 1, delo 52, papka 8, listy 40–3. Cited in Weathersby, "Soviet Aims in Korea," p. 14.

39 Soviet MFA Proposal on Korea, September 1945. AVPRF, fond 0431I, opis 1, delo 52, papka 8, listy 44–5. Cited in Weathersby, "Soviet Aims in Korea," p. 15.

40 Cited in Dmitri Volkogonov, "Sleduyet li etogo boyatsia" (Should We Fear This?), *Ogonyok* (Little Flame), 1993, no. 26, p. 29.

41 See Zi Zhongyun, *Zhanhou Meiguo waijiao shi – cong Dulumen dao Ligen* (American Postwar Diplomatic History – From Truman to Reagan), Beijing: Shijie zhishi chubanshe, 1994, pp. 158–63, 204–5. For material on the Japan Peace Treaty from Russian archives, see B. N. Slavinskii, "San Frantsisskaia konferentsia 1951 g. po mirnomu uregulirovaniiu s iaponiei i sovetskaia diplomatiia" (The 1951 San Francisco Conference: Peaceful Normalization with Japan and Soviet Diplomacy), *Problemy dal'nego vostoka* (Problems of the Far East), 1994, no. 1, pp. 80–100.

42 Telegram from Gromyko to Tunkin at the Soviet Embassy in Pyongyang, September 11, 1949. AVPRF, fond 059a, opis 5a, papka 11, delo 3, list 45. Telegram from Tunkin to Soviet Foreign Ministry, in reply to September 11, telegram, September 14, 1949. AVPRF, fond 059a, opis 5a, papka 11, delo 3, listy 46–53. CWIHP.

43 Goncharov *et al.*, *Uncertain Partners*, pp. 101, 320.

44 Weathersby, "The Soviet Role," p. 433.

45 For former North Korean Lt. Gen. Yu Song-chol's recollections, see Vladimir Petrov, "Soviet Role in the Korean War Confirmed: Secret Documents Declassified," *Journal of Northeast Asian Studies*, 1994, vol. 3, pp. 63–7. Kim, "The Truth about the Korean War," pp. 143–55.

46 Cited in Goncharov *et al.*, *Uncertain Partners*, p. 145. Also see Kim, "The Truth about the Korean War," p. 106.

47 Telegram from Stalin to Mao, May 14, 1950. APRF, fond 45, opis 1, delo 331, list 55. NSA.

48 Telegram from Liu Shaoqi to the Central Committee Secretariat, July 27, 1949. In Zhonggong zhongyang wenxian yanjiushi bian (Chinese Communist Party Central Committee Document Research Office, ed.): *Jianguo yilai Liu Shaoqi wengao* (Liu Shaoqi Documents Since the Foundation of the State), Beijing: Zhongyang wenxian chubanshe, 1998, vol 1, p. 313.

49 Even on the question of whether or not North Korea should establish relations with the People's Republic of China, North Korea sought the view of the Soviet Union. Telegram from Stalin to Shtykov, October 3, 1949. APRF, fond 45, opis 1, delo 346, list 58. NSA.

50 Telegram from Shtykov to Vyshinsky, May 15, 1949. NSA.

51 Telegram from Kovalev to Stalin, May 18, 1949. APRV, fond 45, opis 1, delo 331, listy 59–61.

52 Telegram from Tunkin to Soviet Foreign Ministry, in reply to September 11, 1949 telegram, September 14, 1949. AVPRF, fond 059a, opis 5a, papka 11, delo 3, listy 46–53. CWIHP.

53 For a short treatment of such "collusion" theorists, see Mineo Nakajima, "The Sino-Soviet Confrontation: Its Roots in the International Background of the Korean War," *The Australian Journal of Chinese Affairs*, January 1979, no. 1, pp. 19–47, especially pp. 28 and 43, footnote 472.

54 See Paik Nak-chung, "From the Korean War to a Unified Korea", p. 13. Zeng Kelin: *Rongma shenya de huiyi* (Reminiscences of Army Life), Beijing: Jiefangjun chubanshe, 1992, p. 252.

55 For a detailed discussion of the repatriation of ethnic Korean troops serving in the PLA to North Korea, see Chen Jian, *China's Road to the Korean War*, New York: Columbia University Press, 1994, pp. 109–10.

56 Zhongguo renmin jiefangjun dongbei junqu silingbu, ed. (People's Liberation Army Northeast Military Region Headquarters, ed.): *Dongbei sannian jiefang zhanzheng junshi ziliao* (Military Material on the Three-year War to Liberate the Northeast), October 1949, pp. 76–7 (not available outside China). Telegram from Shtykov to Stalin, September 15, 1949. APRF, fond 3, opis 65, delo 776, list 15.

57 Telegram from Moscow to Shtykov, January 8, 1950. Telegram from Shtykov to Moscow, January 11, 1950. NSA. See also Nie Rongzhen, *Nie Rongzhen huiyilu* (Memoirs of Nie Rongzhen), Beijing: Jiefangjun chubanshe, 1982, p. 744.

58 Military expenditures constituted the major portion of China's 1949 state budget, with 60 percent of expenditures going to military personnel costs. If expenses for combat and logistical supplies are added, the proportion was even higher. In December 1949, Mao proposed using army troops for income-producing economic activity, and, in April 1950, he proposed to begin demobilization. See Zhongguo shehui kexueyuan, Zhongyang dang'anguan bian (Chinese Academy of Social Sciences and Central Committee Archives, ed.): *1949–1951 nian Zhonghua renmin gongheguo jingji dang'an ziliao xuanbian: zonghe zhuan* (Selection of Material from the the People's Republic of China Economic Archives, 1949–51: Summary Volume), Zhongguo chengshi jingji shehui chubanshe, 1990, pp. 114–15, 120. Zhonggong zhongyang wenxian yanjiushi bian (Chinese Communist Party Central Committee Document Research Office, ed.): *Jianguo yilai Mao Zedong wengao* (Mao Zedong Documents Since the Founding of the State), vol. 1, pp. 182–3, 310.

59 Allen S. Whiting, *China Crosses the Yalu: The Decision to Enter the Korean War*, Stanford: Stanford University Press, 1960, p. 44.

60 From the author's July 31, 1996 Moscow interview with Professor Ledovsky. Shen later found one of the two telegrams to which Ledovsky referred. Based on the telegram from Gromyko to Kovalev on November 5, 1949, it appears that, on October 21, Mao sent a telegram to Stalin indicating that he did not believe that North Korea should take military action at that time. Stalin replied that, "We support the view you expressed on this issue, and will share advice in this spirit with our Korean friends." NSA.

61 The consensus of Korean War scholars is that Stalin did not discuss a North Korean attack on the South with Mao during the Chinese leader's winter 1949–50 visit to Moscow. Shi Zhe and Jia Peicai, both of whom were involved Mao's discussions with Stalin, hold this view. See Chen Jian, *China's Road to the Korean War*, pp. 112, 263, and Kim Hakjoon, "North Korean Leaders." Professor Bajanov, who has mastered a major portion of the relevant Russian archives, agrees. See Evgueni Bajanov, "Assessing the Politics of the Korean War, 1949–1951," *CWIHP Bulletin*, 1995/1996, nos. 6–7, p. 87. Bajanov points out that while Stalin was reconsidering his Korea policy during Mao's time in Moscow, and discussed Korea with Mao, "according to all available data the Soviet dictator never mentioned to the Chinese guest his decision to launch an attack on the South as well as his invitation to Kim Il-Sung to come to Moscow."

62 Telegram from Stalin to Mao, May 3, 1950. APRF, fond 45, opis 1, delo 331, list 54.

63 Telegram from Shtykov to Vyshinsky regarding meeting with Kim, May 12, 1950. AVPRF, fond 059a, opis 5a, delo 3, papka 11, listy 100–3. CWIHP. (Translator's note: As related in this telegram, and as told to Ambassador Shtykov by Kim, the North Korean ambassador to Beijing had been rebuked for acting without authorization in discussing with Mao and Zhou Enlai the subject of Kim's requested meeting with Mao. Disagreeing with Zhou, who suggested

Kim's meeting be official, Mao told the North Korean Ambassador that, "if you intend to begin military operations against the South in the near future, then [we] should not meet officially...." Mao also reportedly opined that, "[T]he unification of Korea by peaceful means is not possible, solely military means are required to unify Korea. As regards the Americans, there is no need to be afraid of them. The Americans will not enter a third world war for such a small territory." Thus, whether or not Stalin gave Mao a heads-up on his emerging decision while Mao was in Moscow, Mao had a heads-up from the North Korean ambassador in Beijing sometime (it is not clear when from the record) before Kim came to China to brief him. It is, of course, quite possible that Mao all along knew or suspected more than he was willing to share with his CCP Politburo colleagues in a timely fashion.)

64 Telegram from Roshchin to Moscow, May 13, 1950. AVPRF, fond 059a, opis 5a, papka 11, delo 3, listy 100–3. CWIHP.

65 Telegram from Stalin to Mao, May 14, 1950. APRF, fond 45, opis 1, delo 331, list 55. NSA.

66 Xue Litai has proposed two reasons for Mao's agreement with Kim's plan to attack South Korea: First, in discussing the issue with Mao, Kim overstated Stalin's enthusiasm for an attack on South Korea. Second, Mao had asked for Soviet assistance in an attack on Taiwan. If he had then indicated skepticism about Kim's plan, Mao might have feared that this would stoke Stalin's nervousness about a Chinese Communist attack on Taiwan. See Weathersby, "Conference Report."

67 AVPRF, fond 0100, opis 43, papka 4, delo 302, list 198. Cited in B. Kulik, "Kitaiskaia narodnaia respublika v period stanovleniia, 1949–1952" (The People's Republic of China in the Founding Period, 1949–1952), *Problemy dal'nego vostoka*, 1994, no. 6, p. 75.

68 Zhonggong zhongyang wenxian yanjiushi bian (Chinese Communist Party Central Committee Document Research Office, ed.): *Zhou Enlai nianpu, 1949–1976* (Zhou Enlai Chronology, 1949–1976), Beijing: Zhongyang wenxian chubanshe, 1997, vol. 1, p. 37.

69 Soviet-era diplomat M. C. Kapitsa's memoir provides evidence that the Soviets knew that the Chinese Communist Party Politburo opposed Kim Il-sung's proposal. See Goncharov *et al.*, *Uncertain Partners*, p. 146, where a Soviet diplomat is cited to the effect that, "throughout multiple bilateral talks on Kim's proposal for war, the Soviets knew that the Chinese Politburo opposed the idea." However, Goncharov *et al.* deduce that Mao was forced to respond positively to Kim's initiative, lest he undercut his own argument that the Soviet Union should support an invasion of Taiwan.

70 Xu Yan, *Diyici jiaoliang: kangMei yuanChao zhanzheng de lishi huigu yu fans*i (The First Test: Recollections and Reflections on the History of the War to Resist America and Assist Korea), Zhongguo guangbo dianshi chubanshe, 1990, p. 16. Zhou Jun, "Xin Zhongguo chuqi renmin jiefangjun weineng suixing Taiwan jihua yuanyin chutan" (A Preliminary Exploration of the Reasons for the Inability of the People's Liberation Army to Implement the Taiwan Campaign Plan in the Early New China period), *Zonggong dangshi yanjiu*, 1991, no. 1. pp. 67–9.

71 According to a former high-ranking North Korean supply officer, before the outbreak of the war, all Soviet weapons assistance to North Korea was sent by sea, not over the Chinese rail system. This was done to prevent China from learning about war preparations. Koreans who had returned from China were also excluded from war planning, again to maintain security and keep the Chinese in the dark. See Goncharov *et al.*, *Uncertain Partners*, pp. 153 and 163.

72 All judgments of Stalin's motivation for changing his Far Eastern policy are based on deductive analysis of historical material. No documentary proof has

been found to support such judgments. In historical research on the leadership of a country such as the Soviet Union, it is unusual to find direct documentary evidence with which to interpret leadership motivations. Even when authentic documents are available, it is hard to say that the words recorded reflect the true intentions of the leader of such a political system.

7 North Korea crosses the 38th parallel

1 Peter Calvocoressi, *Survey of International Affairs, 1952*, London: Oxford University Press, 1956, p. 2.

2 Telegram from Shtykov to Zakharov, June 26, 1950. From a collection of Soviet military documents obtained by the British Broadcasting Cooperation in 1994 for a BBC documentary. CWIHP.

3 For further analysis of the U.S. decision to intervene in the Korean War, see Shen Zhihua, "Meiguo shi zenyang juanru Chaoxian zhanzheng de?" (How Did the United States Get Into the Korean War?"), *Shijie lishi*, 1995, no. 3. See also Niu Jun, "Meiguo dui Chaoxian zhengce de yanbian" (The Evolution of U.S. Korea Policy), *Meiguo yanjiu* (American Studies), 1991, no. 1.

4 Telegram from Stalin to Shtykov, July 1, 1950. APRF, fond 45, opis 1, delo 346, list 104. CWIHP.

5 Telegrams from Shtykov to Stalin, July 1 and 4, 1950. APRF, fond 45, opis 1, delo 346, listy 105–7. CWIHP.

6 In 1950, the Soviet Union provided 870 million rubles worth of military materiel to North Korea, almost three times the value of military assistance in 1949. (No foreign currency conversion factor is given.) See Sergei Goncharov, John Lewis and Xue Litai, *Uncertain Partners: Stalin, Mao, and the Korean War*, Stanford, CA: Stanford University Press, 1993, p. 147.

7 Telegram from Stalin to Shtykov, July 6, 1950. APRF, fond 45, opis 1, delo 346, list 140. CWIHP.

8 See Shen Zhihua, *Chaoxian zhanzheng jiemi* (Unveiling the Secrets of the Korean War), Hong Kong: Tiandi tushu youxian gongsi, 1995, pp. 155–77.

9 Nikita Khrushchev, *Khrushchev Remembers*, transl. and ed. by Strobe Talbott, Boston: Little, Brown and Company, 1970, p. 370.

10 Telegram from Shtykov to Stalin, transmitting a letter from Kim to Stalin, July 8, 1950. APRF, fond 45, opis 1, delo 346, listy 143–4. CWIHP.

11 Cited in Dimitri Volkogonov, "Sleduyet li etogo boyatsia" (Should We Fear This?), *Ogonyok* (Little Flame), 1993, no. 26, p. 29.

12 Cited in Evgueni Bajanov, "Assessing the Politics of the Korean War, 1949–1951, *CWIHP Bulletin*, 1995/1996, nos. 6–7, pp. 88–9.

13 Telegram from Stalin to Roshchin, with message for Zhou, July 5, 1950. APRF, fond 45, opis 1, delo 331, list 79. CWIHP.

14 Telegram from Stalin to Roshchin transmitting a message for Mao, July 8, 1950. APRF, fond 45, opis 1, delo 334, list 82. CWIHP.

15 Telegram for Kim, via Shtykov, August 28, 1950. APRF, fond 45, opis 1, delo 347, listy 5–6, 10–11. CWIHP.

16 Three days after launching the war, Kim Il-sung sent a military officer to brief China on the war situation. According to Shi Zhe, Mao Zedong was very unhappy, telling Shi after the briefing that, "They are our close neighbor, but did not consult with us before the outbreak of the war, and only now have come to speak with us." See Li Haiwen, "Zhonggong zhongyang jiujing heshi jueding zhiyuanjun chuguo zhuozhan?" (When did the Chinese Communist Party Central Committee Finally Decide to Send Volunteers Abroad to Fight?), *Dang de wenxian* (Party Documents), 1993, no. 5, p. 85.

17 Lei Yingfu, "Kang Mei yuan Chao zhanzheng jige zhongda juece de huiyi" (Recollections of Several Key Strategic Decisions in the War to Resist America and Assist Korea), *Dang de wenxian*, 1993, no. 6, p. 76.

18 Zhonggong zhongyang wenxian yanjiushi bian (Chinese Communist Party Central Committee Document Research Office, ed.): *Zhou Enlai nianpu, 1949–1976* (Zhou Enlai Chronology, 1949–1976), Beijing: Zhongyang wenxian chubanshe, 1997, vol. 1, p. 52. Zhou Jun, "Xin Zhongguo chuqi renmin jiafangjun weineng suixing Taiwan jihua yuanyin chutan" (A Preliminary Exploration of the Reasons for the Inability of the People's Liberation Army to Implement the Taiwan Campaign Plan in the Early New China Period), Beijing: *Zonggong dangshi yanjiu*, 1991, no. 1, p. 72. On August 11, the Central Military Commission agreed with People's Liberation Army commander Chen Yi's recommendation to delay the campaign plan against Taiwan until after 1951.

19 *Zhou Enlai nianpu*, vol. 1, p. 51.

20 *Zhou Enlai nianpu*, vol. 1, p. 54. As noted above, with no Chinese ambassador in Pyongyang, on July 8, Stalin reminded Mao that he might want to send a representative to Pyongyang, "if, of course, Mao Zedong considers it necessary to have communications with [North] Korea."

21 Zhonggong zhongyang wenxian yanjiushi bian (Chinese Communist Party Central Committee Document Research Office, ed.): *Jianguo yilai Mao Zedong wengao* (Mao Zedong Documents Since the Founding of the State), Beijing: Zhongyang wenxian chubanshe, 1987, vol. 1, p. 428. Li Ping, *Kaiguo zongli Zhou Enlai* (The PRC's First Premier: Zhou Enlai), Beijing: Zhonggong zhongyang dangxiao chubanshe, 1994, p. 247.

22 Xu Yan, *Diyici jiaoliang: kangMei yuanChao zhanzheng de lishi huigu yu fansi* (The First Test: Recollections and Reflections on the History of the War to Resist America and Assist Korea), Beijing: Zhongguo guangbo dianshi chubanshe, 1990, p. 16.

23 Bo Yibo, *Ruogan zhongda juece yu shijian de huigu* (Recollections of Some Important Policies and Events), Beijing: Zhonggong zhongyang dangxiao chubanshe, 1991, vol. 1, p. 43.

24 *Mao Zedong wengao*, vol. 1, pp. 454, 469, 485.

25 *Zhou Enlai nianpu*, vol. 1, pp. 68–70. Li, *Kaiguo zongli Zhou Enlai*, pp. 247–8. Lei, "KangMei yuanChao" (Continuation), *Dang de wenxian*, 1994, no. 1, p. 25. *Mao Zedong wengao*, vol. 1, p. 484.

26 Alexandre Mansourov, "Stalin, Mao, Kim, and China's Decision to Enter the Korean War, September 16–October 15, 1950: New Evidence from the Russian Archives," *CWIHP Bulletin*, 1995/1996, nos. 6–7, pp. 95–6.

27 Report from Vasilevsky to Stalin, September 23, 1950. APRF, fond 3, opis 65, delo 827, listy 81–2. CWIHP.

28 Telegram from Matveyev (General M. V. Zakarov) to Stalin, September 26, 1950. APRF, fond 3, opis 65, delo 827, listy 103–6. CWIHP.

29 Telegram with Instructions from Stalin to Matveyev (General Zakharov) and Ambassador Shtykov, approved by the CPSU Politburo, September 27, 1950. APRF, fond 3, opis 65, delo 827, listy 90–3. CWIHP.

30 According to former Korean Workers' Party Central Committee Secretary Im Un and North Korea ceasefire delegate Lee Sang-jo (North Koreans living in exile), Mao warned Kim to anticipate a U.S. landing at Inchon. According to Im, "Kim Il-sung ignored [Mao's] warnings as matters unworthy of consideration, and ordered his men to keep [Mao's advice] secret." Cited in Chen Jian, *China's Road to the Korean War*, New York: Columbia University Press, 1994, pp. 273, 275.

31 Vladimir Petrov, "Soviet Role in the Korean War Confirmed: Secret Documents Declassified," *Journal of Northeast Asian Studies*, 1994, vol. 3, pp. 60–1.

32 Chen, *China's Road to the Korean War*, p. 161.

33 *Zhou Enlai nianpu*, vol. 1, p. 80.

34 *Zhou Enlai nianpu*, vol. 1, p. 83.

35 Chai Chengwen and Zhao Yongtian, *Banmendian tanpan* (Panmunjom Talks), Jiefangjun chubanshe, 1989, p. 79.

36 Joseph C. Goulden, *Korea: The Untold Story of the War*, New York: Times Books, 1982, p. 281.

37 Li, *Kaiguo Zongli Zhou Enlai*, p. 249. *Renmin ribao* (People's Daily) prominently published Zhou's remarks on October 1. While Li claims the last half of the Chinese warning was added to the draft by Zhou, researchers at the Institute of Military Science told the author that, in fact, this addition to the draft is in Mao's hand.

38 Telegram from Shtykov to Gromyko, September 30, 1950. APRF, fond 45, opis 1, delo 347, listy 46–9. CWIHP.

39 Telegram from Kim Il-sung and South Korean Communist leader Pak Hon-yong to Stalin, via Shtykov, September 30, 1950, APRF, fond 45, opis 1, delo 347, listy 41–5. CWIHP. CWIHP Virtual Archive gives the date of this message as September 29, though the telegram was sent on September 30.

40 Mansourov, "Stalin and China's Decision," p. 98.

41 Petrov, "Soviet Role in Korean War," pp. 60–1.

42 Telegram from Stalin to Mao and Zhou, via Ambassador Roshchin, October 1, 1950. APRF, fond 45, opis 1, delo 347, listy 97–8. CWIHP.

8 China decides: "whatever the sacrifice necessary"

1 Alexandre Mansourov, "Stalin, Mao, Kim, and China's Decision to Enter the Korean War, September 16–October 15, 1950: New Evidence from the Russian Archives," *CWIHP Bulletin*, 1995/1996, nos. 6–7, pp. 95, 106–7 (footnote 30).

2 Chinese officials have told the author that no copy of the telegram published by Russia has been found in Chinese archives. Russian academics told the author at a January 1996 academic conference in Hong Kong that Russian archives hold no copy of the telegram published by China.

3 Zhonggong zhongyang wenxian yanjiushi bian (Chinese Communist Party Central Committee Document Research Office, ed.): *Jianguo yilai Mao Zedong wengao* (Mao Zedong Documents Since the Founding of the State), Beijing: Zhongyang wenxian chubanshe, vol. 1, pp. 539–40.

4 Telegram from Roshchin to Stalin, conveying an October 2, 1950 message from Mao to Stalin, October 3, 1950. APRF, fond 45, opis 1, delo 334, listy 105–6. CWIHP.

5 Chen Jian, *China's Road to the Korean War*, New York: Columbia University Press, 1994, p. 173. In researching his book, Chen extensively interviewed persons with contemporary and other knowledge of the Korean War, gaining the understanding of the situation described here from military figures. The author, through other channels, has confirmed Chen's findings. Xu Yan told the author that his interviews confirmed the same facts.

6 The author gathered information about this situation in the course of interviewing informed sources. These events are also described in Wang Yan *et al.*, ed., *Peng Dehuai zhuan* (Biography of Peng Dehuai), Beijing: Dangdai Zhongguo chubanshe, 1993, p. 400.

7 Chen in *China's Road to the Korean War* (p. 175) states that the October 2 meeting decided to send Chinese troops into Korea on or about October 15, and that Mao suggested before the end of the meeting that he convey this decision in a personal telegram to Stalin. Chen told the author that he wrote this based on the assumption that Mao's October 2 cable (as published by China) had been sent.

8 Shi Zhe, *Zai lishi jüren shenbian: Shi Zhe huiyilu* (Together with Historical Giants: Memoirs of Shi Zhe), Beijing: Zhongyang wenxian chubanshe, 1991, pp. 401–2. *Nie Rongzhen huiyilu* (Memoirs of Nie Rongzhen), Beijing: Jiefang chubanshe, 1984, vol. 2, p. 735. (Translator's note: The English-language edition of Nie Rongzhen's memoirs, *Inside the Red Star: The Memoirs of Marshal Nie Rongzhen*, p. 636, gives a more "heroic" version of the October 4 Politburo meeting, along with reference to Lin Biao's dissent and fear when he was asked to command Chinese troops in Korea. See below for bibliographic information.) Also see Peng Dehuai's October 14 address to high-level cadres of the Chinese People's Volunteers, in Peng Dehuai zhuan ji bianxie zu (Peng Dehuai Biographical Research and Editorial Group), *Peng Dehuai junshi wenxuan* (Selection of Military Writings of Peng Dehuai), Beijing: Zhongyang wenxian chubanshe, 1988, pp. 320–1.

9 Peng Min, chief ed., *Dangdai zhongguo de jiben jianshe* (The Basic Construction of Contemporary China), Beijing: Zhongguo shehui kexue chubanshe, 1989, vol. 1, pp. 4–5.

10 For these and other economic indicators, see Zhongguo shehui kexueyuan, Zhongyang dang'anguan bian (Chinese Academy of Social Sciences and Central Committee Archives, ed.): *1949–1951 nian Zhonghua renmin gongheguo jingji dang'an ziliao xuanbian: zonghe zhuan* (Selection of Material from the People's Republic of China Economic Archives, 1949–1951: Summary Volume), Beijing: Zhongguo chengshi jingji shehui chubanshe, 1990, pp. 23, 28–9 and 65.

11 Zhonggong zhongyang wenxian yanjiushi bian (Chinese Communist Party Central Committee Document Research Office, ed.): *Zhou Enlai waijiao wenxuan* (Selection of Zhou Enlai's Diplomatic Documents), Beijing: Zhongyang wenxian chubanshe, 1991, pp. 25–7. When Indian Ambassador Panikkar told Zhou of press reports that South Korean troops had already crossed the 38th parallel, Zhou noted that China had read a press report that General Walker had led troops across the 38th parallel, but that it was unclear whether these were U.S. or South Korean troops.

12 As late as October 14, when the U.S. and South Korean armies had already broken through the Pyongyang defense perimeter, intelligence in the possession of China was that, "It appears there is no final decision yet on whether and when the Americans will advance on Pyongyang." "The American forces are still at the 38th peninsula." *Mao Zedong wengao*, vol. 1, pp. 558, 560.

13 After extensive discussions with Chinese historians and reading "often self-serving" memoirs of participants in the October 4–5 Politburo meetings, Chen Jian concluded "that it would be safe to say that almost all members of the Politburo, except Mao, expressed reservations in different degrees about sending troops to Korea." See Chen, *China's Road to the Korean War*, p. 281, footnote 78.

14 Interview with Yang Shangkun, July 20, 1984. See Wang, *Peng Dehuai zhuan*, pp. 401–3.

15 Xu Yan, *Diyici jiaoliang: kangMei yuanChao zhanzheng de lishi huigu yu fansi* (The First Test: Recollections and Reflections on the History of the War to Resist America and Assist Korea), Beijing: Zhongguo guangbo dianshi chubanshe, 1990, pp. 23–4. Chen, *China's Road to the Korean War*, p. 185. Wang, *Peng Dehuai zhuan*, pp. 401–3.

16 Memorandum from Gromyko to Stalin, with draft cable to Shtykov, September 30, 1950. APRF, fond 3, opis 65, delo 877, listy 123–5. CWIHP.

17 Telegram from Gromyko to Shtykov, approved by CPSU Poliburo, October 5, 1950. APRF, fond 3, opis 65, delo 827, listy 121–2. CWIHP.

18 Memorandum from Gromyko and Vasilevsky to Stalin, attaching draft cable to Shtykov, October 6, 1950. APRF, fond 3, opis 65, delo 827, listy 126–7. CWHIP.

19 Telegram from Stalin to Kim, via Ambassador Shtykov, October 8, 1950. APRF, fond 45, opis 1, delo 347, listy 65–7. CWIHP.

20 *Mao Zedong wengao,* vol. 1, pp. 543–5.

21 Telegram from Shtykov to Stalin, October 9, 1950. APRF, fond 45, opis 1, delo 347, listy 72–3. CWIHP. Summary of the Meeting between Gromyko and Chu Yong-ha, October 10, 1950. APRF, fond 2, opis 65, delo 776, listy 157–8.

22 Telegram from Roshchin to Stalin, October 8, 1950. RGASPI, fond 558, opis 11, delo 334, list 132. Cited in *Novaia i noveishaia istoriia* (Modern and Contemporary History), 2005, no. 5, pp. 107–8.

23 In the portion that has been redacted from the October 2 telegram that has been released by China, Mao asked Stalin to provide a large amount of military equipment, including tanks, heavy artillery, other heavy and light arms, and several thousand vehicles. He also asked the Soviet Union to provide air support when Chinese forces entered North Korea.

24 Du Ping, *Zai zhiyuanjun zongbu* (In the Headquarters of the Volunteers), Beijing: Jiefangjun chubanshe, 1989, pp. 21–2.

25 Besides the memoirs of Zhou Enlai's interpreter Shi Zhe, China has also published the memoirs of Zhou's confidential secretary, Kang Yimin (see below). Mansourov told the author in October 1996 that, in interviewing Stalin's interpreter, N. T. Federenko, he had learned that Federenko had prepared minutes of the Black Sea meeting that would soon be published. However, to date, no documents from the Russian archives on the Black Sea meeting have been published. There are even different dates cited for this meeting. Zhonggong zhongyang wenxian yanjiushi bian (Chinese Communist Party Central Committee Document Research Office, ed.): *Zhou Enlai nianpu 1949–1976* (Zhou Enlai Chronology, 1949–1976), Beijing: Zhongyang wenxian chubanshe, 1997, vol. 1, p. 85 states that Zhou departed Beijing on October 8, reached Moscow on October 10, met with Stalin on the Black Sea on the afternoon of October 11 and returned to Moscow on October 12. According to Shi Zhe, the meeting took place on October 10–11. Based on Fedorenko's reported minutes, Russian scholars claim the meeting took place on October 9–10.

26 Li Haiwen, "Zhongong zhongyang jiujing heshi jueding zhiyuanjun chuguo zhuozhan?" (When did the Chinese Communist Party Central Committee Finally Decide to Send Volunteers Abroad to Fight?), *Dang de wenxian*, 1993, no. 5, pp. 85–8.

27 See Xiong Huayuan, "KangMei yuanChao zhanzheng qianxi Zhou Enlai mimi fangSu" (Zhou Enlai's Secret Visit to the Soviet Union on the Eve of the War to Resist America and Assist Korea), *Dang de wenxian*, 1994, no. 3, p. 83. Zhang Xi, "Zhongguo renmin zhiyuanjun ruChao qianxi 'turan zhanting' de jingguo" (The 'Temporary Halt' on the Eve of the Chinese People's Volunteers' Entry into Korea), *Dangshi yanjiu ziliao* (Party History Study Material), 1993, no. 1, p. 3.

28 Mansourov, "Stalin and China's Decision," p. 103.

29 For Zhou Enlai's July 31, 1960 Report to the CCP Central Committee Work Conference, see Li Ping, *Kaiguo zongli Zhou Enlai* (The PRC's First Premier: Zhou Enlai), Beijing: Zhonggong zhongyang dangxiao chubanshe, 1994, p. 252. For the explanation given by Mao and Zhou to Kim Il-sung in 1970 regarding China's intent in sending Zhou to Moscow before dispatching Chinese troops to Korea, see Xiong, "KangMei yuanChao," pp. 84–5.

30 See Mansourov, "Stalin and China's Decision," pp. 102–3.

31 Xu, *Diyici jiaoliang*, pp. 23–4. Li, *Kaiguo zongli Zhou Enlai*, p. 250.

32 For Kang's recollection, see Qi Dexue, *Chaoxian zhanzheng juece neimu* (The Inside Story Behind Korean War Policy), Shenyang: Liaoning daxue chubanshe, 1991, pp. 62–3. However, Kang muddies the picture by reporting that,

after Zhou returned to Moscow from the Black Sea, Molotov urged Zhou not to deploy Chinese troops and withdrew the Soviet offer to arm Chinese troops, but that Zhou angrily and successfully fought back against this alleged instance of Soviet cold feet. Quite possibly, Kang confused this alleged event with other aspects of the discussions regarding whether and how to assist North Korea. See also Pei Jianzhuang, *Zhonghua renmin gongheguo waijiaoshi (1949–1956)* (A Diplomatic History of the People's Republic of China (1949–1956)), Beijing: Shijie zhishi chubanshe, 1994, p. 39. Also see Yang Feng'an and Wang Tiancheng, *Jiashi Chaoxian zhanzheng de ren* (The Men Who Conducted the Korean War), Beiing: Zhonggong zhongyang dangxiao chubanshe, 1993, p. 99. (The latter book is not available outside China.)

33 Mansourov, "Stalin and China's Decision," pp. 103, 105.
34 Shi, *Zai lishi jüren shenbian*, pp. 497–8, 500.
35 Nikita Khrushchev, "The Truth about the Korean War," *Far Eastern Affairs*, 1991, no. 1, p. 165.
36 See Li, "Zhonggong heshi jueding," p. 88. Zhang, "Zhongguo 'turan zhan-ting,'" p. 3. Li and Zhang told the author that they were not aware that the October 11 joint telegram from Stalin and Zhou had been found in Chinese archives (but see below), though Mao's telegram to Zhou on October 13 (see below) mentions this earlier telegram.
37 See Xiong, "KangMei qianxi," p. 85. Li, *Kaiguo zongli Zhou Enlai*, p. 252.
38 Telegram from Stalin and Zhou to Mao, October 11, 1950. RGASPI, fond 558, opis 11, delo 334, listy 134–5. Cited in *Novaia i noveishaia istoriia*, 2005, no. 5, pp. 108–9.
39 A 1966 Soviet Foreign Ministry document states that China only sent troops to Korea under Soviet pressure. See Kathryn Weathersby, "The Soviet Role in the Early Phase of the Korean War: New Documentary Evidence," *Journal of American–East Asian Relations*, Winter 1993, vol. 2, no. 4, p. 443. However, this explanation is not in accord with the facts.
40 Evgueni Bajanov, "Assessing the Politics of the Korean War, 1949–1951, *CWIHP Bulletin*, 1995/1996, nos. 6–7, pp. 88–9.
41 Telegram from Stalin to Roshchin transmitting a message for Zhou, July 5, 1950. APRF, fond 45, opis 1, delo 331, list 79. CWIHP.
42 Telegram from Stalin to Zhou or Mao, via Roshchin, July 13, 1950. APRF, fond 45, opis 1, delo 331, list 85. CWIHP.
43 Telegram from Roshchin to Stalin, July 22, 1950. APRF, fond 45, opis 1, delo 334, listy 88–9. NSA.
44 Telegram from Vyshinsky to Roshchin, transmitting a message from Stalin to Zhou, July 25, 1950. APRF, fond 45, opis 1, delo 334, list 90. CWIHP. Telegram from Stalin to Zhou, via Kotov, August 27, 1950. APRF, fond 45, opis 1, delo 334, list 94. CWIHP.
45 At this time Soviet air assets in the region were impressive. According to a July 1, 1950 estimate by the Joint Chiefs of Staff, Soviet air assets in the Far East included 2,200 fighters, 600 attack planes, 1,100 light bombers, 600 bombers, 500 transport planes and 300 reconnaissance planes, for a total of 5,300 aircraft. In addition, the Soviet naval air force in the Far Eastern theater included 550 fighters, 80 transport planes, 350 light bombers and 170 reconnaissance aircraft. See Paul Kesaris ed., *Records of the Joint Chiefs of Staff, Part II: 1946–1953, The Far East*, Washington: A Microfilm Project of University Publishers of America, 1979, no. 9. The newly formed Chinese Fourth Air Force only deployed to its Liaoyang base in late October 1950 and to its Langtou base in Andong (now Dandong) on December 21, and only then did it start training with the Soviet Air Force. The first few Chinese Air Force planes joined the air war over Korea only on January 21, 1951. See "Zhongguo renmin jiefangjun

lishi ziliao congshu bianshen weiyuanhui" (Chinese People's Liberation Army Historical Material Editorial Commission): *Kongjun huiyi shiliao* (Air Force Historical Reminiscences), Beijing: Jiefangjun chubanshe, 1992, pp. 245–50.

46 Wang, *Peng Dehuai zhuan*, p. 404.

47 Telegrams from Roshchin to Stalin, October 12, 1950. RGASPI, fond 558, opis 11, delo 334, listy 140–1. Cited in *Novaia i noveishaia istoriia*, 2005, no. 5, p. 109.

48 Memorandum from Golovko and Fokin to Stalin, October 13, 1950, APRF, fond 3, opis 65, delo 827, list 139. CWIHP.

49 Mansourov, "Stalin and China's Decision," p. 104.

50 Shtykov to Stalin Telegram, October 14, 1950. APRF, fond 45, opis 1, delo 335, list 3. CWIHP. For details regarding Kim's evacuation preparations, see Mansourov, "Stalin and China's Decision," p. 104.

51 I. F. Stone, *The Hidden History of the Korean War*, New York and London: Monthly Review Press, 1952, p. 137.

52 Wang Yazhi, "KangMei yuanChao zhanzheng zhong de Peng Dehuai, Nie Rongzhen" (Peng Dehuai and Nie Rongzhen in the War to Resist America and Assist Korea), *Junshi shilin* (Military Histories), 1994, no. 1, p. 9.

53 *Mao Zedong wengao*, vol. 1, pp. 552–3.

54 Wang, "KangMei yuanChao," pp. 8–9.

55 Chen, *China's Road to the Korean War*, pp. 201–2. Wang, *Peng Dehuai zhuan*, pp. 405–6. According to material cited by Chen, Peng was very angry on learning the Soviet Union would not provide air cover over Korea and even threatened to resign his command. This version of events, however, has not been confirmed in other sources.

56 *Mao Zedong wengao*, vol. 1, p. 556.

57 Li, "Zhonggong heshi jueding," p. 88. Xiong, "KangMei qianxi," p. 86.

58 *Mao Zedong wengao*, vol. 1, pp. 560–1.

59 Telegram from Roshchin to Stalin, reporting a meeting with Mao, October 13, 1950. APRF, fond 45, opis 1, delo 335, listy 1–2. CWIHP. Listed as a "14 October" telegram in the CWHIP virtual archive, but not on the document in translation, this telegram was received in Moscow on October 14. This document in the Russian archives and the telegram sent by Mao on October 13 to Zhou are virtually identical.

60 Telegram from Stalin to Kim, October 13, 1950. APRF, fond 45, opis 1, delo 347, list 75. CWIHP. The date signed by Stalin on this telegram is October 13. However, Stalin only saw Roshchin's telegram on the Chinese dispatch of troops to Korea in the early hours of October 14. This telegram, therefore, should have been dated October 14.

61 Telegram from Stalin to Kim, October 14, 1950. APRF, fond 45, opis 1, delo 347, list 77. CWIHP.

62 For Mao's two October 14, 1951 telegrams to Zhou Enlai, see *Mao Zedong wengao*, vol. 1, pp. 558–61. Also see *Zhou Enlai nianpu*, vol. pp. 86–7; Shi, *Zai lishi jüren shenbian*, p. 502; and Xiong, "KangMei qianxi," pp. 85–7. Xiong in particular presents a very careful, detailed chronology of the messages between the Chinese and Soviet leaderships during Zhou's visit to the Soviet Union to discuss the scope of Soviet assistance prior to the Chinese entry into the Korean War.

63 Wang, *Peng Dehuai zhuan*, p. 407. *Mao Zedong wengao*, vol. 1, p. 567.

64 Allen Whiting was the first Korean War scholar to argue that China proceeded primarily from national security considerations. Allen S. Whiting, *China Crosses the Yalu: The Decision to Enter the Korean War*, Stanford: Stanford University Press, 1960.

65 In *China's Road to the Korean War*, Chen vigorously argued that Mao and the Chinese leadership entered the Korean War primarily for ideological and

"revolutionary" reasons. The Russian scholar Kulik has also supported this view, drawing on Liu Shaoqi's September 21, 1950 discussion with Soviet Ambassador Roshchin. On the question of sending Chinese troops to Korea, Liu said that, "Chinese Communist Party leaders believe the Chinese revolution has still not come to its end. We need several more years to complete the revolution. If we are forced to fight the American aggressors, the date for the conclusion of our revolution will draw closer, since we are convinced that the American aggressors will be defeated." See AVPRF, fond 0100, opis 43, papka 10, delo 302, listy 266–7. Cited in Kulik, "Kitaiskaia narodnaia respublika v period stanovleniia, 1949–1952" (The People's Republic of China in the Founding Period, 1949–1952), *Problemy dal'nego vostoka* (Problems of the Far East), 1994, no. 6, p. 79.

66 See Kim Chullbaum ed., "The Truth about the Korean War, Testimony 40 Years Later," Seoul, 1991, p. 107. Shi, *Zai lishi jüren shenbian*, pp. 496–7. Xu, *Diyici jiaoliang*, p. 22. John Toland, *In Mortal Combat: Korea, 1950–1953*, New York: William Morrow, 1991, p. 238.

67 See also Shen Zhihua, "Zhongguo chubing Chaoxian de juece guocheng" (China's Decision-Making Process in Dispatching Troops to Korea), *Dangshi yanjiu ziliao*,1996, no. 1. (Not available outside China.)

9 A new stage in Sino-Soviet cooperation

1 *Selected Works of Zhou Enlai*, Beijing: Foreign Languages Press, 1989, vol. 2, p. 308.

2 P. Iudin, "Zapis besedi s tovarishchem Mao Tszedunom" (Record of Meetings with Comrade Mao Zedong), *Problemy dal'nego vostoka* (Problems of the Far East), 1994, no. 5, p. 107.

3 Dmitri Volkogonov, *Stalin: Triumph and Tragedy*, transl. by Harold Shukman, New York: Grove Weidenfeld, 1991, p. 540.

4 Jon Halliday, "Air Operations in Korea: The Soviet Side of the Story," in William Williams ed., *A Revolutionary War: Korea and the Transformation of the Postwar World*, Chicago: Imprint Publications, 1993, pp. 149, 163.

5 Telegram from S. E. Zakharov, the Soviet military representative in Beijing, to Stalin, November 2, 1950. APRF, fond 45, opis 1, delo 335, listy 71–2. CWIHP. Andong (now Dandong) is a logistical hub on the Chinese side of the Yalu River. As noted on the CWIHP website, Zakharov was later asked about the accuracy of the information he reported.

6 Telegram from Mao to Stalin, via Zakharov, November 15, 1950. APRF, fond 45, opis 1, delo 335, list 116. CWIHP.

7 Wang, *Peng Dehuai nianpu* (draft), (Peng Dehuai Chronology (draft)), mimeographed copy, pp. 46–7. (Not available outside China.)

8 Telegram from Mao to Stalin, March 1, 1951. APRF, fond 45, opis 1, delo 337, listy 78–82. NSA.

9 Telegram from Stalin to Mao, March 3, 1951. APRF, fond 456, opis 1, delo 337, list 89. NSA.

10 Telegram from Stalin to Mao or Zhou, via Zakharov, March 15, 1951. APRF, fond 45, opis 1, delo 337, list 118. CWIHP.

11 Halliday, "Air Operation in Korea," p. 152.

12 Ibid., pp. 149–50.

13 Ibid., pp. 156–7.

14 Ibid., pp. 159–60.

15 Telegram from Stalin to Soviet Military Advisor in Beijing, Krasovsky, June 13, 1951. APRF, fond 45, opis1, delo 339, list 47. CWIHP.

16 Halliday, "Air Operation in Korea," pp. 154, 161. The lack of coordination between Soviet air cover in both the rear area and the front was confirmed in

Goncharov's interviews: "[Soviet] planes gave minimal help to ground operations, and the Soviet pilots made no effort to coordinate their sorties with those operations. See Sergei Goncharov, John Lewis and Xue Litai, *Uncertain Partners: Stalin, Mao, and the Korean War*, Stanford, CA: Stanford University Press, 1993, pp. 199–200.

17 Zhongguo renmin jiefangjun lishi ziliao congshu bianshen weiyuanhui (Chinese People's Liberation Army Historical Material Editorial Commission): *Kongjun huiyi shiliao* (Air Force Historical Reminiscences), Beijing: Jiefangjun chubanshe, 1992, pp. 251–60, 309.

18 Zhonggong zhongyang wenxian yanjiushi bian (Chinese Communist Party Central Committee Document Research Office, ed.): *Jianguo yilai Mao Zedong wengao* (Mao Zedong Documents Since the Founding of the State), Beijing: Zhongyang wenxian chubanshe, vol. 2, pp. 331–2.

19 Telegram from Mao to Stalin, May 27, 1951. Telegram from Stalin to Mao, May 29, 1951. APRF, fond 45, opis 1, delo 338, listy 95–7, 98–9. Second telegram NSA.

20 *Mao Zedong wengao*, vol. 2, pp. 9–10.

21 Record of Ye Jianying Conversation with Malukhin, June 10, 1951. AVPRF, fond 0100, opis 44, papka 15, delo 322. Cited in Kulik, "Kitaiskaia narodnaia respublika v period stanovleniia, 1949–1952" (The People's Republic of China in the Founding Period, 1949–1952], *Problemy dal'nego vostoka*, 1994, no. 6, pp. 81–2.

22 Shi Zhe, *Zai lishi jüren shenbian: Shi Zhe huiyilu* (Together with Historical Giants: Memoirs of Shi Zhe), Beijing: Zhongyang wenxian chubanshe, 1991, pp. 522–3. Telegram from Mao to Stalin, March 28, 1952. APRF fond 45, opis 1, delo 342, list 129. NSA.

23 Minutes of Conversation between Stalin and Zhou, September 3, 1950. APRF, fond 45, opis 1, delo 329, listy 75–87. CWIHP.

24 Nie Rongzhen, *Inside the Red Star: The Memoirs of Nie Rongzhen*, Beijng: New World Press, 1988, p. 655.

25 Telegram from Mao to Stalin, via Roshchin, October 28, 1950. Telegram from Stalin to Mao, via Zakharov, October 29, 1950. APRF, fond 45, opis 1, delo 334, listy 62–3, 64. CWIHP.

26 Telegram from Zhou to Stalin, November 17, 1950. Telegram from Stalin to Zhou, November 17, 1950. APRF, fond 45, opis 1, delo 335, listy 122–3, 124. CWIHP.

27 Telegram from Zhou to Stalin, February 12, 1951. Telegram from Stalin to Zhou, via Zakharov, February 16, 1951. APRF, fond 45, opis 1, delo 337, listy 58–9, 60. First telegram NSA; second telegram CWIHP.

28 Telegram from Stalin to Mao, May 22, 1951. APRF, fond 45, opis 1, delo 338, list 87. NSA.

29 Telegram from Stalin to Mao, May 26, 1951. APRF, fond 45, opis 1, delo 338, list 91. NSA.

30 Telegram from Mao to Stalin, June 21, 1951. APRF, fond 45, opis 1, delo 339, listy 64–5. CWIHP.

31 Telegram from Stalin to Mao, June 24, 1951. APRF, fond 45, opis 1, delo 339, list 78. CWIHP.

32 See Hong Xuezhi, *KangMei yuanChao zhanzheng huiyi* (Recollection of the War to Resist American and Assist Korea), Beijing: Jiefangjun wenyi chubanshe, 1991, p. 184.

33 The author gathered the detailed information below on the Soviet reequipment of Chinese forces in interviews with Wang Yazhi.

34 Minutes of Conversation between Stalin and Zhou, September 3, 1952. APRF fond 45, opis 1, delo 339, listy 75–87. CWIHP. Later published data are a bit lower, at 38.19 and 45.64 percent, respectively. See Zhongguo shehui

kexueyuan, Zhongyang dang'anguan bian (Chinese Academy of Social Sciences, Central Committee Archives, ed.): *1949–1951 nian Zhonghua renmin gongheguo jingji dang'an ziliao xuanbian: zonghe zhuan* (Selection of Material from the Economic Archives of the People's Republic of China, 1949–1951: Summary Volume), Beijing: Zhongguo chengshi jingji shehui chubanshe, 1990, pp. 872, 891.

35 Zhongguo shehui kexue yuan, Zhongyang dang'an guan (Chinese Academy of Social Sciences, Central Committee Archives): *Zhonghua renmin gongheguo jingji dang'an ziliao xuan bian, 1949–1952: duiwai maoyi zhuan* (Selection of Material from the Economic Archives of the People's Republic of China, 1949–1952. Foreign Trade Volume), Beijing: Jingji guanli chubanshe, 1994, pp. 461–2.

36 Zhou Enlai's Discussion with Roshchin, July 24, 1951. AVPRF, fond 0100, opis 44, papka 32, delo 322, listy 48–9. Cited in Kulik, "Kitaiskaia narodnaia respublika," 1994, no. 5, p. 115.

37 AVPRF, fond 07, opis 23a, papka 18, delo 236, listy 128–37; papka 18, delo 237, list 2. Cited in Kulik, "Kitaiskaya narodnaya respublika," 1994, no. 6, p. 75.

38 *Zhonghua duiwai maoyi zhuan*, pp. 500–7.

39 AVPRF, fond 07, opis 23a, papka 16, delo 221, listy 44–5, 68–74; fond 06, opis 12, papka 22, delo 337, listy 13–14. Quoted in Kulik, "Kitaiskaia narodnaia respublika," 1994, no. 6, pp. 75–6.

40 For more information on the work of Soviet experts in China, see Shen Zhihua, *Sulian zhuanjia zai Zhongguo (1948–1960)* (Soviet Experts in China (1948–1960)), Beijing: Zhongguo guoji guangbo chubanshe, 2003.

41 Odd Arne Westad, "The Sino-Soviet Alliance and the United States: Wars, Policies, and Perceptions, 1950–1961," Paper for the International Conference on "The Cold War in Asia," Hong Kong, 1996.

42 Du Ping, *Zai zhiyuanjun zongbu* (In the headquarters of the volunteers), Beijing: Jiefangjun chubanshe, 1989, p. 141.

43 Nie, *Inside the Red Star*, p. 640.

44 *Mao Zedong wengao*, vol. 1, p. 722.

45 Du, *Zai zhiyuanjun zongbu*, p. 99.

46 Wang Yan *et al.*, ed., *Peng Dehuai zhuan* (Biography of Peng Dehuai), Beijing: Dangdai Zhongguo chubanshe, 1993, pp. 438–9.

47 Summary of a December 4, 1950 Discussion between Gromyko and Wang Jiaxiang, December 5, 1950. APRF, fond 3, opis 65, delo 515, listy 35–7. NSA.

48 Telegram from Roshchin conveying message from Zhou to the Soviet government, December 7, 1950. APRF, fond 45, opis 1, delo 336, listy 17–19. CWIHP.

49 Telegram from Gromyko to Roshchin, transmitting a message from Stalin to Zhou, December 7, 1950. APRF, fond 45, opis 1, delo 336, listy 21–2. CWIHP.

50 CPSU Politburo decision with approved message to Vyshinsky in New York, December 7, 1950. APRF, fond 3, opis 65, delo 828, listy 23–4. CWIHP.

51 *Mao Zedong wengao*, vol. 1, p. 741.

52 See Peng Dehuai zhuan ji bianxie zu (Peng Dehuai Biographical Research and Editorial Group), *Peng Dehuai junshi wenxuan* (Selected Military Writings of Peng Dehuai), Beijing: Zhongyang wenxian chubanshe, 1988, p. 383.

53 Wang Yazhi, "Nie Rongzhen jiangjun zai kangMei yuanChao zhanzhong de liangci tanhua" (Two Conversations with General Nie Rongzhen (About) the War to Resist America and Assist Korea), *Dangshi yanjiu ziliao* (Party History Research Material), 1992, vol. 11, pp. 1–2. (Not available outside China.) Wang Yazhi, "KangMei yuanChao zhanzheng zhong de Peng Dehuai, Nie Rongzhen" (Peng Dehuai and Nie Rongzhen in the War to Resist America and Assist Korea), *Junshi shilin* (Military Histories), 1994, no. 1, p. 11.

54 Wang Yan, ed., *Peng Dehuai nianpu* (Peng Dehuai Chronology), Beijing: Renmin chubanshe, 1998, pp. 465–6.

55 Telegram from Mao Zedong to Stalin, transmitting January 14, 1951 message from Mao to Peng with message for Kim, January 16, 1951. APRF, fond 45, opis 1, delo 337, listy 1–3. CWIHP.

56 For an incisive analysis of this issue, see Xu Yan, *Diyici jiaoliang: kangMei yuanChao zhanzheng de lishi huigu yu fansi* (The First Test: Recollection and Reflection on the History of the War to Resist America and Assist Korea), Beijing: Zhongguo guangbo dianshi chubanshe, 1990, pp. 69–70. Also see Xu Yan, "KangMei yuanChao zhanzhengshi yanjiu shuping" (Review of Historical Research on the War to Resist America and Assist Korea), *Dangdai Zhongguoshi yanjiu* (Contemporary Chinese Historical Studies), 1994, no. 1.

57 Dean Acheson, *Present at the Creation: My Years in the State Department*, New York: W. W. Norton and Company, 1960, p. 513.

58 Chen Jian, "China's Strategy to End the Korean War," Paper for the International Conference on "The Cold War in Asia," Hong Kong, January 1996. Also see Shen Zhihua and Yafeng Xia, "Mao Zedong's Erroneous Decision During the Korean War: China's Rejection of the UN Cease-fire Resolution in Early 1951," *Asian Perspective*, 2011, vol. 35, pp. 187–209. Shen and Xia argue that, "Because of the mistake, China completely lost its advantage on the Korean battlefield and in the international area."

59 Wang, *Peng Dehuai nianpu*, p. 446.

60 Telegram from Mao to Stalin, conveying telegram from Mao to Peng Dehuai, January 29, 1951. Telegram from Stalin to Mao, January 30, 1951. APRF, fond 45, opis 1, delo 337, listy 41–3, 44. CWIHP.

61 Telegram from Mao to Stalin, March 1, 1951, in *Mao Zedong wengao*, vol. 2, pp. 151–3. Telegram from Stalin to Mao, March 3, 1951. APRF, fond 45, opis 1, delo 337, list 89.

62 Xu Yan, *Diyici jiaoliang: kangMei yuanChao zhanzheng de lishi huigu yu fansi* (The First Test: Recollections and Reflections on the History of the War to Resist America and Assist Korea), Beijing: Zhongguo guangbo dianshi chubanshe, 1990, p. 95.

63 Nie, *Inside the Red Star*, p. 641.

64 Xu, *Diyici jiaoliang*, p. 268.

65 Telegrams from Mao to Stalin, June 5 and 9, 1951. APRF, fond 45, opis 1, delo 339, listy 23, 28–9. For the first telegram see CWIHP; the second telegram CWIHP unpublished.

66 *FRUS, 1951*, vol. 7, part 1, pp. 462, 507–11. Acheson, *Present at the Creation*, pp. 532–3.

67 For details on Stalin's discussion with Kim and Gao, see Shi, *Zai lishi jüren shenbian*, pp. 506–8.

68 Telegram from Stalin to Mao regarding meeting in Moscow with Gao Gang and Kim, June 13, 1951. APRF, fond 45, opis 1, delo 339, listy 31–2. CWIHP.

69 Telegram from Mao to Gao Gang and Kim, June 13, 1951. APRF, fond 45, opis 1, delo 339, listy 57–60. CWIHP.

70 Memorandum of the Discussion between Gromyko and Kirk, June 27, 1951. APRF, fond 3, opis 65, delo 828, listy 181–5. Chai Chengwen and Zhao Yongtian, *Banmendian tanpan* (The Panmunjom Negotiations), Beijing: Jeifangjun chubanshe, 1992, pp. 122–8.

71 Telegram from Stalin to Mao, June 24, 1951. APRF, fond 45, opis 1, delo 339, list 78. CWIHP.

72 Telegram from Mao to Stalin, 30 June 1951, APRF, fond 45, opis 1, delo 339, listy 90–1. CWIHP.

73 Telegram from Mao to Stalin, conveying January 22, 1952 telegram from Peng Dehuai to Mao and February 4, 1952 reply from Mao to Peng, February 8, 1952. APRF, fond 45, opis 1, delo 342, listy 81–3. CWIHP.

74 Telegram from Mao to Stalin, July 18, 1952, conveying July 15, 1952 telegram from Mao to Kim and July 16, 1952 telegram from Kim to Mao. APRF, fond 45, opis 1, delo 343, listy 72–5. CWIHP. Telegram from Razuvaev to Vasilevsky sending Kim message to Stalin, July 16, 1952. APRF, fond 45, opis 1, delo 342, listy 65–8.

75 Telegram from Stalin to Mao, via Krasovsky, July 17, 1952. APRF, fond 45, opis 1, delo 348, list 69. CWIHP.

76 Minutes of Conversation between Stalin and Zhou, August 20, 1952. APRF, fond 45, opis 1, delo 329, listy 54–72. CWIHP. Despite this record, the Japanese scholar Wada Haruki believes that at the time when Zhou visited Moscow in 1952, North Korea and the Soviet Union favored a quick ceasefire, but Stalin was forced to accept China's position. See Wada Haruki, "Stalin and the Japanese Communist Party, 1945–1953: In Light of New Russian Archival Documents," Paper for the International Conference on "The Cold War in Asia," Hong Kong, January 1996.

77 Given the paucity of declassified Chinese archival material, it is still difficult to hazard a conclusion about whether there was a basic difference of views between China and the Soviet Union during the process leading up to the end of the Korean War. For a discussion of this issue, see two papers presented at the January 1996 Hong Kong International Conference on China's strategy to end the Korean War: Kathryn Weathersby, "Stalin and a Negotiated Settlement in Korea, 1950–1953;" and Fernado Orlandi, "The Alliance: Beijing, Moscow, the Korean War and its End." For more recent analysis of this issue, see Peng Xianzhi and Li Jie, *Mao Zedong yu kangMei yuanChao* (Mao Zedong and the War to Resist America and Assist Korea), Beijing: Zhongyang wenxian chubanshe, 2000. Also Shen Zhihua, "1953 nian Chaoxian tingzhan – ZhongSu lingdaoren de zhengzhi kaolu" (The 1953 Korean Ceasefire – The Political Calculations of Chinese and Soviet Leaders), *Shijieshi* (World History), 2001, No. 3. (Shen's article is not available outside China.)

Selected bibliography and suggested further reading

Bajanov, Evgueni. "Assessing the Politics of the Korean War, 1949–51," *Cold War International History Project Bulletin*, 1995/1996, nos. 6–7, pp. 54, 87–91.

Casey, Steven, ed. "Special Issue: On the 60th Anniversary of the Korean War," *The Journal of Strategic Studies*, vol. 33, no. 2 (April 2010).

Chen Jian. *China's Road to the Korean War: the Making of the Sino-American Confrontation*, New York: Columbia University Press, 1994.

Goncharov, Sergei, John Lewis and Xue Litai. *Uncertain Partners: Stalin, Mao, and the Korean War*, Stanford, CA: Stanford University Press, 1993.

Mansourov, Alexandre. "Stalin, Mao, Kim, and China's Decision to Enter the Korean War, September 16–October 15, 1950: New Evidence from the Russian Archives," *Cold War International History Project Bulletin*, 1995/1996, nos. 6–7, pp. 94–107.

Merrill, John. *Korea: The Peninsula Origins of the War*, Newark, DE: University of Delaware Press, 1989.

Shen Zhihua, "Chaoxian zhanzheng chuqi Su Zhong Chao sanjiao tongmeng de xingcheng: yi Zhong E jiemi dang'an wei jichu de yanjiu" (The Formation of the Sino-Soviet–North Korean Triangular Alliance in the Beginning Period of the Korean War: A Study Based on Declassified Archives in China and Russia), *Guoli zhengzhi daxue lishi xuebao* (History Bulletin of National Chengji University), 2009, no. 31. (Includes a short English precis.)

Shen, Zhihua. "China and the Dispatch of the Soviet Air Force: The Formation of the Chinese–Soviet–Korean Alliance in the Early Stage of the Korean War," *The Journal of Strategic Studies*, vol. 33, no. 2 (April 2010), pp. 211–30.

Shen Zhihua and Yafeng Xia, "Mao Zedong's Erroneous Decision During the Korean War: China's Rejection of the UN Cease-fire Resolution in Early 1951, *Asian Perspectives* 35 (2011).

Shen, Zhihua and Danhui Li, "After Leaning to One Side: China and Its Allies in the Cold War," Washington, DC: Woodrow Wilson Center Press and Stanford, CA: Stanford University Press, 2011.

Stueck, William. *The Road to Confrontation: American Policy toward China and Korea, 1947–1950*, Chapel Hill, NC: University of North Carolina Press, 1981.

Stueck, William. *The Korean War: An International History*, Princeton, NJ: Princeton University Press, 1995.

Weathersby, Kathryn. Soviet Aims in Korea and the Origins of the Korean War, 1945–1950: New Evidence from the Russian Archives, Cold War International History Project Working Paper no. 8, Washington, DC: Cold War International

History Project, Woodrow Wilson International Center for Scholars, 1993. (www.wilsoncenter.org/program/cold-war-international-history-project)

Westad, Odd Arne, ed. *Brothers in Arms: The Rise and Fall of the Sino-Soviet Alliance (1945–1963)*, Washington, DC and Stanford, CA: Woodrow Wilson Center Press and Stanford University Press, 1998.

Xia, Yafeng. "The Study of Cold War International History in China: A Review of the Last Twenty Years, *Journal of Cold War Studies*, vol. 10, no. 1 (winter 2008).

Yang Kuisong. *Mao Zedong yu Mosike de enen yuanyuan* (Mao Zedong and Moscow – Gratitude and Enmity), Jiangxi renmin chubanshe, 1999. (Yang's endnotes and bibliography provide excellent references to primary source and secondary material in Chinese on Sino-Soviet relations.)

Index